D1710584

34'

# U.S. NAVAL AIR SUPERIORITY

## DEVELOPMENT OF SHIPBORNE JET FIGHTERS
## 1943-1962

## Tommy H. Thomason

Edited by Nicholas A. Veronico

Designed by Connie Nordrum

ISBN-13 978-1-58007-110-9

**SPECIALTY PRESS**
PUBLISHERS AND WHOLESALERS

39966 Grand Avenue
North Branch, MN 55056 USA
(651) 277-1400 or (800) 895-4585
www.specialtypress.com

Printed in China

Distributed in the UK and Europe by:

Midland Publishing
4 Watling Drive
Hinckley LE10 3EY, England
Tel: 01455 233 747 Fax: 01455 233 737
www.midlandcountiessuperstore.com

Library of Congress Cataloging-in-Publication Data

Thomason, Tommy H.
  U.S. naval air superiority : development of shipborne jet fighters,
1943-1962 / Tommy H. Thomason.
    p. cm.
  Includes bibliographical references and index.
  ISBN 978-1-58007-110-9 (alk. paper)
1.  United States. Navy--Aviation--History--20th century. 2.  Fighter planes--United States--History--20th century. 3.  Aircraft carriers--United States--History--20th century. I. Title.

VG93.T56 2008
359.9'44097309045--dc22

2007047067

**Back Cover Top:**
The F5D versus the F4D: Same wing planform, same engine, but no external tanks required and almost 0.5 Mach faster. Even Ed Heinemann could do better the second time around. (National Archives 80-G-677189)

**Back Cover Center:**
An early production F7U-1 and the first production F6U flying over NAS Dallas, which is located in Grand Prairie, Texas. The Vought plant is above the F7U and to the left of the runway. (Jay Miller collection)

**Back Cover Bottom:**
The last vestige of resemblance to the F9F Cougar had disappeared by first flight except for the wing fences. (Grumman Aircraft History Center)

**Inside Front Flap:**
The centrifugal flow compressor resulted in engines of relatively large diameter as seen here, a Pratt & Whitney J42 in an F9F-2. The chief has his right hand on one of the combustion chambers. This photo also illustrates the engine access afforded by removal of the aft fuselage. (National Archives 80-G-419845)

**Inside Back Flap:**
The XF10F was only flown at Edwards AFB, California, and only by Grumman test pilot Corky Meyer. Numerous high-speed taxi tests and "hops" were required to establish that the pitch-control system was adequate for flight, which it turned out not to be. (Grumman Aircraft History Center)

**Title Page:**
The Naval Air Test Center at NAS Patuxent River was the first to receive production aircraft in order to accomplish required service evaluations. The number 751 on the nose is the last three digits of the FH-1 Phantom's Bureau Number, 111751. The "ET" on the nose stands for Electronic Test, one of NATC's test divisions. (National Archives 80-G-390767)

*Dedication*
*For Harold (Hal) Andrews*

# Table of Contents

# Preface

In writing this book I benefited greatly from unpublished reminiscences by two individuals now deceased, George Spangenberg and Albert Metsger: George Spangenberg began his career with the Navy as a civilian engineer at the Naval Aircraft Factory, Philadelphia, Pennsylvania, in 1935. He transferred to the Bureau of Aeronautics (BuAer) in 1939 and retired from its successor, Naval Air Systems Command (NavAir), as director of the Evaluation Division in 1973. Before he died, he dictated a detailed and comprehensive oral history. His daughter Judith B. Currier reviewed it with NavAir's Harold Andrews and then placed it on a website, http://www.georgespangenberg.com/. Long before and until his retirement (some say even after), Mr. Spangenberg was the Navy's de facto chief aircraft engineer and easily the equal of the greatest of the industry's chief engineers in intelligence, experience, and good judgment, if sometimes bluntly expressed.

Rear Admiral Albert B. Metsger was a 1931 graduate of the Naval Academy and a Naval aviator. As a commander, he was the Navy's Fighter Class Desk Officer from 1 October 1945 to 19 April 1949. He wrote a candid and unpublished autobiography, part of which covered this period in some detail, which I had access to because of the unlimited generosity of Hal Andrews. Metsger was not unlike George Spangenberg in terms of firmly held opinions and strong will and bears at least some of the credit for Navy fighters becoming jet-powered as early as possible.

In addition to working with Mrs. Currier to transcribe George Spangenberg's oral history and loaning me a copy of Albie Metsger's biography, Hal Andrews provided me with unrestricted access to his library of BuAer memoranda, technical reports, books, photographs, etc., and also his notes for a book very much like this one that he planned to write. (I already had copies of as many of his articles and books as I could get.) I'm honored that he agreed to not only let me pick up where he left off, but also guide me in writing it. He was the quintessential example of a gentleman and a scholar, recognized as an Honorary Naval Aviator for his many contributions — technical, programmatic, and historical — to Naval aviation. Unfortunately, he was only able to read and comment in general on a rough draft of this book before he passed on, or it would have been better in all respects.

Bob Lawson and Jay Miller have also played key roles in my lifelong interest in Naval aviation history. Both are well-known and accomplished aviation historians as well as writers and photographers. Bob created *The Hook* magazine for the Tailhook Association and served as editor for 15 years. Jay has written and published numerous aviation books and monographs. Most of Bob's photography and memorabilia collection now resides at the National Museum of Naval Aviation in Pensacola, Florida. Jay's library, which includes his photography and reference files, is now at the Aerospace Education Center in Little Rock, Arkansas. Both friends have humored me for many years in spite of my lack of aptitude for what they do so easily and so well.

Three organizations — the Naval Aviation History Branch of the Naval Historical Center at the Washington Navy Yard, District of Columbia; the Vought Aircraft Heritage Foundation in Grand Prairie, Texas; and the Northrop Grumman History Center in Bethpage, New York — merit more than a simple acknowledgement. All deserve recognition for diligently trying to preserve and,

*Mr. George Spangenberg. (Judith B. Currier)*

*Captain Albert B. Metsger, USN. (National Archives 634194)*

*Mr. Hal Andrews. (Mike Hirschberg)*

as importantly, organize and catalog the documentation in their respective organizations that is critical to historians. Moreover, they help researchers and freely share their information. In the many happy hours that I spent in those offices, I was aided and abetted by Joe Gordon at the Naval Aviation History Branch; Dick Atkins, Harry Kent, and Allene Deuson at Vought; and Larry Feliu and Lynn V. McDonald at Grumman, for which I am most grateful. I also want to mention Lois Lovisolo, who previously worked at Grumman and was the best resource I've ever dealt with at an aerospace company.

McDonnell Aircraft was represented by individuals who readily responded to requests for information. At the risk of missing someone, they were current and former McAir team members Chester Braun, Mike Brickman, Joseph Dobronski, William E. Elmore, Greg Kuklinski, Bob Little, David E. Morgan, and Frederick Roos.

Several people provided information and photographs that add to the detail and texture of the book. Particularly helpful were John Connors at the New England Air Museum; Terry Panopolis for pictures of pioneering Royal Navy jets; Dave Ostrowski, editor of *Skyways*; a group of former F8U pilots: William Boardman, Bill Brandel, Dick Cavicke, Dr. Wayne (Bull) Durham, Will Gray, and Tom Weinel; Francesca De Florio at Martin-Baker; Dennis Jenkins for D-558 material; Don Hinton for photos of preserved aircraft; Jan Jacobs; Angelo Romano; Gary Talachan; Gary Verver for China Lake photos and information; Jim Rotramel for Sparrow missile information; and Bob Lorimer for first-hand J40 engine experience. Last but not least, I want to express my appreciation to my sister-in-law Allison Jones and her brother Bruce. They are two of the nicest and most patient people you could ever be blessed to work with. She gently corrected my writing style, and he coached me on how to use the drawing program, Illustrator.

In order to keep this book of manageable size, I have not provided detailed descriptions of any of the aircraft. These are available elsewhere. I recommend Steve Ginter's excellent series on Navy fighters.

In most cases, the aircraft performance, configuration, and weights data that I provide are from the Standard Aircraft Characteristics charts that I have for each aircraft. Although these are the best source for standardized apples-to-apples data, the values I've provided should still be considered as representative, because I didn't always have access to an airplane's chart for the time frame I was writing about. Also, although the charts were periodically updated, it took time for manufacturers' estimated performance data to be replaced by flight test data. The effect of in-service changes might not ever be incorporated, and errors are not unknown.

In any historical account that spans a quarter of a century and begins with events that occurred more than a half century ago, some place names, organizations, designation practices, etc., are going to have changed. I have generally used the names and designations in place at the time. The same applies to the rank or title of an individual to the best of my knowledge. Some examples:

The Navy's aircraft procurement agency was known as the Bureau of Aeronautics (BuAer) from 1921 when it was founded to August 1959, when it was merged with the Bureau of Ordnance to become the Bureau of Weapons (BuWeps). This organization lasted until May 1966, when the Bureau system was reorganized and renamed as a set of Systems Commands, with the aircraft procurement organization becoming the current (at least as of the end of 2006) Naval Air Systems Command.

The United States Department of the Air Force was established in September 1947 as a separate service. Before that, the entity was the United States Army Air Forces (note the plural), which had been created and had absorbed the United States Army Air Corps in June 1941.

Before 11 June 1948, the U.S. Air Force and Army Air Forces fighters were designated "P" for pursuit. After that, their fighter designation was the same as the Navy's had always been, "F."

The National Advisory Committee for Aeronautics (NACA) became the National Aeronautics and Space Administration in October 1958 as part of the United States' response to the Soviet's launch of the Sputnik satellite.

The U.S. Air Force's system of designating aircraft was imposed on the U.S. Navy in September 1962. I have used the original aircraft designation up to that point. In the main, the only aircraft I refer to by the new designations are the F8U, which became the F-8, and the F4H, subsequently known as the F-4. A description of the Navy designation system is provided as Appendix A.

Muroc Air Force Base, the site of many milestones in U.S. aviation, was renamed Edwards Air Force Base in December 1949 for Capt. Glen Edwards, USAF, who was killed along with his crew in the crash of a Northrop YB-49 in June 1948. The site was previously known as Muroc Army Air Field until the establishment of the U.S. Air Force.

At some point, the designations for jet engines, which had become standardized between the Air Force and the Navy in 1947, dropped the dash between the type designation and the number. Not knowing when that occurred, I have simply used the current practice throughout.

Whether to include or substitute values in metrics for speeds, dimensions, and weights was an easy decision. I haven't. In that regard, I also had to decide whether to substitute knots, or nautical miles per hour, for ordinary miles per hour since knots don't seem to have become standard in aircraft reports and documents until the late 1940s. I've chosen to list the value as dimensioned in the original document and sometimes parenthetically provided the counterpart. Where I haven't, a speed of 100 knots equals 115 miles per hour; a speed of 100 miles per hour equals 87 knots.

# Introduction

At a remarkable gathering of aviators and aircraft at Naval Air Station Patuxent River, Maryland, in October 1944, several different fighters were evaluated by test and combat pilots from airplane companies and the military. There was only one jet-propelled fighter in the group, the Bell P-59. The convocation's summary report with respect to "Power Plant" was:

"Increased power with due regard to economy is desired without sacrificing current dependability. The current air-cooled radial engine inspired the most confidence. The use of a conventional reciprocating engine with a supplementary jet or gas turbine in combination was viewed with disfavor. Pure jet propulsion engines were considered promising for future use."[1]

The lack of "Wow – I got to get me one of these!" statements relative to the jet was understandable. The focus of the group was on the near-term improvements to win the air war in the Pacific. The P-59 not only suffered from the inherent limitations of a jet-propelled airplane compared to its propeller-driven, piston engine-powered counterparts, it was an underpowered, first-generation jet on a ramp with some of the highest performance prop fighters extant, representing decades of development, a few still in test before service use.

One of the evaluators, however, a civilian test pilot named A. B. Heller who was representing the Curtiss-Wright propeller division, clearly recognized the jet's potential and in response to a question from the moderator about counter-rotating propellers, said:

"Commander, after just flying the squirt job, I am out of business and I don't think there is any reason why we should talk about dual rotation. If anybody needs a good tug boat captain or something, that is about all I can talk about. I just finished the test in the squirt job and I have about two pages of comments. First I am going to hand in my resignation."

The German Me 262, the first operational jet fighter, was only then making its presence known in the air war over Europe. It did not make a big impact militarily for various reasons, but it did viscerally to the Allied fighter pilots, since it was almost untouchable when up and away on two engines.

The combat superiority of the jet fighter presented the U.S. Navy with a significant problem. Carrier-based aircraft have additional and burdensome design requirements compared to aircraft that do not have to fly on and off carriers. Through experience and innovative design practice by their aircraft suppliers, the Navy had overcome that basing-imposed headwind and were flying propeller-driven fighters that were in no way operationally inferior to their land-based adversaries. Now they had to do it again with a higher degree of difficulty – the innate limitations of jet propulsion could not have been more incompatible with safe and routine carrier-based operation.

Nevertheless, they had made a start. At the time of the conference, McDonnell was building the Navy's first jet fighter, the McDonnell FH-1 Phantom, with a Navy-sponsored jet engine. The service was about to contract for two more, one from North American and the other from Chance Vought.

The successful transition to high-performance, carrier-based jet fighters wasn't just accomplished by the airplane manufacturers, however. Timely and thoughtful innovations in aircraft carrier design, operational procedures, training, and equipment were also necessary.

This is an account of how it all came together.

*Under the watchful eye of the HUP plane guard pilot, an instrumented NATC F7U-3 is about to be launched by steam catapult during Project Steam aboard* Hancock *in June 1954. (U.S. Navy via Hal Andrews)*

## CHAPTER ONE

One of the early concerns about carrier basing jet aircraft was the risk of deck personnel being sucked into the engine intake. In October 1948, Lieutenant A. L. Hall of the Navy's Medical Service Corps therefore donned a parachute harness attached to a restraining line and conducted a qualitative evaluation of the suction at this FJ-1's inlet. He found that he could safely stand two feet in front of the nose, with the measured inward velocity being about 38 knots. (National Archives 706179)

# The Opportunity - Benefits, Problems, and Requirements

## Carrier Basing Requirements

The U.S. Navy has been operating aircraft from carriers since 1922, when evaluations began aboard the small flight deck added to a collier, the *Jupiter*, renamed the *Langley*. In order to ensure stopping within the space available, a hook that could be lowered prior to landing was added to the underside of the aircraft's tail. If all went well, this hook engaged one of the cross-deck wires provided in the landing area of the ship and stopped the aircraft in a very short distance.

After a period of land-based testing, the concept was evaluated aboard the *Langley* and proved workable. Since the deck was both short and narrow, all takeoffs and landings were accomplished with the carrier headed into the wind. Emphasis was placed on launching and recovering a group of aircraft in minimum time, since the wind wasn't always coming from the direction that the task force commander wanted to go. The less time spent going the wrong way, the better.

The landing was the most critical part of the process. The technique developed was similar to a short field landing with no obstacles. The pilot made a low, slow, flat approach with power on. Once landing was assured, he "cut" the power, which produced an immediate descent and touchdown. It was soon recognized that there was great value in having someone on deck giving the pilot guidance on his approach and the all-important point at which to reduce power to idle. This was the Landing Signals Officer, or LSO, who stood at the aft end of the carrier on the port side. With a paddle in each hand and using body language, he would signal the pilot to correct his lineup, height, and speed. Examples are shown in Figure 1.1. At the right moment, just as the aircraft was approaching the ramp, the LSO would dramatically signal a "cut," which was mandatory. The pilot then reduced the power to idle, nosed over slightly, and then almost immediately raised the nose again. This series of control inputs started a descent towards the landing area, and then it checked slightly, putting the end of the tail hook in position to snag a wire.

The basic concept of the tail hook has not changed since the beginning of carrier basing as evidenced by this picture of an F2B tail hook dated October 1926. (National Archives 185784)

The USS Langley was the first U.S. Navy aircraft carrier. In this May 1928 photo, taken while at anchor, its aircraft are spotted for takeoff and its folding funnels are in the upright position. The man ahead of the aircraft pack provides a size reference for the 542-foot-long, 65-foot-wide flight deck. (National Archives 416340)

An LSO is just visible on the flight deck to the left of the landing Vought VE-7 in this photo of the USS Langley. The funnels are now folded down for flight operations. (U.S. Navy)

Going around instead of landing occurred frequently. With a flight of aircraft trying to land in as short an interval as possible, sometimes one would not have cleared the landing area before the next was on final approach. Other reasons were a bad and unsalvageable approach, the ship's motion, and forgetting to

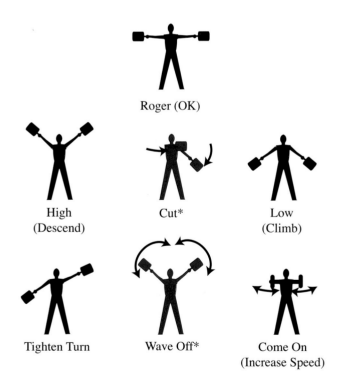

Roger (OK)

High (Descend)   Cut*   Low (Climb)

Tighten Turn   Wave Off*   Come On (Increase Speed)

*Mandatory

LSO Signals
Figure 1-1 (Author)

lower the tail hook. The mandatory "wave-off" to go around again could occur right up to the last moment before the "cut."

Up through the beginning of World War II, takeoffs were usually accomplished by a deck run into the wind, augmented by the ship's speed. Catapults were installed as standard equipment, but they were only used when there wasn't enough space for a deck run with the existing wind-over-deck conditions because it took less time to launch aircraft using deck runs. Later in World War II, use of the catapults became more frequent as aircraft and their weapons loads got heavier, making takeoff runs longer.

For naval flight operations, slow flight capabilities and handling qualities are more important than for land-based aircraft. It wasn't just enough to have a low stall-speed and good stall warning. Approach speed might be dictated by the speed at which roll control became unacceptable or visibility of the LSO was restricted. Since there was an upper landing speed limit imposed by the arresting gear and/or aircraft structural limitations, the lower limit had to be low enough to provide for a margin of error on either side of the target approach speed. Otherwise, the pilot was walking a tightrope with no net. The best the designer could do, however, was to thicken the rope – precise speed control was still critical.

Carrier-basing also necessitated compactness. There were fundamental constraints, like the height of the hangar deck and the dimensions of the elevators, which moved aircraft to and from the flight deck. These dimensions varied somewhat from ship to ship, and elevators were of slightly different sizes, but the box all aircraft had to fit in was roughly 17-1/2 feet high by 48 feet long and 44 feet wide.[1] A specific measurement of compactness was the number that could be crammed onto a specified area. At one point this was defined as the first 200 feet of the 96-foot-wide flight deck – overhang was allowed. As a result, almost all carrier aircraft had folding wings after the transition to monoplanes and were shorter than their land-based counterparts.

The designer of a carrier-based aircraft is therefore presented with a longer list of requirements than for a shore-based aircraft. His design had to have catapult and hold-back fittings and a tail hook, both integrated into the structure to withstand the loads imposed by launching and recovery; a sturdier landing gear because, for example, the deck was sometimes moving up toward the aircraft at the moment of touchdown; folding wings were required to achieve the required degree of compactness; low-speed capability and handling qualities; a clear view of the LSO in approach attitude; and a higher degree of emphasis on corrosion protection and maintenance access in a confined area with minimal support equipment. All these added weight to a carrier-based aircraft design compared to an equivalent land-based one, which made achieving comparable performance in speed and range more difficult.

The hangar deck on a carrier was reserved for crash-damaged aircraft and those undergoing heavy maintenance. Routine maintenance such as work on the ejection seat requiring removal of the canopy was accomplished on the flight deck. (U.S. Navy via Robert L. Lawson collection)

## The Problem With Jets On A Carrier

Other than speed, smoothness, and cockpit noise, the first jets were inferior to propeller-driven aircraft. The jet engine didn't provide much thrust at low speeds. Actually, the first jets didn't have much thrust at any speed. On takeoffs, they seemed to trundle along forever until they were capable of flight. Their rate of climb at low speed was disappointing. During approach to landing, a successful go-around became increasing unlikely as touchdown neared because the engine was slow to accelerate from idle to maximum thrust, as little as it was. The Pratt & Whitney R-2800 piston engine powering the Grumman F8F Bearcat would develop about 7,000 pounds of thrust with a 13-foot diameter propeller at zero airspeed and takeoff power. The total thrust in the first jets was less than half that, even when the engines were new, and old was measured in tens of hours.

It was as if the jet aircraft was a car that had only a top gear and therefore was very slow to accelerate. By contrast, the prop

The difference between low-speed thrust available in propeller-driven aircraft versus jets was in part due to the relative size of the propulsion disk. In this regard, the F8F Bearcat was exceptional. (National Archives 421662)

Propeller-driven aircraft had better wave-off capability than jets, but the power – particularly in a fighter like the F8F Bearcat here – had to be judiciously applied if awkward situations were to be avoided. Note the double-wire barriers stretching across the deck forward of the landing area. (National Archives 704707)

plane had a great first gear, and with the addition of the variable-pitch propeller, supercharging, and water-alcohol injection, something like a second gear and third gear. The development of the afterburner provided the jet with a second gear, but first gear was simply not attainable with the engine alone. There were ways to augment takeoff performance, catapulting being the most practical and rockets another, but the ability to reject a landing at the last moment, the wave off, was critical to a carrier-based aircraft.

Moreover, and particularly significant in carrier-based operations, a propeller-driven aircraft was able to loiter at very low fuel consumption if required to wait out weather or a fouled deck. Thrust is accomplished by accelerating a mass of air and is most efficiently accomplished by accelerating a lot of air a little, which is what propellers do; jets accelerate a little air by a lot, which is far less efficient. Jets couldn't be flown to sip fuel like a propeller-driven aircraft could when required to hold for the deck to be cleared or low visibility to improve. Jets had a very high metabolism. Even at "idle," waiting for takeoff, they were emptying the tanks at a prodigious rate compared to a piston engine.

Up and away, by contrast, jets were a delight in addition to being fast. There was little if any noticeable torque or "P factor," which made piston engine fighters a handful. There was no engine management workload associated with cowl flaps, oil and/or intercooler flaps, supercharger management, propeller rpm, mixture control, etc. The fatigue induced by noise and vibration was absent. The jet engine also provided a ready source of cockpit pressurization and air conditioning, which the piston engine did not.

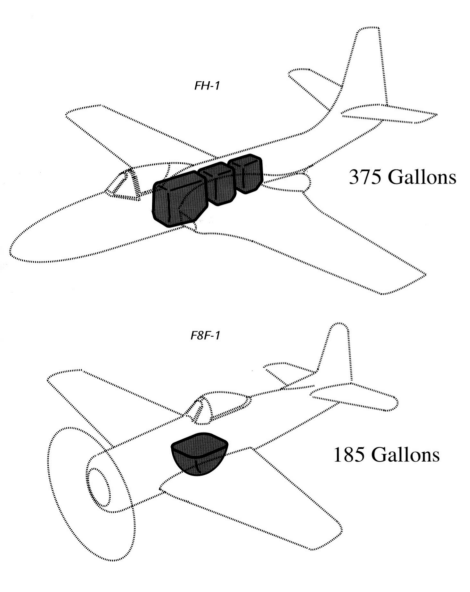

FH-1

375 Gallons

F8F-1

185 Gallons

*Internal Fuel Comparison*
*Figure 1-2 (Author)*

*The hangar deck wasn't big enough to accommodate anywhere near the entire air group. Here the Essex is spotted for takeoff in July 1951, off Korea and about to turn into the wind to launch a portion of the aircraft on deck. (National Archives 432858)*

*An F2H-3 Banshee has been waved off from landing aboard Oriskany in March 1954 off Korea. Note the deck load of aircraft has been pulled forward to conduct landings. (National Archives 642751)*

One key to appreciating and properly operating jet aircraft was that while their fuel consumption was high, their cruise speeds were also high, and optimum cruise altitudes were very high. Propeller-driven aircraft could fly for a long time on internal fuel, but their cruising speed was much slower than their top speed. As shown in Figure 1-2, the Navy's first operational jet fighter, the FH-1, had twice the internal fuel capacity of the contemporary F8F-1 propeller-driven fighter. Because of its higher fuel consumption, the jet had only 60 to 70 percent of the endurance of the piston engine fighter, even though it carried twice the fuel. However, it was only about 20 percent deficient in range when flown on a jet profile because its cruising speed was so much higher.

Another advantage of the jet engine was that no warm-up was required, per se. In the time it took to do preflight checks, much less taxi, the engine was ready to go. Engine run-up requirements, unlike the magneto, carburetor heat, rpm control, and other checks required of a piston engine, were almost non-existent.

The jet pilot's main concern was fuel. Not only was there not much left if the pilot had been anywhere even moderately distant, but there was also a limit on the combination of weight and landing speed from an arresting gear standpoint. That weight limit didn't provide fuel for many wave-offs. A new jet pilot therefore learned to start up, take off, and get to altitude as quickly as possible; know when to start back no matter what; not descend out of altitude until a ready deck was assured; and demand a priority landing if necessary.

Fortunately, consecutive wave-offs were relatively rare, as were deck crashes that required clearing and resetting of the barriers before flight operations could resume, so the jet aircraft's lack of endurance was more of a nuisance than a deal killer. One aspect of early jet fighter development, however, was successive iterations of a design after first flight to add more fuel capacity.

The jet's lack of endurance did force a much stricter operating timetable on flight operations than had previously been the case. A carrier deploys with far more aircraft than can be accommodated on its hangar deck, usually reserved for "duds" being repaired and aircraft undergoing scheduled maintenance that kept them from being readily moved. The ready aircraft are parked on the flight deck. For launches, all the aircraft would be parked on the back half of the deck. When the launch was complete, all the remaining aircraft would be pulled forward so the aircraft aloft could be landed. After the last aircraft that needed to land was recovered, all the aircraft would be pulled aft to be ready for the next launch period. This cycle of launch aircraft, pull the pack forward, recover aircraft, pull the pack aft, and repeat went on for most of the day and meant that there were only specific and limited periods when a carrier deck was available for landings.

The relatively limited endurance of jets forced this cycle to become significantly shorter and less flexible. Since a jet pilot would be out of fuel in something on the order of two hours, the deck had to be ready for recovery about 90 to 120 minutes after his being launched, which forced the cycle of launch/pull forward/recovery/pull aft/launch/pull forward to be about an hour and 45 minutes long.

There were also operational concerns about jet engines on a carrier deck. The intakes were a hazard to deck personnel – a North American mechanic had been killed at Muroc in September 1947, when he was sucked into an F-86 intake from four feet away – and their danger zone was less visible than that of whirling propellers. The exhaust was more intense all the time, hot and high velocity, but in the early jets it was reasonably small, localized, and dissipated quickly. Ultra-sonic vibration was an early concern, because the jet engines were turning at 15,000 rpm or more, but experiments and experience showed that there was no discernible effect on the deck crew.[2]

In the beginning, however, the major worry was about the ability of the jet to take a wave-off due to its low thrust and poor acceleration at approach speeds – a catapult launch would take care of the poor acceleration on takeoff for the most part.

The carrier had to be modified to accommodate the higher rate of fuel consumption and be replenished more often. Additional storage turned out to be not quite as much of a problem as originally feared. Although many of the first jet engines were run on gasoline, it turned out that kerosene, a less volatile fuel, was better. Safe storage of kerosene was less of a burden from a carrier vulnerability standpoint.

One obvious solution to the jet engine's shortcomings for carrier operations was to combine the propeller with a jet. This could be done two ways: 1) put a piston engine driving a propeller in the nose and a jet engine in the tail or 2) use the jet engine exhaust to turn a turbine that drove a shaft that turned a gearbox that turned a propeller. The Navy tried both. The Ryan FR Fireball and the Curtiss F15C were Navy fighter aircraft with "composite" powerplants, separate piston and jet engines. The former saw limited operational service. The latter was not put into production. Ryan also modified an FR with a turboprop engine for a one-off demonstration.

It eventually became clear that jet fighters were superior in air-to-air combat to propeller-driven ones, turboprops weren't much better than piston engines in that regard (although they came to be preferred for some aircraft types), and composite powerplant fighters retained the shortcomings of each engine type to such a degree that they didn't reap the benefits. The Navy simply had to make jets compatible with carriers and vice versa. And it didn't get any easier when it turned out that the swept-wing configuration was de rigueur (with a few exceptions like the F-104) for high-performance fighters, introducing even higher landing speeds and awkward handling qualities.

## The Navy's Fighter Missions

The primary and all-important mission for the fighter is to defend the carrier. Next is facilitating power projection by protecting the strike aircraft from enemy fighters. Finally, if not required to maintain air superiority, fighters were expected to contribute to the effectiveness of the strike itself, by air-defense suppression or as light bombers. At the end of World War II, either of the two existing fighters, the Grumman F6F Hellcat or the Vought F4U Corsair, was capable of performing all three missions. When the requirement to defend the carrier against attacks at night or in poor weather emerged, small numbers of first the Corsair and then the Hellcat were minimally modified with radar equipment and assigned to some carrier air groups for this specific mission.

More specialized fighters were now needed to: 1) defend the carriers against a high-altitude, high-speed bomber attack in all weather conditions 2) escort carrier-based bombers with similar capabilities at standoff ranges and 3) provide air superiority at night. From these three mission profiles, it was determined that the Navy needed an interceptor, a general-purpose fighter, and a night fighter. Each aircraft's operational requirements were envisioned as follows:

The interceptor was initially thought to be the best way to cope with the new near-term threat, a jet bomber postulated to be coming in at Mach 0.9 (520 knots) at 50,000 feet and, in the worst case, not detected until it was only 100 miles away. That meant the bomber was only about 10 minutes away from bomb release. The difficulty of maintaining a 24-hour combat air patrol with jet fighters dictated an interceptor. It would be launched at short notice and have an extremely high rate of climb so as to be in position to shoot down a bomber at 50,000 feet "in all conditions of weather and visibility" before it could drop its bombs. The geometry and limited time for the interception dictated a head-on attack, with a closing speed of 1,000 knots for the bomber and the interceptor. This precluded the use of conventional cannons and gun sight. In addition to climb performance, therefore, the interceptor needed a radar and blind-firing fire-control system, and to be armed with air-to-air missiles. A very limited range and endurance was accepted in order to achieve the low weight necessary for maximum climb performance. It was to be relatively lightly armored compared to other fighters for the same reason.[3]

The general-purpose fighter was to be a single-seat jack-of-all-trades. It was to have much greater range and endurance than the interceptor. Speed and rate of climb were secondary. A small airborne intercept radar and an autopilot were a requirement so it could operate as an all-weather fighter and augment the interceptors in fleet defense. It was recognized that it would have less capability and effectiveness than a dedicated night fighter, but it was still required to be capable of operating in all conditions of weather and visibility. Ordnance-carrying capability and armor were required so that it could be used as a light attack aircraft to supplement the air group's attack squadrons as required. It was also to have "special aerodynamic features to permit relatively low cruising speed for escort missions," since one of the requirements was to accompany and defend medium-range attack aircraft in strikes.[4]

The night fighter was to have long range, a two-man crew, and even more capable radar than specified for the interceptor or general-purpose fighter. It was to be used in an air-to-ground role as well as air-to-air, but the latter was its primary mission. Maneuverability was less important than it was for the interceptor or general-purpose fighter.

As it turned out, these requirements were both ambitious, resulting in protracted development times, and somewhat flawed, not addressing the fighter types that turned out to be needed.

## Engines

The engine has been critical to an aircraft's success since the Wright brothers' Flyer, although it usually only gets publicity if the aircraft is a failure. It has to be light in weight but at the same time reliable and durable. It also has to be efficient from a fuel-

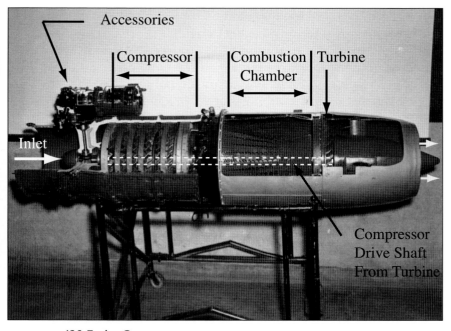

*J30 Engine Cutaway*
*Figure 1-3 (Author)*

# US Jet Engine Family Tree

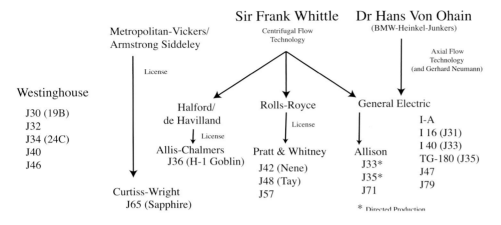

Note: Even numbered engines were managed by the US Navy and odd numbered engines by the US Air Force. However, both services used each other's engines.

*Figure 1-4 (Author)*

consumption standpoint to provide the most range from a given amount of fuel. It has to function properly over a wide range of temperature and pressure conditions. Prompt and smooth response to throttle changes is important, even abrupt ones. These demands forced the Wrights to build their own engine.

Engines have traditionally taken considerable development and subsequent operational time to perfect. Aircraft designers are often torn between selecting an engine of proven performance and demonstrated reliability versus one with better performance potential that does not have a lot of operating time or is still undergoing development. Because of the cost, time, and risk involved in the development of a new engine type, the U.S. military services separately contracted with an engine company for a new engine type and then provided it to aircraft companies as government-furnished equipment (GFE) to design an aircraft type around. As a result, there are fewer engine types than aircraft types.

The jet engine is simple compared to a piston engine. Air is compressed, mixed with fuel, and ignited to create a hot, expanding gas. On its way out of the engine, in addition to providing thrust, the resulting blowtorch of air turns a turbine that turns the compressor by means of an interconnecting shaft. As shown in Figure 1-3, it's the same suck/squeeze/bang/blow cycle of the piston engine – only without the mechanical complexity and reciprocating gyrations of the magnetos, valves, pistons, gearboxes, connecting rods, crankshaft, variable pitch propeller, supercharger, external cooling system, mixture control, etc.

Jet engines remained theoretical for a long time, however, primarily because the technology didn't exist to manufacture turbine parts that could withstand being bathed in the blowtorch coming out of the combustor for any period of time.

The jet engine was independently developed in England by Sir Frank Whittle and in Germany just before World War II. The U.S. military belatedly recognized the potential of the jet engine and initiated its development with companies that did not build aircraft engines but rather steam turbines and/or superchargers, which were similar to some of the inner workings of the jet engine. The British government voluntarily provided the Whittle technology to the United States, giving General Electric a head start in jet engine development, of which they took full advantage. The Navy contracted with Westinghouse to develop an engine independent of the Army Air Forces and General Electric program. After the war, General Electric also took advantage of German experience and technology as well as the knowledge gained by Pratt & Whitney and Rolls-Royce. A summary of the U.S. jet engine family tree is shown in Figure 1-4.

## Navy Aircraft Procurement and Operation

The head of the Navy is Chief of Naval Operations (CNO). His office and staff are referred to as OpNav. One of his direct reports in that office, the Deputy Chief of Naval Operations [DCNO (Air)], is responsible for the Navy's aircraft, to include planning, training, safety, maintenance, and personnel.

From 1921 until 1959, when it was renamed in a Navy reorganization, the Bureau of Aeronautics (BuAer), under the direction of OpNav, was reponsible for the design, development, procurement, and support (training, manual, spare parts, etc.) of Naval aircraft and related systems except for weapons, which were under the cognizance of the Bureau of Ordnance (BuOrd). The successor to BuAer was Bureau of Naval Weapons (BuWeps), which was an amalgamation of BuAer and BuOrd. (BuWeps became Naval Air Systems Command in 1966.)

In the procurement process, the DCNO (Air) is responsible for setting operational requirements and overall force-level needs, including dates for Initial Operational Capability (IOC). The operational requirements and IOC were used by BuAer to plan programs to develop and produce aircraft. Creation of the requirements and IOC was an iterative process, with the draft definition of mission capability and performance going back and forth between OpNav and BuAer to insure that the technology was available to develop and field the aircraft type by the date desired and within the budget available.

BuAer (and to a lesser extent, OpNav) maintained close contact with the aviation industry, particularly the handful of aircraft manufacturers that were its preferred suppliers. Expensive components common to different aircraft types, like engines, were directly furnished to airframe manufacturers as GFE. This practice resulted in lower cost to the government due to quantity procurement and maintenance commonality. Avionics were generally GFE, and, eventually, so were fighter ejection seats, after Martin Baker demonstrated a dramatic improvement in capability.

The Navy's source selection for new aircraft programs prior to 1962 was not a casual or informal process, but it was pragmatic. The Navy kept abreast of emerging technologies and threats, and periodically reviewed and updated its mission requirements. Meanwhile, the manufacturers would be preparing design studies that were shared with the Navy. These discussions would affect both the mission studies and the design studies, with requirements generating design solutions and the projected performance of the contractors' designs shaping requirements. At some point, the need to replace existing aircraft and military funds availability would coincide. OpNav and BuAer also took into account the need to maintain a competent and competitive industrial base for developing and producing carrier-based aircraft. In other words, they spread the development contracts around and even bought aircraft that they didn't absolutely need.

There were three ways the contractor could get a new program – provide the Navy with an unsolicited proposal for a new design, propose an improved version of an aircraft in development or production, or win a formal competition. Of the roughly 21 Navy jet fighter programs started between 1943 and 1956, four were initiated by the Navy or the contractor as new starts with no formal competition, 10 were improvements of existing aircraft, and only seven were the result of formal competitions.

BuAer contracted for improvements to existing models without resorting to the bidding process, in order to expedite the availability of more capable aircraft. Some fairly substantial changes were justified and authorized. It should be noted, however, that during this time BuAer almost always had at least two aircraft-development or improvement programs in progress at different manufacturers at the same time for the same mission requirement. So while there was no formal competition per se, each contractor was well aware that BuAer had alternatives if their price, product, or schedule performance was unsatisfactory.

When the Navy felt the need to have a formal competition, it would issue an invitation to bid, also known as a request for proposal (RFP). It included, among other things, the mission requirements, design specifications, and a list of acceptable engines. Interested manufacturers would respond with proposals. The BuAer-led evaluation team would almost summarily eliminate all but the most promising two or three and then work with the suppliers on the short list to refine their proposed designs. A contract would usually follow for the best one or two

that incorporated a detailed and tailored specification and some performance guarantees. The relatively informal process, controlled almost wholly by BuAer, had been instituted during World War II to expedite improvements. Even though the Armed Services Procurement Act of 1947 stipulated that advertised bids were to be used again, there were exceptions allowed by the act and BuAer took advantage of them. As a result, Navy aircraft development and procurement was much less rule-bound than it later became, when the Department of Defense imposed more structure and insistance on DoD approval of contracts after Robert S. McNamara became Secretary of Defense in 1961.[5]

BuAer was a matrix organization with military officers in charge. Projects were managed by "Class Desks" responsible for each major mission type, like patrol, fighter, attack, etc. The officers assigned to the Class Desks were the focal points for the process and carefully selected for their intelligence, experience, and leadership. As in industry, there were also groups of experts, primarily civilians, responsible for major elements of aircraft design like airframe design, powerplants, avionics, etc. The Class Desks focused on mission requirements and overall program management, while the experts focused on design specifications and evaluation of designs. The design specifications were very detailed and derived from Navy experience, particularly those resulting from career-damaging disappointments. Most of the officers were there for only a few years before they were moved back to operational assignments, whereas the civilians were there throughout their careers, providing the continuity and the institutional knowledge to each newly assigned Class Desk officer fresh from the fleet.

For management and maintenance purposes, each aircraft that the Navy bought or intended to buy was assigned a serial number. It became known as the Bureau Number, abbreviated to BuNo. The Navy was generous with the assignment of BuNos. during the planning phases of development and production programs. As a result, BuNos. were issued for many aircraft that were never built.

## Aircraft Development and Qualification Process

The design and development of a new aircraft began with a contractor preparing design studies of new or derivative aircraft based on existing or potential mission and performance requirements. These studies were based on projected and available engines, avionics, and armament. They used the latest aerodynamic and structures technology available to the contractor. In addition to configuration studies and mission analyses, pre-contract activities often involved mockups and wind-tunnel tests. During this process, the fundamental configuration decisions were based on the known or assumed priorities of the Navy for the prospective mission – top speed might be sacrificed for increased manueverability at altitude, for example.

Eventually, the Navy foresaw the availability of budget combined with a mission capability shortfall and selected one or more contractors to design and develop an aircraft to fill the requirement. To initiate the program, BuAer generally ordered two or three prototypes and a static test article in accordance with a detail specification proposed by the contractor that was reviewed by and negotiated with BuAer. The start of a program was often accomplished with a Letter of Intent, which permitted the manufacturer to begin work that could be charged to the government within stipulated limits. A more detailed contract would follow based on negotiations between the manufacturer and BuAer while the engineers were making progress.

The elapsed time from the beginning of detailed design effort, which often preceded the actual receipt of a contract for various reasons, to first flight was on the order of 18 to 24 months. This varied depending on the amount of effort that preceded the contract award, the degree of difficulty of the new design, the funding available, etc. The essential milestones prior to first flight included approval of the detail specification, design reviews, and at least one mockup review by BuAer. The detail specification could significantly impact the elapsed time between the official go-ahead and first flight if it involved significant changes to the contractor's proposed design, which it sometimes did. A design review consisted of detailed presentations on the aircraft structure, performance, systems, etc., based on wind-tunnel tests, material tests, design analyses, and so forth. At least one of the design reviews would include a detailed mockup of the entire aircraft as well as a cockpit mockup for review of control and instrument placement and the all-important field-of-view.

First flight was a major milestone but usually not a particularly high-risk event. What followed would be about two years of contractor tests to establish the flight envelope in terms of airspeed and altitude, the stability and control at low and high speeds, $g$ capability, range and altitude performance, structural demonstrations, aircraft and mission systems performance and reliability, etc. These were accomplished by contractor test pilots with periodic flight evaluations by Naval aviators, called NPEs for Navy Preliminary Evaluations, to determine progress and compliance with requirements. Changes to the design were inevitable as a result of this process, both because of problems uncovered in tests as well as requirement updates by the Navy. One very important and critical milestone in Navy testing was carrier suitability, invariably accomplished by Patuxent River test pilots rather than contractor pilots. Tests at sea aboard a carrier were preceded by extensive shore-based catapult and arresting-gear tests. In general, Navy flight testing was to spot-check contractor test results, determine suitability for service use, and develop tactics and training for the new aircraft.

At some point, production aircraft would be ordered, often before a prototype had flown. The initial aircraft was used by the contractor to validate the changes that had resulted from prototype flight-test and requirements changes. Subsequent aircraft would go to the Navy for their service-testing requirements, which included a formal process known as BIS Trials. BIS stood for Board of Inspection and Survey, a venerable Navy institution that dated back to 1868. It was founded to periodically inspect ships to ensure that they were seaworthy and otherwise "suitable for service." From an aircraft standpoint, BIS Trials determined whether the aircraft complied with the contract and was suitable for service use. The actual testing, evaluation, and report writing was delegated for the most part to the appropriate Navy test organization.[6]

Various Navy units accomplished operational testing with specific responsibilities for various aspects of aircraft useage. Naval Air Test Center (NATC) Patuxent River was organized into Service Test, Engineering Test, Armament Test, Flight Test, and Tactical Test. In addition to the testing done there, there were development squadrons, of which the most important for the fighter mission were VX-3 at Atlantic City, New Jersey, and VX-4 at Point Mugu, California.

Eventually a configuration would be approved and delivered to operational squadrons. Depending on the amount of overlap of production with flight-test development, there might be a significant configuration break early on in production to incorporate the changes. Avoiding this was the objective of the Fleet Introduction of Replacement Models (FIRM) approach, which the Navy defined in the mid-1950s. The concept was that there would be no prototype, per se. A new model would be produced at a low rate for at least the first three years, with the first six aircraft being used for contractor and subsequent aircraft being used for BIS trials and service tests at Patuxent River. Only after evaluation was substantially complete and a Fleet Introduction Program (FIP) accomplished (six weeks of intensive flying of a handful of aircraft using fleet pilots and mechanics to evaluate the aircraft, manuals, and support equipment in a quasi-squadron environment) would production be ramped up and deliveries begin to fleet squadrons. This was to insure that relatively few aircraft would be produced before the Navy was sure that the design met all requirements while expediting availability if it did.

The sea-going Navy was divided into the Atlantic and Pacific Fleets. There was less communication, coordination, and cooperation between them than you might expect. However, the de facto competition was of some benefit, allowing comparisons to be made of innovations and different practices. The operational aviation organization varied somewhat during the introduction of jet fighters, but in both fleets it basically consisted of carrier air groups to which operating squadrons were assigned. There was

also an all-weather composite squadron on each coast in the early 1950s, VC-3 at Moffett Field, California, and VC-4 at Atlantic City, that provided night fighter and intruder detachments to carrier deployments.

In summary, and very roughly speaking, it might take two years between contract award and first flight, two years for contractor development and qualification ending with delivery of the first production aircraft, a year or more of Navy qualification before aircraft were issued to a squadron, and a year or less of training at the squadron before the first deployment, making a total of six years between the go-ahead for a new aircraft and its operational use as shown in Figure 1-5. However, there was a considerable variation from this timetable, as will become apparent.

## Contrasting and Comparing Navy Jet Fighters

Having carriers nearby when a crisis affecting U.S. interests develops anywhere in the world is primarily accomplished by scheduled deployments. A carrier with an air group aboard will leave its home port for a period of six to eight months at sea with visits to foreign ports in Asia (Pacific Fleet) or Europe (Atlantic Fleet). During the deployment, the carrier and its air group are ready for action, maintaining a defensive posture, and practicing for an offensive tasking. Between deployments, both the carriers and the air groups spend time separately recuperating and regenerating. If not laid up for maintenance, repair, or upgrades, a carrier is available for aviator qualification and proficiency, carrier suitability testing of aircraft, NATO exercises, etc. The carrier air groups will be ashore – restaffing, reequipping, training, etc. - for roughly eight months between deployments. Both carriers and air groups were occasionally called upon for short-term contingency or surge efforts: the Suez conflict in late 1956, Lebanon in July 1958, and the Cuban missile crisis in the fall of 1962 are examples. Since it was unlikely that their major refit and equipment upgrade cycles would be the same in frequency and duration, a particular carrier air group would not always deploy on the same carrier. In fact, when a situation like the Cuban missile crisis required a carrier that was not deployed to sally forth, the squadrons that went with it might not all be from the same air group.

The focal point for deployment planning and scheduling is the aircraft carrier. Periodically, each one has to undergo major maintenance, repair, and upgrade. Some of these yard periods can last up to three years. Based on these requirements, OpNav plans years ahead for carrier deployments in order to maintain the necessary presence. It is critical that each carrier deploys on schedule, because it is replacing one that, after six to eight months on the line, is beginning to lose effectiveness due to normal wear and tear.

The 11-year span between the cease-fire agreement in Korea in July 1953 and the start of the Vietnam War for the U.S. Navy in August 1964 was a relatively stable period from the standpoint of aircraft carrier fleet size and operational useage. There were an average of 12 Navy attack (as opposed to anti-submarine warfare) carrier deployments a year, each lasting about six to eight months. A Carrier Air Group – consisting of fighter, attack, and supporting squadrons or detachments – would be aboard. This meant that, on average, there were three attack carriers in the Atlantic/Mediterranean and three in the Pacific at all times.

The fighter squadron make-up of the carrier air group changed slightly in the mid-1950s. Until then, flying fighters in poor weather and at night – like photo reconnaissance, airborne early warning, and nuclear weapon delivery – was a specialty accomplished by the composite squadrons. In the mid-1950s, one of the two or three fighter squadrons in the air group was assigned the all-weather role and equipped with a fighter designed for that purpose. The other fighter squadron or squadrons was equipped with a so-called day fighter. (Two fighter types powered by different engines were also desirable because of the likelihood that a jet-engine type might develop a serious flaw, so serious that the aircraft it powered had to be grounded.)

It took a great deal of planning and coordination by OpNav and BuAer to insure that there were enough fighters with the right capabilities to equip each of those squadrons. Almost as critical was the need to keep improved and new fighters in development so that the carrier and its attack aircraft were protected by fighters that could shoot down the postulated bomber threat, and so that they were at least a match for the projected land-based fighter opposition. A delay in a development and qualification program – or worse, production – required replanning and work-arounds to ensure that every Air Group deployed with a full complement of fighters that met all its mission requirements, both offensive and defensive.[7]

There are several ways to judge the relative merits of the different Navy jet fighters and whether one that reached fleet serv-

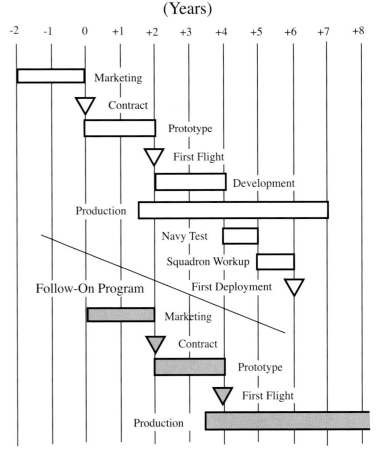

## Notional Program Schedule
### (Years)

*Figure 1-5 (Author)*

ice was a success or a disappointment. The most common and entertaining are anecdotes from the fighter pilots. Another is how many of each type were procured. While these are useful, what may be most meaningful is their duration and extent of service in fleet squadrons, their raison d'être, specifically as measured in terms of carrier deployments. In other words, how valued and useful a particular fighter type was, for carrier-based operations, can be inferred by comparing its deployment history to that of its predecessors, contemporaries, and successors.

For purposes of establishing the set of deployments to be used for determining the number of times a particular fighter type was used, I have eliminated short-term events like NATO exercises and crisis response outings, as well as shakedown cruises of new carriers and voyages that had the sole purpose of repositioning carriers from the Atlantic to the Pacific and vice versa. A summary of the results by fighter type is provided in Chapter 15.

## CHAPTER TWO

To insure that an aircraft that missed hooking a wire did not proceed forward and injure people and damage parked aircraft, a series of wire barriers was placed across the deck just before mid-ship. They were very effective, as illustrated by this picture of a Bearcat in a landing accident aboard Philippine Sea in September 1949. (U.S. Navy via Hal Andrews collection)

# Baby Steps - Initial Testing and Problem Recognition

In September 1941, the U.S. Army Air Forces issued a contract for its first jet aircraft, the P-59A, to the Bell Aircraft Corp. in Buffalo, New York. It was to be powered by two 1,250-lb thrust General Electric I-A turbojet engines that were based on the British Whittle Power Jets Limited Model W.2B engine. First flown in great secrecy in October 1942, its existence was not publicly revealed until January 1944.

Although designed and built in Buffalo, initial flight testing was accomplished in California from Rogers Dry Lake a few miles from what was then known as Muroc Army Air Field. Muroc was in the middle of what was known as the high desert, 2,500 feet above sea level and north of Los Angeles. It was an ideal place to test a secret aircraft powered by an engine of unknown capability and reliability because it was isolated, unpopulated, and featured several large emergency-landing areas in the form of the smooth and flat "dry lakes" that are rejuvenated every spring after the rains.

The P-59A was armed with two 37mm cannons and intended to be an operational fighter. Other than the powerplant, Bell was not pushing the state of the art, in part probably due to having only 12 months from contract go-ahead to first flight. It had a sturdy, simple look to it, unlike its exotic predecessors in the Bell product line. The wing area was relatively large in recognition of the low static thrust of the jet engine. The preference of the jet engine for

high-altitude operation was apparently recognized, because the cockpit was pressurized. The internal fuel capacity was 290 gallons, more than adequate for a propeller-driven aircraft of the same size, but only about an hour's supply for the P-59's engines.

The P-59 did not see much service use. It was underpowered and had a very short range compared to existing propeller-driven fighters. The engines were temperamental and easy to damage. Rapid throttle movements were likely to cause flameouts or compressor stalls. A minor error in starting the engine could result in an overly high temperature, often heralded by a 50-foot tongue of flame out the exhaust, which damaged the turbine and required engine removal. Even if the pilot technique was perfect, the turbine blades did not last long. Balancing the fuel-nozzle flow was difficult, and unbalanced nozzles caused localized overheating and damage to the burner liners, combustion chambers, and nozzle diaphragms. As a result, the initial time between overhaul was only three hours, including time at idle power, although by 1945 some engines were reaching 50 hours before removal. The engine was eventually designated the J31 and its thrust improved to 1,600 lbs.

Even though it didn't go to war, the P-59 more than justified the effort to create it by providing a first-hand introduction to jet propelled flight – it's one thing to be briefed on a novel concept and quite another to experience it. One frequently stated first impression

![An XP-59A cruises over the bombing range at Muroc]

An XP-59A cruises over the bombing range at Muroc. The big wing compensated for the low engine thrust. (National Archives B29838)

The GE I-A engine, based on the Whittle centrifugal-flow concept, is very short and compact so that the shaft between the compressor and turbine could be as short as possible. Most of the engine itself is just behind the main landing-gear door on this P-59. The light-colored tube aft of that is all tailpipe. (National Archives 210420)

The first Naval aviator to fly the P-59A, at Muroc in April 1943, was Capt. Frederic M. Trapnell of the Navy's flight-test branch at Naval Air Station Anacostia. The Navy subsequently acquired P-59s from the Army Air Force and assigned them to the Naval Air Test Center at Patuxent River for evaluation of the concept and pilot training in jet aircraft. The first of two unassembled YP-59As, assigned BuNo. 63960, arrived at Patuxent in November 1943 and the second, BuNo. 63961, shortly after. They were assembled, jet engines installed, and initially flown in January 1944. Cdr. Paul H. Ramsey and Lt. Cdr. Noel Gayler wrote a letter-type flight-test report on the YP-59A dated 14 March 1944 to record results and impressions up to that point. It compared and contrasted the power characteristics as follows:

was how quiet and smooth it was compared to a propeller-driven fighter. (One P-59 feature was a vibrator on the altimeter to keep the needles from sticking.) As General der Jagdflieger Adolf Galland reportedly said after his first flight in the jet-propelled Messerschmitt 262 in 1942, "Al ob ein Engel schiebt" (As if an angel pushes). Another first impression was the lack of acceleration with throttle application and the lack of deceleration with throttle reduction – basically a jet was reluctant to speed up but it also didn't want to slow down.

"The thrust of the propelling units at constant altitude, temperature and rpm is nearly constant, so that the thrust horsepower available is roughly proportional to the true airspeed. This means to the military pilot that the air-

*One of the Patuxent River tests accomplished using the Navy's P-59s was the effect of the jet exhaust on aircraft closely parked behind them. Here an eminently expendable XSB2A-1 is the test subject. (U.S. Navy via Hal Andrews collection)*

plane loses power as it slows down, so that take-off, climb and acceleration are relatively poor, while level and diving performance is relatively good. Speed for best climb is much higher than in conventional airplanes. This power characteristic affect (sic) also the usable turning radius of the airplane. Power available in a slow tight turn is not sufficient to maintain minimum turning radius without rapidly losing altitude. Air temperature has a much greater effect on available power than in conventional engines, amounting to approximately .35 percent per degree Fahrenheit."

The report also noted "the airplane will successfully make a carrier approach and take a wave-off from Vstall plus 5 knots in the landing condition, in cold weather (0° C). Because of the effect of temperature on thrust, opinion is reserved as to its ability to take a wave-off in hot weather." It concluded that:

Because of their fuel-consumption characteristics, the airplanes are best suited for employment as high-altitude interceptors, and are poorly suited for escort of low-altitude missions, and That development troubles in the Bell airplane and General Electric powerplants do not appear to be of sufficient importance to delay seriously the early military employment of the airplanes."

NATC's final report on the YP-59As, issued in September 1945, provided some insights into the ongoing development of design and operational requirements for jet aircraft:

Because of the overall cleanness of the airplane and the absence of a propeller, deceleration requires more time and distance. Some air-braking device is considered desirable for landing.

The absence of propeller slipstream…renders the rudder ineffective for taxiing.

From the results of the jet wake tests it would appear that the maximum temperature of the jet wake aft of the tailpipe nozzle is reduced considerably by natural augmentation. The jet wake velocity decreases at a slower rate and appears to be the critical factor with regard to shipboard operation.

Fly-by tests to determine the tailpipe exhaust flame visibility at night were accomplished with no exhaust flames being visible from any ground observation point. Directly astern the incandescent glow of the turbine wheel and exhaust cone could be seen for an estimated distance of 200 feet.

The limited quantity of fuel on board is a definite mental hazard, for the pilot. A reliable and accurate fuel-quantity gauge or fuel-consumption totalizer is essential.[1]

*In January 1944, an F4U Corsair was almost as fast as the first United States jet aircraft, the Bell P-59, at any altitude. The Navy's new F8F Bearcat was as fast or faster. That would soon change. (National Archives 214027)*

The Navy subsequently acquired three P-59Bs. The first, BuNo. 64100, arrived at NATC in October 1945 and the next two, BuNos. 64108 and 64109, in early 1946. The B was differentiated from the A by having 66-gallon fuel tanks in each of the outer wing panels to increase the fuel capacity.

No attempt was made to evaluate the P-59 from a carrier, as it lacked adequate thrust at low speed. It was put to good use, however, in providing jet experience to Naval aviators since it was very easy to fly. The tricky part was getting the engines started without burning one of them up, particularly unknowingly. Of the Navy's first 100 jet pilots, all but three had their first jet-propelled flight in a P-59. The last of the P-59s was still being flown at Patuxent in January 1948, providing a first jet experience for Ensign Ralph H. Beatle, the 231st known Navy jet pilot.

## The McDonnell Aircraft FH-1

Like all aircraft, the jet fighter is heavily dependent on its engine for success. It is of utmost importance to the aircraft designer that the engine manufacturer meets weight, thrust, and fuel-consumption predictions and develops the engine so it is reliable and durable. The only way for an engine manufacturer to get attention is to fail to deliver in this regard. If everything goes well, the engine is taken for granted. Jet engines don't set speed and altitude records – the aircraft that they power do. As an example, the Westinghouse Electric Company is far better known for the oft-maligned J40 jet engine, which caused delay or worse to a generation of Navy jet fighters, than they are, if at all, for designing and developing the first all-American jet engine.[2] In January 1942, after several months of involvement with a government study group on jet propulsion, they received a letter of intent from the Navy for the design of a jet engine and ran it for the first time in March 1943. They had produced a successful engine in a little more than 13 months, without any prior experience or any contact with the other major Allied jet-engine

Before it designed and built the XFD-1 Phantom, McDonnell's only military project had been the XP-67 for the U.S. Army Air Forces. There is a family resemblance in the shape of the empennage and the use of large fillets at the junctures of the wing to the engine nacelle and to the fuselage. (National Archives B29992)

inventors in England due to the Navy's insistence on secrecy. A further development of that first engine powered the first Navy jet fighter, and a subsequent growth version powered two of the Navy's first operational jet fighters.

In late December 1942, even before the Westinghouse engine had run for the first time, BuAer called James S. McDonnell, founder of McDonnell Aircraft Corp., to come to Washington, D.C. with a small team to discuss a new aircraft program. To develop its first jet fighter, the Navy had chosen a fledgling aircraft manufacturer, with whom nobody had much experience and the Navy had little. At the time, McDonnell was building parts for other aircraft

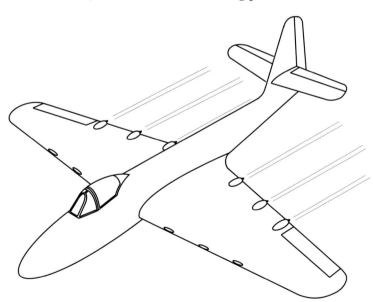

XFD Artists Concept - Six Engines
The Phantom's basic shape is already apparent in this artist's concept of an early layout that incorporated the Westinghouse engines originally intended as auxiliary propulsion for propeller-driven aircraft. They were so small that they could be embedded in the wings. (Author)

companies, producing a target drone for the Navy, and designing and building a long-range, twin-engine, propeller-driven fighter, the XP-67, for the Army Air Corps. However, they didn't have a great deal of work and no follow-on design work after the XP-67, which was as futuristic-looking as any aircraft in an action comic book. Moreover, their lack of experience and therefore prejudices might well have been in their favor.

In Washington, BuAer asked McDonnell and his team for a pre-design study of a carrier-based jet fighter, right there and then. They were first presented with the specifications for a 300-lb thrust Westinghouse engine. It was New Year's Day 1943, in a dilapidated engineering drafting room in the Navy building on Constitution Avenue. McDonnell started with six of the engines, all completely housed within the wings, three to a side because they were so small. That did not provide enough thrust, so two more were added for a total of 2,400 lbs. That was an adequate amount of thrust, but the design team quickly realized that eight throttles were more than a handful for a fighter pilot, among other things.

As Kendall Perkins of McDonnell remembered it, they then thought to ask whether the engine could be made bigger. That was not a problem, so the McDonnell team now used a "rubber" engine in the design study, meaning it could be whatever size suited them from an aircraft standpoint. They first doubled the thrust to 600 lbs, which resulted in a 16-inch-diameter engine but still meant that four engines were required. They then doubled the thrust again to reduce the number of engines to two, which resulted in a 19-inch diameter. They stopped at that point, because they had grown accustomed to placing the engine in the wings, leaving the center of the fuselage open for fuel. Given the amount of fuel required by jet engines, having the fuel tanks located squarely on the center of gravity was beneficial from a weight and balance standpoint.[3]

The Navy, satisfied with the McDonnell concept, sent them back to St. Louis with additional design requirements and the promise of a contract for the XFD-1 (which they finally got in August

1943). Whether by coincidence or because Perkins' memory was faulty, Westinghouse was already working on a 19-inch engine, which they would name the Yankee, in honor of its all-American origin.

Like the Army with Bell, the Navy had no time to allow McDonnell the luxury of a demonstrator. The XFD-1 was not to be a research aircraft. It was to be designed and laden with all the features, requirements, specifications, and necessities of a carrier-based fighter from the beginning. Its mission was combat air patrol, armed with four .50 caliber machine guns. It was equipped with a bulletproof windshield, armor plate, folding wings, catapult hooks, a tail hook, and provisions for JATO (Jet Assisted Take Off, actually solid rockets). The only subsequent jet fighter features that it did not have were a pressurized cockpit and an ejection seat, and that was probably only because BuAer had not thought of them yet.

McDonnell not only didn't have carrier-based aircraft experience, but its one and only prior aircraft program proved to be something of a flop: the XP-67 didn't fly until January 1944, due to problems, including fires, with its untried Continental 12-cylinder, liquid-cooled reciprocating engines. The program was terminated nine months later – before the second aircraft had even flown – due to continuing engine problems, including yet another engine fire.

In contrast to Continental, Westinghouse did a great job with its engine. The resulting Westinghouse 19-B Yankee had a dry weight of 826 lbs, including accessories, and static thrust of 1,365 lbs. It was 104 inches long, including the tail cone and oil cooler. There were six compressor stages and a single turbine stage. The exhaust was variable geometry, with a tail cone that retracted into the engine to provide maximum area for starting and idling and moved out to reduce the exhaust area for higher exit velocity and maximum thrust. In the January 1946 issue of *Aviation*, Managing Editor John Foster, Jr. described it as "the most powerful engine in the world for its size." By comparison to German jet engines, which were also axial flow, he noted that the Yankee was less than half the weight and about half the length and diameter while producing 70 percent of the thrust.

Kendall Perkins, McDonnell's chief engineer, wisely limited innovation on the XFD-1 to the engines and the tricycle landing gear, which was also a feature on the XP-67. Every other design feature was as conventional as possible. The wing leading edge was straight because of the design team's belief that this would provide benign stall characteristics. The wing had a small amount of taper and no twist. The wing fold was simple and straightforward. The horizontal tail had dihedral to clear the high-temperature engine exhaust and also to improve the spotting factor slightly, showing an awareness of carrier-basing requirements in spite of a lack of any experience with them.

*Before an aircraft can be taken aboard ship, it has to undergo shore-based testing, including catapulting. Here the XFD-1 is positioned on the field catapult with the bridle and holdback pendant in tension ready for launch. (U.S. Navy via Hal Andrews collection)*

*The XFD-1 was designed to be carrier based, including folding wings. The dihedral on the horizontal tail was present in part to allow FD-1s to be more tightly packed together. The diameter of the two engine exhausts of the XFD-1 contrasts dramatically with the propeller diameter of the F8F Bearcat, which is about the same gross weight. (U.S. Navy via Tommy H. Thomason collection)*

*Approaching the moment of truth, with gear, flaps, and hook down. Leaving the canopy open for takeoffs and landings would still be standard for many years since it facilitated egress in the event of a water landing. The post in front of the canopy of the carrier qualification XFD-1 was there to engage the actuation strap of the Davis barrier in the event that the nose gear was up or collapsed. (U.S. Navy via Hal Andrews collection)*

The XFD-1 flew for the first time on 26 January 1945, piloted by Woodward Burke. Legend has it that the first flight was with only one of its two engines installed, since only one was available. This is more realistically remembered as a short hop down the runway with ballast in place of the second engine. It's a good story but the daily BuAer status report doesn't mention any high-speed taxi testing on only one engine. [4] However, it is possible that such a hop was made, before or even after the first flight, since engines were in short supply.

Given McDonnell's limited experience with aircraft development and zero experience with carrier-based aircraft, its success with the FH was amazing, particularly compared to that of Vought, one of the most experienced Navy carrier aircraft companies, with its first jet a few years later. Initial performance was claimed to be 420 knots at 20,000 feet, a rate of climb of almost 5,000 feet per minute, and a still-air range of 750 miles. Compared to existing piston engine fighters, these were modest figures but good enough to justify a contract for 100 aircraft in March 1945. However, this was reduced to only 30 aircraft in

*Since the XFD-1 hadn't completed field catapult testing at the time of the carrier qualification aboard FDR, it was deck launched. This proved to be straightforward in the case of the Phantom but was not recommended for subsequent Navy jets. (U.S. Navy via Hal Andrews collection)*

August because the war was ending, but was subsequently increased by another 30 aircraft later that year.

The McDonnell program's initial success was marred by the fatal crash of the first prototype on 1 November 1945, killing Woodward Burke. The aileron installation had been modified before his flight and the result was an aerodynamic lock at full deflection with Burke unable to recover or bail out in time. However, testing continued with the second prototype, BuNo. 48236, and in April 1946, it was ferried to Patuxent River for acceptance testing, including a carrier-suitability evaluation.

In July 1946, after successful shore-based trials, the second XFD-1 was deemed ready for carrier trials aboard *Franklin D. Roosevelt*. Craned aboard in Norfolk, Virginia, the Phantom was flown off for the first time on 21 July by Lt. Cdr. James J. Davidson from a 400-foot deck run. He immediately turned downwind to make an approach and landing, the first for a pure-jet in the U.S. Navy. The landing technique developed in the shore-based trials was very similar to the one used for propeller-driven aircraft, except – in recognition of the jet's reluctance to decelerate – the all-important cut was given a bit earlier when the jet was farther out from the ramp than for a propeller-driven aircraft. Approach speed was 95 mph with a stall speed of 85 mph.

Six takeoffs – all deck runs since shore-based catapult tests had not been accomplished yet – and five landings were accomplished along with one "no-notice" wave-off on approach for evaluation purposes. The wind-over-deck varied from 32 to 40 knots. No problems were encountered, with the deck runs varying between 360 and 450 feet depending on wind-over-deck and gross weight. According to the September 1946 issue of *Naval Aviation News*, "Davidson...reported that acceleration and deceleration were slightly less than in conventional-type aircraft but there was no torque trouble, less noise, and speed and altitude were easy to maintain."[5]

One prominent carrier-suitability test modification to the XFD-1 was the installation of a guard in front of the windscreen to activate the new Davis barrier developed for aircraft with nose

The standard wire barrier wasn't compatible with twin-engine aircraft with nose landing gears, as demonstrated in this test of an unpiloted F7F Tigercat, so the Davis barrier was developed to reduce the likelihood of damage to these aircraft types and injury to the crew. It proved to be satisfactory for jets in most circumstances. (U.S. Navy via Tommy H. Thomason collection)

The Davis barrier was successfully demonstrated in July 1945 with this F7F Tigercat sustaining minimal damage after a 40-knot, engine-running engagement. The Tigercat was stopped with minimal damage in less than two aircraft lengths. (U.S. Navy via Tommy H. Thomason collection)

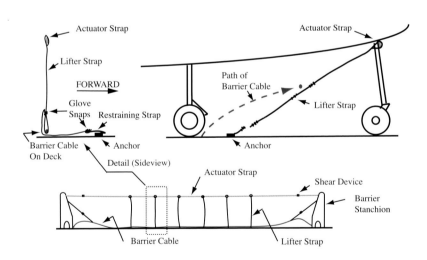

*Davis (Jet) Barrier Operation*
*Figure 2-1 (Author)*

wheels. Barriers, until now a series of pairs of steel cables stretching across the deck, were necessary to protect the people and aircraft forward of them if an aircraft was not "trapped" on landing. They were a very early addition to carrier operations. The cables were mounted on stanchions that could be quickly raised and lowered. They were not intended to be engaged by the aircraft's tail hook – they were there to stop an aircraft virtually in its tracks if it traveled that far up the deck on landing. The pilot was rarely injured beyond being shaken up, particularly after the shoulder harness was added to the pilot-restraint system in 1942 and crash helmets became common after 1947. The pilot was protected from the cables by the propeller and the fact that he was sitting behind the wing leading edge. These and the landing gear took the brunt of the cable damage in stopping the aircraft.

Not only was there no propeller to shield the pilot of a jet aircraft from the existing barrier system, because of weight and balance considerations the cockpit on jets was forward of the wing.

*The Royal Navy was the first to land a jet aircraft on a carrier. Here a Sea Vampire, the production version of that jet, is about to touch down, having taken the cut from the batsman (English for LSO) who is watching closely. For jets, the cut was given farther out. (Terry Panopolis)*

Fortuitously, the necessity for a modification of the existing barrier had already been foreseen for twin-engine aircraft with tricycle landing gear like the F7F Tigercat. S. V. Davis of the Naval Aircraft Factory suggested one that substituted a canvas actuating-strap for the upper steel cable with the lower steel cable lying flat on the deck as shown in Figure 2-1. When the nose gear contacted the actuating strap, lifter straps pulled the barrier cable up off the deck to snag the main landing gear and bring the aircraft to a stop. If the nose gear was not down or failed in a hard landing, the barrier activator in front of the windscreen would snag the strap to lift the barrier cable. A secondary benefit was that it would keep the strap from riding up over the windscreen and into the cockpit.

## Vampire

The honor of operating the first jet aircraft from an aircraft carrier went to the British. The De Havilland Vampire was a small straight-wing aircraft with twin tailbooms, powered by a single 2,700-lb thrust Goblin I turbojet also produced by De Havilland. By October 1945, the third prototype Vampire had been modified with the requisite tail hook as well as larger flaps and dive brakes to provide more drag in the landing approach. Longer landing gear oleos were also incorporated in view of the potential for harder landings aboard ship than to a runway.

After evaluating various approach techniques, the pilot for the first test series, Lt. Cdr. Eric Brown, elected to fly a low, flat, pow-

ered approach, with a throttle chop 150 feet aft of and 30 feet above the deck. A full-stall landing was then accomplished in the landing area to get the tail down to guarantee catching a wire. This procedure kept the engine rpm relatively high so that the sudden application of full throttle for a wave-off would not result in exceeding the Exhaust Gas Temperature (EGT) limits.

Shore-based trials were successfully accomplished in November 1945, and approval given for ship-based trials which commenced on 3 December with a first landing on HMS *Ocean*. Conditions were not ideal, with the flight deck rolling five degrees and pitching 12 feet at the stern. The wind over deck was 38 knots. The pitching deck almost resulted in a ramp strike, but the first landing was successfully accomplished and so were the next two, with the fourth marred by minor damage to the trailing edge of the landing flaps due to inadequate ground clearance. Takeoffs were accomplished by deck runs without incident.[6]

The Sea Vampire, with refinements to the flap system and a slightly more powerful engine, went on to be used in small numbers by the Royal Navy for operational evaluations, brief deployments, and training.

## Mixed Powerplant Alternatives

In 1942, the likelihood of jets being able to operate successfully from aircraft carriers was unknown but very possibly low. In parallel with the FD program, BuAer therefore initiated a competition for a fighter powered by both a piston engine in the nose

*Initially concerned that jet aircraft would be incompatible with carrier operations, the Navy awarded Ryan Aircraft a contract for an aircraft powered by both a piston engine in the nose driving a propeller and a jet engine in the tail. The resulting FR-1 is seen here landing aboard the escort carrier Charger in January 1945. (National Archives 361445)*

*Some in BuAer thought the turboprop engine was more appropriate than the pure jet for Navy fighters. Accordingly, Ryan received a follow-on development contract for the F2R, which substituted a turboprop engine for the front powerplant and retained the jet engine in the rear. No production resulted. (U.S. Navy via Hal Andrews collection)*

*The F15C, Curtiss' last Navy fighter, was another of the Navy's hedges against the possibility that an aircraft powered only by a jet engine might not be carrier compatible. No production resulted. (U.S. Navy via Hal Andrews collection)*

respected that fighters should no longer have propellers. During that time, two different fighters with both piston and jet engines were designed, built, and flown. Enough of one was built to allow extended operations, including exercises at sea, by a fleet squadron. The results were conclusive – the low-speed advantage of the composite-power-plant arrangement was not nearly enough to offset the shortfall in speed compared to jets.

The winner of the competition, Ryan Aeronautical Corp., began design of the XFR-1 Fireball in February 1943. The front engine was a Wright R-1820-72W piston engine rated at 1,425 horsepower for take-off, considerably less powerful than the 2,000-horsepower Pratt & Whitney R-2800 that was becoming the standard for Navy fighters. The rear engine was a 1,600-lb thrust GE I-16 (J31). The prototype flew in June 1944. Other than minor systems problems, development was relatively trouble-free. Production was accomplished in parallel with development, so deliveries began in January 1945, against production contracts for 700 FR-1s and 600 FR-2s with a more powerful Wright R-1820 of 1,500 horsepower. With the end of the war, orders for all but 66 FR-1s were canceled.

One fighter squadron was equipped with the FR-1. It was intended to deploy as soon as possible as part of the air defense against Japanese Kamikazes. The tactical concept was that the FR-1 would loi-

and a jet engine in the tail. The concept was that the "conventional" engine would provide the takeoff and wave-off performance and cruise efficiency that a jet engine could not and the jet would boost the high-speed performance.

As it turned out, pure-jet aircraft were entirely capable of operating from aircraft carriers, but it took several years to convince everybody in the Navy whose opinion had to be

ter on the front engine on a Combat Air Patrol station and then, when the Kamikaze controlling aircraft was identified on radar, the Fireball pilot would light off the jet engine and intercept it. Such was the haste to get the aircraft into service that it was planned for this squadron, staffed with a cadre of very experienced pilots, to become operational ahead of all the usual qualifications and demonstrations that were conducted at

*One of the Navy's P-80As was equipped with an arresting hook, catapult hooks, and a catapult holdback fitting. The Navy's carrier trials P-80 had three catapult hooks for test evaluation, one on each wing for a bridle hookup as shown here, and an alternative one under the fuselage for a pendant. Both bridles and pendants were evaluated for attachment to the catapult shuttle during shore-based testing. (U.S. Navy via Hal Andrews collection)*

Patuxent River. Initially designated VF-66, it was based at NAS North Island, San Diego, where the Ryan plant was located and would be the first squadron to operate a jet-powered, tricycle landing-gear aircraft from an aircraft carrier. Reportedly, the squadron was within a few weeks of deploying when the war ended.

As it turned out, the FR-1 did not have a speed or acceleration advantage over conventional Navy fighters like the F4U or F8F. To further boost performance and in the hopes of a resumption of production, Ryan proposed bigger jet engines to go along with the FR-2's 1,500-horsepower Wright. One proposal was for an FR-3 that would have had the 2,000-lb thrust GE I-20 in the tail. They were successful in getting a contract for an XFR-4 with a 4,200-lb thrust Westinghouse J34. Built using an FR-1 airframe, it flew in late 1944 but was not considered enough of an improvement over future jet fighters from a high-speed standpoint – the presence of the propeller continued to limit high-speed performance.

The little FR-1 was popular with its pilots for its speed, maneuverability, landing visibility, and novelty – they loved to feather the front propeller and astonish onlookers by making fast, low passes and flying away with no visible means of propulsion. The fun ended in June 1947 when a hard landing on *Rendova* resulted in the FR-1 breaking in two at the juncture of the removable aft fuselage and the forward fuselage. All squadron aircraft were inspected, found to have various degrees of structural damage, and grounded for good. The last flyable FR-1 limped into the

Naval Air Technical Training Center, Memphis, Tennessee, in April 1948, to be used as a maintenance trainer.

The BuAer Powerplant Office continued to push for propeller-driven fighter alternatives to the jet engine in light of the perceived need for takeoff and wave-off performance. They were advocates of the turboprop engine, with the jet engine turbine driving a propeller in addition to the compressor. The last experiment was to modify an FR-1 with a 1,700-horsepower GE XT31 turboprop engine in the nose and retain the J31 in the tail. This was designated the XF2R-1. It flew in November 1946 and demonstrated a high rate of climb, but it was actually slower in level flight than the XFR-4 had been. There is no indication that BuAer was seriously considering the aircraft for production. Ryan then proposed that the J31 be replaced by the more powerful J34 to provide a more balanced pair of engines, which generated some interest by the Air Force but not the Navy.

A bigger fighter using the mixed powerplant concept, the XF15C, was initiated at Curtiss in April 1944. It was to be powered by the then-standard fighter engine, the Pratt & Whitney R-2800, and a De Havilland Halford jet engine of 2,700 lbs thrust. It first flew, on the piston engine only, in February 1945. A jet engine was finally made available for flights beginning in May. Contractor flight-testing continued through the fall of 1946 after which the two surviving prototypes were delivered to NATC where they were evaluated and then disposed of in 1947.

By then the Fighter Class Desk, Cdr. Albert B. Metsger, was well on his way to convincing even the most cautious of his superiors that future Navy fighters had to be powered solely by jet engines.

## Lockheed P-80 Shooting Star

While the FD-1 was in development, the Navy was also evaluating the Army Air Forces' P-80A. The Army Air Forces had contracted with Lockheed in June 1943 to build this jet fighter, the prototype being powered by the same Goblin I engine as the Vampire. The P-80A was a redesign using the more powerful GE I-40, which was subsequently designated the J33 and produced in quantity by Allison. It first flew in June 1944, and with 4,000 lbs of thrust it had better high-speed performance than the P-59 and FD-1. In early 1945, the Navy decided to buy two P-80As, assigned BuNos. 29667 and 29668, for evaluation, with 29668 to be minimally modified for carrier suitability evaluation.

The first Navy P-80A, BuNo. 29667, was ferried to Patuxent River from Van Nuys, California, by Lt. Najeeb Halaby in the first transcontinental jet flight, arriving on 29 June 1945, with flight tests beginning a week later. As usual, shipboard trials would only be accomplished if land-based testing indicated adequate performance and handling qualities. However, BuAer provided

The tallest figure with his back to the camera is the late, great Marion Carl, U.S.M.C., World War II ace and postwar test pilot. The P-80A is being fueled for carrier qualification testing from FDR in November 1946 (National Archives 80-G-703311)

some leeway in the project authorization: "The P-80 airplanes concerned…will have control and stability characteristics which may be considered deficient in certain respects according to Navy standards."[7]

In early 1946, an informal air-to-air combat evaluation was conducted at Patuxent River between an F8F-1 and one of the Navy's P-80s. Cdr. Fred E. Bakutis flew the F8F and Lt. Col. Marion Carl, USMC, the P-80. The letter report concluded that the F8F could keep from being shot down, but it could not engage or disengage at will. The P-80 was simply far too fast – climbing, diving, or in level flight. A P-80 pilot was well advised not to try to turn with the F8F – that was a familiar restriction to Carl, who had 18.5 kills in the Pacific war, several being the highly maneuverable Japanese Zero. Instead, the jet pilot simply swooped into and out of the fight with relative impunity until he got bored, was running out of fuel, or the F8F pilot made a mistake and got shot down. In Bakutis' words:

"The results of this short combat evaluation convinced me of the astounding difference in performance between the two types. Actually the P-80 is approximately 100-150 mph faster than the F8F-1. In actual simulated combat this difference in performance is so tremendous that I had no choice in the matter but to wait for Lt. Col. Carl to initiate action. The F8F-1 is without doubt one of the most outstanding performers in the conventional engine field. Yet I felt as helpless as one would feel fighting an SNJ against an F6F. I was completely on the defensive with no option but to counter the P-80's approaches. During one or two of these counters I would have been able to get in a short, fleeting burst. The P-80's rate of closure and departure was so great that very seldom was I able to even get a "snap" shot. Conversely the P-80 was able to make sustained firing approaches. These approaches were at firing ranges that were a little long but very comparable to present standards. At no time was the P-80 able to make a tail shot, but my countering and evasive maneuvers still gave him excellent deflection shots."[8]

The carrier suitability configured aircraft, BuNo. 29668, which had been modified with a tail hook and catapult fittings, was ferried to Patuxent in December 1945, arriving 1 January. The NATC report on initial shore-based flight tests that was issued on 1 March 1946, concluded that:

Due to the absence of braking action of a wind-milling propeller, the airplane is very clean in the power-off landing condition and will not settle on the deck in the same manner as propeller-driven aircraft. For this reason it may be desirable to "fly" into the gear.

"The wave-off rates of climb are of sufficient magnitude for practical use if account is taken of the lag in the build-up of rpm and power after the throttle is opened.

Only slight turns should be made during wave-off due to the deleterious effect on rate of climb.

Once the airplane begins to settle in the approach, a wave-off can no longer be made.

The aileron effectiveness at low speed is good but there is an undesirable lag and lack of feel in the aileron-control system due to the boost device.

Lateral stability in the carrier approach is weakly negative to neutral.

Take-off distances are great and use of catapulting would be required for efficient carrier operation."

Land-based catapult shots were accomplished to determine the best hookup/hold back and pilot technique. After some experimentation, a satisfactory configuration and technique was settled on. Carrier landings, however, proved more problematic. The pilot was advised to avoid three-point landings because of the perceived weakness of the nose gear. However, the P-80 had a tendency to rock forward if landed firmly and nose high, which lifted the main gear and the tail hook clear of the deck. It would then rebound nose high, which resulted in a liftoff, floating past the arresting gear. A longer tail hook was considered but decided against because it would require a redesign and modification of the installation.

After extensive experimentation, the project pilot, Lt. Col. Marion Carl and his LSO, Lt. Earl Lock, established an approach speed – 103 mph, 5 mph above stall – and perfected a landing flare that minimized the rocking forward. The margin above stall speed was minimal but considered acceptable because the P-80A had both good stall warning and benign stall characteristics.

A flight evaluation aboard *Franklin D. Roosevelt* was therefore accomplished on 1 November 1946. A barrier activator was also installed in front of the windshield as it had been on the FD-1. Two catapult launches (the first at sea for a jet), four free deck takeoffs, and five arrested landings were made without incident. However, the deck runs took about 900 feet even with 35 knots of wind, twice that of the FD-1 and most of the length of the *FDR's* deck.

"The final report[9] on these trials concluded:

The P-80 airplane is not considered satisfactory for normal carrier operations for the following reasons:

It does not respond satisfactorily to a wave-off.

It rocks and bounces when landing so that it misses too many wires for normal operations.

In order to operate more than a few planes they would have to be catapulted since they need such a long run for unassisted take-offs. Catapulting a group of jet planes would take longer than normal due to the difficulty in spotting or if spotted by plane handlers it would take two minutes to turn up full power.

Fuel consumption is so high that the P-80 could not delay landing or take as many wave-offs as are often necessary when landing operations are delayed.

The training for pilots would have to be longer since many mistakes made by a pilot qualifying in a conventional plane aboard a carrier would be fatal in a P-80A type plane.

With respect to fuel consumption, it was noted that the P-80A burned 37 gallons of fuel during the three minutes between launch and landing, including the engine start. By contrast, the F4U burned six gallons for the same cycle."

Start of P-80A BuNo. 29668 testing as an "overload fighter" commenced in early December 1946, at NATC and was completed in April the next year. Overload referred to the addition of two 160-gallon tip tanks, which almost doubled the fuel capacity and resulted in a gross weight of 13,600 lbs. It was determined that the P-80A as an overload fighter could not take off from a carrier either by catapult or deck run, precluded from the former by inadequate wing strength with the tip tanks installed and the latter by take-off distance required.[10]

Before the carrier suitability tests, some in the Navy advocated adopting the P-80 instead of buying the FD-1. Lockheed proposed a variant of their P-80B to the Navy in 1947, as a carrier-based fighter to be designated FO-1. It was soon apparent that the better high-speed performance of the P-80A came with an unaccept-

The P-80A was both catapulted and deck launched during the trials aboard FDR, but deck launching was impractical for operational use because of the long takeoff run required with full internal fuel. (National Archives 80-G-703312)

The Navy decided not to buy the P-80 as a carrier-based fighter, but it did buy 52 as shore-based jet trainers, designated the TO-1. These are assigned to VF-52, an early jet training squadron based in San Diego, California. (National Archives 80-G-416544)

able penalty – takeoff and landing capability. For example, the FD-1, which had been designed with carrier-based, low-speed capability as a requirement, could take off in 1,100 feet with no wind, about half the distance the P-80 required. Following these tests, the Navy elected to continue with development of its own

*The Navy briefly evaluated the German Me 262, as did the U.S. Army Air Forces, to compare its technology and performance to that of the American industry. (National Archives 80-G-408619)*

jet fighters. However, they subsequently bought 50 P-80s as the TO-1 to use as shore-based jet trainers and equip one squadron, VF-6A (subsequently VF-52) at San Diego and one USMC squadron, VMF-311 at El Toro, California.

## Me 262

In July 1945, a shipment of German aircraft arrived at Newark, New Jersey. BuAer requested that NATC evaluate these aircraft with respect to performance and "any pertinent or unusual features of arrangement or characteristics."[11] NATC pilots chose two Me 262s that had been assigned BuNos. 121442 and 121444. BuNo. 121444 was used for spare parts for BuNo. 121442, which was flown for 10.2 hours between October 1945 and January 1946. NATC then requested that the project be terminated due to maintenance problems and the lack of spare parts.[12]

## Emerging Conclusions

The four jets described above that were tested at NATC were roughly the same size as the best Navy propeller-driven fighter of the era, the Grumman F8F Bearcat:

|  | YP-59A | XFD-1 | Me 262 | P-80A | F8F-1 |
|---|---|---|---|---|---|
| Gross Weight (lbs)* | 10,500 | 8,626 | 15,448 | 11,400 | 9,386 |
| Total Thrust (lbs) | 3,200 | 3,200 | 3,600 | 4,000 | n/a |
| Thrust/Weight | 0.30 | 0.37 | 0.23 | 0.35 | n/a |
| Wing Span (ft) | 49 | 42 | 41 | 38.9 | 35.5 |
| Length (ft) | 38.8 | 37.2 | 34.8 | 34.5 | 27.8 |
| Top Speed (kts) | 359 | 397 | 453 | 485 | 366 |
| Stall Speed (kts) | 71 | 62 | 94 | 85 | 75 |

*Internal Fuel

To compensate for their relatively low static thrust, the jets had bigger wings. To properly locate the center of gravity, the jet fuselages had longer noses. The aerodynamic tradeoffs were already becoming apparent – the YP-59 with its big wing was slower than the Bearcat. The XFD-1 was paying almost as big a penalty for its carrier compatibility. The Me 262 was the heaviest by far, but still had impressive performance given its low thrust-to-weight ratio. Its relatively thin wing with slats and a modicum of sweep back (probably incorporated more for center of gravity considerations than speed) represented the jet aerodynamics of the future.

Two of the jets, the P-59 and the P-80, were powered by engines with centrifugal compressors. The other two had axial-flow engines. While not immediately apparent, the axial-flow engine, which was independently developed in America and Germany during World War II, was to prove so superior as to relegate the centrifugal flow compressor to small turboprop and helicopter engines.

The two experimental programs that the Navy had initiated to determine the way forward for jet aircraft on carriers, the XFD-1 and XFR-1, each provided results as conclusive as they could have hoped for. The pure jet could be successfully operated to and from existing carriers. The composite powerplant concept was not only unnecessary, but it also provided no significant performance benefit over conventional piston-engine-powered fighters in exchange for its marginally superior carrier compatibility compared to pure jets.

However, it was apparent that a jet equipped for carrier operations and with a large wing for low-speed approaches was inferior to a land-based jet in payload and high-speed performance. This built-in headwind had to be addressed and minimized in future designs.

*A CVL's deck was crowded with a squadron's worth of FHs being prepared for flight operations. The wings were unfolded prior to the carrier turning into the wind and accelerating for the requisite wind-over-deck for launch. (U.S. Navy via Hal Andrews collection)*

# FIRST SQUADRON-SIZED PROGRAMS

The Navy's first jets were produced in small quantities and saw only limited operational use. However, the experience was invaluable, both for the Navy and the manufacturers.

In September 1944, the Navy provided eight aircraft companies with the opportunity to bid on the design and construction of a carrier-based fighter to be powered by any of the following engines:
• General Electric I-16 (J31), I-20 (J39), I-40 (J33) or TG-180 (J35)
• Westinghouse 19XB (J30) or "24C" (J34)

The request stressed that the requirements document "relaxes the usual carrier landing and take-off limitations to the greatest extent considered practicable in an effort to obtain the highest possible performance for a carrier based VF type."[1] Further specifications for the aircraft included:

The maximum folded dimensions as limited by elevator size and hangar deck clearance was 46-foot length, 42-foot span, and 17-foot height. At least 35 airplanes were to be spotted on a portion of the carrier deck 96 feet in width and 200 feet long – overhang of the deck edge was permitted.

Armament was to be either four .50-caliber guns with 400 rounds of ammunition per gun or six .50-caliber guns with 250 rounds per gun. Protection from .50-caliber bullets was required for the pilot except for the bulletproof glass, which only needed to provide protection from .30-caliber fire.

A combat radius of 300 nautical miles was required. In recognition of the jet engine's high fuel consumption, the standard mission was modified to permit returning at an altitude of 5,000 feet, and the reserve was reduced from one hour to 30 minutes.

The stalling speed with 25 percent of mission fuel remaining was not to exceed 90 miles per hour. When loaded with full internal fuel and ammunition with gear and flaps down on a 95° F day, the rate of climb at a speed of 10 miles per hour above power-off stalling speed was to be at least 500 feet per minute. No maximum speed was given – "the maximum performance consistent with the necessity of getting the airplane on and off the carrier is the main objective."

Four of the eight companies submitted proposals – Grumman, McDonnell, North American, and Vought. (Douglas apparently did not propose since they were already working with the Navy on what was to become the D-558 research aircraft program.) All but Grumman were awarded a contract. Grumman's

Design 71 was very similar in size and layout to Vought's V-340 and powered by the same engine, the Westinghouse 24C (J34). To buy both would have been duplication of configurations. The Navy may therefore have decided that Grumman was currently busier than Vought with production and development of Navy propeller-driven fighters. BuAer's feedback to Grumman was that they proposed the thickest wing and the slowest top speed.

McDonnell was provided with a development contract for an improved FD, the F2D soon to be F2H. Separately, they got a production contract for the FD, soon to be re-designated FH. Vought, a very experienced Navy supplier, received a letter of intent for the single-engine XF6U in late December 1944, and North American was awarded a contract for the single-engine XFJ-1 in early January 1945. Fortunately for North American, the Navy accepted its alternate proposal that the FJ-1 be powered by the new and more powerful General Electric TG-180.

*Even before the XFD-1 had flown, the Navy decided to order some for service evaluation and to equip at least one squadron. This lineup at the McDonnell factory includes the XFD-1 on the left identifiable by its different canopy, with its tail probably cropped out because the difference would be more noticeable. (U.S. Navy via Hal Andrews collection)*

This XFJ-1 Fury was already marked for service use. The white lines on the lower side of the forward fuselage are there to provide guidance to the LSO as to the airspeed of the aircraft on final approach to the carrier depending on which one lined up with the leading edge of the horizontal stabilizer. (U.S. Navy via Hal Andrews collection)

The XF6U was Vought's first attempt to design a jet fighter. It had to be small and lightweight because it was powered by a single Westinghouse J34 with only 3,000 lbs of thrust. (U.S. Navy via Jay Miller collection)

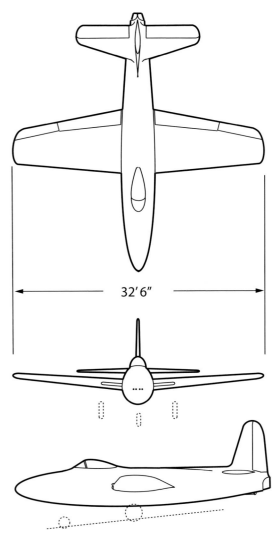

32' 6"

Grumman Design 71
Figure 3-1: Grumman Design 71 Three-View (Author)

Whether by happenstance or BuAer intent, the engine installation for each aircraft was different. The FD/FH was a twin-engine design, with the engines buried in the wing roots. The XFJ-1 had a single engine in the fuselage with the inlet at the front of the fuselage. The XF6U also had a single engine in the fuselage, but the intakes were in the wing leading edge adjacent to the fuselage. Otherwise, the three aircraft were very similar – straight wings and 10,000 to 12,000 lbs gross weight.

The FJ-1 and F6U did not have folding wings, in large part to minimize airframe weight. They knelt instead, on a small auxiliary wheel inserted on the underside of the nose, which allowed the nose gear to be retracted. This enabled the nose of a kneeling jet to be positioned under the tail of another one. In addition to looking silly, there were FOD and maintenance issues and little if any spotting benefit when parked with a non-kneeling aircraft.

Both were shaped by their engines – the F6U being sleeker like its axial-flow Westinghouse J34 that was less than two feet in diameter and the FJ-1 being somewhat more rotund like its bigger Allison J35, which was almost three feet in diameter. Similarly, the F6U was somewhat smaller in size and weight, in part because of the lower thrust of its engine, 3,000 lbs thrust at the Take Off rating compared to the FJ-1's at 3,750 lbs. Both aircraft had the capability to carry tip

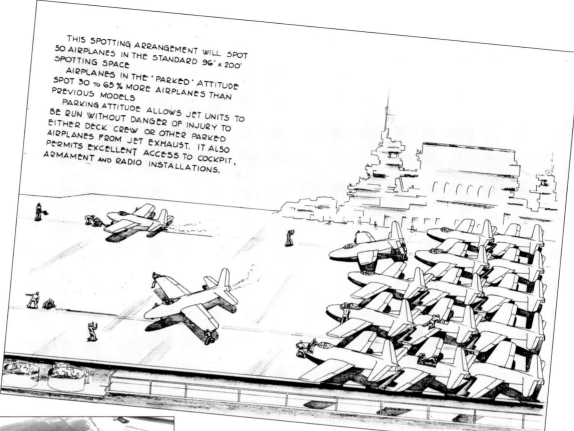

THIS SPOTTING ARRANGEMENT WILL SPOT 50 AIRPLANES IN THE STANDARD 96' x 200' SPOTTING SPACE

AIRPLANES IN THE "PARKED" ATTITUDE SPOT 30 to 65% MORE AIRPLANES THAN PREVIOUS MODELS

PARKING ATTITUDE ALLOWS JET UNITS TO BE RUN WITHOUT DANGER OF INJURY TO EITHER DECK CREW OR OTHER PARKED AIRPLANES FROM JET EXHAUST. IT ALSO PERMITS EXCELLENT ACCESS TO COCKPIT, ARMAMENT AND RADIO INSTALLATIONS.

*The standard metric for deck space compactness for several years was the number of aircraft that could be parked in the first 200 feet of a 96-foot-wide flight deck. Overhang of the deck edge was permitted. In the case of the 1944 jet competition, the Navy apparently encouraged the use of the kneeling concept to conserve deck space. (Grumman Aircraft History Center)*

*Kneeling for stowage was accomplished by installing a small auxiliary nose wheel under the nose of the aircraft and then retracting the nose landing gear. This allowed similarly kneeled aircraft to be stacked close together with noses under tails. (U.S. Navy via Hal Andrews collection)*

tanks to substantially increase the fuel capacity. One difference was that the F6U was to be armed with four 20mm cannons with 600 rounds of ammunition whereas the FJ-1 was the last of the Navy fighters to have the heretofore-standard six .50-caliber machine guns with 1,500 rounds of ammunition.

## McDonnell FH-1 Phantom

The production FD-1 first flew on 28 October 1946. (It became the FH-1 in August 1947; to minimize confusion, it will be referred to as the FH-1 from here on.) There were minor changes to the empennage – the horizontal tail and vertical fin were somewhat enlarged and the tips squared off. The wing tips were also squared off and the wingspan slightly reduced as a result. The four .50-caliber machine guns of the prototype with 1,300 rounds of ammunition were retained. It was flown to Patuxent River for testing in February 1947.

The FH-1 had a gross weight of 10,000 lbs with 2,250 lbs of internal fuel and was powered by two Westinghouse J30 axial-flow engines of 1,600 lbs of thrust each. The J30 was developed from the engine that powered the XFD-1, lighter with a better compression ratio and turbine design. The production Phantom's takeoff and landing performance relative to the other early jets was very good because of its low wing loading – the carrier approach speed was only 85 knots. The weight empty was about 6,700 lbs. It was fully navalized, with folding wings, catapult launch hooks, and a tail hook. However, the cockpit was neither pressurized nor equipped with an ejection seat, since those features had not yet become standard in jets.

The Phantom was notably deficient in performance compared to the Lockheed P-80A that was being delivered to the Army Air Forces at the same time, in part because the P-80 had a more powerful engine with lower fuel consumption. The P-80's maximum speed in level flight was approaching 500 knots

The Naval Air Test Center at NAS Patuxent River was the first to receive production aircraft in order to accomplish required service evaluations. The number 751 on the nose is the last three digits of the FH-1 Phantom's Bureau Number, 111751. The "ET" on the nose stands for Electronic Test, one of NATC's test divisions. (National Archives 80-G-390767)

The first operating squadron to receive the FH-1 was VF-17A based at NAS Quonset Point, Rhode Island. (U.S. Navy via Robert L. Lawson collection)

range. The FH was even worse: even with a 190-gallon belly tank almost doubling the fuel available after takeoff and climb, it had a range of only about 700 nautical miles. The Pilot's Handbook warns that, "About 40 gallons of fuel is required to go around" from a wave-off back to a landing, an indication of how much fuel an early twin-engine jet consumed at low altitudes and high power settings. As a result, FH production was limited to only 60 aircraft in anticipation of higher performance models then in development.[2]

Delivery of production Phantoms began in July 1947 to VF-17A, which became the first Navy jet squadron. The delivery rate was slow, averaging only two per month, but they finally were up to full strength by early 1948. In view of the importance of the introduction, pilots were only assigned to the squadron if they had a minimum of 1,000 hours and 50 carrier landings. After an extensive period of Field Carrier Landing Practice (FCLP), the squadron was ordered to embark aboard the light carrier Saipan off Narragansett Bay in May 1948, for carrier qualifications. The 16 FH-1s subsequently made 200 landings in a three-day period and accomplished combat air patrol and intercept missions, engaging P2V Neptunes sent out for mock attacks. The Saipan's short and narrow deck compared to Essex class carriers was not a problem. Following a very successful qualification period and a demonstration to the press, all 16 aircraft were flown off for the return to their home base, NAS Quonset Point, Rhode Island. Tragically, their commanding officer, Cdr. Ralph A. Fuoss, was killed in a mid-air collision with his wingman while the formation was circling for landing at Quonset.

The results of the VF-17A's qualifications as reported in the August 1949 edition of Naval Aviation News:

Wave-offs were routinely accomplished – "Actually, fewer wave-offs were given the jets than the others, possibly because visibility from the pilot's cockpit is better."

Approach speeds and residual thrust on landing was not a problem – "The Phantoms came in only slightly faster than F6Fs. They caught earlier wires than propeller planes, as a rule, and apparently float no worse than the heavier fighter."[3]

Jet exhaust was acceptable to the deck crew – "Saipan deck crews treated the jet exhaust with proper respect – that is, they did not walk directly behind the engines or touch the hot metal when shut down. They were not timid around them, as they are around a propeller. Some catapult men, chilled by the icy 30-knot wind over the Saipan deck, backed up to the edge of the exhaust aft of

whereas the FH could manage only a bit more than 400. The P-80's initial rate of climb was 4,500 feet per minute compared to the FH's 3,150. The P-80 was acknowledged to be deficient in

VF-17A qualified en masse aboard the light carrier Saipan in May 1948. Relatively few jet operations were conducted from these smaller carriers, with a flight deck that was less than 700 feet long and 100 feet wide. (National Archives 80-G-392020)

Once newer jets were available to reequip VF-17, their FHs were transferred to the Marine Corps, in this case VMF-122, to start their transition to jets. (U.S. Navy via Hal Andrews collection)

the tail and warmed their hands and backs. Force of the blast appeared no greater than ordinary prop wash a short distance behind the plane."

The need for auxiliary start carts did not slow launches – "Two battery jeeps duck around the jets, energizing their powerplants in rapid fashion. Since no warm-up of the engine is required once it starts, rapidity of launching is greater with jets from the time the general quarters gong rings."

Clearing the hook in the presence of the jet exhaust was possible – "By using a sort of gaff stick, *Saipan* deck men cleared the jets just as fast as any other type plane. Many of the hooks cleared of their own accord on the rollback after arrestment."

Jet exhaust did not affect launch or landing intervals – "Some pilots on the *Saipan* used oxygen masks when they took off with open canopies. Planes followed closely on each other at the catapult without damaging the one behind."

The only complaint reported was "the terrific whine of the jet engines was bothersome" to some deck crewmen. The potential danger of being sucked into a jet intake was not mentioned, although the squadron had already had an incident, with a sailor being partially drawn into an inlet.

Although the visibility was better, the proper landing technique was important. Phantom pilots had to be careful to touch down neither too nose-high nor too nose-low. The former risked striking the aft fuselage and the latter resulted in a hook skip ending with a trip into the Davis barrier. However, there was only one barrier engagement during the three days, with no significant damage to that aircraft – it flew off with the rest of the squadron.

Redesignated as VF-171 in August 1948, this same squadron operated from CV-47 *Philippine Sea* that month and from *Midway* and *FDR* in 1949, in each case for very brief periods for refresher training or pilot qualification. In March 1949, they were the first squadron to receive F2H-1s.

Only 60 FH-1s were built, but they were operated in squadron strength in VF-17A/VF-171, VMF-122 and briefly, in 1949, in VF-172. After their active service career, the FH-1s also did yeoman service in several Naval Air Reserve squadrons.

The major shortcoming of the FH-1 was the very limited engine time between overhauls, exacerbated by the degree of difficulty in engine starting. The clumsy or inexperienced could easily over temp the turbine blades, which required engine removal and overhaul. As Cdr. Richard W. Carter, who flew the FH-1 in the Navy Reserve, remembered it:

> My strongest recollections are of the rather elaborate start procedures. Service life of the little Westinghouse engines was limited by the number of start cycles. There were no sophisticated jet fuel controls in those days. The throttle was literally a gate valve, and the start was controlled by easing the throttle up, chasing the EGT (Exhaust Gas Temperature), and the "rumble" the term for what is now called compressor stall.[4]

The JATO feature was used at least once. A VMF-122 aircraft had been belly landed on a beach in the Dominican Republic due to contaminated fuel. The recovery crew simply dug holes in the sand down from the front of the aircraft, extended the landing gear, and hauled the FH-1 up the makeshift ramp. The fuel, some fuel-system components, and inboard flaps were replaced; JATO bottles installed; and a successful takeoff accomplished

*Early jet engines had to be changed fairly frequently. Not only was the allowed time between overhaul low, but adding too much fuel too soon when starting an early jet engine was a common error that damaged the turbine. The photo was taken in September 1947 at NAS Patuxent River. (National Archives 80-G-398696)*

from the beach using the rockets to augment the thrust from the jet engines.

## North American FJ-1

North American submitted carrier-based fighter proposals to BuAer in 1944, for a carrier adaptation of the P-51H and a jet-propelled fighter designed for the Westinghouse 24C (J34) engine with summary studies for the TG-180 (J35) and I-40 (J33) engines. At a 27 November 1944 BuAer conference (attended by George A. Spangenberg), it was decided that "BuAer policy covering jet fighters must be such as to cover the field of available engines. With this view in mind North American Aviation is the logical and desirable choice to undertake a jet fighter using the TG-180 unit because of the probable availability of the engine at a time which would meet the contractor's requirements." The P-51 proposal was "very attractive in certain respects," but BuAer did not want North American to be distracted from the jet-propelled design.[5]

The FJ-1 was developed by North American concurrently with the Army Air Forces' XP-86. Initially the aircraft were very similar in configuration. However, because of the post-war availability of German research on swept wings, the Air Force elected to redirect their program to incorporate this new concept. The Navy, mind-

ful of the prospective low-speed lift and handling-qualities drawbacks of the swept wing, elected to continue with the straight-wing configuration.

North American was ready for an engine in January 1946, only a year after contract go-ahead, since the aircraft was very similar in structure to its existing propeller-driven fighters, particularly the laminar flow wings. The new Allison J35 engine, however, was not available until June, which delayed first flight to September 1946, when Wallace A. (Wally) Lien took off from Muroc Army Air Field. After a relatively trouble-free development phase the three XFJ-1s, BuNos. 39053, 39054, and 39055, were turned over to the Navy in September 1947.

In April 1945, OpNav was increasingly concerned with the Kamikaze threat to the fleet. They directed BuAer to procure 100 FJ-1s in addition to the 100 FD-1s that had just been ordered: "Since this plane utilizes the TG-180, G.E. jet units, rather than the Westinghouse, it appears that it may be available before the FD-1s which use the Westinghouse units."[7] After V-J Day, this order was reduced to 30 aircraft. The first of these was delivered in October 1947 with the last being delivered in April 1948. In parallel with acceptance testing and trials at NATC that included carrier qualification, deliveries commenced to VF-5A based at NAS North Island, San Diego, California, in January 1948. The Navy was eager to get jets into the fleet and short-circuited its usual acceptance process to do so. VF-5A was therefore authorized to commence carrier operations before NATC had completed shore-based testing. Catapult launches were explicitly prohibited. It was noted that the takeoff distance at 11,600 lbs on a Standard Day (59° F) was 680 feet with 35 knots wind over deck.[8]

Following extensive field practice, the VF-5A squadron commander, Cdr. Evan Peter (Pete) Aurand, and Lt. Cdr. Robert Elder, his executive officer, made the squadron's first FJ-1 carrier takeoffs and landings in March 1948, from CV-21 *Boxer*. The technique used was to establish lineup about 200 yards farther out than for propeller-driven aircraft, necessitated by the "cut" being required farther out due to the lack of drag. At the cut, with the aircraft about 35 feet above the deck level, the throttle was reduced to idle and the nose dropped. A flare was accomplished just above the deck, raising the nose and dropping the tail to insure hook engagement. After the trials, which involved a total of 24 landings and takeoffs between the two pilots, Commander Aurand said:

> The visibility is what impresses you most. For the first time I not only knew what I was doing, but actually saw what I was doing in my landing approach. Usually by the time you're down to the deck with a propeller plane you are busy lining up the deck by looking out to the side. It was almost frightening to look ahead from the FJ and see the barriers for the first time. The jet is the easiest plane to land…you just fly it down and there you are.[9]

Aurand was a bit less forthcoming about the takeoff experience. As described by H. L. Elman in the Summer 1968 issue of the AAHS *Journal*:

> The FJ-1 was rolled to the aft end of the flight deck, its wheels just barely on the deck, its tail over the water. The carrier…was brought full speed into the wind and a maximum effort takeoff began… Wheels broke from the deck about 30 feet short of the bow, near the edge of the large "21" painted on the forward end of the flight deck. Loss of ground effect even resulted in a lurch after the plane went over the bow and Aurand was quite concerned over whether the ship would run him down. After that, no one in the Navy wanted to try another jet running takeoff.

Even with a 40-knot relative wind and using the full length of the deck, fly offs (as opposed to catapult launches) were demonstrated to be marginal – successful but still in doubt as the bow approached.

Aurand's squadron lost an aircraft, but not the pilot, on a training exercise to locate and attack ships 150 miles at sea off San Diego in May 1948. In searching for the ships in poor visibility at low altitude, Aurand stayed out a couple of minutes too long, with one FJ-1 running out of fuel and having to ditch just three miles out from North Island; the other three made it to the air station but flamed out before they could taxi in. The incident did reduce concerns that jets, particularly those with nose inlets, would dig in and dive under on contact with the water. The ditching went very smoothly, and the aircraft stayed afloat for more than enough time for the pilot, Lt. (jg) Alfred E. Nauman Jr, to make an orderly exit, inflating his life raft first.

After shore-based training and completion of the NATC carrier suitability trials, the squadron went aboard CV-37, *Princeton,* in May 1948, to qualify. In contrast to VF-17's virtually trouble-free FH-1 qualification aboard a smaller aircraft carrier, it went very badly. The fourth pilot to come aboard landed hard, breaking off the left wing, which was the only part of the aircraft to stay on the deck. The pilot was rescued unhurt. At the end of the second day, the remaining aircraft were all so damaged that they were unflyable and had to be returned on the ship to be craned off in San Diego.

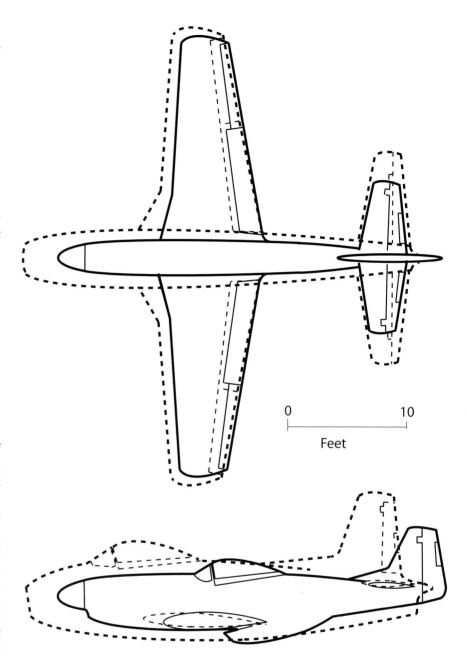

*P-51 vs. FJ-1*

*A comparison of North American's P-51 Mustang and FJ-1 Fury makes clear the heritage of wing and tail planform of the FJ-1. This undoubtedly contributed to the Fury's relatively trouble-free development aerodynamically. Note also the weight and balance considerations that have resulted in the jet's nose being extended farther forward. The relocation of the cockpit and armament and addition of the nose landing gear provided balance for the rearward location of the engine. (Author)*

*Various ways to provide access for engine removal were evaluated. North American's choice for its FJ-1 Fury was incompatible with the limited overhead room on the hangar deck of an aircraft carrier. (U.S. Navy via Tommy H. Thomason collection)*

All was forgiven however, and VF-5A, by then designated VF-51, briefly operated at sea with the FJ-1 at least two more times, aboard *Tarawa* in September 1948 and *Boxer* in February 1949.

Aurand's squadron also competed in the 1948 Bendix Trophy race for jets from Long Beach, California, to Cleveland, Ohio, a distance of a little more than 2,000 statute miles. This was accomplished nonstop by installing longer tip tanks that held twice as much fuel as the standard ones. It was just barely enough – Bob Elder ran out of fuel 50 miles short of Cleveland and glided to a dead-stick landing at the airport. The fastest speed turned in by a finisher, Ens. F. E. Brown, was 489.526 mph. He ran out of fuel while taxiing in and had to be towed to the parking area. Lt. A. T. Capriotti turned in the worst performance. He elected to cruise climb past the 40,000-feet altitude limit imposed by the Fury's oxygen system to get enough range to complete the flight into Cleveland. In short order he became hypoxic. Lost and out of fuel, Capriotti crash landed in a field near Melmore, Ohio, 82 miles west southwest of the Cleveland airport.

A VF-51 FJ-1 could not help but win the race since their six aircraft were the only contestants. A California Air National Guard pilot flying a P-80C – officially a non-competitor since the Secretary of Defense had forbidden competition between the services in races of this type – actually beat VF-51's best time by a little over two mph. He also used larger-than-standard tip tanks. Neither straight-wing jet was that much faster than a civil-registered P-51 Mustang flown by Paul Mantz, who won the propeller-driven class at an average of almost 448 mph.

Fast was demonstrated by Air Force Maj. Dick Johnson in the new, swept-wing sibling of the FJ-1, the F-86 Sabre. He would have set a new world record of 669.5 mph at the Cleveland Air Show that year if one of the recording devices had not malfunctioned.

The FJ-1 would have been hard pressed to get within 80 mph of that speed. It was clear that high-speed performance meant swept wings, a fact that the Navy had already recognized and had programs in place to better understand and implement.

In 1949, VF-51 was reequipped with the F9F-3, and their surviving FJ-1s were distributed to Naval Air Reserve squadrons as jet familiarization and proficiency aircraft. All had been stricken by January 1954. Of the 30 production aircraft built, at least 17 crashed and were written off before then, with VF-5A/VF-51 accounting for nine of them. Both Aurand's and Elder's careers survived all this carnage. In fact, in February 1950, Commander Metsger, who had been the Fighter Class Desk at BuAer during VF-51's operation of the FJ-1, had the Commander Air Force, Pacific Fleet, Adm. T. L. Sprague sign a letter of commendation to then Cdr. Aurand. It cited "realization of the maximum capabilities of the Model FJ-1 airplane" (at least two of the losses were fuel starvation) and cited valuable "lessons learned" (which pretty much covered the remainder).

Aurand went on to be the Fighter Class Desk at BuAer, continuing to champion the Fury – he was responsible for the FJ-4 program. He was the Naval aide to President Eisenhower during Ike's second term and retired as a vice admiral. Elder also had a long career, both operationally and in flight test and retired as a captain. Other VF-5A jet pilots who became notables were Lt. Don Engen, who also became a vice admiral, and Lt. Cdr. John Magda,

*Cdr. Aurand's first landing aboard Boxer was significantly less of a challenge than the takeoff. He was particularly impressed with the cockpit visibility on approach and short final compared to propeller-driven aircraft he had flown aboard. (National Archives 80-G-705095)*

who went on to lead the Blue Angels and then was killed during the Korean War while flying an F9F Panther.

## F6U

Designed and built in Stratford, Connecticut, the F6U's first flight was accomplished at Muroc Army Air Field in view of the experimental nature of its Westinghouse J34 engine. Taxi tests were accomplished at Stratford, and then the newly named "Pirate" was disassembled and flown in a Fairchild C-82 Packet cargo plane to California. Twenty-four minutes into its first flight on 2 October 1946, the F6U's engine accessory drive failed and Vought test pilot Ted Owens had to land on the lakebed. Westinghouse could not provide another engine for 45 days. The troubled start was all too typical of what was to follow.

In February 1947, Vought was finally awarded a production contract for 30 F6Us, well after the contracts for FH-1 and FJ-1. One has to wonder why the Navy bothered, because by then they knew that F6U flight test was not going well. It was probably to provide production work at one of their favored suppliers. (There is also the possibility that it was a backup to the F9F-2 program, Grumman's first jet, a common BuAer practice at the time.) For starters, an unacceptable stall characteristic was uncovered very early on. Then, when the envelope expansion had reached 0.6 Mach, a so-called "rudder jab" due to unsteady flow off the horizontal tail manifested itself, which when fixed allowed a further speed increase only to reveal an unsatisfactory Dutch-roll condition. Because of these problems and poor longitudinal stability, several successive empennage configuration changes were evaluated until a satisfactory solution was finally obtained. The change process was slowed considerably by the fact that the engineering

and experimental manufacturing departments were located in Connecticut and the aircraft in California.

The F6U was also underpowered. It had the same "payload" – pilot, cockpit, armament, and avionics – as the F2H but only half the thrust, since it had only one J34 and the Banshee had two. Moreover, the production aircraft were burdened by emerging jet aircraft requirements – the ejection seat and cockpit heating and pressurization – that the FH-1 and FJ-1, released for production earlier, did not. Vought's solution to the thrust problem was the installation of the first afterburner on a jet engine. The production fuselage was stretched to add the new equipment and 50 more gallons of internal fuel as well as rebalancing of the aircraft following the addition of the afterburner.

After a rough start, VF-5 carrier qualified as a squadron. It never deployed with the FJ-1 but did periodically go aboard for exercises. Here, they are queuing up for takeoff from Princeton in January 1949. (National Archives 80-G-416552)

One of VF-5A's FJ-1s takes off from Long Beach, California, for the 1948 Bendix Race. For this event, the aircraft carried non-standard oversized tip tanks so they had enough fuel for a nonstop flight to Cleveland, Ohio. (National Archives 80-G-416541)

The afterburner was also the only real contribution of the F6U to the development of Navy jet fighters besides what Vought learned from the experience in general. The principle was simple – the exhaust still contained enough oxygen that jet fuel could be sprayed into the tailpipe and burned, increasing thrust significantly, albeit very inefficiently. As a result, the Westinghouse engine, rated at 3,150 lbs of thrust, could produce 4,200 lbs of thrust in an afterburner. During the first in-flight test in April 1949, at 12,000 feet, the afterburner increased the indicated airspeed from 345 mph to 440 mph with no change in engine-operating rpm. This tremendous improvement in performance came with an equally big reduction in endurance. At normal rated (maximum continuous) power, the J34 burned 2,765 lbs of fuel per hour, which would deplete the internal fuel in about one hour. At military power, the rate went up to 3,744 lbs per hour. In afterburner, it went to 12,850 lbs per hour, limited to five minutes of continuous operation from a structural standpoint and less than 13 minutes by the internal fuel capacity.

The afterburner was successfully integrated into the airframe and engine-control system, although it had limited applicability within the flight envelope. It was, for the F6U, a mixed blessing. The additional weight penalized performance when it was not operating, and when it was, it burned prodigious amounts of fuel, exacerbating the existing endurance problem. In addition, the presence of the afterburner hardware in the exhaust reduced the maximum thrust of the basic engine by 100 lbs or so, which the F6U pilot could ill afford.

With production underway but no aircraft completed, Vought management decided to move the company from Connecticut to a Navy-owned facility in Grand Prairie, Texas, southwest of Dallas. Many Vought personnel decided not to move, further affecting productivity. Moreover, government-furnished equipment like engines, afterburners, and other items were behind schedule, and the runway at the Naval Air Station adjacent to the new plant was determined to be inadequate for the F6U. While it was being lengthened, the first flight of the production F6U was finally accomplished at Carswell Air Force Base, west of Fort Worth, in June 1949. (All experimental and production flight testing was subsequently relocated to a former Navy training field near Ardmore, Oklahoma, due to conflicts with the Air Force and Convair at Carswell.)

By the time the first flight finally occurred, all 30 production aircraft were already supposed to have been delivered. VF-171 and VF-51 were starting to receive second-generation jet fighters, F2Hs and F9Fs respectively, to replace their FHs and FJs. As a result of the schedule difficulties, ongoing development work to cure the last of the aircraft's aerodynamic, system, and structural problems, and the resulting modifications that had to be made to the assembled F6Us, by the end of October 1949 the Navy had taken delivery of only two production aircraft, BuNos. 122481 and 122483. Both were used for Board of Inspection and Survey Trials at the Naval Air Test Center Patuxent River to determine contract compliance. Deliveries resumed in December 1949 and were completed in February 1950, with most of the aircraft being temporarily

*The sailor is apparently training pilots on how to operate ground-support equipment. Note the unusually shaped red tow bar and two sets of auxiliary nose wheels (used to accomplish the "kneeling" parking position) under the wing. (U.S. Navy via Robert L. Lawson collection)*

*When VF-5 (now VF-51) started to get F9F Panthers, their surviving FJs were handed down to Reserve Squadrons. Here the Weekend Warriors from NAS Oakland, California, proudly parade (with sequential aircraft numbers) in November 1950 with the Bay Bridge in the background. (U.S. Navy via Hal Andrews collection)*

stashed at VX-3, an Air Development Squadron based at NAS Atlantic City, New Jersey, which developed fighter tactics including weapons employment.

Only a few months later, VX-3 was ordered to ferry its F6Us to NAS Quonset Point for short-term preservation. In November 1950, 27 of the 29 survivors were parceled out to various Navy facilities for ground-test or maintenance training, with two being retained by NACA "for lateral dynamic stability studies." The 30 production aircraft flew only 945 flight hours, a little over 30 hours each. Eight were reportedly only flown for less than 10 hours each, the time required for production flight acceptance and ferry to a disposition point.

There apparently was never an attempt to carrier qualify the F6U, probably because the aircraft was delivered too late to have been of any operational use. A few of the aircraft were useful in other ways – one was used for an evaluation at the Naval Air Material Center of the effectiveness of jet blast deflectors on afterburners, and others were made available for jet barrier evaluations.

The F6U was literally too little and too late. The afterburner cured the thrust problem, but it did not always light off when commanded, and that often left the pilot in an untenable situation. It might have compared favorably with the FH and the FJ if it had been fielded when they were and equipped as they were. Certainly the Fighter Class Desk officer had high hopes for it in August 1946 before its first flight:

> The jet manufacturers' strikes having been settled
> some months ago, we are just on the verge of flying the

*The first flight for the F6U at Muroc Army Air Field in California may well have been the highlight of the Pirate program. It was cut short by engine problems, a harbinger of the difficulties to come. (Vought Heritage Center)*

XF6U and the XFJ. The FJ is now some 1,400 pounds "overweight," but we feel that it should be a very good airplane nonetheless. The XF6U is very close to its weight and if we can get 10 percent extra thrust from the engine as is now expected, this airplane should become fairly attractive.[10]

Unfortunately, coming into service as it did two years later than the FH and the FJ, it was up against the bigger, more capable F9F Panther and the F2H Banshee. Its primary benefit was the introduction of Vought to the jet fighter and as a flying test bed for the afterburning engine concept.

## First Jets – Summary and Lessons Learned

The FH, F6U, and FJ-1 are sometimes lumped together as contemporaries, with a similar conjunction of the F2H-1, F9F-2, and F3D-1. The actual timing was more complicated, as shown in Figure 3-2. The XFD-1 first flight preceded those of the F6U and FJ-1 by almost two years. However, the FH-1 and FJ-1 were operationally evaluated at about the same time while production F6U deliveries lagged behind those of the F2H-1 and F9F-2.

The FJ-1 is sometimes regarded as being superior to the FH-1. From the standpoint of performance that may have been true, but the first Phantom embarrassed far fewer pilots than the first Fury. The FJ-1's reputation stems in part from public relations activity by VF-5, the Navy, and North American, in that its achievements were promulgated widely and embarrassing incidents suppressed. The FH was in fact an outstanding first effort for McDonnell, not only being its first design to go into production,

but for the most difficult of requirements, carrier-based operation. The basic configuration with bigger engines, the F2H, served the Navy well for many years.

One interesting comparison between the F6U and the FJ-1 is the benefit of the former's afterburner on performance using the 1 May 1949, SAC charts for both at combat weight, here defined as full internal fuel. The FJ-1 chart provides data for two power conditions, Military and Normal (maximum continuous); for the F6U, the two conditions were Combat and Normal, with Combat indicating the use of Military power along with the afterburner.

Using its afterburner, the F6U went from being woefully deficient in performance to equivalent in speed and superior in rate of climb and combat ceiling. Although there was an adverse impact on range and endurance, it was very dependent on time spent in afterburner.

| Power | FJ-1 Normal | F6U Normal | FJ-1 Military | F6U Combat |
|---|---|---|---|---|
| Max Speed SL (kts) | 468 | 395 | 510 | 518 |
| SL ROC (ft/min) | 4,750 | 2,385 | 5,660 | 8,060 |
| Ceiling (500 fpm) | 35,900 | 29,000 | 38,000 | 46,300 |

Nevertheless, the F6U was the least successful of the first three Navy jets from an operational standpoint, not only never being deployed with an operating squadron but apparently never even being evaluated aboard a carrier – a very poor showing considering that Vought was the only one of these three companies with carrier-based aircraft experience. When delivered, however, it was more advanced and better equipped than the FH-1 and FJ-1 with its pressurized cockpit, ejection seat, 20mm cannon armament, and afterburner. Unfortunately, it appeared too late for service in

### First Jets - First Flights

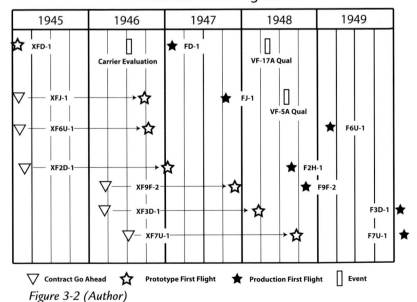

| | 1945 | 1946 | 1947 | 1948 | 1949 |
|---|---|---|---|---|---|
| XFD-1 | ☆ | | ★ FD-1 | | |
| Carrier Evaluation | | ▯ | | | |
| VF-17A Qual | | | | ▯ | |
| XFJ-1 | ▽ | →☆ | | ★ FJ-1 | |
| VF-5A Qual | | | | ▯ | |
| XF6U-1 | ▽ | →☆ | | | ★ F6U-1 |
| XF2D-1 | ▽ | | →☆ | ★ F2H-1 | |
| XF9F-2 | | ▽ | →☆ | ★ F9F-2 | |
| XF3D-1 | | ▽ | →☆ | | F3D-1 ★ |
| XF7U-1 | | ▽ | →☆ | | F7U-1 ★ |

▽ Contract Go Ahead   ☆ Prototype First Flight   ★ Production First Flight   ▯ Event

*Figure 3-2 (Author)*

*A sure indication of problems is the appearance of tufts on a flight-test aircraft. These are short lengths of string temporarily attached to the surface. They are then photographed in flight at test points of interest to provide a better understanding of the localized airflow. (Vought Heritage Center)*

*Vought's problems with the F6U tail weren't because it didn't accomplish large-scale wind-tunnel testing to develop the design. This wind-tunnel model was seven feet long and reconfigurable so it could be tested with the landing gear and flaps up or down, canopy open or closed, and control surfaces positioned. (Vought Heritage Center)*

*The answer to the F6U's need for more thrust was one of the first afterburners. Basically, an afterburner was simply a tailpipe fitted with a fuel spray bar inside and a means to ignite the fuel. The Westinghouse J34 engine is to the left of the gentleman in the hat, and the Solar afterburner is to the right. An XF6U being rebuilt with a new aft fuselage for the afterburner installation is in the background. (Vought Heritage Center)*

*The XF6U modified with afterburner and one of the many vertical fin variations is ready for test. The wide length-wise stripes on the side of the rear fuselage are a special paint, Tempilac, which melts at a specific temperature. This is an inexpensive way to determine what surface temperature was reached in operation. (U.S. Navy photo via Hal Andrews collection)*

an operational squadron and was not assigned to any reserve squadrons either. In spite of the afterburner, which on paper provided superior performance, it had the reputation of being underpowered, which it certainly was without afterburner.

Ejection seats became standard because jets spent a lot more time at airspeeds that minimized the likelihood of a safe bailout. Ironically, the F6U seat failed the one time it was called upon. In January 1950, due to dragging brakes, the long takeoff roll of an NATC F6U at NAAS Mustin Field near Philadelphia, Pennsylvania, resulted in the landing gear being damaged by a retaining wall located beyond the end of the runway. The pilot elected to climb to altitude off the coast, point the F6U out to sea, and eject. When

When development was finally completed, the aft fuselage had changed significantly from the XF6U-1 BuNo. 33532 on the left to the production F6U-1 BuNo. 122481 on the right, with the addition of the afterburner and the final result of empennage changes to eliminate buffet and provide adequate directional stability. Not obvious in this comparison is the lengthening of the forward fuselage as well. (U.S. Navy photos via Jay Miller collection)

the seat did not fire after three attempts, he resorted to rolling upside down and dropping out. He was subsequently picked up unharmed by helicopter. It was later determined from inspection of other seats that the lanyard connecting the face curtain and the cartridge had too much slack in some F6U installations.

Cockpit pressurization became standard because the jet aircraft functioned best at altitudes that were hard on the pilot in an unpressurized cockpit and potentially fatal. Even the FH-1 achieved its best range at 30,000 feet, the upper limit for standard-demand 100-percen oxygen masks. Above that, pressure-demand breathing was required to minimize loss of mental and visual acuity. Pressure demand forced oxygen into the lungs and effort was required to exhale, which was tiring. Fortunately, bleed air from the engine provided a ready source of pressurization. However, a low-pressure differential was provided for various reasons, so the cockpit might be at 25,000 feet when the aircraft was at 40,000 feet.

Another innovation was the use of speed brakes. With no propeller, jets had poor acceleration, but since they also lacked the drag of the propeller when it was windmilling, they had equally poor deceleration. The FH-1 was equipped with a wing-mounted brake that extended from

The F6U saw very limited usage. This one was assigned to Electronic Test at the Naval Air Test Center at NAS Patuxent River. The yellow low-slung jeep-like cart carries the array of batteries needed to start these early jets. (National Archives)

*VX-3 was one of the first squadrons to get a new model of jet aircraft after NATC. This formation with the FH-1 Phantom, then being retired, and the F2H-1, then being delivered, illustrates the bad timing of the F6U production program. It was the same state-of-the-art technology as the FH but finally entered service at the same time as the F2H, powered by two J34s to the F6U's one. (U.S. Navy via Hal Andrews collection)*

At the end of 1948, the good news was that jets had clearly demonstrated carrier compatibility with respect to previous concerns. In fact, the first jets were considered easier to land than the contemporary propeller-driven fighters due to better visibility on approach. Initial aircraft carrier changes required to accommodate jets had been determined and were being implemented. The jet afterburner had the potential to significantly reduce the problem of low thrust at low speeds and dramatically increase rate of climb and high-speed performance. The Navy's first swept-wing jet fighter, the Vought F7U, had just flown, and another was on contract with Grumman. The basic jet fighter specification requirements – dive brakes, cockpit pressurization, wing folding, etc. – had been established.

A training program had also been instituted to transition pilots from propeller-driven aircraft to jets by not only educating them on the critical differences but also providing safe, easy-to-fly jets to learn and practice on. McDonnell proposed a two-seat variant of their FD-1 as a jet trainer, but it does not appear that it was considered necessary. Instead, VF-52 had been equipped with 24 single-seat TO-1s, which were stock Lockheed P-80 Shooting Stars with a Navy designation, and assigned the responsibility of jet pilot training for the Pacific fleet. This increased the number of Navy jet fighter squadrons by 50 percent. It also provided the capability to begin more rapidly and safely increasing the number of Navy pilots flying jets.[11] Although a little more than 400 Navy and Marine Corps aviators had flown a jet at least once by the end of 1948, compared to about 12,000 Naval aviators in total, there were only about 75 jets actually flying day in and out. The transition syllabus took less than a month, with 52 hours of ground school and 21 hours of flight time, solo from the first flight on, a testament to the simplicity of the jet fighter at the time.

the upper and lower surface of the wing; it was very effective and was carried forward to the F2H series as well. The XFJ-1 used a wing-mounted brake similar to the FHs; however, an early failure of one side to deploy in flight test resulted in a change in production to extendible panels mounted on each side of the fuselage like the F6U's.

Engine durability was an early shortcoming. The FJ-1 engine had an overhaul limit of 30 hours. The aircraft would be towed to and from the runway in order to maximize the amount of flight time available. Jet engine durability was in stark contrast to the more developed piston engine, which had overhaul times of 1,000 hours or more. As a result, squadrons operating piston engine aircraft took few spare engines and no overhaul parts on a deployment, only spare and line maintenance parts like spark plugs and fuel pumps. With experience, however, and better fuel controls, overhaul times were increased to a few hundred hours for the next generation of jet engines.

Three aircraft companies, McDonnell, North American, and Vought, had built jet fighters to Navy carrier aircraft requirements and had them evaluated by the Navy in squadron service, although one almost flunked carrier qualification and another didn't even get to the boat. Finally and most importantly, the next generation of the Navy's straight-wing jets, the F2H, F9F-2, and F3D had made their first flights.

## CHAPTER FOUR

*The XF2D was essentially a slight scale-up of the FD-1 to add more powerful engines, more fuel, more features (e.g., cockpit pressurization), etc. However, more power resulted in it flying fast enough to encounter compressibility, which had not significantly affected the development of the Phantom. (National Archives 80-G-395929)*

# SECOND GENERATION - OPERATIONAL AND INTO COMBAT

During most of the transition to and the perfecting of jet fighters, BuAer usually had enough budget to have two in development and two in production for each of its mission requirements. Spreading their bets and fostering competition were to prove effective....

## F2H Banshee

McDonnell built on its FH success with the F2H. The F2H began as the F2D just as the FH had originally been designated the FD. However, in April 1946, Douglas received a letter of intent for its first Navy fighter since its little-known, one-off XFD-1 biplane fighter in 1933. Because the F2D designation had already been assigned to McDonnell and "D" was the letter identifier for Douglas, their new Navy jet was designated the XF3D. The potential for confusion was eventually resolved by changing the McDonnell letter to "H" in Navy Aircraft Circular Letter 81-47 of 28 August 1947.

The XF2D-1 was very similar in configuration to the XFD. However, it was to be powered by Westinghouse's new 24C jet engine (later designated J34), which had almost twice the thrust of the XFD's engines. Internal fuel capacity was increased. The armament was upgraded to four 20mm cannons. It had more wing area and thinner wing sections, but the wing and stabilizer dihedral of the XFD was retained. McDonnell received a contract for three prototypes in March 1945, only a few months after the XFD's first flight. A BuAer mockup review was accomplished only a month later. The Banshee first flew in January 1947, piloted by Robert M. Edholm. Captain Trapnell and Lt. Col. Marion Carl conducted an initial evaluation in March 1947. They were favorably impressed with its climb, takeoff, and wave-off characteristics.

Flight test development was not quite as trouble-free as it had been with the XFD. As the XF2D was flown to higher speeds, the test pilots encountered successive critical Mach number effects. The critical Mach number is the speed at which local flow on the wing, which is moving faster than the aircraft due to the curvature of the airfoil, reaches the speed of sound. When it is exceeded, there is a disproportionate increase in drag with increase in speed as shown in Figure 4-1, as well as an onset of buffet and control problems.

The first encounter was an overall airframe shake or roughness that was clearly compressibility related since the onset at different altitudes was at the same Mach number. It was finally isolated to disturbed airflow at the upper intersection of the wing root and fuselage. The solution was to extend the trailing edge aft and reshape the wing root. This modification allowed an increase to a speed at which a violent roughness of the rudder was encountered. Various fixes, including the addition of a dorsal fin,

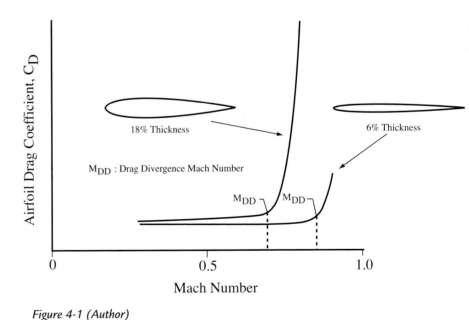

*Figure 4-1 (Author)*
*With jet engines providing the thrust to not only go faster on a routine basis but even faster in a dive with no propeller to hold the airplane back, thick airfoils became a significant liability from a drag standpoint. The drag rise is even steeper than shown, because it is proportional to the drag coefficient multiplied by the square of the velocity. (Author)*

*The most obvious changes resulting from Banshee flight-test development were to the empennage and to the engine compartment fairing, which was extended aft to increase the critical Mach number. The XF2D BuNo. 99858 on the left has dihedral in the horizontal stabilizer and a thicker wing-to-fuselage fillet compared to the production F2H-1 BuNo. 122532 below. (U.S. Navy photos via Hal Andrews collection)*

failed to have any impact on this until a fillet was added to the intersection between the vertical and horizontal tails that extended back onto the rudder, and the dihedral in the horizontal tail was eliminated.

This allowed a speed increase to an encounter with aileron roughness, or buzz, which was finally masked with the addition of a hydraulic actuator. With this restriction lifted, airframe roughness and rudder buffet were again encountered at higher speeds. This time engineering decided that the wing and tail thickness ratios had to be reduced to increase their critical Mach number. (While this was being implemented, another round of fin/stabilizer intersections was evaluated.) The original wing was 13 percent thick from the wing fold to the tip. The new wing was 12

percent thick at the wing fold and only 9 percent thick at the wing tip. The horizontal tail thickness was reduced from 12 percent to 11 percent. The reductions not only eliminated the airframe roughness and the rudder buffet, the aileron buzz had also disappeared. At this point, the limiting condition was an uncontrollable pitch up at transonic speeds attainable only in a dive, so configuration development was declared complete.[1]

As part of the redesign for production to incorporate the aerodynamic changes, the fuselage forward of the wing was extended by about 14 inches. This allowed an increase in the internal fuel capacity from the XF2D-1's 526 gallons to the F2H-1's 877 gallons. An ejection seat and cockpit pressurization were also added. Even though it had folding wings, the F2H-1 was also capable of

VF-171 was the first fleet squadron to take delivery of the new F2H-1 Banshees. After relatively brief operational use, these were replaced with F2H-2s, which had much-needed additional fuel capacity thanks to jettisonable tip tanks. (National Archives 80-G-411576)

The XF2D prototypes were used to develop successive improvements. This is a one-of-a-kind configuration – the short forward fuselage of the XF2D, an interim version of the empennage with a splitter plate at the juncture of the horizontal stabilizer and vertical fin, the thin wing of the F2H-1, and tip tanks similar to those which would be used on the F2H-2. (U.S. Navy via Hal Andrews collection)

kneeling onto a small auxiliary nose wheel like the FJ-1 and F6U. This proved to be of little advantage and was dropped from the F2H-2.

The prototype was delivered to Patuxent River for BIS trials in February 1948. The first production F2H-1 flew in August 1948. In March 1949, VF-171 was the first fleet squadron to get the F2H-1, which replaced its FH-1s. Subsequent production aircraft went to VF-172 with all 56 aircraft on order being delivered by June 1949. Carrier trials were accomplished in May 1949 aboard *Franklin D. Roosevelt*. The same month, an F2H-1 crashed at Patuxent River and the Navy pilot was killed when the left wing came off during a strafing evaluation. The cause was determined to be the pilot exceeding structural limits, but the F2H had a reputation for weak wings from then on. However, it was considered easy to fly, particularly in instrument conditions, and bring aboard the carrier.

The F2H-1 had a short operational career in the fleet. McDonnell had corrected shortcomings identified in development and evaluation for the most part, but there were two more wing failures resulting in fatal crashes in June. These required flight envelope restrictions and the addition of a bob-weight to increase stick force with increasing g. In March 1950, during a landing on *Philippine Sea*, a barrier engagement resulting from a

tail-hook failure resulted in the cutting of the Davis barriers by the main landing gear. All F2H-1s were temporarily restricted from carrier operation. In May, there was a similar incident and additional modifications to both the aircraft and the barriers were made, along with the rapid development and installation of an additional backstop, the "retardation barricade."

The F2H-1 was followed down the production line by the F2H-2, which had uprated J34s, jettisonable wing tip tanks, and external stores stations. The tip tanks increased the F2H-2's fuel capacity to 1,277 gallons, a 140 percent increase over the original design volume. One casualty of the late addition of the tip tanks to the design was the ability to fold or unfold the wings with full tip tanks, a definite drawback particularly when an F2H became a dud (having a problem that meant it could not be launched) on the way to the catapult. It also meant that the wings had to be spread for the tip tanks to be filled, which increased the deck space that had to be assigned to the Banshees before launch.

The first two F2H-2s were delivered to the Navy in November 1949. In May 1950, NATC conducted carrier suitability trials. Both VF-171 and VF-172 traded their -1s in on the -2 before they began their first deployment in September 1950 aboard *Coral Sea* to the Mediterranean. In all, 334 F2H-2s were produced.

With its high aspect ratio wing, the F2H had outstanding altitude capability. During the debate between the Air Force and the Navy about the respective vulnerability of the B-36 and the aircraft carrier, the Banshee played a significant role. The Air Force had claimed that Navy jets couldn't fly as high as bombers and, even if they could, they would not get to altitude in time for an interception. The B-36s, and by extension, Soviet bombers, could therefore attack aircraft carriers with impunity. In an article in the 14 March 1949 issue of *Aviation Week* on the B-36, reporter Robert Hotz stated:

> A series of test interceptions pitting the Lockheed F-80C, Republic F-84, and the North American F-86A against the B-36B had indicated that the fighters are unable to make (a) significant percentage of successful attacks on the bomber and never have been able to make an interception until after the bomber reached its target and dropped its bomb load.

The article went on to claim that radar provided less than 30 minutes warning of a B-36's approach, and it took that long to reach the bomber's altitude of 40,000 feet.

As part of a campaign to repudiate this assertion, the Navy conducted a carrier-based aviation demonstration on 26 September 1949, on *Franklin D. Roosevelt* for the Secretary of Defense Louis Johnson, high-ranking civilian and military leaders of the Air Force, Army, and Navy, and other civilians, including the press. One of the demonstrations was an interception of incoming bombers – four VF-171 F2H-1s were launched in response to a mock attack and climbed to 40,000 feet in less than seven minutes.

There was some thought given to staging an aerial war exercise pitting the B-36 against jet fighters. The House Armed Services Committee was recommending one to provide data for their investigation of Air Force plans for B-36 strategic bombing. The Navy fighter community was eager to participate. McDonnell modified at least one F2H-1 with afterburners, not to increase speed but to cut the time to climb to 40,000 feet in half. However, the Joint Chiefs decided that since it would be impossible to conduct a valid exercise, one would serve no useful purpose.[2]

That did not stop efforts to publicize the altitude capability of Navy fighters. Later that year, an F2H-1 with a cartographic camera mounted in the aft fuselage was flown over Washington, D.C. The objective was to take a picture of the capital from an altitude of 50,000 feet, the height being verifiable by analysis of the photograph and well above the B-36's capability. Lt. (jg) Hugh Tate actually got as high as 52,000 feet but had to descend beneath an overcast to 48,846 feet for the photo. A few days later, Lt. (jg) Frederick C. Turner repeated the flight and took a picture from 51,089 feet.[3]

The Navy realized that its capability to find and attack incoming bombers at night and in bad weather was inadequate. They had contracted for a night-fighter version of the FH but then realized that the type would be obsolete before it was available. They transferred the requirement to the F2H and ordered an evaluation quantity of 14 aircraft as F2H-2Ns. The major changes were the addition of APS-19 search/intercept radar, the same one used by the F4U-5N, in a lengthened nose, which required relocation of the four 20mm cannons. The first at-sea evaluation with an air group was aboard *Franklin D. Roosevelt* as a VC-4 detachment on a shakedown cruise in October 1950. However, BIS trials of the F2H-2N that were finally accomplished in mid-1952 concluded that the APS-19A radar was not effective in jet interceptions. In any event, no more F2H-2Ns were procured.

One operational option with the Banshee was to single up to one engine for extended range and endurance. Reduced fuel consumption resulted because an engine produces power more effi-

*The F2H-2N was a continuation of the Navy's wartime practice of creating night fighters by adding visual-assist radar to existing day fighters. Only a handful of F2H-2Ns were built, but they were deployed without difficulty since they were otherwise identical to the F2H-2. (U.S. Navy via Tommy H. Thomason collection)*

ciently at higher power settings. Shutting one down let the other operate at a higher power setting.[4] In October 1954, Ensign Duane L. Varner of VF-34 made a nonstop, unrefueled, 1,900-mile flight from Los Alamitos, California, to Cecil Field, Florida, in four hours in an F2H-2. The flight was possible in part because he used the single-engine technique to extend his range, but the primary reason was the strength of the tail wind.

## 1945 All-Weather Fighter Competition

The next major competition for Navy jet fighters was held in 1945, as the war in the Pacific was ending. Having jet day-fighter programs in place, BuAer now turned to the night-fighter mission. The new requirement (heavily influenced by the Marine Corps) was for a two-seat, twin-engine, carrier-based night fighter equipped with long-range, high-power radar and armed with four 20mm cannons. Tail warning radar was also required. Maximum speed at sea level was to be at least 475 mph. Internal fuel was to be provided for a 350-mile combat radius or six hours endurance. Side-by-side seating for the pilot and radar operator was requested to improve crew coordination. The proposal request was provided to 12 companies in June 1945.

Five of the companies declined to bid. The proposals from five others were rejected for various reasons like being too large for carrier operations, inadequate high-speed performance, excessive

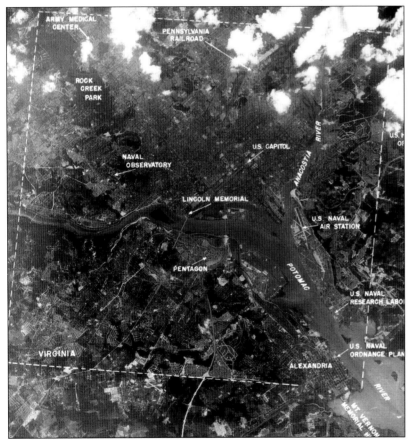

*Even without a big wing and afterburner, the F2H was capable of climbing to and maintaining higher altitudes than most of its contemporaries. This picture was taken by a camera mounted in the aft fuselage of an F2H-1 at almost 50,000 feet over Washington, D.C. to demonstrate that the Banshee could easily climb to any altitude that a bomber could operate at. (U.S. Navy via Tommy H. Thomason collection)*

*The usual approach to creating a carrier-based night fighter was to add a radar to an existing day fighter like the F6F and F4U, shown here with an F3D over the Golden Gate Bridge. These aircraft are all assigned to VC-3 at NAS Moffett Field. (U.S. Navy via Hal Andrews collection)*

development time proposed, or unsatisfactory aerodynamic characteristics. At that point, only the Grumman and Douglas proposals remained. The Grumman Design 75 was powered by four 3,000-lb–thrust Westinghouse J34 engines, two in each mid-wing nacelle, and had the requisite side-by-side seating for the pilot and radar operator. The Douglas design had two J34 engines in pods on the fuselage sides under the wing. Spangenberg recalled:

> (A)wards were made (for) two very different aircraft, the Douglas F3D and the Grumman F9F-1. The Douglas proposal was as expected, with two J34 engines mounted well forward under the wing. Grumman surprised everyone by submitting a four-engine arrangement with (J34) engines. The very different design solutions were due to

the definition of the combat portion of the design mission for the airplane. Historically, all previous problems had required maximum thrust/power to be used but in this competition, the combat (portion) was specified to be at 400 mph, well below the maximum speed of the Grumman design. This came about due to the project officer's insistence that any higher speed could not be used tactically at night with the radar then available and guns as armament. If full power was used for combat the Grumman design was woefully short-legged.[5]

After evaluating these proposals and revisiting their specification requirements, the Navy decided that the Grumman design, with relatively minor changes, had potential as an all-weather

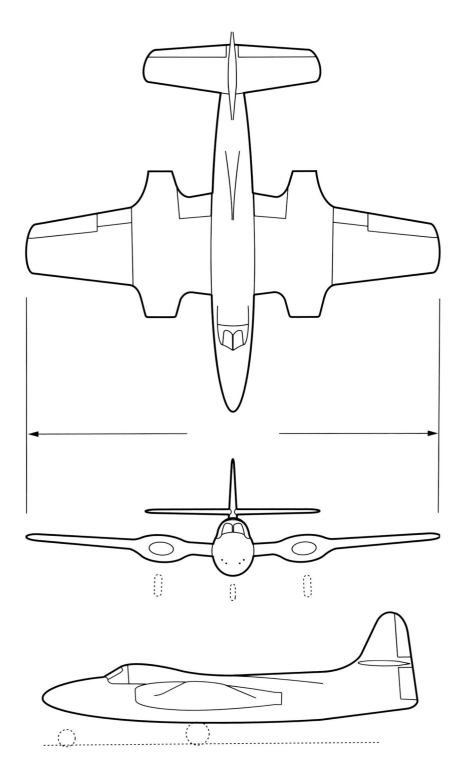

*Grumman XF9F-1*

*The XF9F-1 was intended to be a two-seat all-weather fighter. This three-view represents the post-proposal configuration dictated by the Navy, which deleted the tail-warning radar among other changes. (Author)*

interceptor. The much higher installed power resulted in excellent high-speed and climb performance, offsetting its otherwise unacceptable range based on post-proposal changes to the mission specification. It was to have a maximum speed of 575 mph, an initial rate of climb of 7,000 feet per minute, and a mission radius of 100 miles. In refining the Grumman design, BuAer deleted the tail-warning radar and added "positive crew ejection."

The Navy wanted Douglas to tailor its design to be an all-weather intruder, or attack aircraft, with good range. It would be specified to have a maximum speed of 530 mph, a rate of climb of 4,500 feet per minute, and a mission radius of 350 miles. The tail-warning radar was retained, the nose was to be enlarged to accommodate the APS-21 radar, armament was to be four 20mm guns instead of spin stabilized rockets, and fuel-tank protection (self-sealing) was required for all internal fuel.

Following the submission of revised cost and design proposals in March in accordance with the Navy requested changes, Grumman and Douglas were both awarded Letters of Intent to Contract in April 1946 for three flight and one static test articles, with the Douglas design being designated the XF3D-1 and the Grumman, XF9F-1. The XF3D was to fly in September 1947, and the XF9F-1, in June 1947.[6]

In the meantime, however, Grumman and the Navy were experiencing problems with the big, twin-engine F7F. After extensive shore-based landing tests and three periods of at-sea tests conducted over two years, the F7F was still not carrier-qualified. In a February 1946 test aboard *Shangri-La*, the aircraft had suffered a structural failure during landing. The XF9F-1 was similar in size and weight to the F7F, causing Grumman to reexamine its proposed design and the Navy to issue an XF9F-1 stop work order in June 1946.

## F9F Panther

Fortunately, Grumman was a preferred BuAer supplier and had been updating the single-engine design study rejected by BuAer in 1944. The Navy realized that it had become overly reliant on Westinghouse, with a strike there delaying engines for most of their jet fighters. As of mid-1946, Grumman's Design 79 variations included a single-engine fighter powered by either a license-built Rolls-Royce Nene or the Allison J33 and a twin-engine version powered by Westinghouse J34s or Rolls-Royce Derwents.

The Navy's and Grumman's needs aligned, except that the head of Fighter Design, Cdr. A. B. Metsger wanted the new Grumman to have a swept-wing or at least include a swept-wing variant as one of the three prototypes. Grumman instead proposed to build only straight-wing prototypes and accomplish a swept-wing design study. Metsger's superiors elected to pursue this conservative approach. As a result, in October 1946, BuAer amended the four-engine, two-seat XF9F-1 contract to deliver three single-seat XF9F-2 prototypes instead with no change in contract value. In November, they decided that the new Grumman program would deliver single-engine aircraft, starting with two XF9F-2s to be powered by the Nene and one XF9F-3 by the Allison J33. The J33 was less powerful at 4,600 lbs of thrust (5,400 lbs with water/alcohol injection) than a license-built Nene but considered lower risk from a schedule standpoint.

At the time, Philip Taylor, formerly general manager of the Wright Aeronautical Corp., had an option from Rolls-Royce for the U.S. sales and manufacturing rights for the Nene engine but did not have a firm commitment for a manufacturing facility. With BuAer's blessing, encouragement, and perhaps connivance, Pratt & Whitney bought the option from Taylor and negotiated a license agreement with Rolls-Royce in mid-1947. They had a J42 running in March 1948, only eight months later, in spite of the

need to convert the British blueprints to American standards and acquire new machine tools to build jet engine parts. Some redesign, particularly of the fuel pumps, was required to allow operation on gasoline as well as kerosene, which was the fuel used by the British. Seven months later, the J42 passed its 150-hour qualification test at a rating of 5,000 lbs, and 5,750 lbs with water/alcohol injection.[7]

Grumman moved out quickly on its new project. The mockup review was held in early 1947. The Panther featured leading edge flaps, an innovation that provided extra lift in the landing configuration. Speed brakes were located on the belly forward of mid-fuselage, and some consideration was given to beefing them up so that they would also function as hydro-flaps in the event of a ditching, keeping the jet from imitating a submarine on contact with the water. However, the first actual jet ditchings, including one with the Panther, ended concerns over submarining and engine explosions on contact with the water.

The first XF9F-2 was airborne in November 1947, only a year after contract go-ahead, at Idlewild Airport (now the John F. Kennedy International Airport), powered by Rolls-Royce-built

*With the successor to the XF9F-1, Grumman and the Navy began a decade-long partnership of both success and disappointment in successive programs without the burden and distraction of formal competition. The XF9F-2 fully justified the Navy's trust in Grumman. (U.S. Navy via Hal Andrews collection)*

*The centrifugal flow compressor resulted in engines of relatively large diameter as seen here, a Pratt & Whitney J42 in an F9F-2. The chief has his right hand on one of the combustion chambers. This photo also illustrates the engine access afforded by removal of the aft fuselage. (National Archives 80-G-419845)*

*None of the early jets had enough fuel initially. Grumman's solution for additional fuel capacity was a hard-mounted tip tank that could not be jettisoned. In the event that the pilot needed to make an immediate landing after takeoff, the tip tank fuel could be quickly dumped as shown in this photo of the demonstration of the capability. (U.S. Navy via Hal Andrews collection)*

Nenes. The second XF9F-2 prototype flew only five days later. There were some early problems with directional and longitudinal stability, but Grumman was quick to resolve them with simple fixes. Shore-based arrested landing trials were marred when the removable aft fuselage came off during one engagement, but this embarrassment was also dealt with expeditiously.

As with other jet fighters, fuel capacity proved to be inadequate, so in early 1948 non-jettisonable, wing-tip mounted fuel tanks were evaluated in flight test. These increased available fuel by 240 gallons or 35 percent. They also had a beneficial impact on cruise performance due to their end-plate effect, so they were made standard with the 13th production aircraft. Although non-jettisonable, the tip tanks had a dump capability that emptied them in 40 seconds.

During 1949, VF-51 and VF-52 on the West Coast were the first to receive F9Fs and began developing carrier-based operating procedures, including jet-specific instrument approaches using Automatic Direction Finder (ADF), and tactics. One diversion was its involvement in the budget dispute between the Air Force and the Navy that had pitted the B-36 against aircraft carriers. Cdr. Pete Aurand, then on Naval Air Force Pacific Fleet Staff, gave their Air Group Commander an informal directive to start intercept-

ing B-36s that periodically used San Diego as a target and get gun-camera footage of their mock attacks.[8]

In February 1950, seven VF-51 and VF-52 pilots were the first to night qualify in jets aboard a carrier. The LSO used paddles festooned with flashlight bulbs powered by a 24-volt battery between his feet to provide landing guidance. After four nights of FCLP, the small group flew aboard *Boxer* and successfully qualified. Having proven that they could, with no radar altimeters or proper deck lighting, they sensibly did not try to do it again or qualify any of the other squadron pilots.

Another emerging requirement was coordination of the short cycle times of the jet aircraft with the propeller-driven attack aircraft. The Panthers had to be recovered within 90 minutes after launch, whereas the Skyraiders and Corsairs could easily do twice that or even three times. Another was coordinating the disparate cruise performance on joint missions. What was worked out was to launch the propeller aircraft first and the jets later. The jets would catch up before the strike reached the target area, provide air cover and/or flak suppression, and then hurry back to the carrier to land first.

The first Panthers were armed only with four 20mm cannons, with 200 rounds of ammunition each. The F9F-2B was introduced

with external stores stations in 1950. These consisted of the addition of four racks on each outboard wing panel, one for a 1,000-lb bomb or 150-gallon fuel tank and the other three for 250-lb bombs or five-inch rockets.

The J33-A-8 engine proved to be both unreliable and unpopular because of its lower thrust compared to the J42. The few F9F-3s that were built were re-engined with the J42 and redesignated F9F-2.

The load-carrying capability of the Panther was improved by the change to more powerful engines, the Allison J33-A-16 (-27) in the F9F-4 and the Pratt & Whitney J48 in the F9F-5. The J48, for example, was rated at 6,250 lbs of thrust (without water/alcohol injection) compared to the 5,000 lbs provided by the J42 in the F9F-2. The engines were otherwise very similar in both size and configuration. The J48 was developed jointly by Pratt & Whitney and Rolls-Royce (British-built versions of this engine were known as the Tay). The J33-A-27 continued to lag behind the Pratt & Whitney alternative in performance, having only 5,850 lbs of thrust.

In order to provide an increased fuel capacity to accommodate the more powerful engine, the forward fuselage of the F9F-4/5 was stretched by eight inches, increasing fuel capacity by 80 gallons. The vertical fin was also increased in size to maintain directional stability with the increase in the length of the forward fuselage. The three most outboard wing stores stations were beefed up to handle 500-lb bombs. Finally, the wing was reduced from 12 percent to 10 percent thickness to provide a higher critical Mach number.

*Improvements to the F9F-2/3 were not long in coming. The F9F-5 provided more thrust and more internal fuel. Most importantly, it was qualified in time to deploy for action in the Korean War. This VF-111 F9F-5 is carrying six 250-lb bombs en route to a target in Korea after being launched from Boxer in 1953. (Robert L. Lawson collection)*

The F9F-5 first flew in December 1949, and the F9F-4 in July 1950, due to development delays with the uprated Allison engine. As it turned out, Allison need not have bothered, since – in spite of a spate of J48 engine problems experienced in mid-1952 that resulted in a grounding of the F9F-5 – the F9F-4 suffered the same fate as the F9F-3: the Allison engines were removed and replaced with Pratt & Whitneys.

The initial carrier qualification of the F9F-5 aboard *Midway*, in July 1951, ended badly when the NATC test pilot failed to respond to low signals on his second approach and struck the ramp. The forward fuselage wound up on the flight deck. He survived without serious injury. The crash was attributed to his lack of recent carrier landing experience. However, after acceptance and production deliveries began, the Navy decided that the F9F-5 stall speed was too high. The prompt response from Grumman that provided the necessary improvement was the addition of a wing fence at the inboard end of the leading edge flap.

Grumman built 1,385 Panthers, the last F9F-5 being delivered in January 1953.

## F3D Skyknight

Meanwhile, the Douglas F3D program was on track to provide the Navy with a two-seat, carrier-based jet night fighter. The raison d'être of the F3D was its radar. Actually radars. There was the APS-21 radar with a 30-inch dish in the nose. It could detect an aircraft at a range of up to 20 miles depending on the radar cross section. A smaller radar, the APS-26, was also mounted in the nose forward of the APS-21. It provided the ability to "lock-on" to a target and track it automatically from about three miles on in, providing a firing solution for the guns. Together, they functioned as the APQ-35.

*The prototype XF3Ds can only be differentiated from production F3Ds by their small engine nacelles. The lack of external change is a testament to the skill (and/or luck) Ed Heinemann and the Douglas aerodynamicists implemented in the design of their first jet fighter. (U.S. Navy via Jay Miller collection)*

*The F3D-2 BuNo. 124596 was used to accomplish carrier suitability testing in July 1951 aboard Midway. While successfully qualified, the F3D was rarely deployed in spite of its superior all-weather operational capability. (National Archives 80-G-437139)*

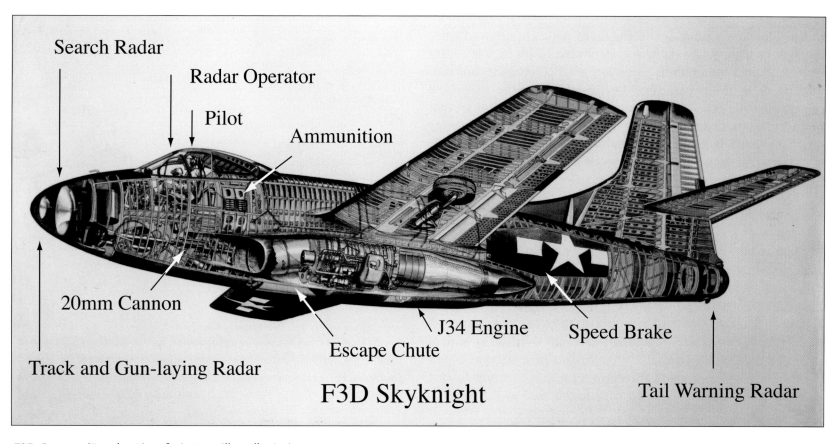

Search Radar

Radar Operator

Pilot

Ammunition

20mm Cannon

Track and Gun-laying Radar

Escape Chute

J34 Engine

Speed Brake

Tail Warning Radar

F3D Skyknight

*F3D Cutaway (Douglas Aircraft via Jay Miller collection)*

*The horizontal white stripe on this NATC F3D is a photographic reference marking used to determine pitch attitude changes on launch and landing. Here the Midway catapult officer is in the process of signaling the enlisted man in the catwalk to fire the catapult. (National Archives 80-G-437141)*

Finally, a small radar, the APS-28, in the tail facing aft, provided warning of an enemy fighter coming in from behind at ranges of up to four miles. It was an adaptation of the small target acquisition radar previously used by propeller-driven night fighters.

Because the size of the fuselage was established by the radar, side-by-side seating could be provided without any additional drag penalty. The big, flat windshield was an additional impediment to high speed but was intended to provide the distortion-free visibility prized at night for airborne intercepts and carrier landings.

The large frontal area did provide plenty of volume for fuel, 1,350 gallons. In any event, Ed Heinemann, Douglas' chief engineer, rejected the use of tip tanks.[9] His primary concern was asymmetric load problems if fuel did not transfer from the tip tanks. There was also the operational difficulty of filling the tanks when the wings were folded and the wing fold actuation loads with the tanks filled. McDonnell and Grumman were not so concerned about these drawbacks, although they were very real. At least one F2H crashed and the pilot was killed when a tip tank broke away during launch, causing loss of roll control.

Ejection seats were ruled out early on – they required a jettisonable canopy, which, together with the weight of the seats and the cockpit pressurization requirement, was too difficult to implement within the weight allotment. Instead, a bailout chute was provided. The bottom door to the chute provided a windbreak. This concept was demonstrated by an extensive series of dummy and live drops. BuAer accepted the concept but it was viewed askance by subsequent generations of pilots.

The fallback in the event of a hydraulic control system failure was an extendible control stick that provided sufficient leverage to handle the higher control loads.

The development of the aircraft was relatively trouble-free. Initial wind-tunnel tests indicated a need for wing-fuselage fillets and wing fences, but none proved to be required in flight tests that began in March 1948, with a first flight by Russ Thaw. The production F3D was therefore essentially identical, externally, to the XF3Ds, with the exception of the engine nacelles. The small engine nacelles on the XF3D were possible because the J34s used were right- and left-handed, but this represented a spares and maintenance burden. For production, Douglas enlarged the nacelles and repositioned them slightly to provide for more internal fuel. It was planned that more thrust be provided by a change to the J46. Unfortunately, J46 development was prolonged and J34s with only 3,250 lbs of thrust (-34) or 3,400 lbs (-36) were installed instead, the same engines that powered the smaller, lighter F2H-2 Banshee.

The sailor standing in the access hatch of this NATC F3D provides a reference for how big the cockpit and the radome were. Access was by climbing up the side of the fuselage where the white stripes are. (National Archives)

Carrier suitability tests were accomplished with the XF3D-1 beginning with shore-based testing in October 1949, and concluding on 1 February 1950. One of the few bright spots in the NATC report was that the big speed brakes were very effective for providing speed control on approach and deceleration on the cut. Otherwise, the carrier suitability pilot basically flunked it and suggested: "Consideration should be given to the employment of a tail-wheel-type alighting gear, with a variable-height tail wheel strut, for this and future carrier-type aircraft to overcome the deficiencies encountered in the subject test and inherent in

*The F3D-2M was carrier qualified but probably never deployed as such. This VX-4 aircraft is participating in Project Steam aboard Hancock. (National Archives 80-G-640359)*

the use of the nose wheel-type alighting gear in carrier operations."

Only 28 F3D-1s, powered by J34-WE-34 engines, were built. The first flew in February 1950. The Navy accepted the first F3D-1 in August and VC-3 received its first Skyknight in December. F3D-1 production was immediately followed by 237 F3D-2s powered by the -36 engines, with the first one flying in February 1951. In addition to the slightly more powerful engines, the -2 had wing spoilers to provide satisfactory rate of roll at high speeds. Aileron application at high speeds resulted in the wing twisting and reducing the roll rate. The -2 was also the beneficiary of an improved search and fire-control radar, tail-warning radar, autopilot, and air-conditioning system.

Initial carrier-suitability tests of the F3D-2 were conducted in July 1951. Follow-on tests were accomplished in early December 1951. The launches were now satisfactory at weights up to 26,660 lbs and the arrested landings at weights up to 22,600 lbs, three tons heavier than the Panthers and the Banshees. It is interesting to note that in the F3D-2 trials, the flat windshield intended to provide good visibility for night landings was faulted for poor visibility during inclement weather conditions.

Most of the Skyknights were delivered to the US Marine Corps, with VMF(AW)-542 at El Toro being the first to receive F3D-1s in early 1951. Some were initially operated by VC-3 and VC-4, the "composite" squadrons on the West and East Coasts, respectively,

for night fighter pilot training and the provision of detachments to carrier air wings during deployments. VC-3 was critical of the F3D-2 mission performance and carrier suitability and did not deploy it. VC-4 only deployed three detachments: *Coral Sea* in 1952, *Midway* on a 1952/53 cruise, and *Lake Champlain* in 1953. Neither the F3D itself nor its after-dark mission was well received aboard those ships. The aircraft was heavy, straining the catapult and arresting gear, and its exhaust was very hard on wooden, oil-soaked carrier decks. The working day on a carrier was already long enough without extending it to midnight or starting it then. Nevertheless, the experience was valuable for VC-4 and the F3D to prove its worth in Korea. VF-11 and VF-14 were equipped with the F3D-2 in the mid-1950s as a placeholder for the F2H-4 and F3H-2N, respectively. They did not deploy with it.

The F3D helped pioneer the concept of the air-to-air guided missile. It was first used as a test platform in missile development at VX-4, since it was big enough to carry the missiles, the radar, and the fire-control system along with a crew member and test instrumentation. Eventually, 12 F3D-1s and 16 F3D-2s were modified to carry and fire the Sparrow I, which resulted in an "M" suffix being added to their designation. The 20mm guns were removed and an APQ-51A radar was installed in a longer nose cone. Four hardpoints were mounted underneath the wings for the Sparrows, two inboard of the wing fold and two outboard. VMF (N)-542 was the only operational squadron equipped with the F3D-2M. They were based at MCAS El Toro, California, and did not deploy. Their Skyknights were replaced with Skyrays in 1959.

### Ready or Not, Navy Jets Go Into Combat in Korea

The Korean War revalidated the usefulness of aircraft carriers and proved the feasibility of carrier-based jet fighters. The Navy was only marginally ready with jets, having the F2H-2, the F9F-2, and the F3D-2 operational. Fortunately, there were few encounters between these straight-wing fighters and the swept-wing MiGs, for while the overall exchange rate was positive, the F3D only fought in the dark where it had a significant advantage, and the Panthers were only tested in a handful of engagements with the MiG.

The Navy had just barely gotten jets deployed in the western Pacific before the Korean War began. *Valley Forge* set out from San

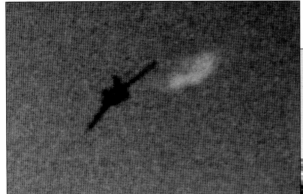

A MiG-15 is taking hits after trying to take advantage of a flight of F9F Panthers in November 1952. (U.S. Navy via Tommy H. Thomason collection)

The sailors are completing installation of a 250-lb bomb on one of the outboard hard points on the F2H-2 Banshee. Two bombs are already hanging from the inboard pylons. Visible on the deck between the sailors and the main landing gear are the straps and cable of a Davis barrier. (National Archives 80-G-432724)

Diego in May 1950 with two squadrons of F9F-3s aboard, VF-51 and VF-52, little more than a month before the start of hostilities. *Valley Forge* was in position off Korea to launch strikes 10 days after the initial North Korean attack. That first day, Panther pilots shot down two propeller-driven Yak-9 fighters.

Panthers were used for all the carrier-based jet missions in Korea until mid-1951, the Banshee squadrons having all deployed on Atlantic Fleet carriers. The first Banshees to arrive were three unarmed photoreconnaissance F2H-2Ps from Composite Squadron 61 (VC-61) aboard *Valley Forge* in June. In August, VF-172, flying F2H-2s, arrived aboard *Essex*, having been transferred from an Atlantic Fleet air group. Their first mission, along with F9Fs, was to escort a flight of Air Force B-29s against North Korean railroad marshaling yards on 25 August 1951. Another Atlantic Fleet F2H-2 squadron, VF-11, arrived with CVG-10 in August 1952 when VF-791 could not get ready in time due to F9F-5 teething problems.

Most of the jet missions were flak suppression or armed reconnaissance. The latter was intended to cut enemy supply lines and was accomplished by patrolling highways and rail lines in flights of two to four aircraft. VF-191 was the first into combat with the F9F-2B in April 1951, launching from *Princeton,* with each carrying four 250-lb and two 100-lb general-purpose bombs for an attack on a railroad bridge.

Panther operations were marginal in no-wind conditions, with the carrier having to generate the minimum 30 knots of wind-over-deck for a successful launch by the H-4B catapult. Early on, more Panthers were lost in bad cat shots than were shot down by anti-aircraft fire. The F2H-2B armed with six rockets needed 33 knots of wind over deck, with two rockets being removed for each knot under 33.

Air-to-air combat was relatively rare, which was not by chance. Except for the night escort missions by the F3D, Navy fighters generally did not operate in areas that MiGs could reach.

In July 1951, a flight of VMF-311 F9F-2s got lost and crossed into Manchuria (Chinese air space) while assigned to cover the effort to recover a downed MiG. Russian-flown MiGs caught up with them after they crossed back into North Korea. The Russian pilots claimed three F9Fs. The United States admitted to only one, with pilot First Lt. Richard Bell, U.S.M.C., ejecting from his F9F-2B and being taken prisoner.

In November, F9Fs from VF-111 got even, accounting for three MiGs, the first one shot down by their commanding officer, Lt. Cdr. W. T. Amen. There was another encounter between Panthers and MiGs on 12 November 1951, when VF-31 was providing escort for a *Leyte* strike on the Sinuiju bridges over the Yalu; the merge was brief and inconclusive, the MiGs choosing not to do more than a fly-by. There were no more MiG kills by carrier-based Navy jets until November 1952, when two more MiGs were shot down and two more damaged in a single engagement with VF-781 F9F-5s flying combat air patrol from *Oriskany*. One Panther was damaged but able to land back aboard. However, the MiGs were clearly superior to the Panthers in speed and rate of climb but not notably inferior in turn capability.

The F9F-5, combined with the new H-8 catapult, finally brought a reasonable load-carrying capability to the fight. In addition to 20mm ammunition, the F9F-5 could carry eight 250-lb bombs even if launched by an H-4B catapult if the wind over deck were 38 knots. However, the more powerful engine also consumed more fuel, affecting its radius of action and combat endurance. The F9F-5 was only just capable of the 90-minute carrier cycle.

The F2H-2 was noted to have a considerably higher service ceiling than the F9F. As a result, when both aircraft were available for combat air patrol or interception missions, the F2H-2 was assigned to cover the higher altitudes. The F2H-2 got high marks in a CVG-4 Action report dated 30 July 1953:

> It is an excellent carrier jet aircraft, and its dual-engine installation possesses definite advantage for modern-day carrier operations. Its range and speed definitely are superior to those of the F9F-5. It was the only carrier-based aircraft in the area which could carry a full bomb-load (four 250-pound and four 100-pound; total 1,400 pounds) to targets on the upper reaches of the Yalu, remain on target about 22 minutes, and return to the task force in 90 minutes.

Some Banshee pilots were reportedly willing to tangle with a MiG as long as the fight was well above 35,000 feet. There was at least one engagement, in March 1952, but it couldn't have been more one-sided. For one thing, the F2Hs were unarmed photore-connaissance -2Ps from VMJ-1. For another, the Marine pilots initially mistook the MiGs making passes at them for Sabres being flown by U.S. Air Force pilots having fun. Then they started being hit, at which point they disengaged by diving away and weren't pursued. McDonnell was justifiably proud that both F2Hs were able to return to their base in spite of very significant damage from the MiGs' cannon. One took a 37mm hit in the right engine turbine section, stopping the engine and starting a fire, and two 23mm hits in the center fuselage. The other took one 23mm hit through the rear spar of the left wing. The one least damaged was repaired in Korea and returned to service.

Ironically, the underpowered F3D not only got the most time in the ring with the MiG, it acquitted itself admirably. The VMF(N)-513 Skyknights were assigned two missions in late 1952, night combat air patrol over the Yellow Sea and B-29 bomber escort. At first, B-29 escort was an every-other-night assignment, alternating with Air Force F-94s. The F-94 apparently did not impress, because the general responsible for the bomber group eventually insisted that only F3Ds be used for escort. The Marine squadron was joined in June 1953, by the VC-4 detachment 44N that had been operating four Navy F3Ds from *Lake Champlain*.[10] A Navy crew reportedly made a kill and then was shot down, the only known air-to-air loss of an F3D against a total of seven kills and one probable. At least two of the kills and the probable were accomplished by firing "blind" as directed by the gun laying radar.

## Post Korean War Status and Lessons Learned

The Navy and its contractors had made progress in many elements of jet-fighter design. Pressurized cockpits, ejection seats, 20mm cannons, gunsights that used radar ranging for accuracy, and irreversible hydraulic controls had all been fielded on operational aircraft. A night fighter with a powerful search radar, defensive tail radar, and most importantly, the ability to shoot down a bogey, sight unseen, had been proven in combat.

Engines were more durable, too. The Pratt & Whitney J42 in the F9F-2 initially had to be overhauled every 150 hours. By late 1951, it was the first jet aircraft engine to be authorized for 1,000 hours between overhauls, approaching that of the better reciprocating engines in propeller-driven fighters. Korean War experience demonstrated that jet engines also had some ballistic tolerance, although nothing like the air-cooled reciprocating engines.[11]

Although jets had now been demonstrated to be compatible with the aircraft carrier, there were more accommodations to be made from a carrier standpoint. For example, one concern

*The advent of jets on carriers required the addition of the blast deflector and nose-wheel steering. The deflector was necessary to protect the people and aircraft that were directly behind the launching jet. This early version retracted directly into the deck and deflected the jet blast up and outboard via turning vanes. Positioning a jet precisely was initially accomplished with a tiller bar that attached to the nose wheel. (National Archives)*

aids were inadequate – night and all-weather landing operations needed to be not only feasible but routinely accomplished by the average aviator.

Most fighter pilots checked out jets at the operational squadron level, but formal jet transition training was being ramped up. Before the Korean War, it was only being provided by VF-52 on the West Coast in the Lockheed TO-1. These aircraft were transferred to the newly formed Jet Transition Training Unit One (JTTU-1), NAS Whiting Field, Florida, in 1949 when VF-52 received F9F-3s and reverted to being a fighter squadron. The two-seat trainer variant of the TO-1, the Air Force T-33, was procured beginning in 1949, as the TO-2, subsequently re-designated TV-2. In August 1951, JTTU-1 moved to Kingsville, Texas, and became Advanced Training Unit Three (ATU-3). Other jet transition squadrons were formed in the next few years, with advanced training still accomplished first in obsolete propeller-driven fighters like the F6F and F8F. As the supply of jet fighters increased, former fleet F9F Panthers were transferred to the advanced training role.

that reemerged when the F9F and F3D deployed was exhaust impingement on the deck. The earlier jets and the F2H had a relatively level sit so the jet exhaust went straight back. The F9F and F3D, however, sat tail low and heated up the deck surface immediately behind them. The F3D would actually start a fire on the wooden flight decks if allowed to stay at power too long. This was only going to get worse with the introduction of fighters equipped with afterburners. As a result, a retractable jet-blast deflector was developed which was to be installed behind the aircraft on the catapult. The deflector incorporated turning vanes set at an angle, so the exhaust was diverted upward and outboard. Metal plates were also installed over the wooden deck aft of the catapult holdback.

There were other changes required as well:

A last-chance barricade was essential – the Davis barrier did not always stop a jet that had failed to catch a wire.

More powerful catapults were necessary – from a temperature standpoint, the Korean operating environment was temperate to freezing cold, which was good for takeoff performance, yet jet mission payloads had to be limited.

Existing lighting and navigation and instrument approach

Fielding a swept-wing fighter as quickly as possible was now recognized to be a high priority. OpNav and BuAer were embarrassed that the Navy had no jet fighters comparable to the MiG, although they couldn't say so in public. In an interview in *U.S. News and World Report* in January 1952, Vice Admiral Cassady, then DCNO (Air), said that the Navy had four new jet fighters that were "superior" in performance to the "very short-range, very short-endurance, strictly defensive" Soviet MiG-15. He noted that they were "flying and in production" not just "blueprint planes" and "have over twice the range and twice the endurance of the Soviet plane." What he didn't say was that every one of the Navy's high-performance fighter programs was behind schedule, in part due to the failure of Westinghouse to maintain its early record of success in jet engine development. The Navy was also guilty of overreaching in terms of mission performance. However, all but one eventually did result in fielded aircraft.

The Navy also continued to fund research and development critical to maintaining parity, if not superiority, in fighter performance and mission capability.

## CHAPTER FIVE

*The Sparrow was the only one of the three guided-missile programs initiated after the war to achieve operational use, and it took almost a decade to be deployable. VX-4's F3Ds did yeoman service in the Sparrow's development, since it was big enough to carry the missile, the outsized avionics, and the research instrumentation. (U.S. Navy photo via Hal Andrews collection)*

# RESEARCH AND DEVELOPMENT - AERODYNAMICS AND ARMAMENT

Two of BuAer's major research and development interests besides engines were aerodynamics and armament (strictly speaking, the responsibility of the Bureau of Ordnance). In aerodynamics, its primary interest was in going faster, but it also had to insure that low-speed capability, including handling qualities, was not compromised. In armament, they were particularly focused on defending the carrier against attack by high-speed jet bombers with little warning. Part of the solution was the development of air-to-air missiles, but turreted guns were also evaluated.

## Aerodynamics

Research aircraft are an economical way of evaluating a high-risk concept before committing to a major development effort for an operational aircraft. During the transition to jet aircraft, three successful programs funded by the Bureau of Aeronautics were the Bell L-39 swept-wing demonstration, the Douglas D-558 Transonic Research Aircraft, and Boundary Layer Control evaluation. These provided valuable information and reduced risk at relatively low cost compared to embarking on a full-scale program involving new technology, as they were to do with the variable sweep-wing Grumman XF10F.

## Bell L-39

One of basic wing parameters that the aircraft designer has to work with is sweep.[1] The benefit of wing sweep is that it increases the critical Mach number. To the air, a wing that is swept appears to be thinner than the same wing if it were not swept because the chord relative to the airflow is greater. A lower thickness ratio is the important parameter in reducing transonic drag, not the thickness per se. An aircraft does not have to have swept wings to break the sound barrier. The Bell X-1 had straight wings, as did the F-104. What the wing has to be is thin relative to its chord, the distance between the leading edge and the trailing edge. However, there are limits as to how thin a wing can be, primarily from a structural standpoint but also in terms of the need for volume for landing gear, control systems, fuel, etc.

The Germans were in the forefront of swept-wing research during World War II. After the war, the former allies all benefited from the discovery and use of German research, most of which was done at an angle of 35 degrees. The majority of postwar swept-wing jets therefore had wings swept at 35 degrees, the North American F-86 Sabre and the MiG-15 being notable examples.

While beneficial from a critical Mach number standpoint, sweeping the wing was otherwise detrimental. Dihedral in a swept wing, for example, increased lateral stability at high angles of attack to the point where the aircraft was too stable. On the other hand, not enough dihedral in a swept-wing aircraft at low angles of attack, i.e., in high-speed flight, adversely affects lateral and directional stability. In addition, as the angle of attack of a swept wing is increased for slow-speed flight or during aggressive maneuvering at high speeds, the wing tip tends to stall first. This was always to be avoided because of the loss of roll control from the ailerons, but in swept wings, there was an added fillip – the center of lift moved forward with the stall of the wing tips. When the center of lift moved forward, the aircraft pitched up, with the increased downwash from the inboard section of the wing adversely affecting the effectiveness of the horizontal tail. This led to the common swept-wing design practice of placing horizontal tails either lower than the wing or much higher. (Later on, the avoidance of the disturbed flow behind the wing of an aircraft flying above its critical Mach number made low tails preferable to avoid pitch-up at transonic speeds.)

The wing tip stall was, in part, caused by span-wise flow at high angles of attack. This rendered the traditionally placed ailerons ineffective. There were different ways of coping with this. One was to move the ailerons inboard; that reduced the trailing edge available for flaps for high lift, although drooping the ailerons as well minimized this. It also reduced loss of aileron effectiveness or even reversal due to the wing torsion at high speeds. Another was spoilers as an alternative or supplement to ailerons. Spoilers allowed more of the trailing edge to be flapped and also avoided the wing torsion problem. Another fix was to add fences to restrict the flow from moving outboard. A more elegant approach was to extend the leading edge of the wing forward

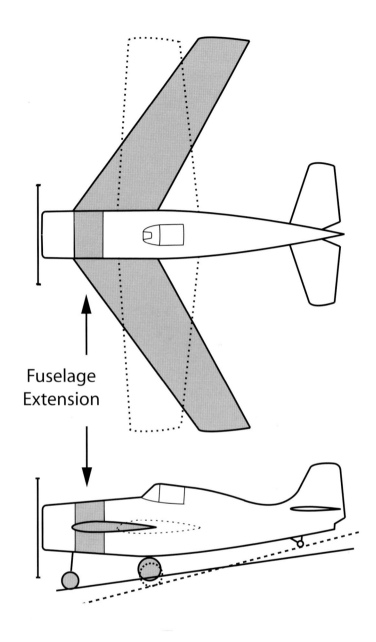

*Grumman Wildcat Swept Wing Demonstrator Design Study*
*In responding to BuAer's request for a low-speed, swept-wing handling qualities demonstrator, Grumman first studied converting an F4F Wildcat. The changes required were significant, and the result did not appear to be as useful as desired. (Author)*

**Fuselage Extension**

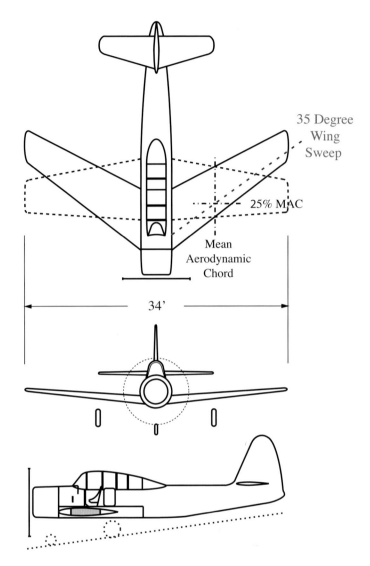

35 Degree Wing Sweep

25% MAC

Mean Aerodynamic Chord

34'

*Proposed Grumman Swept-Wing Demonstrator*
*Grumman's all-new swept-wing demonstrator featured a lower fuselage bay that could accommodate different bolt-on wing configurations ranging from straight to swept. Space was also provided in the cockpit for a second seat. Note the shortness of the nose, the result of the weight and balance impact of the nose-mounted 450-hp R-985 engine. (Author)*

about two-thirds of the way toward the tip, creating a "snag." At high angles of attack, this discontinuity in the leading edge produced a vortex that acted as an aerodynamic fence.

BuAer was rightfully concerned about the swept wing's low-speed capability and handling qualities. These were of signifi-

cantly more importance to carrier-based operations than they were to land-based ones. To quickly ascertain how significant the problems were, they solicited industry bids for a flying test bed. Grumman and Bell Aircraft both responded. Grumman did design studies of a modified F4F and an all-new design and Bell, a modified P-63 King Cobra. Bell's proposal was selected because it was a significantly lower cost, using existing P-63 fuselages.

The modified P-63 would have a wing sweep of 35 degrees with an aspect ratio of 4.5, a taper ratio of 1.8 and no dihedral.

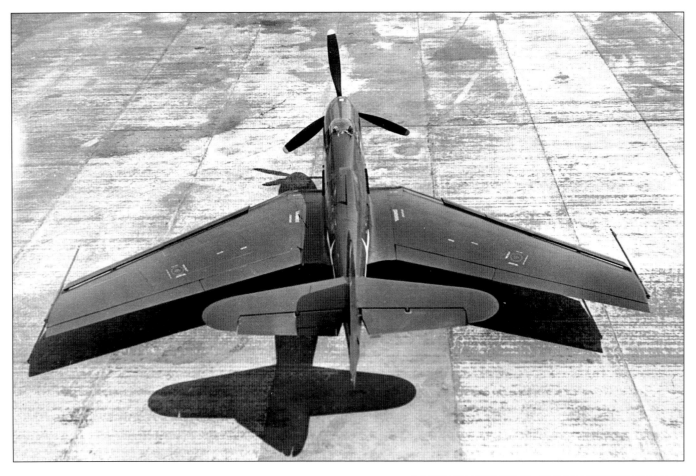

*Bell's low-speed swept-wing demonstrator featured a five-segment leading edge slat. In this picture, the outboard four segments have been opened. (National Archives 80-G-702663)*

The wings were P-63 outer wing panels mounted to sweep aft from a short unswept inboard section and with new wing tips. This unswept section was necessary to correctly position the swept-wing's center of lift with respect to the aircraft's center of gravity. One important addition to the modified wing were five constant-chord slats evenly spaced along the leading edge of the swept portion of the wing, any of which could be positioned open or closed for flight.

In accordance with Navy practice for designation of research aircraft, the two Bell swept-wing demonstrators were designated the L-39, L being the Bell company designator and 39 being Bell's model number for the aircraft. The only significant configuration difference between the two was that the slat on the L-39-1 was somewhat thicker than the one on the L-39-2, so the slot was 56 percent bigger.

The first L-39 was designed and built in only 10 weeks after go-ahead by BuAer and flew in April 1946. In accordance with the low cost and low-speed nature of the flight evaluation, the main landing gear was no longer retractable. After initial flight tests, a ventral fin was added for better directional stability. Since the center of gravity proved to be too far forward, the four-blade pro-

*Because the P-63 already had a nose gear and the engine was mounted in the middle of the fuselage, the L-39 was close to a jet aircraft in configuration. The box on top of the canopy contained a 35mm motion picture canopy that filmed the tufts mounted on the upper surface of the wing. (U.S. Navy via Hal Andrews collection)*

peller was replaced with a lighter, three-blade assembly and the empennage was extended aft by about four feet with a fuselage plug. The second L-39 was completed with the fuselage extension, a larger ventral fin, and the three-blade propeller.

The requisite modifications were expeditiously accomplished and the evaluation began. It was quickly established that an unslatted swept wing had unacceptable wing stall characteristics – abrupt, without any warning, and with a significant amount of roll off. However, with 40 to 60 percent of the leading edge span of the wing slatted as measured from the wing tip, the stall characteristics were acceptable. There did not seem to be any significant difference between the thick and thin slat other than "(The) pilots reported greater difficulty with the (thin) slot in stabilizing the airplane's behavior at low airspeeds."[2]

The Fighter Class Desk Officer, Cdr. Metsger flew the aircraft in June, including simulated carrier approaches and landings. His evaluation put to rest any residual concerns that he had about the compatibility of swept-wing aircraft with aircraft carrier operations. He went back to Washington to complete the evaluation of swept-wing fighter proposals. Among the military and industry pilots who flew the Bell L-39s that summer was Corky Meyer of Grumman:

> My flight in the L-39 with no slats was brief. This bird cavorted like a cat on catnip during the stalls, which required excessive altitude for recovery. The L-39 prototype with leading-edge slats was docile during stalls and accelerated stalls. Both maneuvers could be performed with little wing dropping and minimum altitude loss. These two prototypes made it clear that slatted swept-wings would provide carrier-suitable flight characteristics for swept-wing fighters.[3]

The Navy concluded its testing in August.

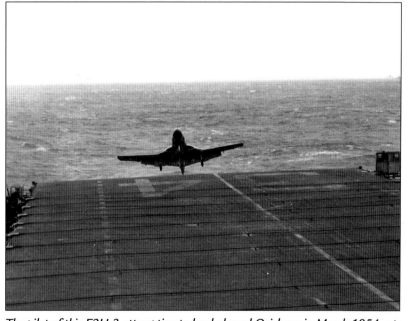

*The pilot of this F2H-3 attempting to land aboard Oriskany in March 1954 gets too slow and can't accelerate enough to climb after getting a wave-off. The resulting ramp strike was horrific, but the cockpit wound up on deck clear of the fire and the pilot wasn't injured. (See Chapter 11, page 80) National Archives 80-G-709153)*

Because the L-39 was propeller-driven, one significant characteristic of the swept-wing configuration was not obvious. By its nature, the swept wing has a low aspect ratio. This results in a steeper "back side" to the aircraft's power-required curve. For a given flap/slat configuration, the power required for level flight decreases with decreasing air speed and then starts to increase again, the so-called back side. Carrier aircraft approaches were made as slowly as possible and therefore on that back side. Being on the back side of the power curve meant that pulling back on the control stick resulted only momentarily, if at all, in a climb – the resulting slower speed increased the power required for level flight, so in the absence of a power increase, the aircraft began to settle, the opposite of pulling back on the stick on the front side of the power curve, which resulted in a sustained climb.

This relationship of speed and power required on the back side was well known to Navy pilots. In a propeller-driven aircraft, it was relatively easy to stop any settling with the throttle because of the thrust available at low speeds. What wasn't immediately appreciated was that the combination of the jet's low thrust at low speed and the much greater increase in power required with decreasing airspeed for a low-aspect ratio wing could quickly result in a situation where there wasn't enough thrust at full throttle to maintain level flight, much less accelerate. The only way to stop descending then was to increase the airspeed, which meant pushing the stick forward and converting potential energy into kinetic energy. That was not an option when on approach only 100 feet off the water. A crash into the water or a ramp strike was inevitable if the jet pilot let his angle of attack get too high on approach.

## Douglas D-558 High-Speed Research Aircraft Program

Transonic flight, defined as beginning at approximately Mach 0.8, was something of a mystery in 1944. Pilots of propeller-driven aircraft had begun to reach those speeds in dives and encountering control and airframe buffet problems. Wind-tunnel testing was not any help because tunnels "choked" at the speed of sound, sooner with a model installed, and could not be made big enough, or very small models made precisely enough, to provide useful data. The answer was a research aircraft specifically designed for high-speed flight test. The project would also provide data to determine the transonic Mach number at which wind-tunnel results began to be erroneous.[4]

The Army and the Navy teamed with the National Advisory Committee for Aeronautics (NACA) in separate programs for this purpose in 1944, with NACA providing a degree of coordination. The Army program's goal was supersonic flight, while the Navy program was to provide data on flight at Mach numbers approaching 1.0, the speed of sound. The Army contracted with Bell Aircraft in Buffalo, New York, for an airdropped, rocket-powered aircraft, the X-1. Some at NACA were against the rocket-powered aircraft because of the likelihood of an explosion and the limited

time available at a test point. BuAer did not want to stray far from a practical operational design, i.e., jet engine power, with its project. However, in the interest of cost and schedule there were to be no provisions for armament, radar, an arresting hook, or any other

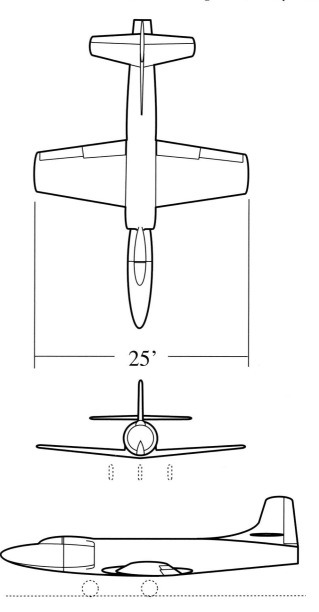

25'

*Douglas Model 558*
*The original D-558 design featured annular engine intakes on the side of the fuselage and a tail wheel. Pictured is the configuration at the first design review that had changed to a tricycle landing gear. After the review, and at NACA's recommendation, the nose inlet, which was to have been incorporated on only one of the six aircraft planned, became the standard on all three that were built. (Author)*

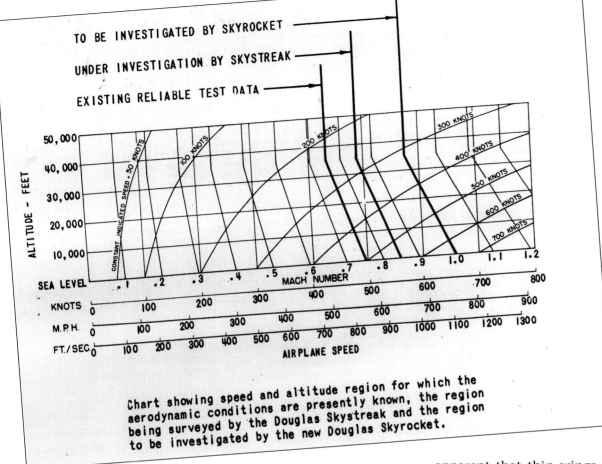

Chart showing speed and altitude region for which the aerodynamic conditions are presently known, the region being surveyed by the Douglas Skystreak and the region to be investigated by the new Douglas Skyrocket.

*D-558 Envelope Expansion Plan*
*(National Archives 80-G-704613)*

- Design and qualification of six research aircraft powered by the General Electric TG-180 (J35) axial flow jet engine, the most powerful available at the time. Maximum speed was projected to be Mach 0.9.
- Modification of two of the Phase I aircraft to change the jet engine to a Westinghouse 24C (J34) and add auxiliary thrust, liquid fuel rocket engines, for speeds of up to Mach 1.
- Design definition and mockup of a combat aircraft based on the D-558.

One of the initial objectives of the program was the evaluation of wing thickness versus high-speed performance. Thick wings were preferred for low-speed lift, but it had become apparent that thin wings had better transonic characteristics. Three different wings were planned. The baseline was a 10 percent thick wing that was projected to have a critical Mach number of 0.75. The thick wing was to have a thickness of 17 percent at the root and 13 percent at the tip, and the thin wing, eight percent at the root and six percent at the tip.

Douglas proposed the D-558 with annular engine inlets along the side of the fuselage aft of the cockpit. These allowed plenty of room in the nose for operational equipment. However, one of the six aircraft was to have a nose intake. The mockup review of the D-558 was held at Douglas' El Segundo, California, facility in early July 1945. NACA representatives were critical of the design, pointing out that it did not have enough volume for data recording equipment, among other things.[6] A second, more successful mockup review was accomplished in mid-August. By this time, German research data on swept-wings was becoming available and discussions during this session resulted in an agreement that Phase II modifications would also include the substitution of a swept-wing for the Phase I straight wing.

Wartime contracting rules and practices were still in place in 1945, allowing considerable latitude in establishing and modifying programs. The Douglas effort smoothly segued into three each of two different research aircraft, the straight-wing D-558-1

operational equipment. The contractor would also not be required to fully comply with the Navy's standard stability and control requirements. Basically, the aircraft was to be the smallest conventional straight-wing airframe that could be wrapped around the most powerful jet engine available, carry a pilot and 500 lbs of research instrumentation, have satisfactory low-speed capability and handling qualities, and fly at speeds of up to Mach 0.85 and altitudes of up to 40,000 feet in level flight.[5]

The Navy contracted with Douglas in 1945 for its high-speed research program. Douglas was interested in high-speed research in part because dive-bomber vulnerability reduction suggested the use of unrestricted diving speeds. However, loss of control incidents and crashes in propeller-driven aircraft doing high-speed dives were increasing. They also hoped that this program would result in a contract for development of an operational aircraft.

The Navy was to provide the funding and contract administration via the Fighter Design Branch of BuAer; NACA, data/analysis, wind tunnel testing, instrumentation, and follow-on flight test; and Douglas, the design and manufacture of the aircraft as well as initial envelope expansion to demonstrate safety of flight. The original contract called for three phases:

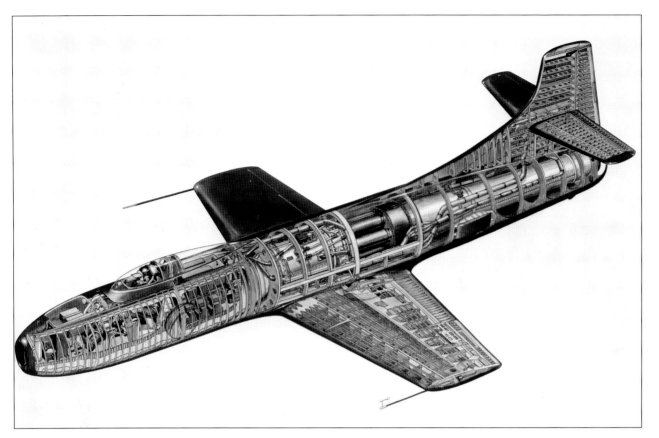

The D-558-1 was the smallest airframe that could be wrapped around the most powerful jet engine available at the time. Much of the fuselage was a four-foot tube of magnesium with relatively few frames. (National Archives 80-G-370135)

It's apparent why the Skystreak was referred to as the crimson test tube. This is one of several color photos that features Marion Carl (on the left) and Turner Caldwell, the military test pilots who flew the D-558-1 to world speed records. (National Archives)

vation at the time, although it may well have been as much or more for the benefit of the engineer's data system than the pilot's comfort.

The design, like most of the early jets, preceded the development and demonstration of the ejection seat. In any event, it was believed at the time that the vertical acceleration required to achieve clearance with the tail fin at high speeds was too much to tolerate. The high-speed bailout provision involved a jettisonable forward fuselage, with the pilot then releasing his seat back to clamber out the opening.

The D-558 Skystreak was about the size and weight of existing jet fighters. All of the fuel was carried in the forward half of the wing from tip to tip, with the interior of the structure being coated with a sealer rather than utilizing separate fuel tanks, thereby maximizing the amount of fuel that could be carried. Depending on power settings, there was less than an hour of fuel, however. Optional tip tanks with a capacity of 50 gallons per side were provided to extend duration by about 30 minutes.

The D-558-1 was being designed in parallel with operational jet aircraft and did not have much performance superiority. The FH-1, F6U-1, FJ-1, and F2H-1 had already flown before the D-558-1's first flight. The Skystreak's major contribution was that it was heavily instrumented for pressures and loads measurement, much more so than production prototypes. There were 400 points at which pressure on the wing and tail could be measured and recorded, another 400 points for structural loads, and the wing was mounted to the fuselage on load cells.

The instrumentation provided data on phenomena like the buffet boundary. This region of flight coincided with the presence

Skystreak, now to be tested with only one wing thickness, and the very different swept-wing D-558-2 Skyrocket.[7] The former was slated to provide data between Mach 0.75 and 0.85 but managed to just break the sound barrier in a dive. The latter was originally expected to be just supersonic with both jet and rocket engines. It was eventually flown out to Mach 2, albeit solely rocket-powered and air dropped from a B-29 as was the Air Force approach to high-speed research.

### D-558-1

The D-558-1 was designed with two features to minimize the known risks of high-speed flight: speed brakes and structural strength. It was obvious that a means of quickly slowing the aircraft down out of a dangerous flight condition was required. Dive recovery flaps that had already been added to some propeller-driven fighters were demonstrated to be ineffective in wind-tunnel tests, so fuselage mounted speed brakes were used.

Also in the interest of safety, and since no payload had to be carried other than research instrumentation and recording equipment, the aircraft was overbuilt. It had a limit load factor of 12 *gs* at a gross weight of 7,500 lbs, versus the usual 7.5. It was also designed for aerodynamic pressures at sea level of Mach 1. The cockpit was pressurized and air-conditioned, a significant inno-

of transonic flow over the wing. At altitudes above 12,000 to 15,000 feet, maneuverability began to be limited not by structural limits, but by strong airframe buffet. The buffet onset occurred at lower and lower gs as altitude increased. D-558 testing demonstrated that the buffet boundary with altitude was roughly proportional to the critical Mach number when plotted against the coefficient of lift.

The buffet boundary became a new criterion for fighters. The onset when pulling gs was like a mild pre-stall buffet, but the aircraft was far from stalling. The buffet built with increasing g, until the aircraft was useless from a gun-tracking standpoint, shaking like a car being driven down a dry washboard road. It quickly became a differentiator among fighters, with good ones experiencing buffet at higher g levels than poor ones, and thus being capable of tighter turns. The Sabre was the benchmark for U.S. fighters, able to pull about 3g at 35,000 feet before it reached the limit for gun platform accuracy.

The D-558-1 first flew in April 1947, piloted by Douglas's Eugene F. May. After only 10 flight hours, the Douglas/BuAer team decided to set a world speed record with it. The program delay and flight risk was justified as "calibration of instrumentation" and to demonstrate "that skilled pilots are able to fly at such speeds close to the ground with complete stability and control." The real reason BuAer approved the flight was to have inter-service bragging rights, the most recent record having been set by Col. Albert Boyd, U.S. Army Air Forces, in a specially prepared, one-of-a kind Lockheed P-80 at 623.604 mph in June.

The speed record course at that time, as defined in the Federation Aeronautique Internationale Sporting Code, was a three-kilometer distance that had to be flown at an altitude of less than 100 meters above the ground. The record speed was the average of four consecutive runs, two in each direction, all of which had to be accomplished within 30 minutes. In the jet age, record attempts in accordance with the altitude restriction were approaching the impractical if not downright dangerous. They also precluded the faster, rocket-propelled XS-1 from setting the official world speed record since it had nowhere near the endurance required.[8]

Cdr. Turner Caldwell, U.S. Navy, then the BuAer D-558 Project Officer, set a new world's speed record of 640.7 mph on 20 August 1947. Five days later, Maj. Marion Carl, U.S. Marine Corps, upped it to 650.6 mph. The results demonstrated the steepness of the transonic drag rise – both of these speeds resulted in the same Mach number, 0.828. When Major Carl flew, the air was 17 degrees Fahrenheit hotter and therefore thinner, which increased the speed of sound.

Another difference with later jet aircraft design practice was that the flight controls were not boosted. Fortunately, this turned out not to be a problem, even though one of the early and significant findings with the D-558-1 was the loss of elevator effectiveness at transonic speeds. In conjunction with the transonic pitch changes experienced at the same time in X-1, Me 262, and YP-80 flight tests, Douglas concluded as early as November 1947 "that it probably will be safer to forget about the elevator at transonic speeds and maintain control at all times with the stabilator."[9]

The D-558-1 was flown supersonically, barely and briefly, in September 1948, a year after Chuck Yeager broke the sound barrier in the X-1. Eugene May made the flight, with a 35-degree dive

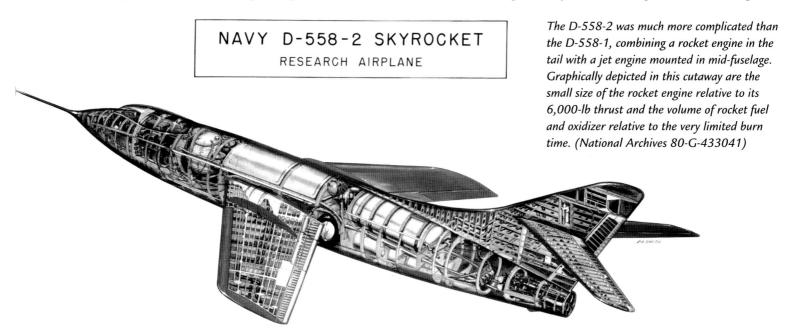

NAVY D-558-2 SKYROCKET
RESEARCH AIRPLANE

*The D-558-2 was much more complicated than the D-558-1, combining a rocket engine in the tail with a jet engine mounted in mid-fuselage. Graphically depicted in this cutaway are the small size of the rocket engine relative to its 6,000-lb thrust and the volume of rocket fuel and oxidizer relative to the very limited burn time. (National Archives 80-G-433041)*

By the time the Skyrocket was rolled out, it had been determined that red was not a high-visibility color in the sky. The flush canopy was also to be replaced by a more traditional one. The jet engine inlets were as flush as possible, with an extendible lip to increase the size of the inlet in low-speed flight. (Dennis Jenkins collection)

No Navy fighter at the time had the performance necessary to chase the D-558-2, which resulted in the use of Air Force F-86s. However, the Skyrocket's markings left no doubt that this was a Navy aircraft. (Dennis Jenkins collection)

With the additional weight of the rocket and its fuel, JATO (Jet Assisted Take Off) was used to increase the amount of thrust available to accelerate to takeoff and climb speeds. However, the higher takeoff speeds increased the pilots' concerns about tire failure. (Dennis Jenkins collection)

From a safety and performance standpoint, being carried aloft by and dropped from a modified P2B-1S (the Navy's designation for the four B-29s it bought for a long-range search mission) finally made a lot more sense than continuing to make conventional takeoffs. (Dennis Jenkins collection)

The first flights were made with the jet engine only with a fairing installed on the aft fuselage. This is an early flight with the original, shorter tail. Performance with the jet engine only was anemic. While the Edwards AFB lakebed was long enough, the pilots grew concerned about the risk of tire failure because of the length of ground roll it took to achieve takeoff speed. (Dennis Jenkins collection)

involved. Of course, the D-558-1 was not intended to be supersonic. That was the province of the redefined second phase of the D-558 Program. NACA flew the third Skystreak once or twice a month up through June 1953 in stability and control and buffet boundary testing.

### D-558-2 Skyrocket

Shortly after the straight-wing D-558 design was frozen and fabrication began on the first article, German swept-wing research became available. Douglas received preliminary authorization for the swept-wing D-558-2 in January 1946, and a mockup review was accomplished in March. A contract amendment for this version of Phase II was not received until March 1947, but in those days, the need for formalization of agreements in Navy contracts was considered far less important on both sides of the table than getting on with the agreed-upon approach.

Since the jet engines at the time were not powerful enough to propel the swept-wing aircraft to the desired speed in level flight, rocket augmentation was required. It proved impossible to simply modify the D-558-1. There was inadequate volume for addition of a rocket engine and fuel even though the requirement was for only about two minutes of run time. The wholly new D-558-2 resulted. The design goal was to exceed Mach 1 in level flight at 30,000 feet. In accordance with the Navy's desire for swept-wing research that reflected its operational constraints, the new aircraft was required to have the stalling speed and low-speed handling qualities of an equivalent straight-wing aircraft. In

*The jet engine exhaust is located in the dark area underneath the national insignia on the aft fuselage. In this photo, the jet engine intake lips are still extended as the aircraft begins to accelerate with the rocket engine firing. (Dennis Jenkins collection)*

*One of the test programs accomplished with the D-558-2 after its transfer to NACA was the evaluation of high-speed stores — drop tanks and bombs. (Dennis Jenkins collection)*

locked in either position if desired. The 10 percent wing thickness of the D-558-1 was retained at the root, but increased to 12 percent at the wing tip for improved stalling characteristics and slat effectiveness.

Since the rocket was to be used for high-speed flight, low-drag jet engine intakes were preferable to high-performance ones, so a flush intake was provided on each side of the fuselage. The jet engine exhaust was located on the bottom of the fuselage, with the tailpipe angled down at about eight degrees. The engine was changed to the Westinghouse J34 with only 3,000 lbs of thrust in order to minimize the fuselage volume required. With just the jet engine installed, the gross weight was about 10,000 lbs, the same as the D-558-1; with the addition of the rocket engine and its fuel, the gross weight increased to about 13,500 lbs.

Once again, the D-558 program was barely keeping up with operational fighters, this time in swept-wing design and development. (It didn't have boosted controls, either.) The XP-86 had already flown in October 1947, four months before John Martin flew the D-558-2 for the first time. Since the XF7U was to fly in late 1948, the Skyrocket was not of any benefit to the Navy's first swept-wing fighter either.

The Navy eventually switched to the less dangerous air launch, the first in September 1950. Deletion of the jet engine allowed more rocket fuel to be carried, although test points continued to be few and brief when a ton of propellant was being burned every minute. However, speeds and altitudes far beyond those originally planned could be explored. Top speed achieved following a ground takeoff was about Mach 1.1. After NACA assumed responsibility for the Skyrockets in August 1951, Lt. Col. Marion Carl flew one to a maximum altitude of 83,235 feet in August 1953. The ultimate speed reached was Mach 2.005, or 1,291 mph, in a shallow dive at 62,000 feet by NACA pilot Scott Crossfield in November.

The D-558-2 demonstrated the classic pitch-up problem at transonic speeds. NACA used the third D-558-2, BuNo. 37975, in a program evaluating the effectiveness of wing slats and leading-edge devices that began in September 1951 and lasted well into the summer of 1953. The Skyrocket was flown with a variety of wing-fence, wing-slat, and leading-edge chord extension

addition, unlike the Air Force's X-1 high-speed research aircraft, it was to takeoff and land under its own power. The D-558-2 retained the jettisonable forward fuselage of the D-558-1 for emergency egress but was designed to a lower limit load factor.

The D-558-2 wing had the then-standard 35 degrees of wing sweep (at a non-standard 30 percent of the wing chord), the maximum that designers were willing to go to given the need for low-speed capability. The wing area was increased to 175 square feet to provide approximately the same stalling speed as the D-558-1. The horizontal tail was swept at 40 degrees to provide a critical Mach number margin between the tail and the wing. In accordance with design practice at the time, the horizontal tail was located partway up on the vertical fin.

In order to provide adequate lift and longitudinal stability at slow speeds, wing slats were included in the design along with a wing fence, called a stall plate by Douglas. The slats were not powered, extending and retracting by aerodynamic loads, but could be

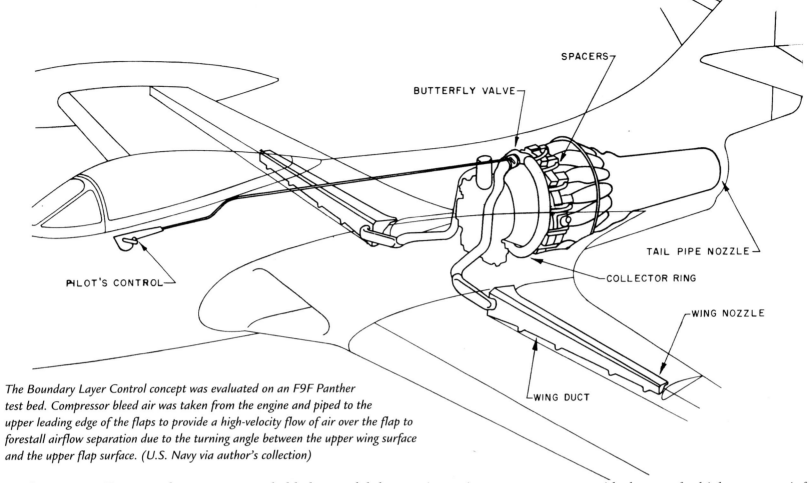

SPACERS

BUTTERFLY VALVE

TAIL PIPE NOZZLE

COLLECTOR RING

WING NOZZLE

PILOT'S CONTROL

WING DUCT

*The Boundary Layer Control concept was evaluated on an F9F Panther test bed. Compressor bleed air was taken from the engine and piped to the upper leading edge of the flaps to provide a high-velocity flow of air over the flap to forestall airflow separation due to the turning angle between the upper wing surface and the upper flap surface. (U.S. Navy via author's collection)*

configurations. However, the tests were probably less useful than NACA or industry might have hoped because the horizontal tail location was a factor in the pitch-up characteristic and immutable.

## Improving Lift in Low-Speed Flight

One simplistic way to think about lift is that it is the result of pushing air down. Going slower means less air is pushed down – an aircraft needs a "bigger" wing for takeoff and landing at reasonable speeds than it does in cruise.

Increasing lift at low speeds with a wing sized for cruise was originally accomplished by adding flaps to the trailing edge of the wing. The effect was further enhanced by the addition of flaps or slats to the leading edge of the wing. These flaps and/or slats increased the curve, or camber, of the wing and its ability to turn the air downward, much as a turning vane does. Unfortunately, there is a limit to how much of an angle air can turn without skidding out like a race car trying to turn a corner at too high a speed. This skidding out happens abruptly (with some exceptions, most notably with delta wings) and in aeronautical terms is called stalling. The aircraft loses lift and begins to descend.

In 1951, a Navy engineer, John S. Attinello, suggested blowing air over the wing flaps to increase the turn angle achievable. The jet engine compressor was an ideal source for high-pressure air for this purpose. After wind tunnel tests with airfoil sections confirmed the potential benefit, BuAer issued a contract to Grumman to modify an F9F-4 with Supercirculation Boundary Layer Control or BLC for short. The modification added a collector around the engine compressor to bleed off high-pressure air, piping leading to slotted ducts located in the wing between the rear spar and the leading edge of the flaps, and a control valve.

Because the tailpipe diameter had to be increased to maintain exhaust temperature at the maximum limit when bleed air was being taken by the BLC system, the amount of bleed air taken off the compressor resulted in a relatively large amount of thrust loss, about 11 percent, with bleed air off. However, this was acceptable for the evaluation of the concept.

Initial testing demonstrated that the stalling speed in a power-on approach was eight knots less with boundary layer control on, a very significant improvement, with no change in flying qualities other than less stall warning and less lateral control at stall. In side-by-side evaluations with an unmodified F9F-4, the BLC Panther became airborne in approximately 100 to 150 feet less distance at approximately 12 knots less airspeed and climbed more steeply even though the engine was producing less thrust. BLC also resulted in a more nose-down attitude (better visibility) on approach and a shorter landing distance.

After shore-based trials, the modified aircraft was tested aboard *Bennington* in 1954. Carrier approaches, landings, and wave-offs were made at speeds 10 to 15 knots slower than without boundary control – the pilot speculated that even lower approach speeds would be possible if lateral control could be retained at the reduced speed. Aircraft takeoff and climb performance were also notably better. One particularly significant result of the *Bennington* tests was the realization that standard F9Fs could not have operated from the ship under the wind-over-deck conditions during the test because of arresting gear limitations.[10]

Supercirculation boundary layer control was touted as being as important a development for low-speed flight as the area rule was for high-speed flight. However, in the mid-1950s, there was not enough excess power to provide the bleed air required. There soon would be with the advent of the new Pratt & Whitney and GE engines. While it did not find widespread use in aircraft design because of the increased complexity and maintenance issues, it was incorporated in some carrier-based aircraft to minimize the approach speed growth inevitable with the higher gross weights needed for more mission capability.

## Armament

The initial response to defending the fleet against jet bombers was the development of high-performance fighters with visual-assist radar to be directed into position to attack by airborne early-warning radar.[11]

However, interception was one thing. Being able to then

The 2.75-inch, unguided, folding-fin rocket was the first air-to-air missile widely used by the military. Its tailfins were spring-loaded to open as the rocket left its launching tube. Several were fired at once to increase the chances that one would hit the target, particularly if it were maneuvering. (National Archives 80-G-641240)

A 2.75-inch rocket hit was devastating. This B-26C has already been hit five times, with this last shot blowing a six-foot hole in the left wing. Prior shots severed the empennage and then the aft fuselage, destroyed the left engine, and blew up the right engine nacelle. Only the cockpit and nose to the upper right are recognizable. (U.S. Navy via Gary Verver)

shoot down the bomber required development of new weapons. During World War II, the standard Navy fighter armament for air-to-air combat was six machine guns firing .50 caliber bullets. This was enough firepower to shoot down the lightly built, minimally armored Japanese fighters and bombers with unprotected fuel systems. However, experience in Europe clearly indicated that a cannon (so-called because it fired a big enough round to contain an explosive) was the minimum firepower effective against better-protected aircraft. Armament specialists estimated that four 20mm cannons had at least twice the effect of six .50 caliber M2 machine guns and weighed little more. Four cannons therefore became the standard armament for almost all Navy jet fighters with 150 to 200 rounds per gun. Up through the F9F Cougar, the 20mm cannon fitted was a Hispano-Suiza M3. Its replacement was the Colt Mk 12, a development of the M3. The principle difference was that the Mk 12 fired a lighter bullet with a larger powder charge, giving greater muzzle velocity, about 3,350 feet per second, and a slightly greater rate of fire, 1,000 rounds per minute. This was considered important in air-to-air combat involving jet aircraft where time on target was often fleeting. The cannon still required closing to a fairly short range and possibly several seconds to deliver a lethal dose.

As jet fighters began to practice intercepts against jet bombers, it became obvious that cannons were inadequate. A head-on pass left too little time to aim and fire accurately and effectively. A slight misjudgment in a pursuit curve left the fighter pilot vulnerable to the bomber's tail guns or out of range for his own. To be effective against jet bombers, fighters needed a longer-range weapon with a higher kill probability.

## Unguided Rockets

Unguided rockets with contact-fused warheads were initially developed in World War II to kill submarines, since it took a combination of velocity and explosive to damage the pressure hull. The rocket was quickly appropriated as a general-use air-to-surface weapon. In air-to-air combat, it offered more range than the cannon, about two miles with rapidly diminishing accuracy, and the prospect of single-hit lethality, which made a head-on attack of a jet bomber viable. The original air-to-air rocket had a 2.75-inch-diameter body, was about four feet long, and weighed 18.5 lbs including a six-lb warhead. The rocket's stabilizing fins folded so that as many as possible could be housed in pods or extendible trays.

The delivery concept entailed flying a precise, radar-guided collision course, with the fire-control system signaling when the target was in range and the time had come to unleash a volley of rockets. The pilot fired and then immediately broke off to avoid merging with the target or its remains. The attack was best accomplished on instruments and therefore unseen, since an aware target that started maneuvering was much harder to hit. Even if it was not, the relatively erratic flight of the rockets required that at least a dozen, preferably more, be fired at the same time to have a reasonable likelihood of one hitting.

However, one hit was all it took. The Naval Ordnance Test Station at Inyokern, California, conducted live-fire testing at a target Douglas B-26 from 27 February to 2 March 1951, to determine how destructive the rocket was. Nine separate shots of a planned 12 were made from a distance of 1,500 feet, resulting in five hits. The first one blew the empennage off. All but one of the next four hits were also judged to be immediate kills. The one that wasn't credited as a kill blew off an engine. After two final misses, likely because the B-26 was a lot smaller than it was when they started, the testers ended the test with three rockets left over.[12]

A very early Sidewinder mounted on an AD Skyraider in February 1951 for test at China Lake, California. The aft fins have yet to be relocated to the end of the missile and reoriented to be in the same plane as the forward fins, but the innovative rollerons used for roll stabilization are already present. (U.S. Navy via Gary Verver)

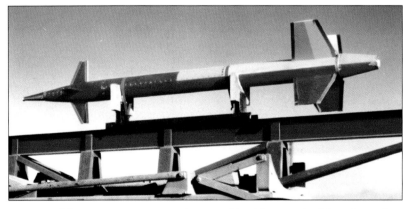

Pictures of the Meteor are rare, and regrettably, this example did not have the booster rocket, which provided the desired range at the expense of size and weight, attached. (U.S. Navy via Tommy H. Thomason collection)

The Sidewinder was not only simple, but little modification and equipment was required to enable an aircraft with a hard point for external stores to carry and fire it. The Grumman F9F-8 was the first Navy fighter to deploy with the missile, but not by much. (National Archives)

*The Oriole was decades ahead of its time, attempting a fire-and-forget functionality that simply wasn't possible with the avionics technology of the early '50s when it was in development. (U.S. Navy via Tommy H. Thomason collection)*

## Guided Missiles

In fleet defense studies, Mach 2+ guided missiles provided the most effective air-to-air capability. As a result, three programs were initiated after the war for short (one nm), medium (5 to 10 nm), and long (25 nm) range missiles.

In December 1946, Sperry received a letter of intent to create the short-range missile by combining a standard five-inch high-velocity rocket with a radar beam-riding guidance and control system; it became known as the Hot Shot. The diameter proved too small, so it was increased to eight inches. Douglas was chosen to build the 12.5-foot-long airframe with a solid propellant motor and a 52-lb blast/fragmentation device with a proximity fuse. The missile accelerated to Mach 2.5 before its motor burned out. The 325-lb missile was designated the AAM-N-2 Sparrow in early 1948, and was eventually re-identified as the AIM-7A Sparrow I. It was first ground-launched in 1948 and air launched in 1950, but the first beam-riding flights did not occur for another two years. (For safety reasons, the first air launch was

from – not at – an F6F drone in July 1952.) The first kill was a QB-17 target drone in December 1952, with the missile fired from a VX-4 F3D-1 based at the Naval Air Missile Test Center (NAMTC), Point Mugu, California.

The intermediate-range missile was contracted to Martin in 1947 as project Oriole. It was to have its own radar so when launched it would home in on the target with no further guidance on the part of the launch aircraft. Until 1950, it was only a guidance development project, which resulted in a requirement for an 11-inch-diameter body to house an X-band radar for all-weather capability. It was 11.5 feet long and weighed almost 400 lbs including a 50-lb warhead, an auxiliary power unit for electrical and hydraulic power, and the requisite electronics to provide automatic target tracking and missile guidance. An evaluation program, including test firings from an F3D-1, was then conducted at NAMTC in 1952 with the missile designated the XAAM-N-4 Oriole. The results did not justify continued development. However, Douglas resurrected the self-guided concept as the company's Sparrow II.

*One of the shortcomings of the Sparrow I was that it had to be fired at fairly short range in visual conditions. A pilot who was alert and flying a reasonably maneuverable aircraft wasn't likely to get shot down by one. (National Archives 80-G-66289)*

passed within six inches of the heat source on a QF6F drone.

The production Sidewinder only weighed 155 lbs, half that of a Sparrow. The seeker head looked straight ahead in a narrow cone, approximately the same field of view as the gun sight. When it detected a heat source it could home on, it transmitted an aural "growl" to the pilot, who just had to determine that the seeker was detecting something he wanted to shoot at and then pull the trigger. The infrared heat seeker was only effective in clear conditions and in the beginning was only attracted to a significant heat source, one of which might very well be the sun. The effective range at launch was only about a mile at sea level but more than four miles at 50,000 feet. The warhead would explode either when the control fins hit something or the proximity fuse determined that the target was within 30 feet. The warhead was relatively small, about 25 lbs, but was still deadly against single-engine jets because it was likely to go off very near the empennage if not actually in the tailpipe. In fact, test shots without warheads sometimes killed the target because they guided into its tailpipe.

Deployments with Sidewinder started in July 1956 with VA-46 flying F9F-8s from *Randolph*. Because of the simplicity of interface, the AAM-N-7 (later AIM-9B) was adapted to every operational Navy jet fighter and even attack aircraft like the A4D.

One of the first squadrons to deploy with the Sidewinder was VF-121 with FJ-3Ms. Their CAG was Bob Elder, of VF-5A fame. During one of its training exercises, they shot down an F6F drone. Elder said of the encounter, "The first missile hit the left wingtip flare; the second hit the right wingtip flare; the third, the engine; and the fourth impacted the falling debris."[13] Fired at a non-maneuvering target from far enough away to arm and guide, it was close to a sure thing. By well-timed hard maneuvering, a pilot might be able to evade it, but not for certain.

The Sidewinder scored for the first time in combat in September 1958, when a Republic of China (Taiwan) F-86 shot down a People's Republic of China (PRC) MiG-17. In a clandestine modification program accomplished by VMF-323, which had Sidewinders on its FJ-4s, the Taiwanese Air Force was provided with the operational capability to even the odds against the higher-performance MiG-17. Caught by surprise, knowing they were well above and out of range of the F-86s' guns, the PRC lost at least four MiGs to Sidewinders. After this engagement, the PRC pilots kept their distance from Taiwanese Sabres.

The long-range missile was part of a project called Meteor that was awarded in 1945 to the Massachusetts Institute of Technology (MIT). Meteor eventually resulted in the AAM-N-5. In order to achieve the range, a solid-propellant booster and a liquid-fuel sustaining motor were both required. Even then, it had to be a high-speed, head-on engagement. The total weight with only a 25-lb warhead was almost 600 lbs. Bell Aircraft was selected to develop and build the airframe. Guidance was semi-active homing, which meant it guided on the reflection of a radar beam from the fighter that fired it. The seeker was captive-flight tested in July 1948 and the missile itself ground-launched in November 1948. Test launches from an F3D began with one in July 1953, followed by four more in early 1954, only the last one being with full guidance. The program was canceled later that year in favor of the shorter-range but lighter and simpler Sparrow III.

The simplest guided missile was developed out in the high desert north east of Los Angeles, California, at the Naval Ordnance Test Station, Inyokern, California. Envisioned in a 1949 study as a "heat-homing rocket" using a five-inch High Velocity Aircraft Rocket as a motor, it soon became known as the eponymous Sidewinder, both for its heat-seeking capability and sinuous path in flight as it homed in at Mach 2. After more than a dozen failed shots, in September 1953, a prototype successfully

*The F3H-2's radar, with its electronics, took up almost all the nose and a good part of the forward fuselage. This VF-213 fighter has had its 20mm cannon removed to reduce weight. It was also equipped with Sidewinder capability as evidenced by the inboard pylons. (U.S. Navy via Robert L. Lawson collection)*

*The F3D radars provided the ultimate in night fighter capability in the early '50s, ashore or afloat. In order to provide both long-range search and short-range tracking and gun-laying, two different radars were required as shown here. The big dish was capable of shaking the aircraft at high scan rates. (U.S. Navy via Jay Miller collection)*

*The F2H-3 and -4 were deployed with different search and track radars, providing both the Navy and their manufacturers with valuable operational experience. (National Archives 80-G-1031404)*

The Sparrow I was also deployed in 1956, initially on the F7U-3M and then on the F3H-2M.[14] It established the feasibility of having a big supersonic missile available as an air-to-air weapon against an incoming bomber raid. As finally qualified, the pilot had to use the gun sight to precisely aim the radar beam while the missile was in flight, reportedly within 0.25 degrees for about eight seconds. This effectively made it a relatively short-range, clear-weather weapon against a non-maneuvering target. Its operational shortcomings, combined with the availability of the Sidewinder, which did not require any post-launch guidance, and the Sparrow III, which was effective in all-weather conditions, resulted in it being withdrawn from service beginning in 1958.

The AAM-N-3 Douglas/Bendix Sparrow II was the Oriole self-guided concept repackaged into the Sparrow I airframe body that Douglas was already responsible for. Its guidance system would receive targeting information from the radar in the missile carrier and then home on the target using data from its Bendix APQ-64 radar. With all the extra electronics, it weighed about 420 lbs, including a 45-lb warhead. It was first air-launched in July 1952. In August 1954, it made a kill in a shot involving multiple targets.

Although the Sparrow II's fire-and-forget capability was very desirable, the size of the missile body limited the radar to K-band, which had a very limited ability to penetrate clouds and less in rain. With all its vacuum tubes, it was also expensive and complex, meaning not very reliable. Closely associated with the Douglas F5D program, it was continued by BuAer as a possible weapon for the F4D for a while after the F5D was terminated, but it, too, was eventually canceled as well.

The Raytheon Sparrow III guidance system turned out to be the most practical approach for fleet defense. It used semi-active radar homing, meaning that it used the reflected energy from the interceptor's radar to guide itself to the target, even a maneuvering one. The first air launch was accomplished in November 1952, followed by the first full-guidance flight on an F3D in February 1953. The first live warhead shot was on August 1955, which resulted in destruction of the target drone. VX-4 began operational evaluation of the Sparrow III in February 1958. In December, VF-64 flying F3Hs from *Midway* accomplished the first deployed firing. One subsequent milestone was a successful head-on shot from a supersonic F4H at a supersonic Regulus II target in May 1962, demonstrating the long-desired capability to kill a supersonic bomber as far out as possible.

## Airborne Radar

The major improvement in mission avionics that paralleled the development of jet fighters was airborne radar, although improved navigation capability was appreciated as well. U.S. military radars received standard avionics designations, e.g., AN/APG-30. "AN" simply stood for Joint Army-Navy Nomenclature System. The second "A" was for Airborne. The "P" designated the unit as a radar, since "R" was already used for *Radio*. The third letter for fighter radars wasn't very descriptive – "A" was for Auxiliary equipment, "G" designated a fire-control capability, "S" meant the radar was for search and detection (range and bearing), and "Q" stood for a multi-purpose or combination capability. In terms of increasing capability (and cost, weight, and complexity), radars and fire controls systems would:
- Determine range to a target ahead of the aircraft.
- Allow the pilot or radar operator to locate and close on a bogey after being vectored into its vicinity and pointed at it.

*The whole nose section of the gun turreted Panther rotated and the guns pivoted within it so that they could be pointed in virtually any direction in the forward hemisphere. (U.S. Navy via Tommy H. Thomason collection)*

*A small radar in the nose of the Emerson Electric turret rotated with the machine guns to track the target and determine range. (U.S. Navy via Tommy H. Thomason collection)*

- Automatically track a designated threat.
- Direct the pilot into position to effectively shoot in the blind with guns or unguided rockets.
- Allow the pilot (or radar operator) to designate a bogey with a radar beam for guidance of a missile.

Night fighters in World War II were equipped with a short-range radar, the APS-19. It could scan a small portion of the sky in front of the fighter. An intercept in weather or at night was dependent on ship- or land-based radar, with a ground controller vectoring the fighter pilot into position close enough behind the bogey to acquire the threat with his radar. He could then close to within visual range for a conventional attack with his guns. After the war, advancements in radar range and scope readability were steadily accomplished, accompanied by electronically coupling the radar to the aircraft's armament, so that the pilot could fire his cannons or shoot his missiles blind, i.e., without ever seeing the target.

When the first Navy jet fighters deployed, they were equipped with range-finding radar that provided data to the gun sight for improved firing accuracy. It was aimed forward along the gun line and reported the distance to the closest thing that came into view. The fire-control system then used that value to correct the gun sight in elevation to account for the bullet's drop over that distance. Prior to that, the pilot had to know or guess the target's wingspan and dial that in to the gun sight so the presentation would compensate for the range to the target when he adjusted the sighting ring.

Longer acquisition ranges, lower-workload interceptions, and blind-firing capability required bigger radar dishes, automatic tracking, and file cabinets full of electronic gear. These capabilities significantly affected the development time and cost for night/all-weather fighters, both initially for the systems themselves and during integration into the aircraft. Missile guidance further increased the complexity of the design of the radar and the fire-control system and weight and volume of the installation. However, without them, all-weather defense of the fleet against jet bombers was not possible.

The inevitable result was that bigger fighters were required. The day-fighter's four 20mm cannons, 600 rounds of ammunition, and an APG-30 radar ranging gunsight weighed on the order of 1,000 lbs. Four Sparrow missiles, the Sparrow pylons, a search radar, and the requisite fire control system totaled more than twice that. As a result, while subsonic day fighters weighed about 20,000 lbs, the first all-weather fighters carrying guided missiles as well were going to have to weigh 30,000 lbs or more. There was some thought given to equipping day fighters with a simple, lightweight radar emitting the continuous-wave signal the Sparrow III needed to engage a target. However, as with the Sparrow I, the pilot would have to provide visual aiming of the radar beam using the gunsight. In practice, the Sidewinder was a much more effective alternative for the day fighter.

## Turreted Cannons

The speed of jets resulted in less time on target in firing passes both air-to-air and air-to ground. With little speed advantage over jet bombers, the jet fighter pilot was also unable to keep his fixed guns on target for very long when coming in from a beam position. The firing window was brief and did not reopen until he was behind the bomber, which meant dueling with the tail gunner. The obvious answer was to adapt the bomber's gun turret to the fighter, so its guns could lead the target independently of the fighter's fuselage orientation.

In June 1949, the Navy contracted with the Emerson Electric Co. for a four-gun, .50 caliber turret for evaluation on an F9F-3. This was a roll-traverse type turret, which meant that it rolled about a fore and aft axis with the guns pivoting within the turret to point as much as 20 degrees aft of vertical. It could roll at 100 degrees per second while the guns traversed at 200 degrees per second and included 1,400 rounds of ammunition.

To improve accuracy, a small gun-laying radar was located in the nose turret and pivoted to parallel the gun line. All the pilot had to do was point the guns within five degrees of the target using an articulated sight and the fire-control system could begin automatic tracking. Initial flight tests, in September 1951, indicated that there was no adverse effect on handling qualities of speed due to either turret motion or gun firing. Unfortunately, the requisite electronics were about the size of a kitchen stove with a big oven, and there was no place to put all of it. (Emerson seemed a little miffed that Grumman would not let them fill the outboard wing panels, apparently unaware that they would have to repackage the system into something like 50 shoeboxes to do so.) The project was canceled in early 1954.[15]

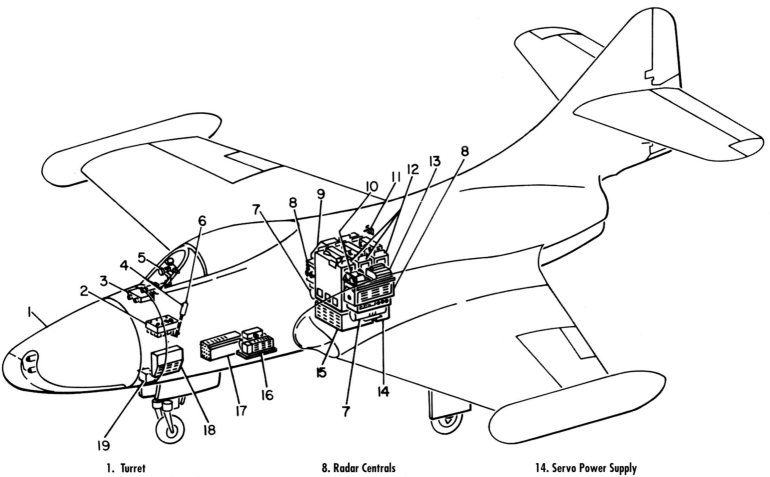

| 1. Turret | 8. Radar Centrals | 14. Servo Power Supply |
| 2. Main Control Panel | 9. Fuselage Terminal Box | 15. Servo Central |
| 3. Operational Control Panel | 10. True Airspeed and Relative Air Density | 16. Three Phase Inverter and Filter Unit |
| 4. Trigger Button | Detector | 17. Computer Auxiliary Amplifier Assembly |
| 5. Sight and Control Assembly | 11. Power Terminal Block | 18. Fire Control Terminal Box |
| 6. Track Button | 12. Computer Centrals | 19. Stable Vertical Gyro Erection Amplifier |
| 7. PU7/AP Motor-Generators | 13. Magnetron Overload Assembly | |

*This drawing depicting the electronics required for full implementation of the nose turret illustrates the difficulty with incorporating the concept in a day fighter the size of the Panther. (U.S. Navy via author's collection)*

*Not only did Vought have to install Allison J35 engines in the first 16 F7U-3s, at some points during production they had more than 30 F7U-3s completed without engines and parked on the ramp at the plant. (Vought Heritage)*

# DISAPPOINTMENTS FROM OVERREACHING

Aviation history is littered with program failures and disappointments. The Navy had its share during the development of carrier-based jet fighters – some were the result of their misplaced confidence in and reliance on Westinghouse as an engine developer. Fortunately, the U.S. Air Force was funding the development of jet engines at other companies. Others were the result of overly ambitious attempts to develop jet fighters with significant increases in range, endurance, and/or other mission capabilities. Better became the enemy of good enough. For their part, the contractors were all too willing to be optimistic to get contracts.

## Westinghouse Stumbles and Falls – The J40 and J46 Engine Programs

Development of a new engine that challenged the state of the art had to be started earlier than the aircraft that it was intended to power because it took longer to develop an engine and prove it safe for flight than it took to design and build an aircraft. To keep an engine problem from causing a costly delay in aircraft development, the military would generally not start a new aircraft program until the new engine had been through its initial flight-rating tests. However, in the race to field the most capable and highest-performing fighters, the military services usually initiated new aircraft programs before that milestone was accomplished, but not too much before. The problem with this approach is that the failure of an engine to meet expectations would affect all the aircraft slated to use it. The Westinghouse J40 and J46 engines were to exemplify the downside of betting that a new engine will be flight qualified on schedule at the planned ratings.

The Navy and the Air Force shared responsibility for engine development and coordinated their programs, with the Navy's engines having even number designations and the Air Force odd. Moreover, an engine manufacturer tended to be aligned with either the Air Force or the Navy. However, there does not seem to have been any bias in either service for using "its" engines.

After successfully developing very capable jet engines literally from scratch in the early 1940s, Westinghouse lost its touch. The outright failure of the J40 engine program and J46 delays in the early 1950s had a huge impact on Navy aircraft programs then in

development. The experience reinforced the prejudice against designing a new aircraft with an unproven engine. It also resulted in a redefined approach to aircraft production planning in the Navy

### J40 Engine Program

The genesis of the J40 was a Bureau of Aeronautics initiative in early 1946 to develop a new turbojet engine rated at 7,500 lbs of thrust without afterburning. The basic engine was to power long-range attack aircraft. With afterburner, the J40 would be a fighter engine. After considering proposals from four engine companies, BuAer contracted with Westinghouse Electric Corp. in June 1947 for its development. The company's proposal committed to

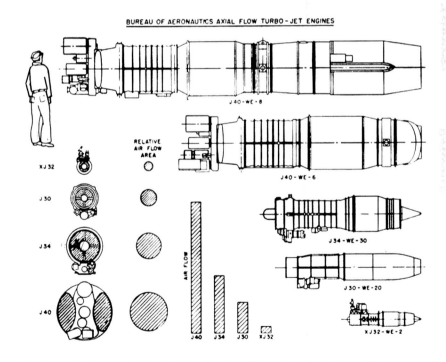

Westinghouse had succeeded in doubling the size of its engines beginning with the XJ32 and expected to do it again with the J40. Note that the afterburner on the J40-WE-8 almost doubles its length compared to the non-afterburning J40-WE-6. The J46, not shown, was in between the size of the J40 and the J34. (U.S. Navy via author's collection)

Westinghouse delivered the first J34s to McDonnell in late 1946 for the XF2H Banshee. When the Navy selected the J40, the Banshee had already flown and its engines were doing well. (U.S. Navy via Hal Andrews collection)

The engine first ran in late October 1948, little more than a year after go-ahead, so all must have seemed well. In early 1949, Lt. Cdr. Neil E. Harkleroad of BuAer's Power Plant Division reported: "The engine has been operating successfully to date." As of that writing, the 50-hour flight substantiation test was to be completed by June 1949, and the 150-hour qualification test by December 1949.[1] If the schedule had been met, there would have been no impact on the new fighter and bomber programs that BuAer planned.

The new engine incorporated several design features to increase the compressor pressure ratio (to 4.6:1) and overall engine efficiency to provide a better thrust-to-weight ratio, improved specific fuel consumption, and less loss in performance above 35,000 feet. The inlet guide vanes on the 11-stage axial flow compressor were internally heated by bleed air for anti-icing, "to burn its own way through ice" according to Westinghouse publicity. (Axial flow compressor engines were more susceptible to icing than centrifugal flow compressor engines.) The annular combustion chamber was relatively long to provide for more efficient fuel burn at altitude. A two-stage turbine drove the compressor. The variable-area exhaust nozzle for the afterburner consisted of two clamshell-type shutters opened sideways by electric actuators. Even the non-afterburning engine was to have a variable exhaust nozzle to optimize performance over a wider range of airspeeds and altitudes and decrease the time needed to go from low thrust to high thrust. All engine control, including the nozzle area, was to be accomplished automatically with an electronic engine control, another innovation since prior jet engine fuel controls were mechanical.

With afterburner, the J40 was 22.5 feet long and narrow, a little over 40 inches in diameter – 42.25 inches high and 45 inches wide. To maintain a minimum engine diameter along its entire length, the J40 was configured to have a bifurcated inlet so the accessories – generator, starter, fuel and hydraulic pumps, etc. – could be mounted on the face of the engine instead of on the side. The accessories added 2.5 feet to the length for a total of 25 feet. Total weight was about 3,366 lbs.

Without afterburner, the J40-WE-8's maximum thrust was to be 7,400 lbs; with afterburner, it was 10,900 lbs, a 47-percent increase. However, fuel burn went from 7,400 lbs per hour, one lb of fuel per lb of thrust, to 27,250 lbs per hour, two and one-half lbs of fuel per lb of thrust.

qualification of an engine with more thrust in less time and at less cost than the others. Given Westinghouse's proven track record, it was not a difficult decision.

Westinghouse was originally asked to develop jet engines in 1940 because of its experience and expertise in designing and manufacturing industrial and ship turbines. It proved to be a good choice, with Westinghouse successfully qualifying three jet engines for the Navy, the J30, the XJ32, and the J34. The J30 powered the FH-1; the diminutive XJ32, the KDN-1 target drone; and the J34, the F2H, F3D, F6U, F7U-1, and D-558-II as well as some U.S. Air Force aircraft. The J40 was similar in configuration to those engines – axial flow compressor, annular combustion chamber, and two-stage turbine. It was, however, significantly bigger.

Westinghouse successfully doubled the thrust of the J30 with the J34. It had received a contract in June 1944 for the J34 and run the first engine within a year. It was already flying in early 1947, when BuAer made its selection. Doubling the thrust again with the J40 must have seemed a relatively low risk. An afterburner was also planned that would increase the basic engine thrust by almost 40 percent.

Engine dash numbers are used to designate specific configurations and thrust ratings associated with different aircraft. The J40-WE-1 was to power the Air Force's X-10 Navaho long-range missile. The -3 was the non-afterburning J40 for Douglas's XA3D, a twin-engine, carrier-based, long-range bomber. The -5 was the proposed engine for the B-66, the Air Force variant of the A3D, which was to use the non-afterburning -6. The afterburning engine for single-engine fighters was to be the J40-WE-8.

BuAer soon asked for more thrust for even better fighter performance. Westinghouse obligingly committed to a more powerful J40 model incorporating a 14-stage compressor for a higher-pressure ratio and matching turbine. The J40-WE-10 was to have a normal rating of 8,330 lbs and a military rating of 9,275 lbs, a 25-percent increase over the -6/8. The afterburning thrust of the -10 was to be 13,700 lbs, a 19-percent increase, with a new iris-type variable-area nozzle replacing the -8's clamshell nozzle. This was a significant up-rating for a new and unproven engine, too much as subsequent events demonstrated.

The J40 was chosen to power all of the new Navy single-engine carrier-based fighters: the Grumman F10F variable sweep wing, general-purpose fighter, the McDonnell F3H-1 interceptor, and the Douglas F4D interceptor. Growth to more than 15,000 lbs of thrust in afterburner was projected. In December 1948, Westinghouse had committed to the specifications for both the J40-WE-8 and the even more powerful -10.

Unfortunately, development of the big engine was protracted. The all-important 150-hour qualification test of the -6, which was to have been completed in December 1949, was not passed until January 1951, more than a year behind schedule. The afterburner was particularly troublesome – the afterburner version, the J40-WE-8, did not pass its 150-hour qualification until August 1952. As a result, the start of flight test was not only delayed by the non-availability of the engine, initial flight test of the fighters had to be accomplished with interim engines or J40s without afterburners, causing program delays.

By its nature and the limitations of engine test stands at the time, the engine manufacturer's qualification test only establishes the initial durability of an engine. It does not subject the engine to realistic inlet airflows or other operating conditions. Compatibility with a given airframe installation, particularly at altitude and when maneuvering, can only be determined in flight. In the case of the J40, compressor stalls were all too common in some installations. Afterburner light offs were erratic, and blowouts at altitude were frequent and unpredictable. Because development and production J40 engines were both being tested in the Westinghouse facility in South Philadelphia using the same three test stands, evaluating and fixing flight-test problems sometimes took a back seat to production demands. Because of the development problems, engines that had been built had to be recycled through production to install

*Because the F4D had no aft fuselage, per se, to remove for engine access, the J40 afterburner was taken out aft and the basic engine was dropped out the bottom. This is a detailed mockup engine provided to Douglas for evaluation in the F4D mockup. Note the accessory section that was located between the bifurcated intake. (U.S. Navy via Tommy H. Thomason collection)*

new or modified parts, which required a rerun on the limited number of test stands. The engines themselves were less durable than expected, causing early removals and in-flight failures. The engine availability situation was made worse by the fact that four aircraft programs in the Navy and two in the Air Force were planning to use the J40, all starting within a year of each other, further straining Westinghouse's production capability. One aircraft test program after another was first waiting on engines to proceed and then slowed by engine problems.

According to Robert W. Lorimer, the supervisor of J40 engine test in south Philadelphia at the time, a serious problem discovered in flight test was the "rotating stall." A blade stall on a compressor stage would affect the aerodynamics of the next blade on that stage, setting up a vibration around the circumference of the stage that resulted in high blade loads and failure, followed by engine failure.

Grumman test pilot Corky Meyer complained that the J40 took 20 seconds to accelerate from idle to 100 percent thrust, much longer than the five to six seconds maximum for other jet engines.[2] The J40 specification requirement was eight seconds from 40 percent of military thrust to maximum thrust, but in June 1953, engines that took 20 seconds from idle to maximum thrust were being accepted in desperation.

Early on, Westinghouse had transferred J34 engine production to a facility in Kansas City leased from the government since the south Philadelphia plant was too small for the production volume involved. Westinghouse attempted to minimize competition for resources by transferring all aircraft engine development and production to this facility, separate from the ship and industrial turbine engineering and manufacturing, and increasing the number of test stands available. As might be expected, this transition initially hurt more than it helped.

When J40-WE-10 development was protracted and threatened to delay F3H development and production, the Navy and Westinghouse came up with the -22 engine, which was simply the less powerful -8 engine with the -10's gearbox, which was configured to drive the production F3H-1's hydraulic pumps and electrical generators. It was also derated slightly. Later, when the electronic fuel control proved unsatisfactory, it was agreed that the first production engines would be delivered with the electronic control as the -22A, but the -22 production standard would have a hydro-mechanical fuel control.

A phased thrust recovery program, so called Block II and III production engines, was planned for the -10 configuration to get to the ratings originally committed to. These were designated the -24 and -26. None were ever delivered. Westinghouse was never able to get the higher-pressure ratio compressor to operate properly.

| | J40-WE-8 | J40-WE-22 | J40-WE-10 | J40-WE-24 | J40-WE-26 |
|---|---|---|---|---|---|
| Max | 10,900 | 10,900 | 13,700 | 12,050 | 13,100 |
| Military | 7,400 | 7,250 | 9,275 | 9,275 | 9,640 |
| Normal | 6,700 | 6,500 | 8,330 | 8,330 | 8,610 |

The engine weight also increased to 4,218 lbs for the -24. Specific fuel consumption (SFC) stayed the same in afterburner at two and one-half lbs of fuel per lb of thrust per hour, but Normal and Military SFCs increased about 10 percent during development. The required acceleration time from idle to maximum thrust was increased to 10 seconds, but apparently 20 was the best that could ever be achieved with delivered engines, another major deficiency.

The J40 never did become operational. All J40-WE-10 development work was canceled in September 1953, with less than 200 hours of engine test time accumulated. Due to uncertainty about the availability of the J71, production of an order for 107 J40-WE-22 engines and spare parts was continued through to completion. However, the J40-powered F3Hs were grounded for good in July 1955, following a fatal crash at St. Louis.

### J46 Engine Program

It's an ill wind that blows no good. The J40 problems may well have saved the Vought F7U-3 program from cancelation. It was briefly terminated in early 1951, and considered for termination in late 1951, but it survived into production because all of the other big new Navy single-seat fighters were powered by the J40.

The lack of progress in these programs meant the Navy was ill advised to cancel the only one powered by a different engine, albeit from the same manufacturer.

Westinghouse's somewhat smaller J46, developed during the same period, was to power the F3D-2, the F2Y Sea Dart, and the F7U-3 Cutlass, all twin-engine fighters. With 6,100 lbs of thrust in afterburner, it was between the J34 and J40 in size. Two would provide roughly the same total thrust as one J40-WE-10. It also experienced development problems and was fielded too late for the F3D-2, which had to make do with an uprated J34. Westinghouse eventually qualified the engine and produced it for the F7U-3 Cutlass program.

Vought complained frequently and bitterly to BuAer about Westinghouse engines, beginning with the afterburning version of the otherwise satisfactory J34. In a 19 June 1951, letter, F. O. Detweiler, Vought's general manager, wrote:

1. The contractor has been attempting to prepare F7U-1 airplanes for delivery for the past several months under the handicap of unsatisfactory powerplants. The J34-WE-32 engines have been well over a year late and have not achieved any reasonable degree of reliability. Engine deficiencies called to the attention of the engine manufacturer have not been fixed, nor have promised for fixes been forthcoming.

2. The delay in the powerplants has not only delayed airplane deliveries, but has made it impossible for the contractor to follow production and flight-test plans. The delay has been costly and now promises to be beyond the contractor's ability to support financially. In addition, the delayed F7U-1 work is conflicting with the contractor's F7U-3 project.

3. Accordingly, the contractor wishes to advise the Bureau that no F7U-1 flight operations with J34-WE-32 engines will be conducted after 30 June 1951, until more positive assurance is received that the J34-WE-32 engine is airworthy and suitable for the completion of the flight-test program or a satisfactory alternative has been agreed upon.

4. The contractor respectively requests a conference at BuAer as soon as possible to review the remaining F7U-1 program in light of the powerplant situation and to discuss possible alternate powerplant arrangements. It is considered desirable to review the F7U-3 powerplant situation at the same time.

Both Vought with its F7U-3 and Convair with its F2Y were obligated to use another engine for first flights. Vought wound up producing the first 16 F7Us with J35s, and a few aircraft flew with one J35 and one J46. The first 150-hour J46 was supposed to be at Vought in mid-1950. It was finally received two years later. By the end of 1953, Vought had built almost 100 F7U-3s and Westinghouse had delivered less than one engine per airframe. In order to be fair to Vought, the Navy was accepting F7Us "conditionally," in other words, without the government-furnished engines.

The original engine for the F7U-3 was to be the J46-WE-2. It was to have 6,100 lbs of thrust in afterburner, with the expectation of development to more than 7,000 lbs of thrust by the time the F7U entered service. In 1951, Vought conducted a study of single-engine alternatives for the two J46s, which included the J57-P-1 and the J40-WE-10. It concluded that the J46 was still the best choice, if it met specifications. Westinghouse came close, but the Navy was forced to accept a derating to 5,800 lbs of thrust as the J46-WE-8. Not only was thrust a disappointment, but specific fuel consumption was higher than expected. By Vought's scorekeeping, the primary reason it didn't achieve F7U performance guarantees was the Navy-furnished engine. The F7U should have had 2,750 lbs more thrust (two times the difference between the projected 7,100 lbs of thrust and the 5,725 of the J46-WE-8) and 105 more nautical miles of radius of action.[3]

## Westinghouse Epilogue

Somehow Westinghouse had lost its way in jet-engine development and production. It may very well have been a leadership problem – as evidenced by a public denial of any responsibility for the F3H crashes. At the October 1955 Congressional hearings, the Westinghouse division manager stated that there was no proof that any of McDonnell's crashes had been caused by an engine failure. He went on to say: "I want to make very clear that all the engines we delivered did meet the Navy's thrust specifications."[4] While this was correct, strictly speaking, it was because the Navy waived or changed the specifications in order to get any engines at all. He was also disingenuous in pointing out that most of the accidents occurred in the heavier aircraft that were supposed to be powered by the J40-WE-10 engine, not the lower thrust -8 engine. The lower thrust did not affect safety of flight in the test and development phase. He did acknowledge that Westinghouse did not initially staff up, adequately fund research, or build enough test facilities or engines, "no doubt because of some complacency resulting from our almost immediate success with the J30 and J40 engines."[5]

Westinghouse didn't immediately get out of the engine business after the J40 cancelation. They went on to produce and support the J46 for the Cutlass. They invested in the development of a 6,000-lb thrust engine, the J54, which was a derivative of the Rolls-Royce Avon, but failed to sell any. It was never selected for an application, not even the U.S. equivalent of the Avon-powered Canberra, the Martin B-57. The J34 stayed in production for several more years. Westinghouse received a contract to uprate it in 1957, to power the Navy's new jet trainer, the single-engine T2J-1. However, as J34-powered aircraft flying hours dwindled (the T2J continued in production, but with two non-Westinghouse engines), so did Westinghouse's engine business. By 1962, they had exited the market.[6]

## Trouble-Free Engine Programs Are Exceptional

There was clearly a significant difference between the results delivered by the Westinghouse of the early 1950s and the Westinghouse of the early '40s. However, it would be wrong to think that only Westinghouse stumbled and fell. Each of the other engine companies – Allison, General Electric, Pratt & Whitney, and Wright – had embarrassments and difficulties as well.

Allison was only in the jet-engine business because the Army Air Forces had awarded them the production contracts for the General Electric I-40 (J33) and TG-180 (J35) engines to keep government-owned facilities in use and to help Allison get into the jet-engine business. Its J33 engine had been the second source for three generations of the F9F and had been inferior every time to the Rolls-Royce equivalents produced under license by Pratt & Whitney. The Allison T40 turboprop engine – a jet engine driving a propeller – was as big a disappointment as the Westinghouse J40. None of the projects that it powered reached production, in part due to other shortcomings, but engine problems adversely affected its development. The company's first in-house project, the J71, was also a disappointment.

General Electric was savaged in a May 1953 letter from ARDC's Maj. Gen. D. L. Putt to C. W. LaPierre, vice-president and general manager of GE's Aircraft Gas Turbine Division concerning the status of the J79 engine program and reminding them of prior disappointments:

> General Electric's past performance on new engine developments has been such as to discourage Air Force optimism toward *any* new GE development, even if it were pursued with an evident enthusiasm and vigor. The first 200 J-47s were subsequently modified at a cost of approximately two-thirds of the purchase price. The J-73 was scheduled to pass its 50-hour qualification test in November 1950. It has only recently completed this test. This engine [also] came out weighing approximately 30 percent more than the originally quoted weight. The J-53 development was also overweight by about the same percentage… The J47-17 engine was originally promised to have completed its qualification test by July 1950, and to be in production by September. It passed an acceptable 150-hour qualification test in December 1952, [on the sixth try] after several hundred engines were shipped which were not qualified.

Pratt & Whitney didn't seem to have major problems like the other manufacturers, but they still went through valleys. Initial F9F Panther flight operations in Korea were marred by J42 fuel-pump problems with gasoline. The Air Force had its F-94Cs grounded by J48-P-5 afterburner problems after it had successfully passed its 150-hour qualification test. F9F-5 Panthers were grounded in early 1952 by J48-P-8 engine problems.

In 1953, Roy Hurley, Curtiss-Wright's board chairman was castigated by Lt. Gen. Rawlings, USAF Air Materiel Command, in a letter dated 22 September:

> From the inception of the YJ and J65 programs there has been an apparent lack of appreciation by your management of the magnitude of the job you have undertaken. There has also been inadequate control over: tooling for the job, manufacturing processes and techniques, quality control, test programs, both at Wright Aeronautical and at subcontractors.... This has been demonstrated by the following:
>
> a. Test schedules have been established without knowledge that parts and facilities were available for their accomplishment.
>
> b. Production schedules have been quoted which, with a minimum of examination, proved to be impossible.
>
> c. Engines have been shipped with damaged and improperly manufactured parts.
>
> ...Many of the theories presented by your Engineering Department in explanation for failures have proved to be unfounded. Engineering changes have been proposed and incorporated, in our opinion, to correct manufacturing [practice] deficiencies.

Fighter engines proved to be a very tough product to develop and build successfully. Of the U.S. engine companies, only Pratt & Whitney and General Electric continued in the fighter-engine business. Allison continued to develop and produce jet engines but never built another fighter engine after the J71. Wright's engine business effectively ended with the J65.

## Grumman XF10F Jaguar

The Grumman XF10F almost became the Navy's first general-purpose fighter. It began as a swept-wing study that was part of its XF9F-2 contract. That resulted in its Design 83, which was submitted in late 1947. The nose resembled the Panther's, but the wing was a small clipped-delta with a thick airfoil. The horizontal stabilizer and elevator, mounted on the top of the vertical fin, was a smaller version of the same shape. The engine was the same as the XF9F-2's except that it had an afterburner; and the fuselage was extended under the vertical fin to house it. Mission equipment included an APS-19A radar. Design 83 was designated the XF10F-1 on 9 January 1948.

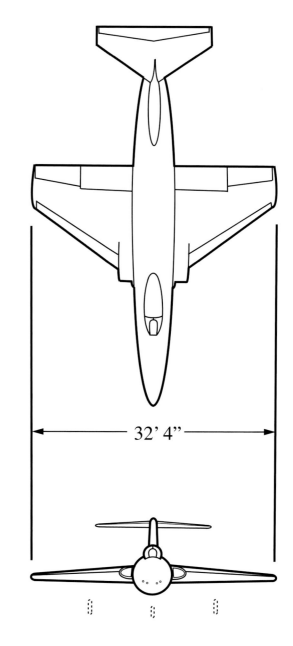

32' 4"

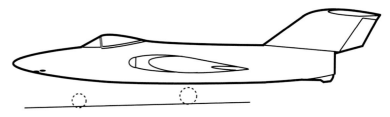

*Grumman Design 83*
*1 August 1947*
*The XF10F began as a swept-wing variant of the Grumman F9F-2. Unlike the later Cougar, only the nose and canopy are recognizable as being of Panther heritage. (Author)*

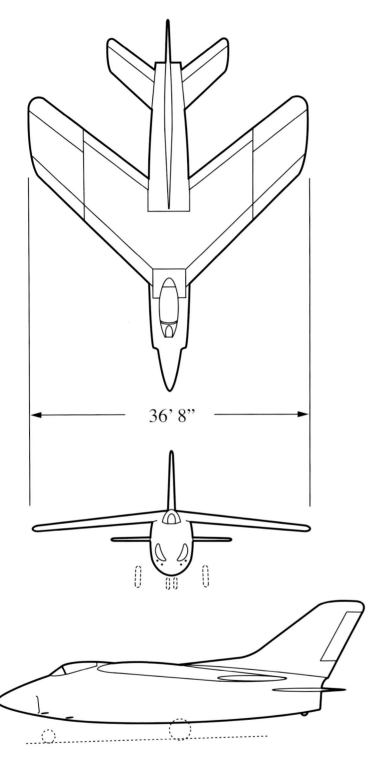

36' 8"

Grumman XF10F-1
Variable Incidence Wing
As the Navy's mission requirements grew, so did the XF10F. At this stage of the design iteration, the aircraft had a high wing so variable incidence could be used for better visibility from the cockpit for landing. (Author)

Grumman received a letter of intent in April 1948 for two XF10F prototypes based on the Design 83, with its first flight slated for August 1949. The delta-wing design was determined by wind-tunnel tests to have too much drag, however, so a revised design was proposed with swept wings and the more powerful J48 engine. This new configuration, as defined in July 1948, was projected to have a combat radius of 288 nautical miles for an escort mission and was equipped with an APS-25 search radar with a 30-inch antenna. The radar alone resulted in a 500-lb weight increase. However, subsequent wind-tunnel tests cast doubt on its all-important low-speed capability.

In any event, BuAer was not done developing the mission requirement. It increased the mission radius to 650 nautical miles, more than double the original. A larger radar antenna, 35-inch diameter instead of 30-inch, was also stipulated. The increased take-off weight, 26,991 lbs, dictated an increase in wing area from 360 square feet to 450 square feet, and the substitution of the new, more powerful Westinghouse J40-WE-8 engine for the J48. The design now featured a variable-incidence wing for takeoff and landing without an excessively nose-high body angle.

The detail specification for this iteration of the F10F was completed in January 1949. The mockup review was held in April. However, changes coming out of the mockup review caused the mission gross weight to increase yet again, to 29,199 lbs. Safe operation from existing carriers was now in doubt. Grumman therefore proposed to replace the variable-incidence swept wing with another innovation, the even more complicated variable-sweep wing. Although the wing sweep mechanism increased the empty weight by about 1,900 lbs, it reduced the landing speed and provided a significant increase in endurance. As George Spangenberg remembered it:

Thinking about it now, I'm inclined to believe we really didn't do a good job on that design, but it was anything but a clear-cut case for or against. We were still in the early part of the jet age. Technical data was becoming available on the drag reduction possible with swept wings at high Mach numbers. Some of the data was coming out of Germany. As with the jet engine, increased sweepback did not come easy for the Navy, as it decreased maximum lift but also increased the angle of attack for maximum lift, aggravating our takeoff and landing problem. To be competitive at the high subsonic and supersonic mach numbers, we had little choice but to use the concept. One solution might be to build variable sweep wings… A problem with airplane balance became obvious between standard and swept wing positions. That could be solved by translating the wing, done subsequently on a research airplane, but it meant weight and complexity on the F10F.[7]

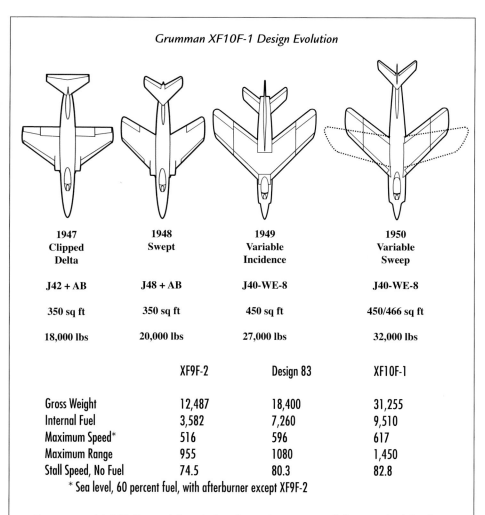

## Grumman XF10F-1 Design Evolution

| | 1947 Clipped Delta | 1948 Swept | 1949 Variable Incidence | 1950 Variable Sweep |
|---|---|---|---|---|
| | J42 + AB | J48 + AB | J40-WE-8 | J40-WE-8 |
| | 350 sq ft | 350 sq ft | 450 sq ft | 450/466 sq ft |
| | 18,000 lbs | 20,000 lbs | 27,000 lbs | 32,000 lbs |
| | | XF9F-2 | Design 83 | XF10F-1 |
| Gross Weight | | 12,487 | 18,400 | 31,255 |
| Internal Fuel | | 3,582 | 7,260 | 9,510 |
| Maximum Speed* | | 516 | 596 | 617 |
| Maximum Range | | 955 | 1080 | 1,450 |
| Stall Speed, No Fuel | | 74.5 | 80.3 | 82.8 |

\* Sea level, 60 percent fuel, with afterburner except XF9F-2

*Four years, 14,000 lbs, and four designs later, Grumman and the Navy had finally settled on the size and configuration of the XF10F. (Grumman Aircraft History Center)*

*Except for the low tail and the wing tilt, the overall configuration is very similar to the final one. Unfortunately, at this point Grumman elected to design the aircraft without hydraulically boosted flight controls. (Grumman Aircraft History Center)*

The definition of the variable-sweep configuration was accomplished by October 1949, and detail design finally began. Little remained of the original Design 83 but a similarity to the aft fuselage and empennage. The XF10F was now two and one-half times heavier than the fighters then entering service, instead of a more reasonable increase of 50 percent.

Since variable-wing sweep was an idea well ahead of its time, there was very little design experience to go on – even less than for swept-wing technology. Messerschmitt was in the process of building a variable-sweep jet aircraft (the Messerschmitt *Projekt* 1101) when World War II ended. The Army Air Forces had brought it to Wright Field, Ohio, for examination in 1945. Concurrently, NACA at Langley had done some wind-tunnel work in conjunction with using a variable-sweep wing on Bell's forthcoming X-2. Bell didn't want to burden the X-2 program with the concept, but it was interested enough in it to propose completing the Messerschmitt airframe with a U.S. jet engine. The result was the Bell X-5 variable-sweep wing-research program, which was conducted in parallel with Grumman's uncharacteristically innovative production effort.

The XF10F wing-sweep system was located high on the fuselage, giving the Jaguar a hunchbacked appearance. It provided a minimum wing sweep of 13.5 degrees and a maximum of 42.5 degrees. The mechanism was heavy and complicated because the wing not only had to pivot, but the pivot point also had to move forward when the wing was swept aft to maintain the center of lift in the correct relationship to the aircraft's center of gravity. To maximize lift at approach speeds, the wing was equipped with leading edge slats and trailing edge flaps. To maximize the flap span, the ailerons were small and roll control was augmented with spoilers. As if the wing wasn't complicated enough, it also folded and was equipped with a swiveling pylon for a 300-gallon drop tank, rocket pod, or 2,000-lb bomb.

In what turned out to be a misguided attempt to avoid the weight and complexity of hydraulically boosted flight controls and the requisite manual backup capability, Grumman decided late in the design phase to use a pitch system that did not require hydraulic power. A small, pilot-controlled surface positioned the stabilator itself, similar to a tab on an aileron being used to move the aileron. In Grumman's defense, it was demonstrated in a 1950 wind-tunnel test to be effective from a pure control-power standpoint. NACA rocket-powered model

Grumman made extensive use of wind-tunnel models in developing the XF10F configuration. The results from the test of the innovative pitch-control system were particularly misleading. (Grumman Aircraft History Center)

A full-scale mockup of the variable-incidence design was built for evaluation. Note that the open canopy tilted along with the turtle-deck located just forward of the wing. (Grumman Aircraft History Center)

Initial taxi tests were conducted at Grumman's Bethpage, Long Island, New York, facility. In this picture, taken at Edwards Air Force Base, the wing is swept fully forward as for takeoff and landing. The small triangle on the front of the horizontal stabilizer fairing is commanding the stabilizer leading edge up, but with no airflow, the stabilizer won't move. (Grumman Aircraft History Center)

The XF10F was only flown at Edwards AFB, California, and only by Grumman test pilot Corky Meyer. Numerous high-speed taxi tests and "hops" were required to establish that the pitch-control system was adequate for flight, which it turned out not to be. (Grumman Aircraft History Center)

The wing sweep turned out to work pretty much as hoped, although as implemented with a heavy translating pivot point, the benefit probably wasn't worth the cost and weight. However, in 1950 BuAer wasn't sure if an aircraft as heavy as the XF10F could safely land at the speeds resulting from the swept-wing configuration. (Grumman Aircraft History Center)

tests had also confirmed its effectiveness at supersonic speeds. The contrary indication was from flight test of a small radio-controlled model, which could have been caused by scale effect.

Less than two months after the start of the Korean War, in late June 1950, 12 production F10Fs were ordered. Production orders followed for 70 aircraft in February 1951, and 30 in October 1952.

Even after the configuration was finally established, progress was slow due to the Navy's priority on a swept-wing derivative of the Panther. It was further delayed by the decision to test the Jaguar at Edwards AFB (an extensive series of high-speed taxi runs and brief liftoffs to be sure that the unique pitch control system would work), and grounding of the J40 engine. Finally, on 1 May 1952, Corky Meyer took off for the first official flight and immediately had second thoughts about it. The aircraft was all but uncontrollable due to the lag in pitch response. Unfortunately, neither test nor analysis methods at the time were capable of predicting control-system dynamic response. The "spoilerons" were also ineffective, in part due to the routing of the control system across the wing sweep mechanism, but not dangerously so for test flying. Rudder control was also unsatisfactory. Ironically, the variable-sweep mechanization worked fairly well.

Not a great deal was accomplished during the year the XF10F was on-flight status other than the basic expansion of the flight envelope and ongoing efforts to sort out the control-system and handling-quality problems. No one but Meyer ever flew it – he apparently never considered it ready for a Navy Preliminary Evaluation (NPE) and nobody at BuAer appears to have disagreed. An afterburning J40 was never installed, so its maximum speed capability was never established.

The projected performance of the F3H-1 and F10F-1 performance in the general-purpose fighter mission could be directly compared since both aircraft were to be powered by the J40-WE-22:

|  | F3H-1 | F10F-1 |
|---|---|---|
| Takeoff Gross Weight (lbs) | 29,168 | 31,937 |
| Combat Radius (nm) | 280 | 345 |
| Average Speed (kts) | 484 | 398 |
| Rate of Climb at SL (ft/min)* | 12,850 | 10,810 |
| Rate of Climb at 35K feet (ft/min)* | 4,000 | 3,250 |
| Max Speed at Sea Level (kts)* | 621 | 612 |
| Max Speed at 35,000 feet (kts)* | 558 | 545 |

*Combat weight with maximum thrust

Corky Meyer stated that the stall speed of the F3H-1 was 96 knots[8] and that of the XF10F, 78. He went on to state that since a straight-wing aircraft could be flown at an approach speed "much closer to the stall" than a swept-wing aircraft, the benefit of a variable geometry wing for carrier suitability was more than this 18-knot difference.[9]

In summary, there was a measurable and arguably significant advantage in range and stall speed of the variable-sweep wing. The weight penalty hurt rate-of-climb and speed somewhat. Overall, the benefits weren't compelling, however, particularly since it was now apparent that swept-wing aircraft approach speeds and handling qualities were acceptable.

The pitch control became acceptable for the last four flights by a switch to an F9F-6 horizontal stabilizer but, by then, neither BuAer nor Grumman was enthusiastic about continuing the program, particularly with the J40 engine.[10] Grumman was busy producing the F9F-6 Cougar and the Navy didn't lack for general-purpose fighter candidates with the F7U-3 Cutlass and F3H-1 Demon in development. George Spangenberg said, "The (XF10F) cancellation effort was led by the project officer, a most unusual happening, as project

*Grumman finally gave up on the unpowered horizontal-stabilizer approach and installed a conventional-powered horizontal stabilizer from the F9F Cougar. This provided a significant improvement in pitch control, but the XF10F had fallen too far behind its competitors for the general-purpose fighter mission to recover. (U.S. Navy via Hal Andrews collection)*

The F2Y mockup included the radome that was part of the production design. Note the horizontal white line that was the equivalent of a ship's Plimsoll line. (U.S. Navy via Tommy H. Thomason collection)

The F2Y featured small beaching wheels at the aft end of the skis and on the aft fuselage so it could be towed or taxied into and out of the water. (National Archives)

officers and program managers are almost universally sales managers who try to keep their programs despite all faults. 'Red Horse' Meyer rated high in my book."[11]

The last of 32 "official" flights was accomplished on 25 April 1953. In addition to terminating the test program, the Navy officially canceled the production contract for 100 F10Fs and stopped the construction of 11 more that were being built, a second prototype and 10 pre-production aircraft.

## A Sea-Based Alternative

In addition to their work on carrier-based jet fighters, in 1948 the Navy initiated a program for a supersonic seaplane fighter. This aircraft was to provide a fighter complement for transport, patrol, and strategic nuclear-attack seaplanes. It also addressed concerns that a supersonic fighter was incompatible with carrier takeoff and landing limitations. The result was a contract to Convair, in January 1951, for the twin-engine, delta wing F2Y-1 Sea Dart, the first and almost certainly last supersonic seaplane fighter.

With two Westinghouse J46-WE-2 afterburning engines, it was projected to have a top speed of 805 knots (Mach 1.4) at 35,000 feet at combat weight. Takeoff gross weight with full internal fuel of 1,000 gallons was to be 24,373 lbs. Armament was to be forty-four 2.75-inch folding fin rockets carried in retractable launchers. An APQ-50 search and fire-control radar would provide an all-weather interception and attack capability.

The Sea Dart wouldn't have looked out of place in Jules Verne's *20,000 Leagues Under The Sea*. Eschewing the high-drag floats used on most seaplane fighters, it floated in the water and was lifted out on takeoff by long, thin hydro-skis that retracted for high-speed flight like landing gear. It was expected that these would allow takeoff and landing in Sea State 3, i.e., with waves up to five feet high. The mockup review was held in August 1952, and the design accepted. The XF2Y Sea Dart first flew in April 1953, from San Diego Bay, California. Although designed for the Westinghouse J46, it was first flown with an interim engine, the Westinghouse J34.

It was immediately apparent that developing a supersonic aircraft to take off and land from the sea was going to be every bit as demanding as developing one to operate from an aircraft carrier. The pounding of the skis even on relatively calm water was far beyond what the Navy and Convair expected. Even before the first of four preproduction YF2Y-1s flew in mid-1954, the rest of the production Sea Darts on order had been canceled. However, the Navy continued to fund the test program, although only enough to fly two of the four YF2Ys built.

The lack of area ruling precluded the Sea Dart from being supersonic in level flight even with the afterburning J46s installed. However, the first YF2Y did break the sound barrier in

a dive in August 1954. Tragically, it disintegrated during a high-speed pass at a public demonstration of Navy/Convair aircraft in November 1954. The cause was a massive structural overload resulting from a previously unencountered pilot induced oscillation (PIO) in pitch.

Various ski shock strut and single- and double-ski designs were evaluated through 1957 on the two surviving Sea Darts. One proved to be acceptable, with a successful, albeit very rough, landing and takeoff accomplished in conditions approaching Sea State 5, far above the requirement and essentially an open-sea condition. By then, however, the program had been overcome by events – sea basing was being abandoned and supersonic fighters were demonstrably compatible with carrier basing.

For some reason, the last YF2Y was not formally stricken until July 1962, which is apparently why it was included in the Department of Defense aircraft designation system as the F-7.

*The XF2Y-1 looked very much in its element as it taxies out from the launching ramp at Convair's facility in San Diego. Water rudder panels on the aft fuselage similar to speed brakes provided for steering during water taxi. (National Archives 80-G-708799)*

*Takeoff and landing proved to be a hard ride. A ski development program was therefore necessary. It wasn't as successful as necessary to overcome all the other impracticalities of sea-based operation, and it was canceled even before the P6M, the seaplane bomber whose operating sites it was intended to protect, was canceled. (National Archives 80-G-708780)*

*The F7U-3M was the final variant to reach the fleet. It could carry four Sparrow I guided missiles in addition to being armed with four 20mm cannons. Note also the blunt trailing edge on the ailevators, an early attempt to improve the maneuver buffet boundary. (U.S. Navy via Gary Verver)*

# F7U CUTLASS -
# NEVER QUITE SHARP ENOUGH

In June 1945, BuAer initiated a high-performance, carrier-based, day-fighter program in parallel to the night-fighter requirement that produced the F3D. The goal was to combine, for the first time, the 600-mph performance of the swept wing with the low-speed capability and good handling qualities necessary for carrier landings.

It took 10 years for the Cutlass to be ready to deploy. Even then, it was a year too soon to avoid a final black mark on its reputation, because the F7U proved to be too difficult to consistently land without incident on axial-deck carriers. What began as an innovative fighter at the very leading edge of the aeronautical state of the art wound up as a temporary fill-in that was unceremoniously retired after a handful of deployments.

## The F7U-1 Cutlass

It is hard to imagine that any of the other dozen or so proposed designs in the Navy's 1945 jet fighter competition were more radical than one of Vought's. It had no horizontal tail. Pitch control was provided by the control surfaces that on a conventional aircraft wing would be the ailerons – Vought called these ailevators. Since there was no horizontal tail, the wing lacked flaps, as there was no means to counter the nose-down pitching moment that extending flaps would cause. To compensate, the Cutlass had a relatively low wing loading. Leading-edge slats allowed the Cutlass to fly at still slower speeds, but at a high fuselage body angle. As a result, the F7U had an unusually long nose gear.

Although clearly unconventional, from a high-speed standpoint BuAer considered the tailless design to be the less risky of the two proposals (see Figure 7-1) that the Navy rated first and second. The runner-up, also proposed by Vought, was a swept-wing aircraft with a tail. At the time, aerodynamicists considered the conventional empennage to be something of a liability at transonic speeds – causing buffet and losing pitch-control effectiveness. As a result, Capt. Walter Diehl, head of BuAer Aerodynamics and Hydrodynamics, favored the tailless design.[1]

Vought received a contract in June 1946, for three XF7U-1 prototypes powered by two afterburning Westinghouse J34 engines and armed with four 20mm cannons. It was to be the first U.S. Navy fighter designed from the outset with afterburners, which Vought had introduced on its F6U Pirate to bolster the inadequate thrust of its engine. The pilot was provided with an ejection seat in a pressurized cockpit. Total internal fuel was 971 gallons. An automatic fuel-transfer system maintained the desired center of gravity since not having a horizontal tail limited the allowable center-of-gravity (cg) range.

The Vought landing-gear design was very innovative in order to accommodate the F7U's unusual configuration and takeoff and landing attitude.

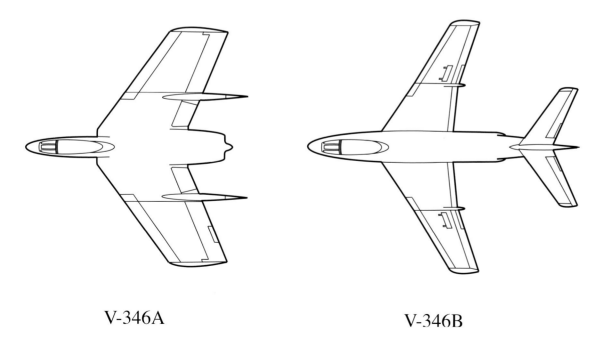

V-346A          V-346B

*Figure 7-1 Vought Proposals V-346A and V-346B (Author)*

*An early production F7U-1 and the first production F6U flying over NAS Dallas, which is located in Grand Prairie, Texas. The Vought plant is above the F7U and to the left of the runway. (Jay Miller collection)*

*Figure 7-2  F7U-1 Alternative main landing gear positions. (Author)*

Air Line to
Pre-rotation
Turbine

Turbine on
nose wheel

*Gadgetry was the hallmark of the F7U. The tail hook was actually stowed on top of the fuselage and extended aft and down when deployed for landing. All six speed brakes are also open in this photo. The insert shows the air line and turbine that spun up the nose wheel for landing. (Jay Miller collection)*

The main landing gear struts pivoted at their mounting point to move the wheels 20 inches between their forward and aft positions. For takeoff, the struts were angled forward to provide a longer lever arm for the ailevators. This landing-gear position also lowered the tail for a more nose-up attitude and therefore higher lift. When the landing gear was extended for landing, it automatically reverted to the aft position, which reduced bounce on touchdown and the risk of tip-back during ground handling. The pilot selected the wheels-forward takeoff position after engine start. (If the wheels were fixed in place by wheel chocks at the time, the F7U would make a very unusual and dramatic rearward lurch and sit back on its haunches.)

The nose gear was extendible for catapult launch, increasing the nose-up attitude from 10.5 degrees with the main landing gear in the forward position to almost 14 degrees. Even more unconventionally, for landing the nose wheel was spun up to approximately the rpm at which it would be rotating shortly after touchdown. This minimized the load on the nose-gear actuating strut that occurred when the nose wheel touched down far below it. The nose wheel was rotated by engine compressor bleed air from a line leading from the wheel well down to a set of vanes on the nose wheel hub.

High-speed flight had necessitated the introduction of powered controls. Initially, only one hydraulic source was usually provided for the hydraulic actuators. If that failed, the pilot was to still be able to fly the aircraft to a safe landing without hydraulic power. Artificial representation of control-stick loads, or control feel, was also necessary because the control surface hydraulic actuators were irreversible. Otherwise, at high speed, fluctuating air loads on the control surfaces would feed back to the cockpit controls. In the event that hydraulic pressure was lost, an automatic reversion system switched the pilot's controls to spring-loaded tabs on the ailevators. (The rudders, like those on most transonic fighters, were not boosted.)

In July 1948, before the first flight, Vought received an order for 19 production F7U-1s. A small lot of production aircraft was often ordered at that point so there was less of a gap between development and introduction into service if the new aircraft met expectations. The first order would provide aircraft for further development and service evaluation. A follow-on order, usually a year later, would be placed if flight tests were proceeding satisfactorily. These and subsequent annual orders would provide the aircraft for operational use.

The three XF7U-1s were built at Vought's Stratford, Connecticut, plant. When the first one was completed, it was put

*The public debut of the Cutlass was well covered because it was such an exotic configuration at a time when every jet fighter was somewhat exotic. The long booms on the wingtips, which were for flight-test instrumentation, were removed after the first few flights because they weren't stiff enough. A traditional nose boom was substituted. (Vought Heritage Center)*

on a barge to be taken to NAS Patuxent River for its first flight, which occurred in September 1948, with Vought's chief test pilot J. Robert Baker at the controls. Capt. F. M. Trapnell flew it publicly for the first time on 18 November. It was a sensational demonstration, as much for the F7U's unusual configuration as its performance, even without afterburners. At that time, the Navy announced that the F7U would be called the Cutlass in keeping with Vought's tradition of naming its aircraft for occupations or things of a buccaneering nature.

On 14 March 1949, the second prototype was lost when Vought chief test pilot H. B. Millar took off for a planned air-to-air photo flight and disappeared over the Chesapeake Bay. From the pieces of the wreckage eventually found, investigators speculated that the aircraft had crashed into the water gear down and slats out in a left roll. No cause for the accident was ever proven, but it was subsequently suspected, after investigation of another fatal F7U-1 accident, to have been the result of a design flaw in the automatic reversion to the manual control system. If pressure were lost in the single hydraulic system for any reason, the control system was designed to automatically revert to the manual mode. Two separate mechanical changes took place – one was the boost actuators going into bypass so the controls were free to move; the other was the actuation of a changeover mechanism that unlocked a spring tab on the ailevators and connected it mechanically to the pilot's control stick. Both were required to accomplish the changeover, which took three to four seconds. If only one occurred, the pilot would not be able to control the aircraft in pitch.

With Vought's move from Connecticut to its new facilities in Grand Prairie, Texas, subsequent F7U development testing was accomplished in Texas. However, while the runway at the adjacent naval air station was being lengthened, test operations were initially conducted at Carswell Air Force Base west of Fort Worth and then at Ardmore, Oklahoma.

The first formal Navy XF7U-1 evaluation was accomplished in June 1949, on the third prototype. Five Navy pilots made 21 flights for 14 flight hours. Their comments validated the changes that Vought testing had identified as necessary. Taller fins and rudders were necessary to improve directional stability and control. A yaw damper was to be added and the artificial control feel system modified to place the feel units in the wings. The speed brakes were redesigned as well, including addition of a second set under the forward fuselage. The original wing speed brakes were judged inadequate to decelerate the aircraft quickly enough if a hydraulic control-system problem resulting in reversion were to occur at high speed, to a speed at which the pilot could cope with the control loads.

In addition to the flying qualities and systems problems, the XF7U-1 was well over weight in spite of the generous use of a relatively new material, magnesium, in the structure. The empty weight had soared from a guarantee of 9,711 lbs at contract award to an actual of 11,874 lbs in October 1948. Vought could only attribute 26 lbs of the increase to Navy changes. The rest were errors, omissions, or optimism on Vought's part. The weight continued to grow because of changes, with the F7U-1 to have an

The most obvious F7U-1 configuration change resulting from flight test was that the original short vertical fin was replaced with a taller one to improve directional stability. The first production aircraft like BuNo. 122474 here were built with the short fin and subsequently modified with the taller vertical fin. Note also the steps that opened on the side of the fuselage when the canopy was opened. These provided access to a more forward panel that was then opened to allow entry to the cockpit. (Vought Heritage Center)

empty weight of 12,387 lbs. The Westinghouse engine ratings were increased to compensate for the weight growth, with the original J34-WE-22 at 3,700 lbs of thrust in afterburner becoming the J34-WE-32 at 4,900 lbs for production F7U-1s. Unfortunately, Westinghouse had trouble qualifying the more powerful engine and delivering any afterburner-equipped engines at all. Vought was forced to use J34-WE-34 engines, which had less thrust and no afterburner.

Although the June flight evaluation was generally favorable, the weight growth and Westinghouse engine problems were serious concerns. At its empty weight, the aircraft was maneuvering and landing at 2,000 lbs heavier than allowed for in the structure's design. Westinghouse clearly needed more time to develop the engine. The Navy was also in the midst of an inter-service budget battle that escalated with the incoming Secretary of Defense's cancelation of the Navy's first super carrier, *United States,* in April.

The F7U's high angle of attack on approach and landing is apparent in this photo taken at the moment of touchdown. The ailevators are deflected well up. Note also the mast in front of the canopy that extended when the tail hook was lowered. It was there to engage the actuation strap of the Davis barrier in the event of a nose gear collapse or failure to extend. (National Archives 80-G-42162)

Faced with both near-term budget and F7U-1 technical problems, BuAer decided not to commit to any more than the 19 already on order. The potential of the design was still evident, however, and the fleet was still in need of a high-performance fighter as soon as possible, so Vought received a contract in September 1949 to modify the design and build 88 F7U-2s to be delivered between June 1951 and January 1953. The F7U-2 was to have a structural beef-up, control-system changes, better maintenance access, and improved cockpit visibility for carrier landings. The contract included two F7U-3s intended to be a further improvement on the -2 design, substituting higher thrust engines and adding search radar.[2]

Vought test pilot and future company president Paul Thayer crashed the first XF7U-1 while attempting a takeoff in September with a simulated 150-gallon drop tank on the right-hand pylon and a new differential rudder-control system. Thayer was not seriously hurt, but the aircraft was destroyed.

There was worse to come. In October, following the "Revolt of the Admirals" in Congressional hearings, the House Armed Services Committee supported the Air Force and sided with the Secretary of Defense over the cancelation of *United States*.[3] The Cutlass program then became one of the sacrifices necessitated by the fiscal year 1950 and projected 1951 defense budget retrenchment that particularly affected the U.S. Navy. The budget reduction, combined with concern at OpNav over the XF7U's flight characteristics as reported in Navy pilot flight evaluations up to then, resulted in BuAer canceling the just-issued F7U-2/3 contract.

That ended any chance of the fleet having a swept-wing fighter in the sky over Korea in 1951. The only good news was that BuAer elected to continue to let Vought complete the order for 19 F7U-1s for development and evaluation purposes.[4]

The production F7U-1s were built at the Grand Prairie plant. In what was to become an ongoing problem, the afterburning J34 engines scheduled to be delivered in late 1949 were not available for the first flight of production F7U-1 on 1 March 1950. The next Navy evaluation was also accomplished that month at Ardmore on an XF7U-1 that did have afterburning engines. Although the modifications since the first evaluation corrected most of the deficiencies found then, others replaced them, primarily longitudinal stability and control issues. One climb in full afterburner was made to 30,000 feet in five minutes from a standing start: the J34s consumed approximately one-third of the total internal fuel in those five minutes.

Boone Guyton, Vought's test pilot on the XF4U Corsair, ferried the second production F7U-1 from Hensley Field at NAS Dallas to Ardmore. His flight was only 35 minutes long and did not exceed 8,000 feet and Mach .73, but he used his firsthand experience to suggest selling points in a 25 April 1950 memo to Vought management and engineering. "It is recommended that we emphatically point up the ease of flying, excellent stall, low-speed approach and landing characteristics, and good ground handling qualities of this airplane." He noted that the F4U had established Vought's reputation as "a company that can provide

an excellent high performance airplane but one which is generally more difficult to fly at or near stalling speeds, during takeoffs, during approaches to and carrier landings, and during normal field landings."

In May 1950, the Navy elected to end F7U-1 production at 14 aircraft instead of 19 because the J34-WE-32 had failed to pass qualification tests at Westinghouse. This was somewhat disappointing for Vought but not a major concern because it was not a reflection on the F7U-3.

On 1 July 1950, the remaining XF7U, BuNo. 122474, went supersonic, diving to Mach 1.006. Any celebration would have been short-lived, as the second production F7U-1

crashed at NAS Dallas on 6 July during a single-engine emergency landing. Vought test pilot Warren P. Smith was killed when, on final approach, one of the two elements of the automatic boost-control changeover system activated due to momentarily low hydraulic pressure and the other did not. Before the F7Us were grounded to modify the control system to insure complete changeover to the manual operation, one of the now-supersonic XF7Us was lost during an air show at Patuxent River on 7 July 1950. An afterburner fuel leak resulted in a massive in-flight fire, requiring Paul Thayer to reluctantly demonstrate the Vought-designed ejection seat for the first time.

Another of the 14 production F7U-1s crashed in September when Vought chief test pilot William Harrigan drowned after his aircraft ran off the runway into the lake at the end of the runway at NAS Dallas. His accident was attributed at least in part to the effects of anoxia following an oxygen-system failure. Unfortunately, he kept the canopy closed for his landing. When the aircraft overran the end of the runway, damage to the nose-gear retracting strut upper attachment jammed the canopy closed, keeping the rescue team from getting him out of the cockpit quickly enough. The long nose strut and its mounting would later cause problems in the F7U-3 as well.

During carrier-suitability tests, the aircraft is often topped up with fuel to maintain a specific gross weight. Note also the man kneeling on the access panel that provided access to the cockpit when a ladder was not available. (National Archives 80-G-432151)

Lt. Cdr. Edward L. "Whitey" Feightner finally accomplished the at-sea carrier suitability tests aboard *Midway* in late July 1951, with the first production F7U-1, BuNo. 124415. It had been a year-long process, much longer than usual, due to aircraft problems starting with the F7Us being grounded from 7 July to 24 August 1950, for the flight-control system rework. In addition, the aircraft was down for replacement of fuel cells and then for a vibration investigation program. The complicated fairing over the arresting gear had also failed three times during shore-based tests. It was eventually removed. Since the Westinghouse schedule status hadn't improved, it was flying with -34 engines, i.e., with no afterburners. (F7U-1s were sometimes flown with an afterburner on one engine and just a tailpipe on the other.)

According to Whitey Feightner, the aircraft was very easy to bring aboard in one respect: "In the carrier-landing configuration, the F7U-1 was really stable. The airplane's drag was so high that you sat on the power all the time. You controlled your altitude by moving the throttle and the airspeed with the stick by bringing the nose up or down. You could change it one knot at a time. It

was great to bring aboard in that respect."[5] Catapult launches up to the gross weight and wind-over-deck speeds tested were also acceptable. Otherwise, the F7U flunked – the pilot couldn't see the deck on final approach, resulting in inconsistent sink rates, and late wave-offs were problematical due to slow engine response. The landings on *Midway* were terminated by a fuselage structural failure due to the high sink rates experienced.

Most of the F7U-1s were only for Vought test and Navy evaluation, with a notable exception being a brief stint with the Blue Angels. Two were forced on the flight demonstration team as an adjunct to their existing complement of F9F-5s. This proved to be a blessing when the F9F-5s were grounded during the early part of the 1952 season for fuel-control problems. The F7U demonstration was spectacular, showing off its afterburners and 540-degree-per-second roll rate. Unfortunately, the pilots experienced a series of problems and emergencies, some not design-related but most associated with the hydraulic system. One time, the two-position main landing gear lowered with one wheel in the landing position and one in the takeoff position, which fortunately turned out not

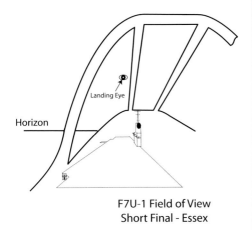

F7U-1 Field of View
Short Final - Essex

*Surprisingly, the lack of visibility of the carrier deck from the F7U cockpit doesn't seem to have been realized before the at-sea tests. As this subsequent Vought analysis demonstrates, no part of the carrier, including the LSO platform on the portside aft, was visible to the pilot when he was in the groove 150 feet out. This was also the case initially with another famous Vought product, the F4U Corsair. (Author)*

to be a difficulty on landing. When the Blue Angels were able to resume performances in the F9F-5s, the Blue's maintenance officer and the F7U pilots agreed to put the two F7Us on the ground permanently. After their flight demonstration at Naval Air Station Memphis, Tennessee, home of the Navy's Technical Training Center, they left without their F7Us, which became, most appropriately, maintenance trainers.[6]

Vought, looking for opportunities to keep the production lines going, proposed the F7U-1, as is, to the Air Force, which evaluated it in early 1952 at Eglin AFB, Florida. Air Force pilots dove it through the sound barrier and considered its transonic handling qualities to be excellent, with the exception of a transient pitch down at Mach 0.91. They found it to be inferior to the F-86 in maximum $g$ capability at 40,000 feet and Mach 0.82 and, like the Navy pilots, considered it to be underpowered unless the afterburners were being used. Although the Air Force's overall impression was favorable (they thought the visibility and ground handling to be superior to their fighters, for example), they passed on acquiring any.

One F7U-1, BuNo. 124422, was assigned to the missile test facility at Point Mugu in 1952 for evaluation with the Sparrow I missile. Some non-firing flights were made with the missile in 1953, but availability suffered from the lack of spare parts. A sec-

ond F7U-1 was flown out to Point Mugu in early 1953 to be used for spare parts, but very little seems to have been accomplished.

The last flyable F7Us were farmed out to non-flying duties in September 1953. BuNo. 124418 was ferried to Memphis to join the former Blue Angels F7Us, 124420 to the Naval Air Technical Training facility at Jacksonville, Florida, and 124425 to the Naval Air Material Center near Philadelphia, Pennsylvania. One of its last hoorahs was Lt. Cdr. Ron Puckett's demonstration at the Dayton National Aircraft Show that month, which included an inverted pass at 200 feet and 500 miles per hour.

## F7U-3 Cutlass Development and Qualification

It's easy to wonder, given the outcome, why BuAer kept funding the F7U program. The answer is probably that it was the only one of its pre-1950 fighter programs that wasn't powered by the J40. BuAer considered the F7U-3 and the XF10F to be its general-purpose fighter candidates according to an article by Cdr. Noel Gayler in the April 1950 *Naval Aviation Confidential Bulletin*, including the italics:

In some respects, the size of these aircraft will prejudice their employment, but this much can confidently be stated: *One or both models will provide the Navy with carrier-based general-purpose fighters of combat performance second to none.*

*Vought convinced the F7U supporters in BuAer and OpNav to assign two F7U-1s to the Blue Angels in early 1952 for demonstrations at air shows. This publicity stunt mainly demonstrated that the F7U-1 was not ready for prime time from a reliability standpoint, but when it was working, the F7U-1 was a sensational performer. (Jay Miller collection)*

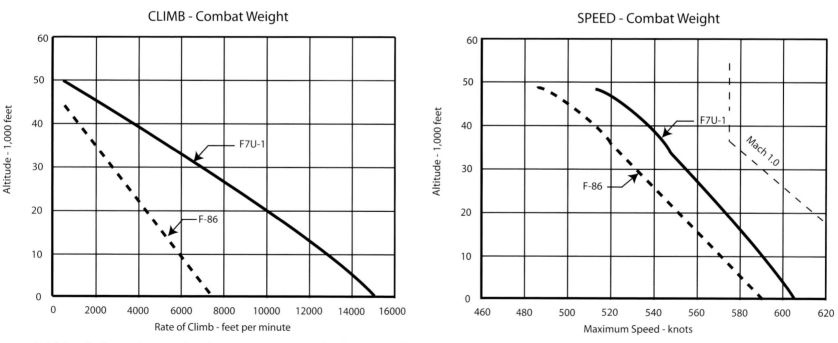

CLIMB - Combat Weight

SPEED - Combat Weight

*With its afterburner in operation, the F7U-1 was projected to have a significantly higher rate of climb than the F-86. The F7U-1 also had an advantage in speed over the F-86, but only in afterburner due to the thickness of its wings. As it turned out, it was inferior to the F-86 in turn performance at altitude for essentially the same reason — a low critical Mach number. (Author)*

The F7U-1 assigned to VX-4 at Point Mugu for an initial evaluation of Sparrow missile compatibility wasn't as useful as hoped, primarily because of parts shortages. Note the open access panel, which provides the final step to the cockpit when a ladder is not available. (Jay Miller collection)

Vought was confident enough that the F7U-3 would be reinstated that it resumed engineering work in 1950. A fuselage-only mockup review was held for the Navy in April, and funding was reinstated later that year as expected, with a go-ahead for 28 aircraft. The bigger, better F7U-3 was clearly a derivative of the F7U-1 but very different under the skin. The flight controls were now powered by two separate hydraulic systems, each pressurized to 3,000 psi by two separate pumps, one on each engine. Along with hydraulic system and avionics changes, the cockpit was raised; the fuselage enlarged to accommodate the bigger engines and more fuel; the 20mm cannons moved from the nose to a location above the engine inlets; and many new access panels added to improve maintainability, which had been another F7U-1 shortcoming.

The landing gear and arresting hook were redesigned. The two-position main landing gear feature was deleted. Two wheels replaced the single wheel on the nose gear but the pre-rotation feature was retained. A much simpler and more conventional V-frame tail hook was substituted for the upper aft fuselage-mounted stinger hook.

As originally designed, the F7U-3's visibility was better than the F7U-1's and about on a par with the F4U-5's. However, after a visit and lecture from Lt. Cdr. Feightner, immediately following his July 1951 carrier qualification testing of the F7U-1, a study was launched that resulted in a new nose and canopy.

Progress in tooling and fabrication was somewhat impacted by industry priority on Korean War requirements. Vought also had to design an interim, non-afterburning Allison J35 engine installation to be used for the first 16 aircraft since Westinghouse couldn't meet the Vought schedule for J46s. Nevertheless, the first aircraft was completely through the shop in late November

1951. Vought chief test pilot John McGuyrt took it up for the first time in December.

First flight is always an uplifting milestone for the company and the program team, but it was particularly gratifying for Vought. The year 1951 had been a very rough year for the reinstated F7U-3 program. In late April, three weeks after an impromptu OpNav/BuAer review at Vought, BuAer canceled all F7U-3 orders after the first 28. The decision came after the Department of Defense had substantially reduced the Navy's

It was probably fortunate that the F7U-1 didn't get a thumbs-up from BuAer for additional production for operational use. But BuAer may have guessed wrong in spending its money on the XF10F instead of quick fixes that would have resulted in a more reliable, carrier-compatible F7U-2 day fighter. (U.S. Navy via Robert L. Lawson collection)

request for FY51 supplemental funding and FY52 funding. The F7U-3 was deemed less likely to meet the Navy's general-purpose fighter requirements than their other programs. BuAer specifically cited the inability to launch the F7U-3 in no-wind conditions with existing catapults. However, Vought was successful in convincing the new BuAer chief, Admiral Combs, to reinstate the production order pending the outcome of the upcoming flight-test program. Vought and BuAer also instituted a weight-reduction program to include deletion of mission equipment like the visual-assist radar.

OpNav was also still second-guessing the decision to continue with the program but was supportive of Vought as a Navy contractor. In December 1951, Vought was informally asked whether it would be willing to produce F3Hs as a second source to McDonnell instead of the F7U. Vought's general manager was less than enthusiastic but couldn't just say no: "If the Navy will not permit us to make F7Us and needed us to produce additional F3Hs, we would have little choice but to do the best we could for the Navy."[8] Fortunately, development problems with their competitors' fighters continued to keep BuAer from being confident enough to pull the plug on the Cutlass program. The swept-wing Douglas F3D-3 was terminated instead.

Nevertheless, the F7U-3 was a fighter in search of a mission. It had been beefed up from its original day-fighter configuration to meet the new requirement of general-purpose fighter. Then it was determined to be too heavy to be launched as a general-purpose fighter so it had been stripped of radar and other equipment to make it a day fighter again. However, in that role, it was rightfully being criticized as too big, complicated, and expensive. The demonstration of the more powerful steam catapult in early 1952, and its immediate acceptance by OpNav undoubtedly helped save the F7U by eliminating launch weight as a concern.

*The removable belly pack housed 32 2.75-inch rockets in two rows. The open slots by the man's right hand were the exhaust ports for the first row. (Jay Miller collection)*

|  | F7U-1 (J34-WE-32) | F7U-3 (J46-WE-2) |
|---|---|---|
| Total Thrust |  |  |
|     Afterburner, lbs | 9,800 | 12,200 |
|     Military, lbs | 6,740 | 8,160 |
| Combat Weight, lbs | 17,707 | 24,068 |
| Wing Area, ft² | 496.0 | 535.5 |
| Thrust to Weight | 0.55 | 0.51 |
| Time to Climb to 30K ft., min | 2.8 | 2.3 |

*The first F7U-3 taxis out on F7U-1 landing gear. (Note the openings in the main landing gear doors to provide clearance for the wheels when retracted.) The lack of paint reveals the different materials that the skin panels were made from. The bulb nose and small canopy were about to change as a result of a reexamination of the visibility from the cockpit on approach to the carrier. (Vought Heritage Center)*

*Because of early concerns that the heavier F7U-3 could be catapulted at a high enough speed, a complicated holdback arrangement was devised to maximize its nose-up attitude at launch. This was evaluated on an F7U-1. Note the pressurized main gear struts, the "grocery-cart wheel" under the fin fairing, and the compression of the tires from the holdback tension. The protective steel cover was to protect the holdback pendant from the heat of the afterburner. (U.S. Navy via Tommy H. Thomason collection)*

In late 1951, Cdr. Pete Aurand, then in charge of the Fighter Class Desk, was campaigning to use the F7U-3 as an interceptor because of the F4D program slippage.[9] With its afterburning engines, it had the necessary rate of climb and it was big enough to carry the radar and fire-control avionics. In January 1952, on a visit to Grand Prairie, he informally told Vought that he wanted to incorporate a search radar into the 17th and subsequent F7U-3s. With this mission assignment, F7U-3 production would only total about 200 aircraft, ending in mid-1954 when the F4D was expected to become available. Vought was relieved that BuAer did not finally implement the change until they had committed to almost 200 F7U-3 day-fighters.

In June 1952, NATC pilots conducted a preliminary qualitative evaluation of the three different F7U-3s at the Chance Vought plant. At this point in F7U development, the engines were non-afterburning J35s, the landing gear was still the F7U-1 design, there were two different artificial-feel systems among the aircraft, and modifications to the nose and canopy to increase visibility over the nose had not yet been incorporated. Overall, performance was regarded as similar or slightly superior to the F9F-6 except for the buffet boundary, which was not only "disappointingly low" but "considered to be a major deficiency." It was noted that the NATC F-86A-5 being used for chase and pace during this evaluation "demonstrated a significant margin in maneuvering performance."

As was customary in these evaluations, there was a long list of unsatisfactory items, most related to handling qualities, and no speculation about the benefit of forthcoming changes like afterburner. There were no other potential showstoppers but it was noted that: "The radius of action of the airplane with a maximum fuel load of 1,140 gallons is extremely short."[10]

The evaluation was tragically marred by the death of one of the Navy pilots, Lt. Cdr. B. L. Hendrickson. For some reason, on his fourth evaluation flight, he failed to extend the wing slats for takeoff and crashed off the end of the runway into the lake. However, since it was clearly pilot error, the accident did not appear to affect the NPE evaluation – it wasn't directly mentioned in the letter report from NATC to BuAer, not even in the paragraph recommending changes to the slat operation for safety of flight.

On 26 July, NATC pilots again flew BuNo. 128451, now modified with blunt trailing edge ailevators, F7U-3 landing gear with improved wheel brakes, improvements to the feel system and yaw damper, and the tailpipes tilted up two degrees for a lower thrust line. They reported some improvement in the handling qualities but "little significant improvement in the buffet boundary."[11]

The Flight Test division was assigned the fourth J35-powered F7U-3 for initial carrier suitability tests. It had the new radome with the upper surface slanted sharply downward to improve the all-important view of the LSO on approach, but it did not yet have the new higher canopy, which allowed the ejection seat to be raised and moved forward for landing.

Initial carrier suitability tests with BuNo. 128454 commenced aboard *Midway* in August 1952. Vought was told that the approach, landing, and wave-off characteristics were satisfactory. The other good news was that it not only achieved the predicted minimum wind-over-deck value for launch, the results indicated that it could be reduced by five knots with more aggressive pilot technique. After a week aboard, 128454 was returned to Vought for the next set of modifications. In November, a second set of trials was accomplished aboard *Coral Sea* with 128454. With the proviso that it wasn't wholly production representative, the NATC report concluded, "the test airplane is satisfactory for catapult launchings and arrested landing up to the limits tested."

In September 1952, Vought management seriously considered suggesting to the Navy that the last four of the 16 J35-powered F7U-3s be sent to Korea the following March for a land-based combat evaluation. After further discussion about the degree of difficulty and the risks involved versus the projected reward, they decided not to pursue the effort. One concern, harking back to an earlier publicity stunt, was: "The way the Blue Angels' F7U-1s were thrown out of Corpus Christi is an illustration of the rapid way things can happen, entirely out of our control."[12]

In December, Vought test pilot William Sunday was killed on a production test flight when an aileron control linkage became disconnected on short final. The aircraft began an uncommanded roll, caught a wing tip, and cartwheeled to destruction.

A carrier flight deck operation was labor-intensive. This photo was taken during the Cutlass' first carrier-suitability tests. By then the nose had been changed and the canopy bulged slightly. (U.S. Navy via Hal Andrews collection)

Following its carrier-suitability tests, BuNo. 128454 was modified with the final configuration canopy and multi-position ejection seat. (Vought Heritage Center)

The F7U finally flew with a J46 engine in April 1953. Since there were concerns at Vought about its reliability, the left engine was still a J35. Flight test was not without problems, including compressor stalls. The engine didn't pass its 150-hour qualification test until July 1953, two years behind schedule. In August, there were 11 F7U-3s assigned to the BIS activity at NATC, but only four were powered by the J46. Engine modifications further delayed deliveries, resulting in the storage of up to 64 "gliders" at Vought.

The first at-sea testing with a production-representative Cutlass occurred aboard *Coral Sea* from 4 to 6 October 1953. (Aboard at the same time were the XF4D and the XF3H.) It was configured with afterburning J46 engines, the revised radome, and a canopy/ejection seat configuration that provided better visibility on approach – the seat bucket could be positioned upward and forward – as well as other carrier-suitability specific modifications like nose-wheel steering.

Additional testing was accomplished in February 1954 aboard *Lake Champlain* and in June aboard *Hancock* that had the C-11 steam catapult and the Mk 7 Mod 1 arresting gear. Although the single-engine landing approach characteristics were not considered satisfactory, the F7U was accepted for service use with some further changes.[13] The maximum arrested weight was limited to 24,200 lbs from a desired 26,180 lbs, however.

The Navy went all out to make the F7U-3 introduction to the fleet as smooth and trouble-free as possible, building on past transitions and lessons learned. In early 1954, it was one of the first aircraft to go through the Fleet Introduction Program (FIP). The

FIP got off to an awkward start on 17 March, the first day of flying, when a Navy pilot managed to do something that hadn't been done before – he spun it at 25,000 feet while doing his third clean condition stall, was unable to recover using the recommended recovery technique, and ejected. Vought immediately reevaluated the spin entry and recovery maneuver and sent a message to BuAer on 31 March recommending ungrounding the Cutlass: "Contractor confident no risk."[14] However, a week later, test pilot John McGuyrt, after more than 100 attempts, was successful in forcing an F7U into an inverted spin, up to and including the ejection since his spin-recovery parachute ripped off.

Like most aircraft going through BIS in parallel with ongoing contractor development of fixes for known problems, the F7U-3 was criticized for deficiencies like gun-gas ingestion, low engine thrust, limited cross-wind capability, inadequate visibility over the nose, and excessive maintenance hours. One piece of good news from the BIS report was that Vought had overcome one of the most worrisome F7U deficiencies, the low buffet boundary. The F7U-3 could "better (both the FJ-2 and F9F-6) in air-to-air combat." The F9F-8 "is far superior in turning ability" but the F7U-3 "has a decided edge in rate of climb, acceleration, and Vmax."

The report also stated: "The F7U-3 will be a satisfactory interim interceptor and medium-speed attack plane when equipped for in-flight refueling or with external fuel." However, it went on to recommend, "The F7U-3 should not be employed as a carrier-based day fighter" because of its lack of range and endurance. In a subsequent contract dispute, Vought agreed that there had been a significant shortfall (combat radius on internal fuel had been cut in half) but that most of it was due to the

*The problem with achieving enough over-the nose visibility on approach is apparent in this photo of the initial carrier-suitability testing aboard Coral Sea. (U.S. Navy via Hal Andrews collection)*

*All the worry about having enough angle of attack for launch and work on special holdback arrangements turned out to have been unnecessary as the Cutlass took to the air with no difficulty off the catapult. (National Archives 80-G-630064)*

engine's SFC being higher than specification. A 220-gallon belly pod had already been developed to offset some of the deficiency.

Fortunately, BuAer and OpNav had found a mission match for the Cutlass in their procurement planning. Pete Aurand's plan to make it an interceptor was realized when BuAer elected to complete what turned out to be the last 98 with the Sparrow I missile. In need of a high-performance, missile-firing fleet defense fighter as soon as possible, BuAer contracted with Vought in early 1953 for the F7U-3M, a Cutlass with a Sperry APQ-51 radar and armed with four Sparrows, two on launchers on the existing inboard wing hard points and one on each outer wing panel. In partial compensation for the lack of in-flight refueling capability (it had to be deleted to accommodate the radar), fuel cells with a 124-gallon capacity were added to each outer wing panel. Gross weight increased to about 33,000 lbs.

First flight of the -3M was accomplished 12 July 1954. Unfortunately, the carrier suitability qualification was delayed by a shore-based landing accident, which meant the aircraft were almost all completed before the F7U-3M's shortcomings for carrier operations became apparent. When returning back aboard with four missiles and full ammunition, the gross weight was about 25,000 lbs, which meant an approach at close to full military power. Any settling from the conventional flat approach often had to be stopped with afterburner, which wasn't modulated, meaning it was either on or off. This resulted in an over-correction when needed and was dependent on afterburner light offs being 100 percent reliable. NATC decided that the power-on, straight-in approach using the recently demonstrated mirror landing system would require less power and be less likely to require the use of afterburner for other than a wave-off. This was evaluated aboard *Shangri-La* in late-1955 following its conversion to the angled-deck configuration. It wasn't much of an improvement. The only answer was to limit landing weight to 23,500 lbs, which precluded returning with Sparrows.[15]

Endurance was a problem with the F7U-3M as well. Carrying Sparrows limited the external fuel to the 220-gallon belly pod. Even with the pod, mission time with the drag of four Sparrows was only one hour and 23 minutes, less than the 1+30 minimum normally used for the carrier operating cycle. The F7U-3M was therefore assigned operationally to attack squadrons although its Sparrow capability was available if needed.

As shown in Figure 7-7, the Navy, Westinghouse, and Vought were never able to reach a satisfactory balance between engine thrust and the requirements that drove the weight. The gross weight kept going up while the thrust, initially satisfactory, went down. Although this was not atypical, in the case of the Cutlass it went too far. A modified engine intake developed in 1955 for the F7U-3M did provide an improvement in thrust below 125 knots, providing a greater margin in approach and wave-off.

## Operational Use

In parallel with the Fleet Introduction Program at Patuxent, Project Cutlass was set up at NAS Miramar, California, to gain "operational familiarization, maintenance knowledge, and logistic data prior to the Cutlass's assignment to the first operational squadron." Fleet Aircraft Service Squadron 12 was formed for this purpose. The first Cutlass arrived in February 1954. They also participated in Project Steam, the steam-powered catapult qualification aboard *Hancock*.[16] In late 1954, some of its personnel were temporarily assigned to Project Checkout with VC-3 at NAS Moffett Field, California. VC-3 had been given the ongoing task to train officers slated to command F7U squadrons and senior pilots and key enlisted men who were to be the cadre for those squadrons. The first class from Project Checkout graduated in January 1955, the pilots having received 150 hours of ground school and 50 flight hours in the Cutlass.

It's not clear how much more spin-recovery work was done between McGuyrt's April 1954 accident and VC-3's restriction of the aircraft from aggressive maneuvering following the loss of two of their F7U-3s in January 1955. Part of the problem was that the Cutlass didn't spin so much as tumble, confusing the pilot as to what to do with the controls, which turned out to be just letting them go. Vought quickly finished the spin-recovery program and demonstrated it to the Navy on 2 March 1955. A flight handbook revision and briefings to Cutlass squadrons followed. "Post-stall gyration" was added to the aeronautical lexicon and another blot appeared on the Cutlass' escutcheon.

Getting deployable Cutlasses to the fleet was a long, drawn-out process. In May 1954, VF-83 was the first fleet squadron to receive an F7U-3, but deliveries were almost immediately halted following completion of the FIP, progress reports from BIS, and the VC-3 experience. In June 1954, BuAer convened a conference to review the readiness of the F7U-3 for delivery to operating squadrons and the recommended configuration in light of all the changes, product improvements, and ongoing development. This wasn't unheard of for a program, but the Cutlass seemed to have an unusual number of deficiencies that delayed introduction into the fleet. In December, another review of the configuration was accomplished in light of the shore-based operating experience, sea-trials and training, and the development status at Vought.

The first Pacific Fleet F7U-3 squadron, VF-124, was formed with a cadre of personnel from Project Cutlass and Project Checkout. The workup for its first deployment was tragically marred in July 1955, when Lt. Cdr. Jay Alkire was killed in a horrific ramp strike, which served to reinforce the warning against getting low and slow in the groove. They deployed aboard *Hancock* in August 1955, only to suffer two landing crashes before the month was up. Worse was to come. In November, Lt. (jg) Milliard

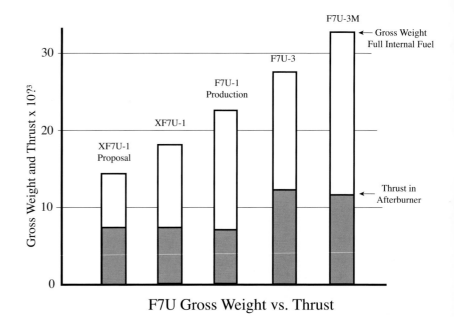

Figure 7-7 F7U Gross Weight vs. Thrust (Author)

*All eyes are on the new arrival on the ramp at NAS Miramar, California, for the start of Project Cutlass. (Vought Heritage Center)*

was killed in a bizarre sequence of events following a poor landing on the ship. He had crashed into the barricade after engaging the second barrier. A vertical strap on the barricade fouled low down on the nose gear, causing failure of the nose gear actuating strut attachment, which resulted in the actuating strut going up through the canopy deck, knocking off the canopy and then firing the ejection seat. Milliard was propelled up the deck into a parked aircraft. The Cutlasses were shore-based in Atsugi for the rest of the deployment.

The second fleet squadron on the East Coast to be assigned the F7U-3 was VF-81 at NAS Oceana, Virginia. VF-81 pilots had problems qualifying aboard *Ticonderoga,* still an axial deck carrier in the spring of 1955. After three accidents and a hurried review by BuAer and Vought, it was determined that the difficulties were caused by a combination of LSOs giving a late cut and the pilots diving for the deck and over flaring, which tended to result in hook skip. After LSOs began to give the cut farther out and pilots simply held a constant attitude after the cut, trusting that the resulting descent would put them squarely in the landing area, the squadron qualified successfully. When the squadron deployed aboard *Ticonderoga* to the Mediterranean in November 1955, as VA-66, one of its aircraft suffered a nose-gear failure during a carrier landing. VA-66, too, was shore-based at NAS Port Lyautey, French Morocco, for the balance of the deployment.

VF-83 became VA-83 on 1 July 1955, with the receipt of the F7U-3M, which replaced its F7U-3s. With the F7U-3Ms, VA-83 deployed on *Intrepid,* then an axial-deck carrier, in March 1956, to the Mediterranean – the first Sparrow I deployment. The axial deck and the Cutlass continued to be incompatible. They had strike damage to four aircraft and had major damage to two more due to nose-gear collapses. Most of the time while in the Med,

they only had four aircraft on the ship with the rest ashore at Point Lyautey.

Ironically, launches turned out to be the least of the F7U concerns, since the Cutlass only deployed on carriers with steam catapults, which induced the heavy Cutlasses to fly with no difficulty. The problem was axial deck landings. It was a bit too hard for the average fleet pilot to land consistently from the standard flat approach with a cut. Avoiding the very real hazard of

*The engine inlet underwent several changes during the course of development. This F7U incorporates the boundary layer fence inside the inlet and associated vent above, the vents for the 20mm cannon, and the lower inlet lip extension. It also has the in-flight refueling probe. (Robert L. Lawson collection)*

*A beautiful day to be at sea in October 1953 aboard Coral Sea. (National Archives)*

The F7U-3 retained the self-boarding concept of the F7U-1. However, the path between the top of the intake and the cockpit was via two small foot pegs that extended out from the side of the upper forward fuselage when the canopy opened. (Vought Heritage Center)

being low and slow without an adequate power margin to accelerate, the pilot tended to be high and/or fast. (Even if the aircraft wasn't high, it certainly looked that way from the pilot's viewpoint when it really wasn't.) All too frequently, the result was the pilot pushing over to get down to the deck after the cut, resulting in a hard landing, often nose wheel first.

This problem was already apparent as the first deployment began. The landing accident statistics, for the period 1 July 1954 to 30 September 1955, demonstrated that the Cutlass was off to a bad start:

| Model | Carrier Landings | Accidents | Accidents/1,000 Landings |
|---|---|---|---|
| FJ-2/3 | 2,264 | 5 | 2.2 |
| F2H | 24,920 | 48 | 1.93 |
| F9F-2/5 | 17,289 | 55 | 3.18 |
| F9F-6/8 | 25,609 | 107 | 4.18 |
| F7U-3 | 886 | 6 | 6.77 |

*On 14 July 1955, Lt. Cdr. Jay Alkire of VF-124 had made one successful landing on Hancock but had gotten low and slow on approach for his second. When he didn't appear to respond to the LSO's "low" and "come-on" signals, he was given a wave-off. He finally went into afterburner but too late to avoid a ramp strike. Alkire was killed, but there were no serious injuries to those on deck, including the LSO who made a hasty and unusual exit from his platform after giving the wave-off signal. (U.S. Navy via Tommy H. Thomason collection)*

It couldn't be argued that it was unfair to compare a new aircraft's accident rate to that of those with many more landings because of the FJ-2/3 data. Moreover, the Cutlass accidents were far more severe than the average. Of the six accidents, one was fatal and two resulted in serious injuries. There was a second fatal accident on 1 October, the day after the reporting period ended. Of the seven total, three were hard landings and two were ramp strikes.

Unfortunately, the Essex/Ticonderoga Class carriers being modified with angled decks were only beginning workups when the Cutlass squadrons were finally ready to deploy. As a result, the aircraft's first three deployments were on axial deck carriers. All were marred by nose-gear failure incidents and the banishment to shore stations of most if not all the Cutlasses for some part of the deployment. The deployments on angle-deck carriers, which allowed for a descending, constant angle-of-attack approach as opposed to taking a cut and then maintaining a fine line between floating up the deck and diving at it, were much less colorful. The nose landing gear was also beefed up.

For example, VX-4 provided a detachment of four F7U-3Ms to CVG-2 aboard *Shangri-La* for Sparrow I missile capability tests during its deployment to the western Pacific from November 1956

to May 1957. According to one of the pilots, "We made a full deployment, met every hop that was scheduled, shot down six drones, and in general had a most enjoyable cruise during which we accumulated many hundreds of carrier landings. I don't think there was any concern among us that the airplane was difficult to bring aboard."[17] VA-116 made the last F7U-3 deployment from the same ship, *Hancock*, which hosted the first one. In sharp contrast to *Hancock's* experience with VF-124, VA-116 claimed 343 flights and 458 flight hours in a three-month period. The difference was that *Hancock* now had an angled deck.

Of the Navy's jet fighters that were produced in any quantity and deployed operationally, the F7U was the least used. About 250 aircraft flew the majority of the 55,000 hours amassed by the F7U-3 fleet, an average of little more than 200 hours each. Some were flown for only 50 hours before being stricken, because the F7U-3s were retired almost as soon as the F7U-3Ms became available.

## The Cutlass Legacy

The successful final deployments were too late to save the Cutlasses' reputation. It will always be known as the Gutless Cutlass (certainly compared to what it would have been if Westinghouse had been able to increase the J46's thrust as expected) and the Ensign Eliminator (deservedly so when flying onto axial deck carriers). In comparison to the safety records of its contemporaries in the early to mid-1950s, which weren't particularly good, it had the worst. Cutlasses were involved in 78 accidents between July 1952 and August 1956, with an accident rate of about 17 per 10,000 hours. The average for all Navy fighter and attack aircraft during that time was 9.8. The last F7U was delivered in 1955, and the last operational service use was just two years later. Few who flew it and wrote of the experience seem to have held it in very high regard, but there are a few. For one thing, the basic airframe is remembered as being incredibly strong – no one ever broke a Cutlass in flight.

The main benefit for Vought (and by extension the Navy) was the experience. In 1946, development of a carrier-based, swept-wing transonic jet fighter approximated going over Niagara Falls in a barrel – nobody had the requisite information to design for it. It turned out that a high-performance jet fighter needed a stabilator, irreversible flight controls with artificial control feel, redundant hydraulic systems, pitch and yaw stabilization, afterburners, pressurization, ejection seats, air-conditioning, engine inlets with boundary layer air removal, and nose-gear steering, among other things. Vought learned all about those systems and features with the F6U and F7U. They then embodied them, a low-thickness-ratio wing, a great engine, and all the lessons they had learned about what not to do in the F8U Crusader.

*One of my most vivid memories from hours spent beside the runway at NAS Sangley Point, Philippine Islands, was seeing one of these VF-121 F9F-8 Cougars. It was like a duckling imprinting on a falcon. (U.S. Navy via Robert L. Lawson collection)*

# PLACEHOLDERS

In a 13 December 1949 memorandum, the chief of the Bureau of Aeronautics, Rear Admiral A. M. Pride, felt compelled to communicate the following to his boss, the Chief of Naval Operations:

Opinions

1. Reciprocating engine fighters cannot successfully engage jet fighters, either offensively or defensively.
2. Reciprocating engine fighters cannot successfully attack jet bombers.
3. Reciprocating engine fighters cannot successfully escort attack aircraft of any type in the face of jet fighter opposition.
4. Reciprocating engine fighters are of doubtful value against reciprocating engine bomber or attack aircraft

The Air Force's first swept-wing jet, the XP-86, flew for the first time in October 1947. It conclusively demonstrated the superior performance of the swept-wing configuration and that its low-speed handling qualities were acceptable. The design was qualified and put into production with remarkably few changes, given its groundbreaking configuration. (National Archives B30505)

escorted by jet fighters, unless they have sufficient numerical superiority to carry out the mission in spite of all the losses the enemy jet fighters can impose.
5. Reciprocating engine fighters can be used against reciprocating engine bomber or attack aircraft if the latter are unescorted or escorted only by reciprocating engine fighters, but in all such cases jet fighters would have a greater combat advantage.
6. Turbo-prop fighter studies do not show sufficient performance (compared to jet fighters) to warrant building a prototype at this time.
7. Reciprocating engine attack aircraft, or reciprocating engine fighter (sic) used as attack aircraft, can carry out attack and ground support missions when effective air opposition is not present or when sufficient jet fighter cover is provided.
8. The cruising performance of turbo-prop attack aircraft approaches that of jets sufficiently so that it should be possible for the jet fighter escort to accompany turbo-prop attack aircraft on a strike.

Recommendations

1. No consideration should be given to the development of new reciprocating engine or turbo-prop fighters at this time.
2. The reciprocating engine fighter should be considered obsolete for fighter missions, and jet aircraft should be procured in the necessary numbers for all fighter tasks, including night fighter and photo-reconnaissance, so as to modernize our fleet air forces as rapidly as possible.
3. Reciprocating engine attack airplanes, and reciprocating engine fighters capable of attack and ground support missions, should be retained in the numbers required for these missions.
4. The development of turbo-prop and jet attack aircraft prototypes should be vigorously pursued but production should not be initiated until the prototypes have been evaluated.

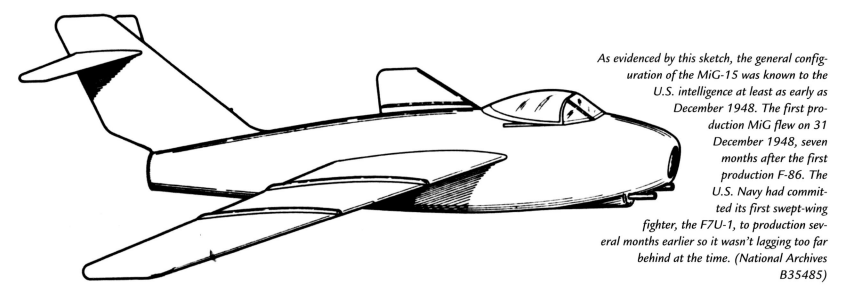

*As evidenced by this sketch, the general configuration of the MiG-15 was known to the U.S. intelligence at least as early as December 1948. The first production MiG flew on 31 December 1948, seven months after the first production F-86. The U.S. Navy had committed its first swept-wing fighter, the F7U-1, to production several months earlier so it wasn't lagging too far behind at the time. (National Archives B35485)*

This unequivocal position statement was required in part because of concerns being voiced, both inside and outside the Bureau of Aeronautics, about the operational suitability of the carrier-based jet fighter compared to other types. There was disagreement at high levels in the Navy that jet fighters were even needed. In a 1950 meeting of the Air Board, AirLant Chief of Staff Capt. J. H. Flatley advocated procurement of additional reciprocating engine F4U-5s instead of jet fighters. This recommendation was based on the Atlantic Fleet's limited operational experience with the FH-1. AirLant's position was countered by Cdr. Peter Aurand based on his FJ-1 experience and not accepted by OpNav.[1]

As events were to prove, the BuAer position paper did not go as far as it should have. Not only were reciprocating engine fighters obsolete, but also straight-wing jet fighters were inadequate for air superiority when up against swept-wing jet fighters. There are few timeouts in international affairs, however. When the MiG-15 came across the Yalu River in Korea in November 1950, the Navy, unlike the Air Force, did not have a comparable fighter even close to ready for deployment. The shortfall was not for a lack of evidence elsewhere of swept-wing success and the benefits. The Air Force's F-86 Sabre flew for the first time in October 1947. It was 80 mph faster than F9F-2 with the same thrust. It had even more of a speed advantage in a dive because of its higher critical Mach number. The British De Havilland Swallow first flew in 1946, and the Supermarine Swift, in

1948; both were swept-wing versions of straight-wing jets, the Vampire and Attacker, respectively. The MiG itself had been accurately described in 1948, and had been observed at air shows in Russia in 1949. Based on the numbers seen, it was clearly in production.[2]

It was not due to a lack of effort by individuals within BuAer to understand and promote swept-wing fighters. Even before the

*This Supermarine Type 510 isn't landing with the nose landing gear up — it doesn't have one. An odd combination of the old and new, it was a swept-wing fighter with a tail wheel. Visible under the wing roots are takeoff rockets, a common practice in the Royal Navy at the time. As usual, the Brits scored a first with these swept-wing aircraft landings aboard Illustrious in November 1950, and then fell behind in fielding one. (Terry Panopolis collection)*

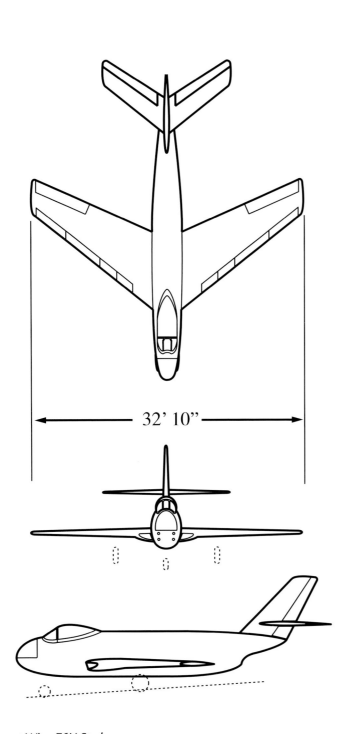

*Vought Swept-Wing F6U Study*
*Of all the possibilities for an early deployment of a Navy swept-wing fighter, the F6U was probably the least worthy of consideration. The change would have had to include a more powerful engine, among other things, and Vought had its hands full with the F7U at the time. (Author)*

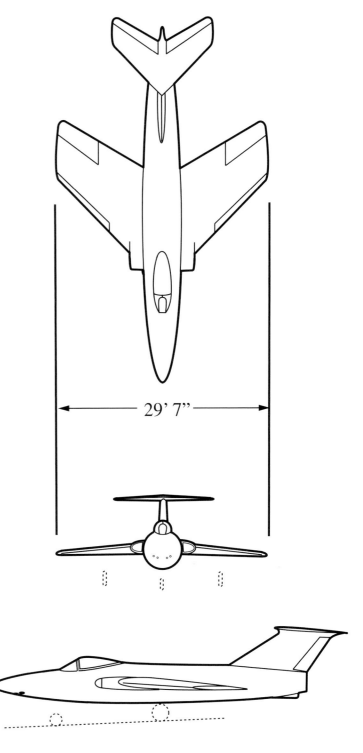

*Grumman Design 83*
*February 1948*
*Although Grumman was able to turn the Panther into the swept-wing Cougar in record time in 1951, when working toward the same objective in 1948 the evolving Navy requirements caused them to go off on a tangent that led to the XF10F. (Author)*

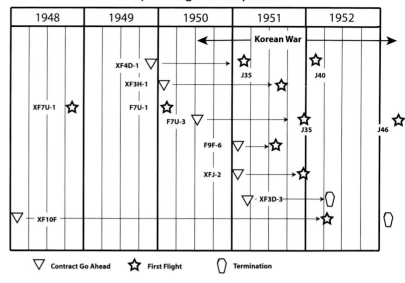

Figure 8-1 Swept-Wing Development (Author)

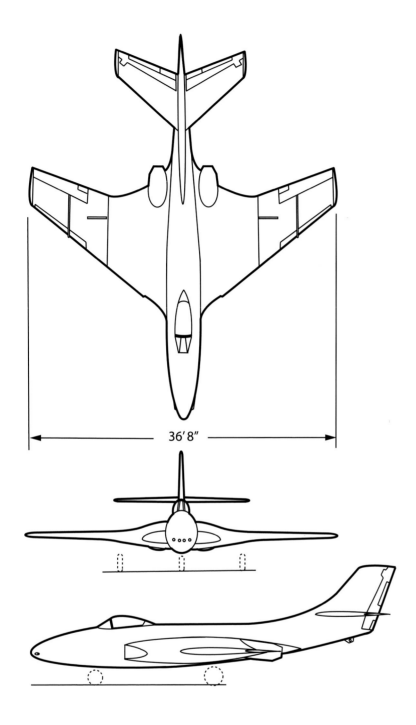

McDonnell "F2H-5"

*McDonnell probably was in the best position in 1947 to quickly create a swept-wing carrier-based fighter. It informally proposed putting F-88 wings, empennage, and afterburners on a Banshee. If it flew as well as the F-88, it was likely to have been acceptable to the BuAer and NATC. (Author)*

F-86 flew, tests of the Bell L-39s in mid-1946 demonstrated that the swept wing could have acceptable low-speed characteristics if equipped with slats. BuAer gave Grumman a contract to do a swept-wing fighter design study and had one of its test pilots fly the L-39. In January 1947, BuAer modified the Douglas D-558 high-speed research program to include a swept-wing version, which flew for the first time in February 1948. The Navy's first swept-wing fighter, the XF7U Cutlass, had flown only 11 months after the F-86. Since its engines were to have afterburners, it would have even better performance.

It certainly was not a lack of initiative on the part of the Navy's aircraft contractors. Vought unsuccessfully suggested a swept-wing version of the F6U as a quick way to achieve higher performance. McDonnell did design studies of a swept-wing variant of the F2H Banshee in 1947 that incorporated features from its Army Air Forces F-88 design, including afterburners, but didn't get a contract modification to proceed.[3]

The Navy did not have a dog-fighting, simply equipped, swept-wing aircraft in November 1950, because its focus was on defending the battle group against high-speed, high-altitude bombers with interceptors, and escorting medium-range carrier-based bombers to the target in all-weather conditions. As a result, the jet fighter programs initiated in the late 1940s after the F7U start were either short-range, fast-climbing, all-weather, rocket-armed, point-defense, bomber-destroyers, or big general-purpose fighters. A simple (e.g., no search radar), lightweight fighter did not fit into these plans.

Therefore, even though almost all of the Navy jet fighter producers were working on a swept-wing fighter in the late 1940s, none of the Navy-funded programs was intended to be a light-weight day-fighter or even to fly until 1951. They were:

- The variable-sweep wing Grumman XF10F Jaguar, a general-purpose fighter and complicated to a fault
- The second coming of Vought's F7U Cutlass as a general-purpose fighter
- A pure interceptor, the Douglas F4D Skyray, as radical as the F3D was pedestrian
- An interceptor become general-purpose fighter, the McDonnell F3H-1 Demon

New Westinghouse engines powered all of them, which was part of the problem. Although it took much longer than expected, all but the XF10F was to achieve operational status. No attack carrier deployed in the early to late 1950s without at least one of these types on board. The F4D and F3H soldiered on aboard the carriers into the early 1960s. More often, two were present and sometimes three, particularly if attack squadrons equipped with fighters were counted.

However, in the interim, BuAer had to scramble to bridge the gap between the small, straight-wing jet fighters that were in production and the big, high-performance fighters that were taking longer to develop than expected. Figure 8-1 shows the relative times between contract go-ahead and first flight for the first Navy swept-wing fighters including the F9F-6 and FJ-2.

## McDonnell F2H-3/4

In the fall of 1951, an evaluation of the single-place F2H-2N versus the two-place F3D was accomplished by VC-4, the East Coast night-fighter specialist squadron. Two NATC F2H-2Ns and two VMF(AW)-513 F3Ds were operated from NAS Atlantic City for the trials. VC-4 pilots with all-weather fighter experience flew the F2H-2Ns. Equally qualified crews flew the F3Ds. The results were mixed – the F3D detected threats at a greater distance with its bigger radar, but the F2H could generally complete the interception further away from the point being defended. The F3D was significantly handicapped from a performance standpoint by the burden of its bigger radar and two-man crew while being powered by the same engines as the smaller and less well-equipped, single-seat F2H. However, the results of the evaluation may well have justified single-seat all-weather fighters for far longer than appropriate. Ironically, BIS trials, concluded in mid-1952, found that the F2H-2N was not acceptable for service use as a night fighter, although the primary problem was its unreliable and limited-capability APS-19 radar.

The Navy contracted for a swept-wing F3D-3 but it was canceled in February 1952 with two prototypes under construction. Various reasons have been cited, but the likeliest is that in light of the Korean War, funds were not available for all the Navy

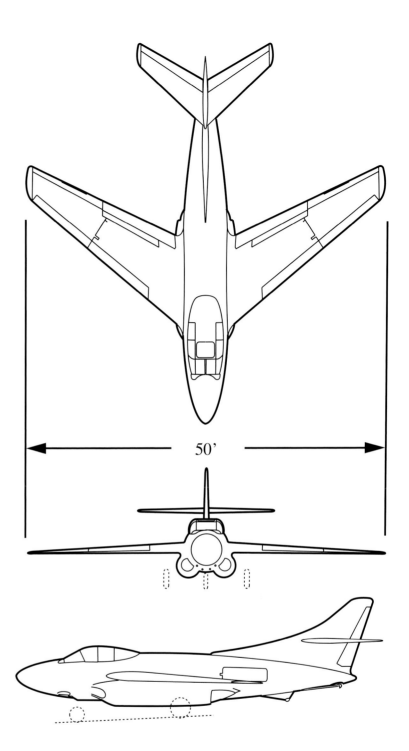

*Douglas F3D-3*
*Douglas would undoubtedly have been able to successfully develop the swept-wing F3D-3, but a big, two-seat aircraft was turning out to not be what the Navy wanted in an all-weather fighter. The program was canceled in early 1952 following late 1951 VC-4 trials that concluded that a small, single-seat night fighter was as good or better than a big two-seat one. The Navy had both the F3D-2 and the F2H-3 in work with the budget for fighter development under pressure because of the need to fund the Korean War. (Author)*

fighter programs under way. Its J-46 engine was also behind schedule.

| | F3D-2 | F3D-3 |
|---|---|---|
| Gross Weight (lbs)* | 25,414 | 26,735 |
| Engine | J34 | J46 |
| Total Thrust (lbs) | 6,800 | 8,400 |
| | | |
| Wing Span (ft) | 50 | 50 |
| Length (ft) | 45.4 | 51 |
| Top Speed (kts) | 452 | 529 |
| Stall Speed (kts) | 82 | 91 |
| *Internal Fuel | | |

The next interim all-weather fighter, yet another derivative of the F2H, was already in the works. McDonnell received a contract in July 1950 for an F2H modified to incorporate a 28-inch-diameter radar dish for improved detection range. In order to reduce workload during all-weather interceptions, the autopilot of the F2H-2N was retained. McDonnell once again stretched the fuselage, this time by more than six feet, to increase internal fuel capacity from 877 gallons to 1,108 gallons, even though the stub tanks outboard of the engines were deleted. The tip tanks were slightly smaller than the -2's, so total fuel with tip tanks only increased by 169 gallons, or 13 percent. The 20mm cannons were relocated to accommodate the bigger radar and additional rounds added. The horizontal tail was repositioned lower and farther aft, and dihedral was reintroduced.

Because of these changes, the gross weight increased to more than 20,000 lbs. The wing area was enlarged to compensate for the increased gross weight by extending the trailing edge aft beginning from just outboard of the wing fold to the fuselage. A beefed-up main gear was installed. A new nose gear was installed that provided a selectable 16.5-inch extension for acceptable catapult-launch performance at the higher gross weight. The engine remained the Westinghouse J34, but it was uprated.

An aerodynamic prototype that flew in 1951 was created from one of the F2H-2Ns, BuNo. 123311. It retained the F2H-2N nose. At one point, it was fitted with afterburners and even more wing area for an evaluation of the resulting reduction in time-to-climb. Two different versions of the bigger "Banjo" were produced, the F2H-3 with the Westinghouse APQ-41 radar and the F2H-4 with the Hughes APG-37. The aircraft were otherwise essentially the same. Initial carrier suitability tests of the F2H-3 were accomplished aboard *Midway* in August 1952, only five months after first flight. Deliveries to VC-3 and VC-4 followed, with the Navy accepting the last of 250 in October 1953. The first of 150 production F2H-4s flew in December 1952, with VC-4 taking deliveries in early 1953.

*One of the Banshee iterations that led to the F2H-3 was this modified F2H-2N. It had afterburning engines, an extended fuselage to provide more fuel for its afterburners, and a trailing edge extension inboard of the wing root fillet. Only the lengthened fuselage and a much smaller trailing edge change were carried over to the F2H-3. (McDonnell Aircraft via Fred Roos)*

*McDonnell test pilot Chester Braun made the first flight of the F2H-3. (McDonnell Aircraft via Chester Braun)*

The Westinghouse APQ-41 radar in the -3 was not as well regarded as the Hughes APG-37 in the -4. For one thing, the Hughes presentation provided a stabilized horizon line, whereas the Westinghouse scan banked with the aircraft in turns. The radar could also lock on to a selected target and provide a steering dot. The more user-friendly Hughes radar presentation provided three

*Follow-on carrier suitability testing of the F2H-3 was accomplished aboard Coral Sea along with the F7U-3 Cutlass and the XF3H-1 Demon in October 1953. (National Archives 630038)*

*The F2H-3/4 was also armed with the Sidewinder. Because of its speed disadvantage, this provided even more of an increase in its air-to-air lethality than it did for a faster swept-wing fighter. (Robert L. Lawson collection)*

ranges, the longest 200 miles and the shortest, about 10. Lt. Blair McDonald remembered, "I could pick up the fleet at 200 miles, pick out my carrier at 100, spot propeller aircraft over 50 miles away, and jets within 20."[4]

The Navy didn't bother completing the formal BIS evaluation until early 1954, after all the aircraft had been delivered and even some deployments accomplished. Although it did not have the performance of even the F2H-2, the bigger Banjo was stable on instruments and was one of the easiest jets to land aboard. That and twin engines made it less challenging to fly at night and in all

weather conditions. The only hiccup in its career was an aft fuselage aeroelastic problem that was discovered early on. The fix was a brace added between the front spar of the horizontal tail and the fuselage to stiffen the aft fuselage laterally. A triangular fillet covered it.

For the first time, the fleet was provided with a jet fighter capable of interceptions in all weather and visibility conditions that it was willing to deploy. All F2H-3s and -4s were also capable of ground attack, up to and including delivery of nuclear weapons. The so-called Big Banjos were first assigned to composite squadrons that provided all-weather fighter and nuclear bomb delivery detachments to carrier air groups being deployed. Both VC-3 and VC-4 sent out F2H-3 detachments on deployments in mid-1953, the former on *Kearsarge* to the Pacific and the latter on *Franklin D. Roosevelt* to the Mediterranean. However, the Navy was already starting to equip one of the two or three fighter squadrons in an air group with an all-weather fighter instead of sending out detachments for this mission. VF-193 was apparently the first to deploy with the F2H-3 in September 1953, aboard *Oriskany* to the western Pacific. VF-31 went out aboard *Midway* in January 1954, for the first extended Atlantic Fleet deployment of the F2H-3. The deployment of VC night-fighter detachments ended in 1956.

The F2H-3s and -4s had to provide all-weather capability for longer than expected, but they were eventually replaced by F4Ds and F3Hs. The last Banshee deployment was VAW-11's Detachment Papa, which provided both airborne radar and fighter cover for *Hornet* for its cruise as an ASW carrier from April to October 1959.

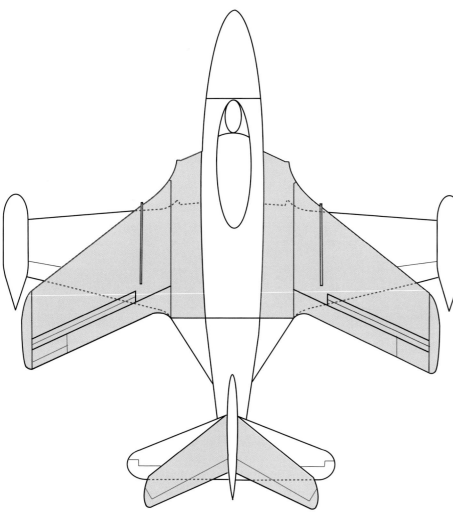

*F9F-5 vs. F9F-6*
*The Navy's first swept-wing fighter that entered the fleet was a quick conversion of the existing F9F-5 Panther. It was accomplished in months rather than the years it was taking for the Navy's swept-wing fighters being developed from scratch. (Author)*

## The Cougar

On occasion, Grumman demonstrated the ability to design, build, develop, and deliver a fighter in far less time than usual. The Cougar was an example. This was the second contract they had received to convert the Panther to a swept-wing configuration. In 1947, the goal was only to use the nose and center sections unchanged: "After laying out a number of arrangements it became evident that the airplane could not be suitably balanced without changing the fuel and powerplant arrangements of the XF9F-2. This immediately implied the necessity for releasing the

study from the restriction of using the XF9F-2 center section without change."[5] Even then, Grumman engineers were unable to come up with an acceptable configuration and the design gradually metastasized, due to the Navy's desire for a substantial increase in mission equipment and range, into the XF10F.

This time, Grumman not only used the nose and center sections of the Panther, they simply pulled three F9F-5 fuselages off the production line and minimally modified them to build the two flight-test aircraft and a static test article. Grumman test pilot Fred Rowley flew the first F9F-6 Cougar in September 1951, only six months after contract award. Although there doubtless was some design work accomplished before then, it was still a significant achievement and one in sharp contrast to the company's inability in 1947 to conceive of a simple conversion.

In profile, the F9F-6 very closely resembled the F9F-5. It used the same engine, landing gear, and other systems. The major difference was the 35-degree swept wing and horizontal tail and the extension of the wing root and inlet fairing forward to properly position the center of lift of a swept wing. Slats were substituted for the Panther's leading edge flaps, but the basic Panther trailing edge and fuselage flap design was adapted to the new wing. The fuselage-mounted flaps were modified to incorporate another pair of speed brakes to augment the existing ones. The two 120-gallon tip tanks could not be retained, but tanks were added in the wing to limit the reduction of internal fuel capacity to about 80 gallons. Only one stores pylon was provided on each wing.

Development was expeditious, with problems either fixed quickly or accepted in view of the urgent requirement. As a result, the first delivery to a fleet squadron occurred in November 1952, little more than a year after first flight, an extremely fast-paced program by any standard. With the aid of others in the industry and close observation of other swept-wing designs, Grumman worked very quickly through all the unique aspects of swept-wing-induced handling quality problems. For starters, both the roll and pitch controls failed to meet requirements.

The original roll control was provided by a combination of unboosted ailerons and hydraulic-powered spoilers called flaperons. If hydraulic pressure was lost, the ailerons were expected to provide adequate roll control for landing. Unfortunately, the mechanical linkage was not stiff enough to keep the ailerons from introducing erratic inputs in high-speed flight. They were therefore deleted and the flaperons extended inboard and outboard to make up for the loss of roll-control power. The flaperons were also divided in half along their length with the aft half on a separate hydraulic system to provide roll control in the event the primary hydraulic system failed. A small aileron-like control surface on the left wing provided roll trim control.

*Although quick, the Cougar's development required modification to the original roll-control concept among other things. The aircraft was designed and first flew with ailerons and wing spoilers as shown here. To correct roll-control problems and retain control in the event of a hydraulic failure, the original F9F-6 ailerons were eliminated except for a small "feeler" aileron on the left wing, and the spoilers were extended and split into two parts, the aft half of which was powered by a backup hydraulic system. (Hal Andrews collection)*

The use of flaperons avoided the loss of roll control at high angles of attack from the span-wise flow characteristic of swept wings but not the pitch-up problem. This was cured by the addition of a large wing fence, the same solution used on other early swept-wing jets. The high-altitude buffet boundary was improved by the simple expedient of a higher and longer wing fence and recontouring the upper aft portion of the large wing-to-fuselage fillet – the fillet height was increased about four inches to delay flow separation to a higher angle of attack. The leading edge of the wing just outboard of the engine air intakes was rounded as part of the stall improvement.

Pitch control using a conventional elevator and a trimmable horizontal stabilizer proved to be inadequate for high-speed flight. For that fix, Grumman test pilot Corky Meyer went to Edwards AFB in April 1952 to fly North American's new F-86E that had a "flying-tail" positioned by a redundant hydraulic system, in which the horizontal stabilizer moved in conjunction with the elevators. It was clearly superior in control power and handling qualities in transonic and supersonic flight to a conventional tail. Grumman adapted it to the Cougar, only with a single hydraulic system that reverted to an electrically trimmed stabilizer and unpowered elevator for low-speed flight and if hydraulic power were lost. Early production aircraft that had been delivered with

*After initiating four swept-wing programs in the late '40s and having nothing on the carriers to show for it, the Navy finally deployed one that was a relatively straightforward conversion of one of its existing straight-wing fighters. (U.S. Navy via Jay Miller collection)*

Panther, the otherwise identical F9F-7 was produced with the Allison J33-A-16A, which only had 6,350 lbs of thrust. As it turned out, the last 50 of the 168 F9F-7s originally ordered were delivered with the J48. The F9F-7 wound up being deployed once and foisted off on the reserves. Any unit that received them substituted the J48 for the J33 if possible.

VF-32 at Cecil Field, NAS Jacksonville, Florida, was the first unit to receive an F9F-6, and they deployed with it aboard *Tarawa* a year later in November 1953. VF-24 on the West Coast was the first to deploy with the new Cougar in August 1953, aboard *Yorktown*, to the western Pacific, just missing the Korean War.

The Navy always considered the F9F-6 to be an interim aircraft. For one thing, it wasn't able to turn with the MiG-15 at 40,000 feet due to buffet. In late 1952, the production order was cut back by 18 percent in anticipation of the availability of higher-performance fighters beginning in 1954. The last of 814 F9F-6/7s was delivered in July 1954. The last deployment of the F9F-6 was with VF-142 on *Boxer,* which ended in February 1956. The F9F-6 went on to serve in Navy and Marine Corps reserve squadrons.

In early 1954, the F9F-6, equipped with the new in-flight refueling probe and refueling once from an AJ Savage over Hutchinson, Kansas, was used to establish an unofficial speed record for a transcontinental flight from San Diego, California, to New York City. The fastest time of the three pilots from VF-21, based at NAS Norfolk, flying a "routine training flight" over the 2,430-mile route was three hours, 45 minutes, and 30 seconds. The existing record of four hours and four minutes had been set in January with an F-86F flying nonstop and unrefueled.[6] Except for the refueling, which had to be conducted at 25,000 feet, the F9Fs cruised at 40,000 to 45,000 feet to take advantage of the eastbound jet stream.

The F9F-8 was the ultimate Cougar, first flying in January 1954, and powered by the J48-P-8 like the F9F-6. The wing was redesigned with a fixed, extended, and cambered leading edge in place of the wing slats and an extension of the trailing edge for more wing area and a higher critical Mach number. The leading

the original elevator control system were modified to the flying tail.

Notwithstanding the teething problems and shortcomings, Grumman's new swept-wing feline was an amazing step forward in such a short period of development. Some pilots believed it to have better handling qualities at approach speeds than the straight-wing F9F-5. The critical Mach number was increased from 0.79 at sea level to 0.86 and to nearly 0.90 at 35,000 feet. What's more, the F9F-6 was capable of breaking the sound barrier, a first for an operational carrier-based fighter. It was something of an unnatural act, since it started with a full-power vertical dive begun at 45,000 feet. The sound barrier was broken at 32,000 feet and, even with no reduction of throttle or dive angle, unbroken at 25,000 feet. What the maneuver demonstrated to Navy pilots accustomed to transonic Mach number limits imposed by the handling qualities and/or buffet unpleasantness of their straight-wing jets was that the Cougar had no such restrictions.

After the first 30 Cougars had been delivered with the 7,000-lb thrust J48-P-6A with water injection, the remaining Cougars were powered by the 7,250-lb J48-P-8 without water injection. In keeping with the alternate engine practice instituted with the

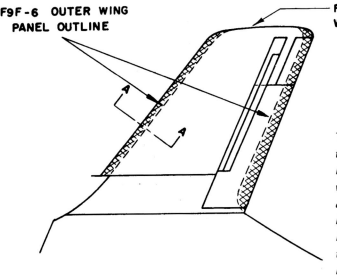

F9F-6 OUTER WING
PANEL OUTLINE

F9F-8 OUTER
WING PANEL

A

A

5% LEADING EDGE EXTENSION
( NO SLAT )

WING CHORD (REF)

SECTION A-A

*The F9F-8 wing was the fix for the few F9F-6 shortcomings with high angle-of-attack and transonic handling qualities. It also eliminated the leading edge slat mechanism and provided wing volume for more fuel capacity. (Author)*

edge extension stopped at the wing fence, creating a snag, but this was probably just a convenient place to end the change, not an aerodynamic consideration. Four more wing-store stations were added. Internal fuel capacity was increased by 144 gallons, to a total of 1,063 gallons, by the incorporation of tanks in the wing leading edge and the lengthening of the forward fuselage by eight inches. The large inlet/wing root fairing was extended all the way aft to the tailpipe opening to decrease its thinness ratio.

The F9F-8B was qualified to carry a nuclear store in addition to more conventional weapons. It also became the first Navy fighter to carry Sidewinder missiles operationally

The F9F-8 outer wing panel was evaluated on an F9F-6 in a short flight-test program at NATC in early 1955. The report recommended that this modification be retrofitted to F9F-6s to improve their pitch-up characteristics in normal and accelerated stalls, transonic behavior (better acceleration), and buffet boundary (better maneuverability) without any deterioration of stability and control or performance.[7] It does not appear that this recommendation was ever acted on, but it is yet another example of the benefits to be realized from continuous improvement of a design.

VX-3, the unit responsible for developing weapons-delivery techniques and operational evaluation of tactical aircraft equipment, carrier qualified in the F9F-8 aboard *Midway* in late 1954, with 10 aircraft. At about the same time, VF-13 at NAAS Cecil Field, Florida, was the first operational squadron to receive the

*VA-46 was the first to deploy with the Sidewinder with ATG-202 aboard Randolph in July 1956 even though it was an attack squadron. Ironically, the F2H-4 in the foreground, assigned to VF-102, is fitted with the pylon for the Mk 7 nuclear weapon. (U.S. Navy via Robert L. Lawson collection)*

The other swept-wing fighter initiated in desperation in 1951 was the FJ-2 Fury. Contrary to the designation implication, it was really a derivative of the Air Force's F-86 Sabre, not the Navy's FJ-1 Fury it is in formation with here. (U.S. Navy via Hal Andrews collection)

The most significant change from the Sabre was the landing gear. The black and white striped bar is a fairly rare feature, a retractable device to insure engagement of the Davis barrier cable. The North American test pilot is Bob Hoover. (U.S. Navy photo via Hal Andrews collection)

NATC accomplished XFJ-2 carrier-suitability testing aboard Midway in April 1954. U.S. Navy)

F9F-8. However, VF-121 was the first to deploy, in August 1955, aboard *Hancock* to the west Pacific.

## Sea-going Sabre

In 1945, the Air Force decided to develop a swept-wing version of the North American jet that became the Navy's FJ-1 Fury. It proved to be an excellent and timely decision, resulting in the F-86 Sabre. Some Navy pilots who had flown or flown against it had recommended buying a navalized version early on. However, most in OpNav and BuAer were convinced that they had fighters in development that would be superior to the Sabre. After the Korean War began, dispatches from there made it obvious that BuAer needed to expedite a swept-wing fighter. The Sabre was an obvious choice. To make it compatible with carrier operations,

*An XFJ-2 is prepared for launch during carrier-suitability testing. Self-boarding access from both sides of the fuselage was rare. Usually it was only provided from the left side. (National Archives)*

North American redesigned the landing gear for a maximum sink rate of 24 feet per second, or more than 16 mph. They also added a tail hook and supporting structure along with wing-folding capabilities, and better visibility over the nose. In addition, the armament was changed from the Air Force's six .50 caliber machine guns to the Navy's standard armament of four 20mm cannons. The F-86's J47 was retained. The first of three prototypes was produced with only the armament change, and it flew in December 1951. The first with the required carrier takeoff and landing modifications flew in February 1952, and went to sea for suitability tests aboard *Coral Sea* in December of that year.

North American had proposed a Wright J65 variant of the Fury as early as July 1951, and the Navy was seriously considering it in December. It had already become clear that the J47's 6,000 lbs of thrust was not enough. Adding the carrier-basing hardware had resulted in a roughly 1,000-lb higher empty weight. In addition to more thrust, the Fury needed another round of structure beef-up and handling quality improvements at approach speeds. As a result, in late 1952 the Navy cut back the FJ-2 production order by a third, having ordered a Wright J65-powered variant as the FJ-3 earlier in

*Of the first two deployable swept-wing fighters, only the F9F-6 went to sea. The FJ-2 was relegated to land-based U.S. Marine Corps squadrons. The FJ-2 was deployed only once, apparently as a fill-in by a USMC squadron for a fighter squadron requirement. Here the two rivals are side by side on the Hancock's deck-edge elevator as part of the evaluation of its steam catapult. (National Archives 80-G-640361)*

*The FJ-3 had the additional thrust that the Fury needed to be acceptable for carrier-basing. It went out for carrier-suitability testing aboard Coral Sea in February 1955. (U.S. Navy via Hal Andrews collection)*

In 1952, the Air Force began to modify its F-86s with a wing modification that deleted the slats and extended the leading edge six inches at the root and three inches at the tip. This change added 1.5 $g$s to maneuverability at 35,000 feet but increased the stall speed in the landing configuration by 12 percent. The FJ-2 retained the original F-86 wing that had leading edge slats because low approach speed was critical. The first FJ-3s had the same slatted wing as the FJ-2. Production then transitioned to a new leading edge similar to the F9F-6/7 to F9F-8 modification – the leading edge slats were deleted in favor of a "hard" wing with a cambered leading edge. This increased the buffet boundary at high altitude but minimized the stall speed increase.

This leading edge change also partially addressed another of the FJ-2's shortcomings, internal fuel capacity, by allowing the addition of 124 gallons of fuel in the wing leading edge. However, 200-gallon drop tanks, which almost doubled the fuel available, were still required operationally. These eliminated some of the speed advantage over a straight-wing fighter but could be dropped for maximum performance if necessary. The new, fixed leading edge also incorporated anti-icing using compressor bleed air.

the year. As so frequently happened with aircraft that had been ordered by the Navy but turned out to be disappointing, the FJ-2s were handed to the Marines Corps, who were happy to get them. However, the FJ-2 was carrier qualified. FJ-2s from VMF-235 participated in Project Steam trials aboard *Hancock* in July 1954, and VMF-122 deployed with Air Group 17 aboard *Coral Sea* to the Mediterranean in 1955.

One of the FJ-2s was modified in 1953 to replace the J47 with a Wright J65 rated at 7,800 lbs of thrust. It flew for the first time in July 1953. The first production FJ-3 powered by the Wright J65-W-4 flew in December 1953. North American was a bit slow in ramping up FJ-3 production, possibly because it was one of the first aircraft to be procured under FIRM, but by July 1954, 24 had been delivered and the FIP was ready to begin at NATC. Using pilots from VC-3 and VF-173, as well as some of their maintenance personnel, the requisite hours were flown between 7 August and 17 September. Although one Fury crashed due to an engine failure from an undetermined cause and another was ditched after the pilot got lost and ran out of fuel, the FJ-3 was considered to have passed. Carrier qualification was accomplished aboard *Coral Sea* in February 1955.

The FJ-3's entry into service was marred and somewhat delayed by engine problems that had not been apparent in development, qualification, or the Fleet Introduction Program. The first East Coast squadron to receive the FJ-3 was VF-173 at Jacksonville, replacing its F9F-6s beginning in late 1954, albeit temporarily. Cdr. J. F. "Tut" Tuttle, remembers it this way:

I was ordered to VF-173 as XO in early 1955, and served in that billet until early 1957. We were one of the first squadrons to receive the FJ-3 Fury and considered it an outstanding aircraft. However, there were problems with the J65 engine. Squadrons on both coasts were experiencing an excessive number of flameouts and seizures. Pilots were squirting out in alarming numbers. Air Pac decided that the FJ-3 was not operationally ready for shipboard deployment so we transitioned to the F9F-8 Cougar about four months prior to embarking in *Wasp* for a very successful eight months WestPac Cruise.[8]

Because of the J65 engine problems, the FJ-3 was grounded off and on through most of 1955. Just when a particular problem seemed to have been solved, there would be another cluster of

*The first FJ-3s retained the wing slats of the FJ-2. This was changed to a hard leading edge that had been developed for the F-86. The hard wing leading edge change roughly corresponded to the change from blue to a gray/white paint scheme. Note that at the time this photo was taken, the Navy's front-line fighter was a derivative of North American's F-86 while the Air Force's was the supersonic North American F-100 in the background. (U.S. Navy via Robert L. Lawson collection)*

engine failures and the aircraft would be grounded again. However, all seemed to have been resolved by early 1956, and the FJ-3 was deployed as a day fighter through 1959.

## Comparing the First Swept-Wing Day Fighters

In December 1951, the BuAer Aircraft Division director sent a memorandum to the chief of BuAer that reviewed all the day fighters with production contracts. He recommended that production of both the F9F-6 and the F7U-3 be ended in mid-1953 in favor of the FJ-3. His analysis was based on assumptions and projected performance, since the F9F-6 had only just flown a few months before, the F7U-3 was about to fly for the first time, and the XFJ-2 with carrier-basing modifications wasn't to fly until February. He dismissed the F9F-6 since, "It inherits some deficiencies…from its ancestors, chiefly a tendency to Dutch roll, poor longitudinal stability and control at both low and high speeds, and inadequate ground clearance under the tail cone." He considered the F7U-3 too big, too complex, and too expensive without any redeeming performance benefit except for rate of climb – it was only slightly faster in level flight and deficient in combat radius compared to the other two. The FJ-3, on the other hand, "has the benefit of the operating experience of the FJ-1 and the hundreds of F-86s which have preceded it."[9] The recommendation was not accepted – BuAer continued with the development and procurement of all three fighters. As it turned out, continuing all three was a wise choice.

Figure 8-2 shows when the deployments of the first swept-wing fighters began, including the F4D and F3H all-weather fight-

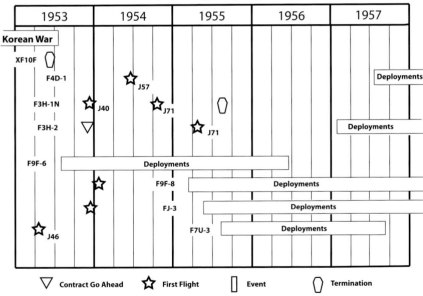

*Figure 8-2 Swept-Wing Deployment (Author)*

ers as well as the placeholders that preceded them to the fleet. The first swept-wing fighters to deploy represented a throwback to traditional air-superiority fighters and a postponement of the implementation of the general-purpose fighter concept. These were strictly day fighters, with no visual-assist radar. While they could be flown in all weather conditions, any combat had to be

*The day fighter's effectiveness was significantly improved by the addition of the Sidewinder missile. Commander F. Ashworth poses here beside the missile at China Lake. (U.S. Navy via Gary Verver)*

accomplished on a strictly visual basis. The only missile armament was the Sidewinder.

Too late for the Korean War, the hastily conceived Cougar and Fury successfully filled the overlooked role of day fighter until the Navy developed better ones. (A swept-wing McDonnell F2H might have been equally capable as well as available for the Korean War.) As predicted, the F7U-3 was too big and short-legged to be a day fighter and was only deployed once or twice in that capacity.

|  | F9F-8 | FJ-3 | F7U-3 |
|---|---|---|---|
| Gross Weight (lbs) | 20,098 | 19,360* | 26,840 |
| Speed SL (kts)** | 561 | 599 | 606 |
| Speed 35K (kts/MN)** | 515/0.89 | 530/0.92 | 540/0.94 |
| Rate of Climb SL (ft/min)** | 5,570 | 9,400 | 14,240 |
| Rate of Climb 35K (ft/min)** | 2,200 | 3,030 | 4,980 |
| Combat Range (nm) | 1,050 | 995* | 800 |
| Mission Time (hrs) | 2.06 | 1.70* | 1.31 |
| Approach Stall (kts) | 93.8 | 94.4 | 93.2 |
| Spot (200 ft) | 25 | 28 | 18 |

Internal fuel only except as noted by * which includes two 200-gallon drop tanks and ** which is at combat weight.

The F9F-6 did not have any swept-wing competition for the first two years of its operational use. The improved models of the Cougar and the Fury, the F9F-8 and the FJ-3, as well as the F7U were first deployed in 1955. The FJ-3 was to deploy a little more often and longer than the F9F-8 (in fighter squadrons) even though it was held back from some planned deployments early on due to J65 engine problems.

Of the day fighters, Corky Meyer of Grumman is insistent that the Fury was inferior in every respect to the Cougar:

(The) Combat Air Patrol mission was for two hours on station at 150nm from the carrier. This required 2+30 takeoff, cruise, and landing endurance plus reserves. The F9F-6 could perform a three-hour CAP mission on internal fuel. The FJ-2 and -3 with external tanks had less than 1+30 mission time and the FJ-4 just met the mission requirement. The FJ-2 only had 2,200 pounds of fuel, less than half the Cougars'. External tanks were required to equal the Cougar's internal fuel capacity. With tanks, FJ-2 was not much faster than F9F-5. The FJ-3 had 600 more pounds of fuel than the FJ-2, but total fuel with two 200-gallon external tanks was still only slightly more than Cougar internal fuel. Its limit dive speed was only Mach 1, with or without tanks, and it had a six-*g* maneuvering limit. The Cougar could dive to 1.2 mach and had 7.5-*g* limit.[10]

The reason that the FJ-3 was deployed longer and a little more often (19 times vs. 16) in fighter squadrons than the F9F-8 probably wasn't because it was the better fighter. More likely it was because it had minimal capability as an attack aircraft, whereas the F9F-8 was good for that too, including nuclear-weapon delivery. In effect, the F9F-8 was a jet attack placeholder along with the F7U-3M while the pipeline was being filled with FJ-4Bs and A4Ds. As a result, the FJ-3 was the designated day fighter by default on most deployments.

Ironically, both Grumman and North American not only fell short in providing a follow-on to the F9F-8 and the FJ-3, but their proposals in the 1953 supersonic day-fighter competition were also judged inferior to Vought's.

*After the Navy's first two swept-wing jets had gone through further development and teething problems with the Fury's J65 engine were resolved, the Navy began to deploy more Furies than Cougars in air groups. In this instance, Air Group 12 went out on Lexington in April 1957 without either its FJ-3s in the foreground or VA-126's F7U-3s in the background. (Robert L. Lawson collection)*

## CHAPTER NINE

*By the mockup review, the initial configuration concept had been refined to closely resemble that of the first flight aircraft. The white markings on the tail are for the LSO's benefit in judging the approach angle of attack. (Tommy H. Thomason collection)*

# F4D Skyray:
# Optimized Interceptor

Since jets had limited endurance, the wartime practice of a combat air patrol with fighters loitering on station did not seem practical. One alternative was the use of deck-launched interceptors. These would be catapulted following radar warning of incoming raids and rapidly climb to altitude to intercept them. All-weather capability was a necessity with at least enough on-board radar capability to detect and close on a hostile aircraft after being coached into position.

The emerging threat after World War II was an incoming jet bomber at 50,000 feet and Mach 0.9 (520 knots), detected only 100 miles – about 12 minutes – away from the carrier. The best defense was projected to be a very fast-climbing, radar-equipped, all-weather fighter with a new type of fire-control system and rocket armament. The fighter would not be launched until the raid was detected and would then climb to 40,000 feet in five minutes or less. The unprecedented climb performance was to be achieved two ways – first, with more than 10,000 lbs of thrust from the new Westinghouse J40 engine with afterburner, and second, a reduction in required endurance/range that minimized the weight of the fuel system and the fuel on board. Total mission time, including 20 minutes of loiter following return to the vicinity of the carrier, was to be only 75 minutes.[1]

The aircraft's search radar would be used to locate an incoming bomber after initial vectors. The fire-control system would then direct the pilot on a collision course until it determined that the moment had come to fire a salvo of unguided 2.75-inch folding fin rockets. The pilot would then be free to break away. The collision course and rockets were necessary because there was not enough time to position the fighter for a classic attack with guns.

It was all theoretical, since none of the key elements of the proposed scenario existed. The Navy intended to develop the APS-25 Airborne Intercept Radar, the Aero IA Fire Control System, the Westinghouse J40 engine, and the folding fin rocket armament in parallel with its new interceptor.

## Douglas D-571-1

The F4D began as a Navy-funded Douglas design study for a very fast-climbing interceptor. The initial result was the Douglas D-571-1, which had a delta-wing planform for low wing loading and was to be powered by two Westinghouse 24C (J34) turbo-jet engines with 4,750 lbs of thrust each in afterburner for outstanding climb performance. The wing was very thick, with no separate fuselage other than a pod containing the cockpit and four 20mm cannons that extended forward of the wing. The engine inlets were located in the leading edge of the wing on each side of the fuselage pod. The vertical fin, rudder, and tail bumper resembled the future F4D's. There were retractable skids on the wing tips, similar to those that would be briefly seen on the first XF3H. Spin-stabilized rockets were being considered as an alternate armament, and a jettisonable nose section was planned for emergency egress.

The configuration was based on research and designs done by the German aerodynamicist Dr. Alexander Lippisch, an advocate of the delta-wing concept. Douglas engineers Gene Root and A.M.O. Smith were among those who had the opportunity to review German technical reports after V-E Day. The delta-wing benefits resonated with Douglas' Ed Heinemann since he and Jack Northrop had worked on flying wing designs in the late 1930s before Northrop and Douglas parted ways.

The D-571's gross weight was projected to be 16,140 lbs including 582 gallons of fuel and 800 rounds of 20mm ammunition. With a wing area of 701 square feet, the wing loading was only 23 lbs per square foot. The initial rate of climb was estimated to be 21,630 feet per minute. The time to climb to 40,000 feet was estimated to be three minutes from a standing start. The critical Mach number was originally thought to be 0.95 or better because the wing, although thick, was considered thin relative to its chord.

In June 1947, the Navy contracted with Douglas for "preliminary investigation and engineering development up to and including the mockup." It was expected that the configuration would "be very flexible until mock-up which is tentatively scheduled for June 1948." This proved to be prophetic as among other things, the wing thickness, planform, and the engine choice were to change.

Heinemann determined from wind-tunnel tests that the Lippisch wing was far too thick for near sonic flight. The wing was therefore dramatically thinned. It was also reduced in area

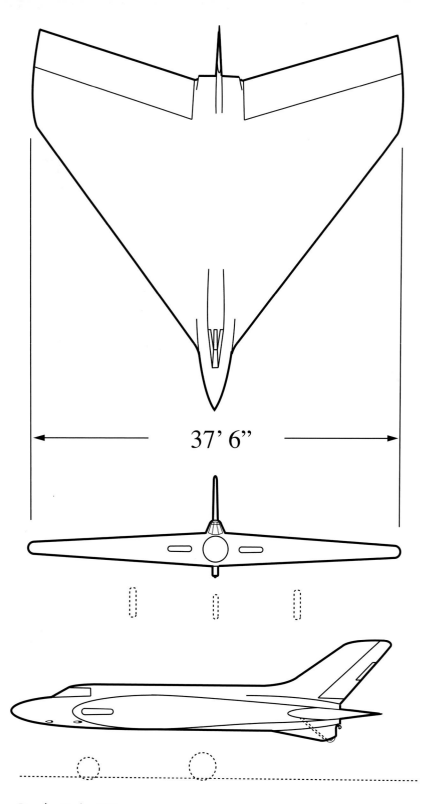

37' 6"

*Douglas Design 571*
*The F4D was the result of a Douglas design study based on German technical reports, but Ed Heinemann was already knowledgeable about the delta wing concept. At this point, the aircraft was to be powered by two afterburning engines. (Author)*

to 557 square feet, still providing a low wing loading for climb and low speed on approach. The trailing edge was now slightly swept instead of perpendicular to the centerline. Since it was a tailless configuration like the F7U, there were no flaps, but there were leading edge slats, in this case aerodynamically actuated rather than being powered.

Pitch and roll control were both provided by the same surfaces, called elevons by Douglas (a different combination of the words elevator and aileron than Vought's) on the trailing edge of the wing. The elevons were hydraulically powered with an artificial feel system. Inboard of those, on the after part of the fuselage, were very thick control surfaces that have been mistaken for elevators but were really giant longitudinal trim surfaces, electrically driven. The rudder was conventional and not boosted. Since only one hydraulic system was provided, in the event of loss of hydraulic pressure the elevons had to be literally manhandled, for which the stick grip could be extended to provide the pilot with an increased mechanical advantage over the control loads.

Another change was the substitution of one J40 engine for the two J34s. Total thrust with afterburning went from 9,500 lbs to 10,900 lbs, and the gross weight increased to 17,000 lbs. The primary armament became the folding fin rockets, housed in pods mounted on pylons under the wing. The 20mm cannons were relegated to provisions located in the wings.

## Interceptor Competition

In 1948, OpNav formally created an Operational Requirement for an interceptor, and BuAer initiated a development program. All of the Navy's fighter suppliers bid on the competition. Douglas appears to have been considered the winner even before the proposals were reviewed. The others were just vying to be the backup. McDonnell proposed a brand new design, very different from its existing straight-wing, twin-engine jets. Vought and Grumman bid variations on their existing fighter projects, the F7U-1 and F10F, respectively. Vought was apparently dropped from consideration early because the F7U, like the D-571, was "tailless" and the Navy preferred a more conventional configuration to be the backup to the Douglas design. After the wheat had been separated from the chaff, only Grumman and McDonnell were left to be compared.

### Grumman Design 86

Grumman proposed its Design 86, which was similar in configuration to the J40-powered XF10F as it looked in 1948.

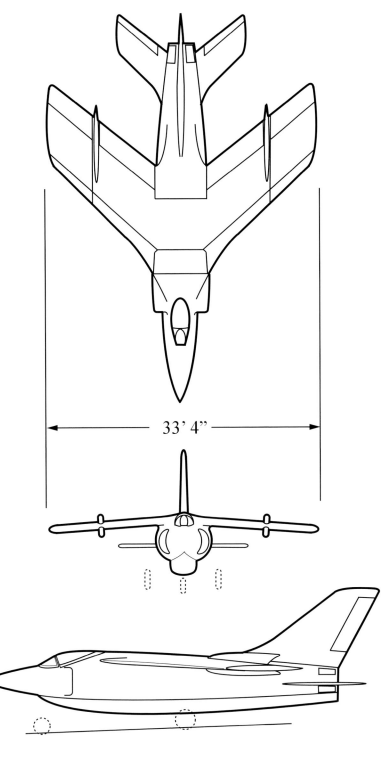

*Grumman Design 86*
*Grumman tailored its XF10F design to the Navy's 1948 interceptor competition by adding a rocket engine for climb performance and rocket dispensers over and under the wings. Choosing between it and the McDonnell's proposal was not easy. (Author)*

33' 4"

The main difference was the addition of a long ventral fairing that contained a 5,000-lb thrust rocket motor and tanks of liquid oxygen and water-alcohol. The other unique feature was the 2.75-inch, folding-fin rocket stowage. In lieu of pods or a retractable launcher, the Grumman proposal housed 24 rockets in batplane-like fairings located above and below each wing at mid-span.

The wing had 42.5 degrees of sweep at the quarter chord. For increased lift on takeoff and landing, it was equipped with large trailing edge and leading edge flaps. For good visibility on approach and lower body angle on takeoff and landing, the wing incidence was increased eight degrees, pivoting at the rear spar.

The rocket was the key differentiator. Estimated time to climb to 50,000 feet was two minutes and three seconds. Vmax at 50,000 feet with the rocket firing was projected to be Mach 1.5, although in hindsight this was unlikely from both critical Mach number and area rule standpoints. The endurance exceeded the requirement by 18 percent.

### McDonnell Model 58

The McDonnell Model 58 certainly looked fast. It was sleek, with a sharply pointed nose and a wing swept at 45 degrees when most designers were hesitant to go beyond 35 degrees. The engine intakes were almost as deep as the fuselage but very narrow in width, a novel configuration little used before or since, probably because of the boundary layer problems that accompanied it.[2] Auxiliary inlets were provided in the side of the fuselage aft of the intakes to provide additional air to the engine at low speeds – they opened when the landing gear was extended and closed when the gear was retracted or there was no hydraulic power. For high lift at slow speeds, the wings had leading edge slats and trailing edge slotted flaps. There were fuselage-mounted speed brakes located just aft of the wing. The flight controls were powered, but the horizontal tail was initially conventional, with an elevator and adjustable horizontal stabilizer.

The XF3H-1 was to have the same engine, the Westinghouse J40-WE-8, and avionics as the XF4D and meet the same interceptor mission requirement. However, there was no provision for guns – it would be armed only with unguided rockets carried internally until the moment they were deployed and fired. The mission gross weight with full internal fuel was projected to be 22,595 lbs, somewhat more than the XF4D.

### And The Winners Are. . .

Source selection documentation from the 1948 interceptor competition only addressed the Grumman and McDonnell proposal, since Douglas already had a contract for its D-571.

| | Douglas | Grumman | McDonnell |
|---|---|---|---|
| Mission Weight | 16,821 | 22,311 | 18,200 |
| Time to 50,000 ft (min) | 4.0 | 2.0 | 5.5 |
| Vmax (kts) | | | |
| Sea Level | 651 | 646 | 620* |
| Altitude (ft) | 574 (40K) | 865 (50K) | 550* (35K) |

\* Flight test

BuAer rated Grumman's design highly because of its rocket-assisted climb performance. However, the lighter McDonnell design was capable of being catapulted with a tailwind and the heavier Grumman wasn't, so the Grumman's time to climb was penalized for its launch having to wait for the carrier to turn into the wind at times. That, the consequences of mishandling the rocket fuel, and the need for Grumman to focus on its existing XF10F contract weighed against Grumman. As a result, the McDonnell design was picked. In the Navy's written evaluation, which did not include the Douglas D-571, the Model 58 was characterized as the smallest possible fighter with the required

equipment built with the largest possible engine – a jet-powered version of the F8F Bearcat.[3]

BuAer awarded McDonnell a contract for development of the XF3H in January 1949, as the second interceptor. Having two designs in development significantly reduced the risk of not meeting the fleet requirement if the best proposal did not meet expectations, particularly since it was an unproven "tailless" design. It also kept Douglas from becoming complacent and lax, since production was not a given. In this case, both fighters eventually reached the fleet as all-weather fighters at about the same time, neither with the J40 engine, but the Demon's road was arguably rockier and filled with more twists and turns.

## F4D Program

Because of all the configuration changes, the Douglas mockup review slipped almost a year to March 1949. One major revelation during the review was that while the design met the downward visibility requirement over the nose of 18 degrees below the horizon, the predicted nose-up attitude of the Skyray on approach was higher than anticipated by the specification. The windscreen and radome were therefore changed to provide

*Douglas test pilot Bob Rahn on the right congratulates Navy test pilot Lt. Cdr. James Verdin after his successful world-speed-record flight on 3 October 1953. Rahn was to set the 3-km closed course record later that month. Verdin was also to accomplish the initial carrier-suitability testing with the XF4D. He became a Douglas test pilot and was killed in an A4D crash. (National Archives 80-G-628712)*

Several innovative features that were on the mockup did not survive to the prototype, much less to production. One of the more interesting ones was this integration of the tail bumper and the arresting hook. (Tommy H. Thomason collection)

Legend has it that Douglas recognized just prior to the mockup review that the specification angle for downward forward vision didn't take into account the approach body angle of a delta wing. This resulted in a last-minute modification of the mockup to droop the nose. (THT collection)

21 degrees down visibility and re-reviewed in April. It was also recognized at the mockup review that the J40 would likely not be available for some months after the planned first flight, and an interim engine was incorporated into program planning. Douglas subsequently received a follow-on contract in December 1949 for wind-tunnel models, a static test article, and two flight articles.

As expected, the airframe was projected to be ready for flight before its J40 was, so a non-afterburning Allison J35 with 5,000 lbs of thrust was substituted for the first flight that took place in January 1951. Douglas test pilot Larry Peyton kept it brief and reportedly refused to ever fly the Skyray again. He had agreed to make the first flight on the manual flight-control system. This was probably a bad idea even before he discovered, after takeoff, that Engineering's estimate of the longitudinal trim surface position for climb was incorrect – he had to hold full forward stick without any hydraulic assistance until he could establish the correct trim position. Russ Thaw made the second flight.

The J40 was finally installed, without afterburner, but still with 2,000 lbs more thrust than the J35, for flights beginning in February 1952, more than a year after first flight. In mid-1952, a Navy Preliminary Evaluation was accomplished with the BuAer test pilots being Maj. Marion Carl, Cdr. Bob Elder, and Lt. Cdr. Bob Clark. They were very impressed by the maneuverability at altitude, with the XF4D capable of 3+ g turns in level flight at 40,000 feet – conventional swept-wing jets at the time were considered good if they could achieve a 2 g turn without encountering buffet, much less maintain altitude. Bob Rahn, who had taken over flying responsibilities from Thaw, finally exceeded Mach 1 in dive the following month. A second NPE was held in November 1952, which cleared the aircraft for carrier suitability tests that began in July 1953, and culminated at sea aboard *Coral Sea* in October.

In September 1953, an afterburning J40-WE-8 had finally been installed in the XF4D. The first priority with the additional thrust available appears to have been setting an official absolute speed record. According to Federation Aeronautique Internationale (FAI) rules at the time[4], this entailed making four separate passes, two in each direction, over a three-kilometer distance, with the aircraft not to exceed 100 meters (328 feet) in altitude above the ground on the course or 500 meters (1,640 feet) in the turns. Douglas' Bob Rahn developed the technique for accomplishing the record flight using only internal fuel. The record was actually set by Lt. Cdr. James B. Verdin, who was to fly the carrier suitability tests aboard *Coral Sea*. The amount of fuel was a major concern because of the time spent in afterburner accelerating up to

The Navy revisited the mockup in April 1949 to review the visibility in the approach attitude with a modified forward fuselage. Note how the white stripes on the vertical fin line up with the leading edge. (Tommy H. Thomason collection)

As initially reviewed, the mockup's instrument panel contributed to the forward visibility problem. The revised instrument panel, shown here, flattened the upper edge at the expense of moving the radarscope, an essential instrument for the F4D's mission, even lower than it was originally and more behind the control stick. (Tommy H. Thomason collection)

maximum speed for each run and making the turns before each pass – it took less than 10 seconds to fly the three kilometers. To maximize the amount that could be pumped into the Skyray's tanks, the fuel was cooled with dry ice to a temperature of about 35° F to decrease its volume.

Ironically, a high ambient temperature was as desirable as cold fuel was necessary because the speed of sound increases with air temperature. The higher the speed of sound, the higher the critical Mach number was in terms of miles per hour and therefore the faster the Skyray could fly. The course was therefore laid out at the hottest nearby location, the Salton Sea, a dry lakebed in Southern California. It had the added benefit of slightly increasing engine thrust because it was 2,600 feet lower than Edwards Air Force Base, slightly lower than sea level.

After the first attempt did not produce a high enough speed to supersede the newly established record of 737 mph set by a Supermarine Swift in the Libyan Desert, the Skyray was cleaned up and taken out again by Verdin on 3 October. This time he averaged 753.4 mph, more than exceeding the required margin over the Swift's speed and therefore setting a new absolute speed record – the first time that it was held by a carrier-based aircraft. Later that month, Bob Rahn was rewarded for his efforts to develop the procedures for the three-kilometer record by being designated to set the 100-kilometer, Closed-Course record in the Skyray. This was an established circular course around Edwards Air Force Base marked by 12 poles. The circuit had to be flown at a very low altitude above the ground, so tires

Because of its low wing loading, the F4D didn't need the large slats or the high angle of attack that the F7U Cutlass did. Its main shortcomings on approach were its unusual handling qualities, different from almost all the other jets. Note also the spats in front of the main landing gear wheels, which were there to guide an activated Davis barrier cable up onto the main gear struts. (Hal Andrews collection)

The Skyray motion during launch was also unusual. Because of the relationship of the catapult hooks and shuttle, the initial stroke of the catapult pulled the nose down and then the nose strut rebounded, causing a somewhat disconcerting bobble during the catapult stroke. (National Archives 630130)

were burned at each pole to provide an aiming point. Rahn used 70-degree banks to make a heading change of 30 degrees at each pole and then flew straight for the 15 seconds or so it took to fly between poles. The flight lasted a little more than 10 minutes from takeoff to touchdown during which roughly 600 gallons of fuel were burned, all but 40 gallons of the total available. The new record was 728 mph.

An attempt was made in December 1953 to beat the world's altitude record of 63,668 feet. Unfortunately, the J40's afterburner would not cooperate. Rahn was unable to climb much above 50,000 feet, and Jim Verdin could not even get the afterburner to light on his flight. However, enough had been accomplished with speed records to justify the award of the Collier Trophy at the Wright Memorial Dinner that December to joint recipients Ed Heinemann of Douglas for the Skyray and Dutch Kindelberger of North American for the Air Force F-100, the first operational fighter that was supersonic in level flight.

The XF4D demonstrated the potential of the tailless configuration, with an excellent rate of climb and maneuverability at altitude, but it was

The F4D first flew with an interim engine, the Allison J35, but even at this point in the program, October 1953, the first XF4D was still flying with a J40 that lacked an afterburner. (National Archives 80-G-628705)

plagued by tail buffet and rudder buzz at speeds over Mach 0.9. In addition, the trimmer position required to counter a nose-down pitch change that began at Mach 0.91 was causing high drag. Moreover, as the failed altitude record attempts demonstrated, the J40 was not ready for flight envelope development, much less operational use. Continued problems with the engine finally resulted in Douglas being able to convince BuAer to switch to the Pratt & Whitney J57 with afterburner for production Skyrays. The production aircraft would also have two separate hydraulic systems powering the elevon actuators but retain the manual reversion capability. The rudder was split into an upper and lower surface, the upper one controlled by a yaw damper and the lower one a traditional rudder controlled by the pilot. The fire-control system was now to be the Aero 13F, consisting of an APQ-50 radar, an Aero 5B armament control system, and an optical gun sight as shown in Figure 9-1.

The first XF4D, the second XF3H-1, an F7U-3, and an F2H-3 were all aboard Coral Sea for carrier-suitability testing in October 1953. Lt. Cdr. Verdin and Cdr. Marshal Beebe, Director of the Flight Test Division at NATC flew the XF4D, which had been repainted white and now had an afterburner. (National Archives)

The second XF4D pictured here was the first to get an afterburner and was the aircraft used to set the speed records in October 1953. (National Archives 80-G-628710)

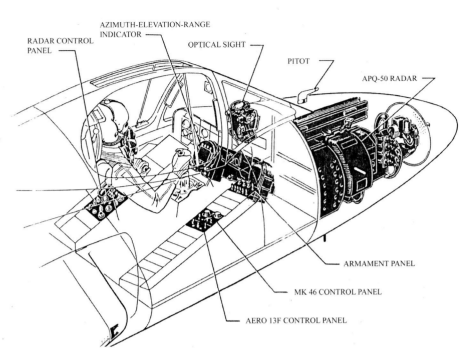

Figure 9-1 F4D Fire Control System (Author)

## The Pratt & Whitney J57

Pratt & Whitney was not able to do much with jet engine technology before the end of World War II because its piston engines were in such high demand. Nevertheless, Frederick Rentschler proved to be as visionary and committed about the jet engine as he was the piston engine. He had resigned as president of the engine manufacturer Wright Aeronautical in 1924, because he felt that his board was not investing enough money in engine development. He easily interested the U.S. Navy in his ideas for an advanced air-cooled engine and convinced the Pratt & Whitney Co., makers of precision machine tools, to invest in that engine. The result was an outstanding product line of air-cooled radial piston engines – Pratt & Whitney built about half the engines produced for the U.S.-built aircraft in World War II. A saying among pilots of Pratt-powered aircraft was: "You can fly a Pratt & Whitney farther than you can ship an Allison."

As the war was winding down in 1945, Rentschler directed Leonard "Luke" Hobbs, who was his head of Engineering, to begin jet-engine development work. His objective was to catch up to the competition technically in five years and be the dominant jet engine company, as Pratt & Whitney had been in piston engines,

in 10. Pratt & Whitney benefited enormously when BuAer decided on the Rolls-Royce Nene to power Grumman's first jet and helped stage manage Pratt & Whitney's acquisition of the U.S. production license in 1946. With his long-term view, Rentschler wasn't disheartened when the Navy selected Westinghouse for its 7,500-lb engine instead of Pratt's JT3-6, also an axial-flow engine with the "6" standing for its compressor pressure ratio. Instead, he continued development of his engine. Needing a customer and aircraft to tailor it to, Hobbs found one in the Air Force's new long-range bomber program. The Air Force had not decided whether a turboprop or a turbojet engine would power it. They therefore had Wright Aeronautical developing a T35 turboprop with the Navy's Westinghouse J40 as the probable choice if they decided that their big bomber was to be jet propelled.

Hobbs sold the Air Force on supporting another, bigger turboprop having the compressor/turbine core of a jet engine with better efficiency and more thrust than the J40. It was designated the T45. His approach was to increase the compressor pressure ratio to 8:1 to improve the specific fuel consumption. Since this would make the engine harder to start and reluctant to accelerate, he elected to make it a dual-spool compressor/turbine, allowing the front (low pressure) and rear (high pressure) section of the compressor to turn at different speeds, each driven by a separate turbine wheel. The jet engine counterpart (the T45 never actually ran as a complete engine) was to be designated the J57.

When the U.S. Air Force decided in late 1948 that its new bomber, the B-52, would be jet propelled, Boeing proposed that it be powered by eight J57s, an engine manufacturer's dream aircraft. Even before the JT3-8 was run in mid-1949, Hobbs had decided that the target-specific fuel consumption required a 12:1 compressor ratio, twice the industry baseline but possible with his dual-spool design. The JT3 compressor was redesigned yet again and run for the first time in January 1950. It became the first jet engine to achieve 10,000 lbs of thrust. First flight of the B-52 occurred in April 1952.

Being the biggest, most powerful jet engine available at the time, the J57 was quickly modified with an afterburner to become one of the engine alternatives for the Air Force's forthcoming Century Series of fighters.

## F4D and the J57

Ed Heinemann claimed that he had deliberately designed the F4D's engine compartment to be larger than required for the J40, large enough for any engine then being planned.[5] True or not, the ability to fit the J57 into the F4D turned out to be crucial to the Skyray's success, given how the J40 turned out. The first production F4D-1 flew in June 1954. Early on, it was flown up to 50,000 feet and, in a 45-degree dive, reached Mach 1.5 at 35,000 feet. However, the F4D inlet and the J57 were not a good match initially, necessitating a redesign and flight-test development followed by a retrofit of the aircraft already produced. Extensive flight-testing was also required to reconfigure the aft end of the fuselage to eliminate the tail buffet and rudder buzz at high indicated airspeeds and reduce drag. The flight-control system continued to be tweaked, and the armament system developed all through 1955, 1956, and most of 1957.

However, initial carrier-suitability tests with a production aircraft were accomplished on

*Ticonderoga* in September 1955. BIS trials had been completed by late 1955. Even though it was still in the midst of a development program almost two years after first flight, the F4D was considered ready for a Fleet Introduction Program in April 1956. The FIP was accomplished at NATC over a six-week, 600-flight-hour period with six F4Ds. VC-3, the West Coast all-weather squadron, then received the first deliveries. An El Toro, California-based Marine squadron, VMF-115, took delivery of a Skyray just a few days later, but within a few weeks it was lost in a crash, killing the squadron commander, Lt. Col. Flickinger. Because of crashes, groundings, and modifications to incorporate problem fixes and design improvements, it ended up being almost two years before the squadron, by then redesignated VMF(AW)-115 for all-weather, would be deployable to Japan.[6]

For example, the final fix had not yet been established for transonic pitch trim change, a consequence of the basic F4D configuration. For the first four years of flight test it had just been an annoying characteristic, but in February 1955 it suddenly became

*A second series of carrier suitability tests with BuNos. 130746 and 130747-shown here, was required for the J57-powered F4D Skyray. (Hal Andrews collection)*

a great deal more. Bob Rahn was on a relatively routine test flight to confirm pitch-trim adequacy at maximum speed at sea level – about .98 Mach at 100 feet over the Pacific Ocean. At the test point he canceled afterburner somewhat more snappily than usual at a higher speed than before and without beginning to retrim nose down because of the proximity to the water. The resulting change in the pitch trim requirement as the aircraft rapidly decelerated caused it to abruptly nose up at 9 *g*s, well over structural limits. Fortunately, Rahn only momentarily lost consciousness, and the F4D held together and remained flyable. This incident necessitated the development of a transonic trim-change compensator to reduce pilot workload and eliminate the potential for violent pitch-up under the same circumstances.[7]

As of March 1957, about 110 F4Ds had been completed, but Douglas and the Navy were still in the process of perfecting the trim-change compensator and completing envelope expansion, avionics and armament tests, and the structural demonstration. A powerplant program to improve high-altitude afterburner performance and re-light envelope was being conducted. Douglas also spent an inordinate amount of time trying to get the F4D to break the sound barrier in level flight. It proved to be a futile exercise, as the drag of the thick wing was just too much to overcome. The

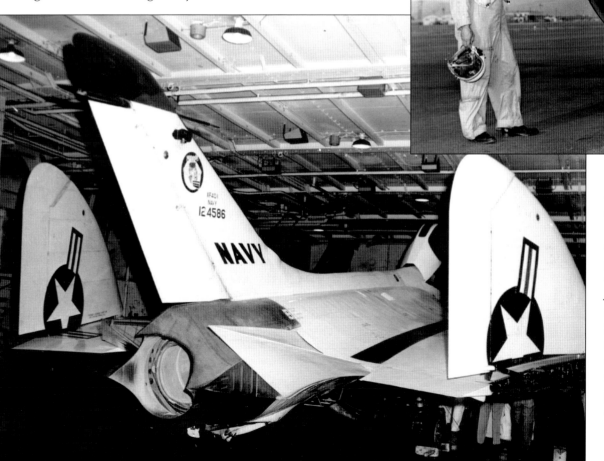

When folded, most of the Navy's carrier-based aircraft demonstrated the limitation on height necessitated by the 17-foot, six-inch overhead of the hangar deck. Note that the trimmers are positioned to provide nose-up pitch. During the Coral Sea trials, the J40-powered XF4D sported one of several failed attempts at fairing the aft fuselage to reduce drag enough to allow the F4D to sustain supersonic speeds in level flight. Contrast that with the picture of the penultimate J57-powered production F4D aft fuselage. (Hal Andrews collection)

*Afterburner was not normally required for a successful F4D launch, and since its operation consumed fuel at an enormous rate and added greatly to the wear and tear on the deck, it was generally not used for launch. In this instance, the ship was at anchor and the assistance of afterburner was necessary. (Robert L. Lawson collection)*

set with what was otherwise an all but permanent F4D appendage, two 300-gallon drop tanks which almost doubled the fuel capacity. By definition, a fighter designed to the 1948 Interceptor mission requirement would not have much fuel – a normal fuel load would have reduced the climb rate that was essential to the mission profile. The tanks themselves were not that much more drag – with tanks and rocket pods, the F4D was only 20 knots slower in level flight in afterburner than it was without them.

Takeoff performance was sensational in afterburner although it was discouraged because of fuel consumption. With enough wind over deck, the F4D could actually be deck launched given the front half or so of the deck for a takeoff run. This was actually done once after VF-101's Lt. Max Morris landed his F4D on the British carrier *Ark Royal* in a cross-decking exercise from *Saratoga* in late 1957 and discovered that his holdback fitting was damaged. He only used 600 feet of deck even with full internal fuel.

The F4D's usefulness as an all-weather fighter was limited by its armament. As Jacque Naviaux recalled of his experience in the Skyray in VMF(AW)-542:

> A working radar, which was not all that rare, could detect a fighter at 24 nm, and track it at 20 nm. The plan was to fire a salvo of four 19-shot pods on a 110-degree lead collision course, with a firing range of 1,500 feet. Whether or not we would have hit anything on a regular basis is a matter for conjecture, but I think not, although I did manage to shoot down a drone at Point Mugu for one of the only recorded kills.[8]

Even if the pilot flew as precisely as the system designer expected, the radar was finely tuned, and the target cooperated by not maneuvering, the accuracy of the unguided rocket left a lot to be desired. It was loaded into tubes with the fins folded for minimal frontal area. The fins unfolded into position once the rocket was on its way. It was therefore not only unguided, but for a short distance after launch, also unstabilized. The effect was rather like firing birdshot from a shotgun. However, in August 1952, a drone controller B-17 was mistakenly shot down by an F-86D firing rockets with inert warheads at what he thought was the drone B-17 target.

One theoretical advantage of the unguided rockets over the guided missiles is that the former could be fired by eye, and there is at least one example of a successful eyeball-only aerial kill with an

Navy was pressing on with the fleet introduction, however. Two squadrons had commenced carrier qualifications, VF-74 out of NAS Oceana aboard *Roosevelt* and VF-141 out of NAS Miramar aboard *Lexington* and *Essex*. Test firing of the Sidewinder heat-seeking missile was about to begin at China Lake.

In 1958, an F4D piloted by the BuAer project officer, Maj. Edward N. LeFaiver, set five time-to-climb records, including one to 49,215 feet (15,000 meters) in two minutes, 36 seconds from a standing start. It was, of course, specially prepared for the record flights, being stripped of all unnecessary hardware, powered by a modified J57 and filled with just enough fuel for that particular flight. Each of the altitudes required a unique profile to minimize the time to a particular altitude, with the 15,000-meter flight being the most complicated – accelerate to .9 Mach and climb to 10,000 feet, climb at .79 Mach to 40,000 feet, and then pull up at 1.5 *g*s into a zoom climb, all the while in afterburner. At 43,000 feet the afterburner would blow out, at 46,000 feet the engine would flame out, but the aircraft would still coast up to 50,000 feet at a 60-degree nose-up angle and arrive indicating about 70 knots. At that point, the aircraft would pitch over into a dive. Going through 25,000 feet, the engine would be restarted.

None of the impressive speed and time-to-climb records was

*The F4D was a terrific interceptor up until the point of interception, where it lacked a viable kill capability in bad weather. This VF-23 Skyray has had its guns pulled and will likely be armed only with two Sidewinders if required to defend the ship. After this 1958 deployment aboard Hancock, the squadron turned in its F4Ds for F3Hs. (Robert L. Lawson collection)*

unguided rocket during the Vietnam War. The more likely outcome was exemplified in 1956 in what has become known as the Battle of Palmdale. Two Air Force F-94 pilots were tasked to shoot down an errant, placidly circling F6F drone that had been launched from nearby Point Mugu, California, and headed east instead of west on its own. Neither was able to get a lock-on with their automated fire control system, so they hosed it by eye with 208 rockets expended in three attacks by each aircraft. There were hits, but only on the vegetation, two houses, and an automobile in and around Palmdale, California. Fortunately nobody on the ground was injured. Untouched, the F6F finally ran out of fuel and crashed in the desert. The last of the brush fires ignited by the F-94s' rockets was brought under control two days later.

Skyray pilots loved the rate of climb and ability to turn inside other fighters at 40,000 feet. Their cockpit wasn't as roomy or well laid out like the Demon's: their mission-critical radarscope was located behind the control stick (a periscope was created to make the radar presentation more accessible). Anecdotally, they felt less comfortable than Demon pilots when landing aboard a carrier, particularly the *Essex* class, even in the best of conditions, not to mention on a dark and stormy night. Rear Admiral E. L. "Whitey" Feightner, the F7U-1 carrier-suitability and Blue Angel demonstrator pilot, was very critical of the F4D based on his experience as Commander Air Group 10 from 20 March 1959 to 18 March 1960 with VF-13 F4Ds aboard *Essex*:

> The F4D was too much airplane for the catapults and arresting gear of an *Essex*-class carrier…Most of the time the ship was unable to get enough wind over the deck to permit launching the F4Ds with external fuel, so many of

the flights were very short, 30-40 minutes, because of limited internal fuel in the aircraft. This routine, of course, played havoc with schedule cycle times and deck handling procedures. An F2H-3 or -4 squadron would have been more effective and saved all the hassle.[9]

The F4D was also the last of the Navy jet fighters to be retrofitted with in-flight refueling, in this case a probe extending from the left drop tank. It was a poor location for determining the relative position of drogue and probe during engagement and limited the fuel transfer to the drop tank capacity. On the other hand, it was 300 gallons of fuel. VF-74 had created the capability by fitting an A4D probe to one of its drop tanks. After two test flights ashore, they further developed the plug-in technique and the probe (the length was increased from 31 to 48 inches) and qualified all their pilots on the probe-equipped prototype during the first part of its deployment aboard *Intrepid* in late 1960.

A total of 419 production F4Ds were built, all -1s. A -2 with a J57-P-14 engine was considered but not proceeded with. However, a redesign to reduce drag that was also briefly designated F4D-2 became the supersonic F5D. The last squadron to operate the F4D was also the first, now VMF(A)-115. The squadron retired its last Skyray on 29 February 1964, while in the process of transitioning to the F-4B (F4H-1).

The F4D flew on a while longer at the Navy's Test Pilot School. There, its unusual handling qualities were valued since fledgling test pilots could be safely exposed to an aircraft that flew very differently from what they were accustomed to. The Ford fun finally ended in August 1966.

## CHAPTER TEN

*Roll control on the first XF3H was by conventionally located ailerons augmented by a small spoiler. The large wing fence was to prevent span-wise flow at high angles of attack. The pitch control was also conventional, with an elevator and adjustable stabilizer that was linked to the elevator so that it repositioned itself, slowly, when the elevator was deflected more than one degree. Note that the afterburner was not yet installed. (Jay Miller collection)*

# F3H Demon:
# Patience and Persistence

The F3H Demon program began as the backup interceptor to the F4D Skyray. Before its first flight, it also became a backup to the Navy's two new general-purpose fighter programs. The risk to McDonnell was that trying to cover two disparate missions would result in a fighter not good enough for either compared to the competition. Surprisingly, the F3H eventually proved to be better at fleet defense than the F4D and a better fighter than either the F10F or the F7U.

## F3H-1

McDonnell received a contract for the XF3H in January 1949. A mockup inspection was accomplished in July 1949, and resulted in a request for engine accessibility changes requiring a revisit in October. Design progress was also set back later that year when the Navy requested provisions for the installation of the more powerful J40-WE-10 that required more inlet air and fuel

capacity than the -8. As a result, first flight was rescheduled for April 1951. As it happened, the first XF3H was ready for an engine in February 1951 but one was not available, Westinghouse having experienced delays in development. Unlike Douglas, McDonnell did not substitute an interim engine. A flight-worthy J40 engine, albeit a -6 without afterburner, was finally delivered and installed for ground tests in July and a first flight in August.

Meanwhile, the Korean War and concern over the pace of Grumman's XF10F program had resulted in a major redirection of the F3H program. In June 1950, the Navy had four high-performance fighter development programs on contract – the F7U-3, F4D, F3H, and F10F. Of these, the two interceptors were closest to first flight and the F10F the farthest, with the F7U-3 somewhere in between and attracting criticism within BuAer. BuAer considered the F4D to be the better interceptor even though neither had flown. Lacking confidence that either the F7U-3 or the F10F, both high-risk configurations aerodynamically, would be successful,

*Like the Cutlass and the Skyray, the Demon was an attention-getter. It looked like it was going a thousand miles per hour, with its sharply pointed nose and 45°-swept wings. The annular intakes added to its sleek look. The windscreen was cleverly integrated into the inlet design so the forward and downward visibility was excellent, but the canopy protruded only minimally. (Hal Andrews collection)*

The first photo released of the XF3H was professionally airbrushed to reduce the size of the engine inlets. This was done to prevent the Soviets from being able to estimate its engine thrust by measuring inlet size. (Jay Miller collection)

BuAer decided to have McDonnell modify the F3H design for more payload and range so that it could also be used as a general-purpose fighter in addition to fulfilling the interceptor mission. Therefore, as of January 1951, the F3H was no longer to be a 22,000-lb lightly armed and armored interceptor with limited range – it was to be redesigned as a 29,000-lb general-purpose fighter, with an increase in internal fuel capacity from 1,148 gallons to 1,506; substitution of four 20mm cannons for the rocket launchers; and addition of eight external stores stations under the wings and fuselage. In recognition of the 33-percent gross weight increase, the Demon was to be powered by the higher-thrust

The second XF3H, shown here, now has inboard ailerons with a small fence. The large wing fence has yet to be deleted. Pitch control has changed to a stabilator with a trim tab, and the afterburner is installed. (National Archives 80-G-627739)

J40-WE-10. Although the thrust ratings were not being increased by as much as the aircraft's weight as a general-purpose fighter, the F3H's alternate mission as an interceptor (with a reduced fuel load) only represented a gross weight increase of about 16 percent. The increased J40-WE-10 thrust more than made up for that, so it would still have interceptor climb performance.

The really good news was that the Navy wanted to rush the F3H into production – in addition to 150 aircraft placed on order with McDonnell in March 1951, Goodyear was to build 100 as a second source, an order subsequently transferred to Temco due to the need for Goodyear blimps. The Temco contract, which had been increased to 160 aircraft in July 1952, was canceled in May 1953, before any had been built. (Temco did build F3H wings as a subcontractor to McDonnell.)

The flight test of the two XF3Hs was to be accomplished as planned but they would now only approximate the aerodynamics of the production aircraft, since a redesign of the fuselage was required for the additional fuel and the change in armament. The wing area was also increased to accommodate the higher gross weight by adding nine inches to the leading edge. These changes necessitated a larger horizontal tail. A mockup review of the revised design was accomplished in July 1951.

At this point, McDonnell called the Navy's attention to the probability that the J40-WE-10 would not be available when required. They submitted design studies of five alternate afterburning engines of similar weight and thrust. The Navy was not receptive to the change, which would have meant a development cost increase and a schedule delay. Instead, they were counting on Westinghouse to develop and produce the improved engine with minimal schedule slippage.

If McDonnell had been concerned about the J40 engine from a schedule standpoint before beginning flight test in August 1951, they were even less enthusiastic about it when they started flying. The flight envelope was restricted to only 25,000 feet by violent compressor stalls, and engine development/qualification had continued to slip. However, McDonnell was distracted by problems of its own – its 45-degree swept wing was susceptible to Dutch roll and its aileron design was ineffective. Aileron effectiveness could not be improved with fences to keep the flow from moving spanwise, so the ailerons were moved inboard at the expense of flap area. The revised wing was installed in March 1952.

The -10 engine schedule slippage was partly alleviated by the Navy's decision in late 1951 to supply a modified -8 engine, the J40-WE-22, to McDonnell for the first 12 production aircraft. In April 1952, after a March meeting with BuAer at Westinghouse where it was apparent that the -10 availability was still uncertain, McDonnell went back to the Navy, this time recommending that the J40 be replaced with the Allison J71, which was very similar in size to the J40 but had more thrust than even the J40-WE-10. James S. McDonnell himself stated in writing to BuAer that a J40-W-22-powered F3H would result in a "disappointingly underpowered combination in comparison to the performance potential of the airplane."[1] The Navy rejected this proposal too, again because it would increase development cost and delay the fighter's availability. Navy officials also did not have a high opinion of Allison based on its Grumman F9F Panther experience.

Unfortunately, Westinghouse was not having much luck turning things around, and the engine continued to disappoint. In May 1952, BuAer notified McDonnell to expect to deliver F3Hs with J40-WE-22 engines until otherwise advised, but to retain provisions for the retrofit of J40-WE-10 engines. In August 1952, the first XF3H was damaged when it was dead-sticked to a landing short of the runway after a catastrophic engine failure shortly after takeoff. By December, the Navy realized that the J40's bright future might never be realized and that McDonnell needed to begin a redesign to incorporate the J71. However, Westinghouse was to continue J40 development and NACA was to get involved with altitude facility testing at its Lewis facility in Cleveland, Ohio, to help solve the compressor stall problem and reduce afterburner fuel consumption. The afterburning J40-WE-8 finally became available in late 1952, with flight tests beginning in January 1953 in an XF3H.

In February 1953, an NPE was accomplished with the second prototype, BuNo. 125445. The highlight of the report was that, "The handling qualities and flight characteristics of the XF3H in 1 G (sic) dives to transonic and supersonic Mach numbers are outstanding." The maximum speed achieved was Mach 1.25. The second XF3H was then laid up for instrumentation for the upcoming accelerated carrier-suitability program, which concluded with an evaluation in October aboard *Coral Sea*.

Meanwhile, the production design had been modified to cant the forward fuselage down by five degrees to provide better visibility at the high angle of attack required on approach. The forward, non-sliding portion of the canopy was also built as one

*Blast off – with a catapult assist – on the last launch from Coral Sea. (National Archives 80-G-630037)*

piece, eliminating the windscreen frames. The radome was made shorter and blunter to improve transmissivity. At some point, a simple range-only radar, the AN/APG-30, was substituted for the AN/APQ-50 search radar for initial production aircraft. These were designated F3H-1N in June 1953, with the follow-on F3H-1M to be equipped with the Sparrow I missile system and associated radar.

In July 1953, BuAer finally directed McDonnell to incorporate provisions for alternate installation of Allison J71-A-2 engines in the 61st and subsequent F3Hs. J71-powered aircraft were designated F3H-2.

In September 1953, the Secretary of the Navy publicly announced that F3H production would be delayed, with 91 fewer aircraft delivered that fiscal year (July 1953 to June 1954) than had been planned. His reason was that the Navy wanted to wait for improved engines for the Demon. It had also become apparent to all involved that the J40-WE-24 that was based on the -10 was not forthcoming. McDonnell would have to make do with the lower-thrust J40-WE-22, which powered the first production F3H-1N, BuNo. 133489, during its first flight on Christmas Eve, 1953. This aircraft was delivered to the Navy on 8 January 1954, but was retained at St. Louis for development testing by McDonnell, during which it was twice successfully dead-sticked back into Lambert Field after engine failures.

March 1954 started well but ended with all the Demons grounded. On the 4th, the first XF3H was dived to Mach 1.31 starting from 43,000 feet in full afterburner. Maximum true airspeed in the 70-degree dive was 800 knots at 15,000 feet. Only five days later, it blew up in flight, but McDonnell test pilot Gilbert North parachuted to safety, either thrown clear or ejecting — he didn't remember. This resulted in the grounding of the other XF3H. It was eventually decided that all the flight test benefit had been obtained

*The additional fuel capacity made the Demon a little less svelte, but it was still attractive. Tilting the nose down by 10 degrees and substituting a one-piece windscreen had increased forward and downward visibility. (Hal Andrews collection)*

from the prototypes, so 125445 was shipped to the Naval Air Development center at Johnsville, Pennsylvania, later that year for a barricade engagement evaluation. A week later, another McDonnell pilot, Chester V. Braun, made 489's first dead-stick landing at St. Louis after his engine seized following an oil-line failure. Only two days after that, an NATC pilot, Capt. Nicholas J. Smith III, ejected following an in-flight fire during the first F3H-

1N NPE flight. All F3Hs were grounded for the next three months to deal with the engine problems. Flights resumed in July with the third F3H-1N going to NATC for carrier-suitability testing accomplished in September 1954. At that point, it had been decided that the F3H-1N was going to be limited to one service tour with no overhaul. In November, the F3H-1N NPE was finally completed. The original production contract for 150 aircraft was being revised to be for 60 F3H-1Ns and 90 F3H-2Ns.

The following year, 1955, got off to a bad start when an NATC pilot, Cdr. K. D. Smith, was killed in January at Patuxent River during an F3H-1N simulated engine-out landing. For some reason, he slowed below the ability of the air-driven emergency hydraulic system pump's ability to provide enough hydraulic flow to the flight controls. (The XF3Hs and the first 10 production aircraft had a battery-powered electrical auxiliary pump; the 11th, which Smith was flying, and subsequent production aircraft used a ram-air-driven pump.) However, BIS trials started in February 1955, although all J40 engines with over 60 hours total time were grounded at the time due to oil line failures.

Possibly inspired by VF-33's attempt with an FJ-3 to unofficially better the existing time-to-climb record from a standing start to 10,000 feet, McDonnell test pilot Chester Braun posted

*In accordance with one of its many missions as a general-purpose fighter, the F3H was to have an air-to-ground role. Low-drag bombs were not yet widely available, so this Demon is loaded with six 500-lb World War II vintage bombs. (U.S. Navy)*

The pod underneath this F3H-1N, the third one built, is a self-contained gas turbine compressor unit to provide high-pressure air for the J40 engine start. It could be hung on an external-stores pylon for stops at airfields where jet engine ground-start capability was not available. (Robert L. Lawson collection)

an unofficial time-to-climb mark of 71 seconds on 13 February at St. Louis. This would have broken the record, but any much-needed rejuvenation of the F3H's reputation was very brief – all the J40-powered Demons were grounded on the 18th to modify the turbines and a McDonnell test pilot was killed doing a supersonic flight in a J71-powered F3H-1 five days later. In any event, on 23 March, Douglas' Bob Rahn, with no prior practice or flight profile optimization, climbed 10,000 feet in 56 seconds, "just for the hell of it" on a climb out for a routine F4D test flight at Edwards AFB.[2] (In 1958, with somewhat more preparation, the Skyray set a 3,000-meter [9,843 feet] record of a little more

The F3H also had a nuclear weapon delivery capability. This Mk 7 dummy store has just been subjected to a dead-stick landing courtesy of the lack of Westinghouse J40 engine reliability. (Joe Dobronski collection)

than 44 seconds.) The F3Hs were ungrounded as their J40s were modified, beginning in late March. BIS was finally completed in May, with the J40-powered F3H-1N now considered suitable only for shore-based pilot-familiarization training in advance of F3H-2 availability.

Engine-related accidents continued, all involving McDonnell test pilots. Robert Strange was killed in May 1955, at St. Louis following a J40 compressor stall and flame out. He either didn't want to use the ejection seat or it failed, and he hit the horizontal tail when he bailed out. When Joe Dobronski's engine failed in late June toward the end of a test flight in 489, he was able to suc-

cessfully dead-stick back into Lambert Field. The last straw for the J40-powered aircraft was a second fatal crash, this time involving an attempted flight by Albert Seawell from Lambert Field in St. Louis on 7 July 1955. His afterburner blew out unnoticed on the takeoff roll. He got on the backside of the power curve on the initial climb out and only got another mile before coming back to earth in a fiery crash. The Navy finally threw in the towel. (It was rumored that the McDonnell test pilots refused to fly the J40-powered F3H any more.) In any event, the Navy grounded all the F3H-1Ns permanently and terminated the J40 engine program. More than 400 F3H-1 BuNos. assigned to production were canceled.

After the J40-powered F3H-1s were permanently grounded in July 1955, the completed aircraft were stored at McDonnell until disposition instructions were received. There are 22 F3H-1Ns pictured here. (Tommy H. Thomason collection)

They also had to be ignominiously carted away or stricken, stripped of useful equipment and disposed of wherever they happened to be when they were grounded. At least three were shipped to NAMC at Philadelphia for barricade, catapult, and gunfire vulnerability tests.

The three surviving J71-powered F3H-1s were not grounded. BuNo. 133519 was used for various flight-test duties at McDonnell through mid-1958, before being ferried to San Diego and stricken. BuNo. 133521 was ferried out to Edwards AFB in July 1956, and stricken in September. BuNo. 133522, the second -2N prototype, was eventually assigned to NAOTS (Naval Aviation Ordnance Test Station) NAAS Chincoteague, Virginia (now the Wallops Island Test Facility).

It was a program and public relations nightmare for McDonnell, Westinghouse, and the Navy. Congress made the most of the opportunity, with hearings that extended into 1956, to investigate why the Navy did not recognize that the J40-powered F3H was a failure sooner. They had spent more than $265 million (roughly $2 billion in 2007), for 56 production aircraft, most of which never flew, and 107 J40-WE-22 engines, most of which were never installed in an aircraft. The Navy's answer was that in late 1950, they needed a high-performance fighter quickly to counter the Russian MiG. Based on Westinghouse's past performance, they believed that the J40 engine would meet the specification and be available on time. As a result, the Navy had Westinghouse build engines and McDonnell airframes as quickly as possible, betting that development and integration problems would be minimal. They lost.[3]

To avoid future debacles of this type, the Navy had implemented its new Fleet Introduction of Replacement Models (FIRM) program. The concept was to hold the production rate of a new aircraft at a low level until development and Navy acceptance was complete and then ramp up production to equip the fleet. In the event of another Korea, according to testimony to the United States Senate Preparedness Investigating Subcommittee in early 1956, the Navy's approach would be:

First, to accelerate production rates of proven models now coming off the production lines and keep those models in high-volume production until replacements of high-performance models are phased into the production;

Of the 60 production F3H-1Ns, four had been completed with J71 engines, and one of those crashed. Of the remaining 56, only 18 appear to have been completed with engines. Five of those crashed, with three fatalities, two were damaged in shore-based carrier-suitability testing, and one was damaged in a dead-stick landing after engine failure. The remaining 38 did not have engines installed but were contractually delivered to the Navy, the last one in June 1955, and then stored at St. Louis awaiting disposition. The Navy considered completing the last 26 with J71 engines, but since they had been built with the F3H-1 wing, BuAer determined that it would be uneconomical to complete them as F3H-2s with the bigger wing and all the other changes required. Twenty-one of the F3H-1Ns that had been stored at McDonnell (it would appear that the other 17 were scrapped in place at St. Louis, but some of the structure and components may have been used in F3H-2 production) were famously towed through the streets of St. Louis in late December 1955. They were then loaded aboard barges to be delivered to NAS Memphis as maintenance trainers, joining some of the remnants of the small F7U-1 fleet. The event was traumatizing for McDonnell and long remembered.

The few F3H-1Ns that the Navy was flying were not even allowed a one-time ferry flight to their ultimate destination.

A young Dave Ostrowski took this picture of F3H-1N BuNo. 133507 on 28 December 1955 as it was being towed along Natural Bridge Road in St. Louis, Missouri, on its way to be loaded on a coal barge for shipment to a Navy mechanics training school in Memphis, Tennessee. (Dave Ostrowski)

At least 21 of the F3H-1Ns — most of which not only had zero flight time but also never had an engine installed — were ignominiously shipped down the river to ground-based roles. (Joe Dobronski collection)

Second, to accelerate tests and evaluation of improved models now flying so that they could be placed in volume production at the earliest practical moment;

Third, to increase the tempo of development of new, very high-performance types.

## Allison J71

Fortunately, the Navy had formally authorized McDonnell to proceed with a backup design of an Allison J71 installation in the F3H much as Douglas had opted to substitute the J57 for the J40. In mid-1953, the Navy finally decided that the J40-WE-10 was never going to be qualified and terminated the development contract in September. Production of the J40-WE-22 continued for the F3H-1N. The four engines compared approximately as follows (published ratings varied over time):

This engineless, brand-new F3H-1N is parked beside an F7U-1 hulk that is missing its outer wing panels. Another F3H-1N can be seen between the two. It is fitted with red engine-run screens, so it appears to have been used for ground-run training of mechanics. (Robert L. Lawson collection)

|                   | J40-WE-10 | J40-WE-22A | J71-A-2 | J57-P-2 |
|-------------------|-----------|------------|---------|---------|
| Maximum (lbs)     | 13,700    | 10,900     | 14,400  | 14,800  |
| Military (lbs)    | 9,275     | 7,400      | 10,000  | 9,220   |
| Normal (lbs)      | 8,330     | 6,500      | 8,700   | 8,000   |
| Dry Weight (lbs)  | 3,968     | 4,218      | 4,390   | 4,735   |

The only difference between the -22 and the -22A was the fuel control. The original electronic fuel control had proved to be unreliable, and a hydro-mechanical control was to be used in production. However, it was in short supply, so initial engines were to be delivered with the original fuel control.

The J71 weighed little more than the J40 but had significantly more thrust and burned nine to 16 percent less fuel for the same thrust. In November 1953, BuAer predicted that the F2H-2 would have a mission radius of 320 nautical miles compared to 285 for the F3H-1, a 12 percent improvement.

The F3H and the J71 were made for each other, but not in a good way. In late 1952, McDonnell was desperate for an engine for the F3H, and Allison was desperate for an application for the J71, the Air Force having canceled most of the expected requirements for the engine. Allison had gotten into the jet-engine business the easy way, selected as the primary manufacturing source for the GE redesign of the Whittle engine, the I-40 (J33), and the GE developed axial-flow TG-100 (J35). With its J47, GE was finally able to break away from Allison from a production standpoint. By then, Allison had enough experience to design engines on its own. The company's first, begun in April 1949, was a derivative of the J35, which the Air Force designated J71.

Like the J57, the first prospective application for the J71 was a bomber, in this case a four-engine version of the B-47 proposed to the Air Force by Boeing in 1950. Before the B-47 re-engine program was canceled, the Air Force had decided to use the J57 instead. Almost nothing else panned out either. The only exception was the J71 being selected instead of the J57 in a 1952 competition to power the Air Force's Douglas B-66, a derivative of the Navy's A3D. The J71's subsequent problems gave the Air Force reason to regret the decision. Development and in-service problems with the engine resulted in all the other aircraft that were to use the J71 winding up with another engine instead, often the J57. It was planned that the J71 would power the Air Force's F-105 but weight growth forced Republic to use the J75 instead, with the J57 as an interim engine due to the J75's development schedule. In the early 1950s the J71 was selected to power an enlarged version of the Air Force's unmanned B-62 Snark cruise missile; it was eventually replaced by the J57, reportedly because of the J71 problems. The Air Force also had Northrop modify one F-89 to replace its afterburning J35s with non-afterburning J71s in the expectation of more power and less fuel consumption; the XF-89E flew in June 1954, but failed to demonstrate enough improvement to justify the change in production. Finally, the J71 powered the first several Navy P6M Seamaster seaplane bombers (originally proposed with J40s), the first of which flew in 1955; in production, the J71s were replaced with Pratt & Whitney J75s primarily due to the need for more thrust.

Of course, the Navy and McDonnell knew none of this when they agreed to replace the J40 with the J71 in late 1952. Neither the J57 nor the J71 had much of a track record up to that point. If anything, the J71 could have been viewed as a lesser risk. It was a derivative of an existing engine, while the J57 was an all-new engine with a novel compressor design that had just been flown for the first time. It is also likely that McDonnell and the Navy selected the J71 over the J57 for the same reason that the Air Force did when ordering the B-66 — J57 development and production was oversubscribed. The J57 continued to be popular. More than 20,000 J57 engines were built, compared to less than 2,000 J71s.

## F3H-2

The J71-powered derivative of the F3H-1 was designated the F3H-2. In November 1953, following a successful mockup review in August, McDonnell received a contract change to build four of the 60 F3H-1Ns with the J71 engine instead of the J40. The requirement for the lowest possible approach speed and better maneuverability at altitude begat yet another wing area increase, this time accomplished by extending the chord at the wing root by 40 inches aft of the F3H-1N trailing edge. The new trailing edge formed a straight line to the original F3H-1N wing tip. This wing-area increase required no change to the wing torque box as the changes were aft of the main spar – it did result in a small reflex in the airfoil section and slightly decreased both the wing thickness/chord ratio and sweep angle. BuNos. 133519 (#31) and 133521 (#33) were modified for the J71 installation only. BuNos. 133520 (#32) and 133522 (#34) were completed with both the J71 and the bigger wing so they were aerodynamically representative of the F3H-2.

A subsequent contract amendment provided for all Demons after the 56th J40-powered F3H-1N to be powered by the J71. The first F3H-2 variant to be produced was the F3H–2N, which was equipped with the Hughes APG-51A radar and armed with four 20mm cannons, with Sidewinder missile capability added later. The next version, the F3H-2M, was to have the APQ-51A radar and be armed with the Sparrow I missile. Ns and Ms were produced in parallel. The final and definitive version, the F3H-2, was the standard all-weather fighter, equipped with the AN/APG-51B radar that provided guidance for its Sparrow III missiles. It could also fulfill the general-purpose fighter role, with wing stations for

*The first F3H-2Ns were very similar to the -1N except for the engine and the bigger wing. This one is carrying a Mk 7 nuclear store on one of the fuselage stations. It still has the one-piece windscreen and the auxiliary engine inlet of the -1N. (Credit) [Insert credit]*

*F3H-2 BuNo. 133572 pictured here has all the late production modifications, including the wing spoilers. The -2 was the production model that was armed with the Sparrow III missile in addition to 20mm cannon and Sidewinder. U.S. Navy)*

up to 6,000 lbs of ordnance for ground attack, although it was seldom if ever used in that mission. There were 459 F3H-2 variants built, 140 F3H-2Ns, 80 F3H-2Ms, and 239 F3H-2s. Most, if not all, surviving F3H-2Ns were eventually modified to have Sparrow III capability. F3H-2Ms appear to have been assigned to other duties after their relatively brief operational career, primarily F3H familiarization training.

The development and qualification of the J71-A-2 was not smooth. In fact, the Navy approached Westinghouse in December 1953 in revisiting its decision to cancel the J40-WE-10. Westinghouse wouldn't commit to being able to qualify an engine soon enough, so the Navy elected to continue with the J71 for the 61st and subsequent F3Hs. McDonnell finally received its first YJ71 engine in September 1954, four months late, and installed it in BuNo. 133519. The first flight was made the following month, and for a time both J40- and J71-powered F3H-1Ns were flying at St. Louis.

In November 1954, the Navy reportedly canceled orders for more than 200 F3H-2s of the almost 500 aircraft that had been on contract. The F3H-2Ps were deleted. The Navy attributed the cancelations to lags in the J71 engine-development program. The F3H-2 aerodynamic prototype, BuNo. 133520, flew in January 1955; unfortunately, it was lost a month later on a supersonic test flight and the McDonnell pilot, John Todnem, was killed. The cause was not determined, but it was speculated to be a failure of the one-piece windshield, possibly from a bird strike, that had been introduced on production F3H-1s. In any event, the windshield was redesigned to be more conventional in structure. An NPE was accomplished using the other F3H-2N prototype at St. Louis in late March – the resulting report was complimentary about the increased performance and high-altitude maneuverability. The first production F3H-2N, BuNo. 133549, flew in April 1955. It was subsequently lost (for a few hours, literally) in October after McDonnell test pilot George Mills ejected from what he thought was an unrecoverable inverted spin. The aircraft then recovered and flew off, keeping McDonnell in some suspense until the Iowa State Police called and asked if they were missing an aircraft. It had belly landed in a farmer's field after it ran out of fuel.

Development and Navy evaluation and acceptance went relatively smoothly after that. The J71 finally passed its qualification test in July. BIS trials began in September 1955, which included carrier suitability evaluation on *Ticonderoga*. They were completed in November. While there were several deficiencies to correct and product improvements to incorporate, such as an in-flight refueling probe installation, the aircraft was cleared to begin the Fleet Introduction Program in January 1956. NATC pilots and mechanics familiar with the aircraft conducted a two-month, 600-flight-hour program with pilots and maintenance personnel from VF-14, VC-3, VX-3, and other organizations operating and maintaining six F3H-2Ns.

The Demon was spared the fire-control system development effort that was partly to blame for the delay in the introduction of the F4D. The F3H-2N had a relatively straightforward search radar and armament system not that different from the F2H-3s and -4s that it was replacing in the fleet. The F3H-2M's Sparrow I missile and the associated radar and fire-control system had already gone through a teething period in the F3D-2M and the F7U-3M.

The first operational squadron, VF-14 at NAS Cecil Field, Florida, received six F3H-2Ns in March 1956. All finally seemed to be going well with the F3H in service except for compressor stall incidents beginning in July 1956, and occasional failure of the afterburner nozzle to open or close properly. The susceptibility to compressor stall was reduced by minor engine changes and operating instructions. The more serious of the nozzle failures was that it stayed open when afterburner was canceled, because this significantly reduced engine thrust. This failure mode was addressed by providing the capability for emergency afterburner modulation throughout the entire throttle range. VF-14 departed to the Mediterranean as part of CVG-1 aboard *Forrestal* in January 1957, and VF-124, the first Pacific Fleet F3H squadron, deployed aboard *Lexington* in April.

At that point, the engine problems began to be more frequent, with six accidents attributed to engine failures between May and September 1957. Most troubling was the loss of two VF-31 F3Hs in June. While flying 150 miles off the Georgia coast in a thunderstorm at 28,000 feet, both suffered near simultaneous engine failures. Both aviators ejected. Unfortunately, one pilot lost his life. Within 30 days, another flight of two had near simultaneous engine failures at 18,000 feet and crashed at sea following flight into what was believed to be similar conditions. As a result, in September 1957 the F3H was grounded yet again. When the grounding was lifted, it was with a restriction from flying in possible icing conditions, an unacceptable limitation for an all-weather fighter.

To determine the cause of the engine failures, Allison and the Navy conducted inlet icing tests at the Mount Washington environmental facility in New Hampshire and at Edwards AFB. At Mount Washington, it was discovered that under severe icing conditions, pieces of ice would break loose and be ingested by the engine. Large enough pieces would cause a

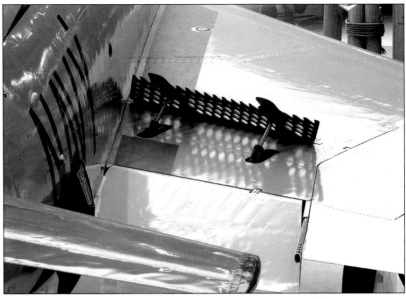

*The addition of the F3H-2 roll-control spoiler is the epitome of low-cost modification of an aircraft already in production. It was simply a perforated plate of metal attached to a hinge fastened onto the upper surface of the wing. Holes were cut in the upper wing surface through which the actuators protruded. The two rounded "fingers" extending aft on the spoiler are simply there to cover up the holes cut out for the actuators. (Don Hinton)*

*The F3H-2M was armed with the Sparrow I air-to-air missile, which proved to have limited effectiveness. Note that this early production aircraft does not have the inboard spoiler modification. (U.S. Navy)*

momentary drop in engine rpm and tailpipe temperature, but there was no engine failure or extended loss of thrust. Additional in-flight tests were conducted behind a B-29 equipped with a water spray rig. Eventually it was concluded that the engine failures were induced by ingestion of a very high volume of water, which

On nice days like this one, the Sidewinder was almost as good as the Sparrow III and better against a maneuvering threat. Note the pilot's incredible downward visibility. The upper 20mm cannon has been removed from this aircraft, an often-seen modification to reduce weight. (Robert L. Lawson collection)

VF-124 was the first West Coast squadron to deploy with the first production variant, the F3H-2N. The -2N was armed with four 20mm cannons and the Sidewinder missile. (Robert L. Lawson collection)

caused compressor-case distortion and compressor-blade rub. The initial fix was to adjust the compressor bleed valve schedule to improve the stall margin and trim the compressor blades slightly because of apparent rubbing on the compressor case when it shrank in cold and wet conditions. Modified engines were installed in two NATC F3Hs, and two test pilots were sent off to fly in clouds at altitudes between 22,000 and 30,000 feet to see if the fix was adequate, i.e., whether their one and only engine flamed out or not. One of them, Roger Carlquist, was successful in not only proving the fix did not work as hoped, but

also dead-sticking the F3H back into NAS Key West, Florida, so the seized engine could be examined. As a result, another trim was made to the compressor blades to finally eliminate the potential for rub when the compressor case shrank. This modification proved to be successful if a bit detrimental to thrust.[4]

The Demon was finally rid of its demons and served for several years thereafter. The Sparrow I missile proved to be a disappointment, and the F3H-2Ms were apparently little used operationally. Its successor, the Sparrow III, was a more accurate, longer-range missile. First fired in flight in late 1952, it became operational on the F3H-2 in 1958, following Operational Evaluation by VX-4 at Point Mugu and onboard *Midway* and *Bon Homme Richard*. VF-64 operating from *Midway* made the first Sparrow III shot from a deployed carrier-based F3H in December 1958.

Until the arrival of its successor, the F4H, the Demon was the only all-weather, radar-missile-armed fighter in the fleet, and it probably would have acquitted itself well against Soviet bombers if called upon. During *Coral Sea*'s 1960-61 deployment, VF-151 fired 16 Sparrow IIIs at targets towed by FJ-3 Furys. There were 14 hits, one near miss, and one abort by a pilot who thought he might be tracking the tow plane.

The last F3H-2 was delivered to the Navy on 28 April 1960. Counting the 60 F3H-1Ns, some of which never flew, McDonnell built 519 production Demons in addition to the two XF3Hs. Unlike most Navy fighters, none was used operationally by the Marine Corps.

This F3H has an external tank on a fuselage pylon and a Sparrow III on the outboard pylon. Because of interference drag, the Demon reputedly couldn't fly any farther with two external tanks than with one. This is a possibility but in any event, the F3H had an excellent cycle time on internal fuel alone. (Robert L. Lawson collection)

After the false starts in interceptor and general-purpose fighter missions and the early engine problems, the F3H became the first and only credible all-weather guided-missile-armed fighter the Navy could deploy for five and a half critical years. (U.S. Navy via Hal Andrews collection)

The last fleet squadron F3H, refueling probe raised to return the salute, is piped over the side on 21 September 1964 at NAS Miramar. The F4Hs that replaced it are on the flight line in the background. (U.S. Navy via Hal Andrews collection)

Although characterized by George Spangenberg as "not a good fleet airplane," the F3H had by far the greatest carrier-based use of the four big fighters of its generation. It made 44 deployments between 1957 and 1964, with the last one departing VF-161 for its resting place in the Arizona desert in September 1964. Not only was seven years on the front line as long as any Navy jet fighter type had served up to then, it deployed two and half times more than the F4D, six times more than the F7U, and, of course, an infinite number of times more than the F10F. Moreover, the Demon's successes and failures paved the way in McDonnell and the Navy for its successor, the F4H. It was replaced on the remaining Essex-class carriers by the limited all-weather F8U-2N, resulting in two Crusader squadrons in the air group. It was replaced on the bigger carriers by the F4H.

## CHAPTER ELEVEN

*The barricade height was raised from about 12 feet to 21 feet with the deployment of the F7U and other tall jets. The extra height has come in handy in this instance. The aircraft has jumped the barriers (catching its tail hook on one) but is about to be stopped by the barricade. Note that the left breakaway fitting on the upper strap suspension has just released. (U.S. Navy via Tommy H. Thomason collection)*

# CARRIERS EVOLVE

When jets fighters were first becoming operational, there were four basic carrier types in terms of size – Escort, Light, Essex, and Midway:

| | Escort | Light | Essex[1] | Midway |
|---|---|---|---|---|
| Approximate Displacement (tons) | 10,000 | 15,000 | 35,000 | 60,000 |
| Flight Deck (ft) | | | | |
| Length | 500 | 600 | 862 | 924 |
| Width | 80 | 96 | 108 | 113 |
| Speed(kts) | 18 | 32 | 33 | 33 |

There were no jet operations from escort carriers and few from light carriers, the most notable being VF-17's qualifications aboard CVL-48 *Saipan* in FH-1s.[2] The light carriers were small and were being phased out or relegated to other duties.

All had hangar deck heights of 17 feet, 6 inches. The elevators, a constraint with respect to aircraft size, varied in number, location, size, and weight capacity even within a given ship class. Catapults and arresting gear also varied in capacity. The least capable catapult when jets began to operate was the hydraulic-powered H4B. It could give a 13,000-lb aircraft an end speed of 74 knots, to which the wind-over-deck was added. Arresting gear had similar limitations. Early jet fighters were not particularly big or heavy, but their takeoff and landing speeds strained catapult and arresting gear. The jets' high rate of fuel consumption also drained the carriers' fuel-storage capacity more quickly.

New aircraft carriers were being designed to accommodate the big, long-range bombers that provided the Navy's strategic nuclear weapon capability, but the majority would still be Essex-class. On 1 February 1952, the CNO approved an Essex-class modification known as 27C for more powerful arresting gear, higher-performance catapults, and the replacement of the aft centerline elevator with a deck-edge elevator of greater capacity. The accommodation of jets had begun.

One of the first changes to the carrier to accommodate jets (or any tricycle landing gear aircraft like the new F7F Tigercat) was the addition of the Davis barrier as described in Chapter 2. Some barrier stanchions were rigged for jets and some for propeller-driven

*The turn from base leg to entering the groove (short final right behind the ship) on an axial-deck carrier looked like this. (National Archives 80-G-659035)*

*The landing Banshee has just been given the cut. Note the dents in the end of the flight deck from "ramp strikes." (National Archives)*

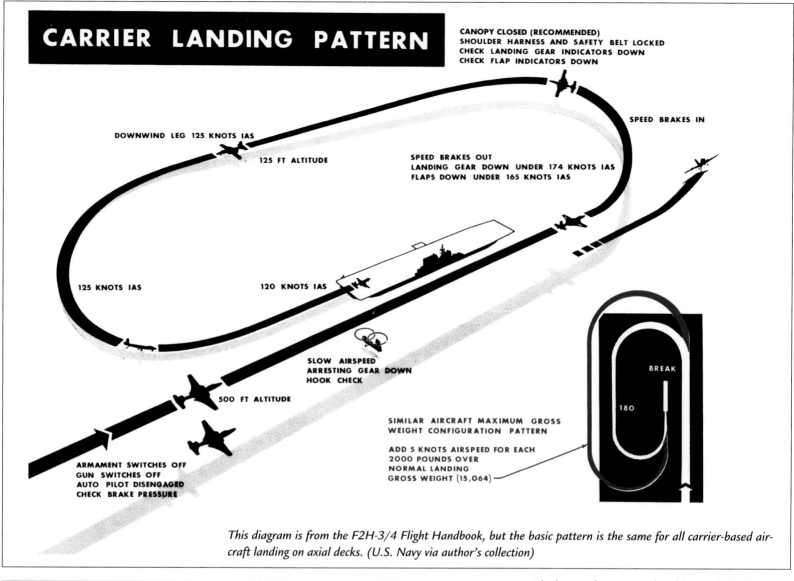

# CARRIER LANDING PATTERN

CANOPY CLOSED (RECOMMENDED)
SHOULDER HARNESS AND SAFETY BELT LOCKED
CHECK LANDING GEAR INDICATORS DOWN
CHECK FLAP INDICATORS DOWN

SPEED BRAKES IN

DOWNWIND LEG 125 KNOTS IAS

125 FT ALTITUDE

SPEED BRAKES OUT
LANDING GEAR DOWN UNDER 174 KNOTS IAS
FLAPS DOWN UNDER 165 KNOTS IAS

125 KNOTS IAS

120 KNOTS IAS

SLOW AIRSPEED
ARRESTING GEAR DOWN
HOOK CHECK

500 FT ALTITUDE

ARMAMENT SWITCHES OFF
GUN SWITCHES OFF
AUTO PILOT DISENGAGED
CHECK BRAKE PRESSURE

SIMILAR AIRCRAFT MAXIMUM GROSS
WEIGHT CONFIGURATION PATTERN

ADD 5 KNOTS AIRSPEED FOR EACH
2000 POUNDS OVER
NORMAL LANDING
GROSS WEIGHT (15,064)

BREAK

180

*This diagram is from the F2H-3/4 Flight Handbook, but the basic pattern is the same for all carrier-based aircraft landing on axial decks. (U.S. Navy via author's collection)*

*The barricade was raised and lowered like the barriers. It therefore was on the deck during operations and subjected to significant wear and tear, as well as being a trip hazard. The protection it afforded to the people and planes forward was more than worth the aggravation. (Robert L. Lawson collection)*

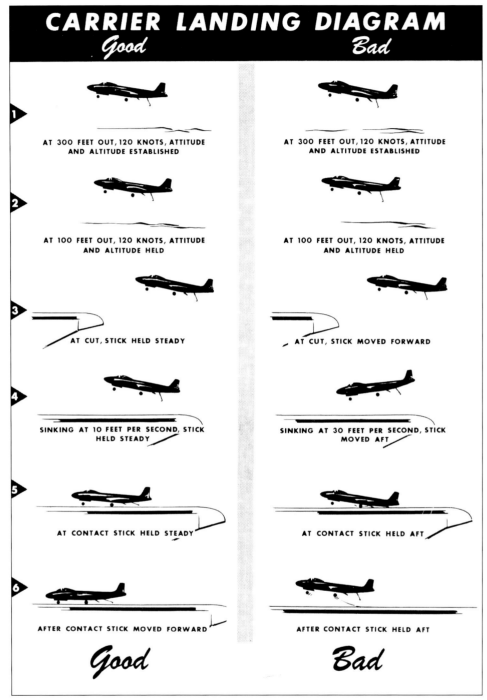

## CARRIER LANDING DIAGRAM
### Good — Bad

**Good**

1. AT 300 FEET OUT, 120 KNOTS, ATTITUDE AND ALTITUDE ESTABLISHED
2. AT 100 FEET OUT, 120 KNOTS, ATTITUDE AND ALTITUDE HELD
3. AT CUT, STICK HELD STEADY
4. SINKING AT 10 FEET PER SECOND, STICK HELD STEADY
5. AT CONTACT STICK HELD STEADY
6. AFTER CONTACT STICK MOVED FORWARD

**Good**

**Bad**

1. AT 300 FEET OUT, 120 KNOTS, ATTITUDE AND ALTITUDE ESTABLISHED
2. AT 100 FEET OUT, 120 KNOTS, ATTITUDE AND ALTITUDE HELD
3. AT CUT, STICK MOVED FORWARD
4. SINKING AT 30 FEET PER SECOND, STICK MOVED AFT
5. AT CONTACT STICK HELD AFT
6. AFTER CONTACT STICK HELD AFT

**Bad**

*The F2H-3/4 Flight Manual depicted both good and bad pitch-control practices following the cut. (As a point of reference, the maximum design sink rate was on the order of 20 feet per second.) However, there were proponents of doing something in between. Also, if, as was often the case, the flight deck began to heave or subside at or following the cut, adlibbing was often resorted to. (U.S. Navy via author's collection)*

aircraft. The Davis barrier system was determined by painful experience in 1949 and early 1950 to be insufficient in some instances. There were incidents where a nose-high attitude resulted in the nose gear not engaging the strap. A nose gear or actuator strap failure sometimes resulted in the barrier being defeated. To everyone's surprise, some landing-gear features could cut the seven-eighths-inch steel cable before it did much retardation. (A second cable was added as part of the fix.) The interaction of the actuator strap and the cable also limited the ability to snag the landing gear to speeds between about 40 and 80 mph. If a jet hit the barrier too fast, the cable was not pulled high enough in time to snag the landing gear. If it went through too slowly, the cable would come up and fall back before the main gear arrived to be snagged.[3]

The solution was the addition, beginning with *Midway* in 1951, of a "retardation barricade" beyond the last barrier. It consisted of a nylon strap running across the deck about 12.5 feet up between two retractable deck edge stanchions with vertical engaging straps about five feet apart running down to another cross-deck strap located on the deck. This webbing was connected to an arresting engine located below the flight deck like the cross-deck pendants and the Davis barriers. Swept-wing aircraft were fitted with little "fences" on the wing leading edge to provide something for the barricade straps to snag on and provide symmetrical loading so the aircraft did not veer off into the island or the port catwalk. With the introduction of the F7U-3, the F3H-2, and the A3D, all of which sat much higher than earlier jets, the barricade height was increased to 21 feet. This had the added benefit of reducing the likelihood that an aircraft would vault it and crash into the pack forward. It also reduced the possibility that the top strap would enter the cockpit if the canopy were slid back for landing and strangle the pilot.

### British Innovations: Steam Catapult/Angled Deck/ Mirror Landing System

The Royal Navy pioneered the major aircraft carrier innovations that significantly increased the safety of operation of jet aircraft and were quickly adopted by the U.S. Navy.

*Although the landing area looked very short on approach and was in fact short, it was not quite as short as it looked. (National Archives 80-G-432532)*

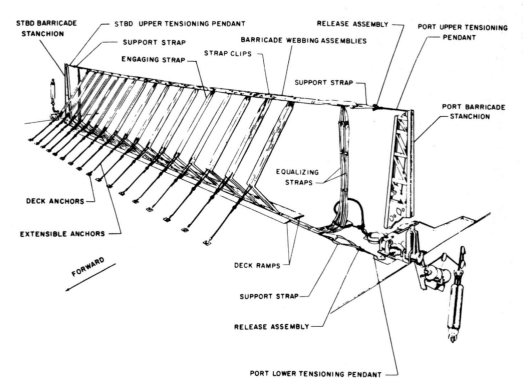

STBD BARRICADE STANCHION

STBD UPPER TENSIONING PENDANT

SUPPORT STRAP

ENGAGING STRAP

BARRICADE WEBBING ASSEMBLIES

STRAP CLIPS

RELEASE ASSEMBLY

PORT UPPER TENSIONING PENDANT

SUPPORT STRAP

PORT BARRICADE STANCHION

DECK ANCHORS

EXTENSIBLE ANCHORS

EQUALIZING STRAPS

FORWARD

DECK RAMPS

SUPPORT STRAP

RELEASE ASSEMBLY

PORT LOWER TENSIONING PENDANT

*The Davis barrier was not effective above or below a certain speed range for a given aircraft or in stopping an aircraft when its main landing gear was retracted or badly damaged. As a result, the barricade was developed as the third and final means of arresting the landing aircraft. It was similar to the Davis barrier in appearance but not in function. (U.S. Navy via author's collection)*

*This F9F-2 hooked the next to last cross deck pendant. In cases like this, the barrier operator had very little time to decide whether to drop his barrier to prevent an unnecessary engagement. (Note that the Panther was traveling so slowly that the cable rose and then fell back before the main landing gear arrived.) There is a second Davis barrier ahead of the Panther. There are also two propeller-aircraft barriers in the picture, one just behind the F9F and the other under its nose wheel. (U.S. Navy via Tommy H. Thomason collection)*

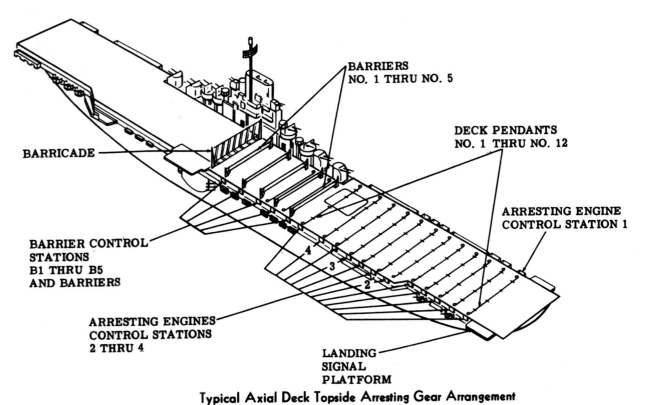

*The defense in depth of the forward portion of a typical axial- deck carrier consisted of cross deck pendants (arresting cables), barriers, and finally the barricade, which was only for jets. (U.S. Navy via author's collection)*

BARRIERS
NO. 1 THRU NO. 5

DECK PENDANTS
NO. 1 THRU NO. 12

BARRICADE

ARRESTING ENGINE
CONTROL STATION 1

BARRIER CONTROL
STATIONS
B1 THRU B5
AND BARRIERS

ARRESTING ENGINES
CONTROL STATIONS
2 THRU 4

LANDING
SIGNAL
PLATFORM

**Typical Axial Deck Topside Arresting Gear Arrangement**

A jet crash into the barrier or the barricade would generally disrupt flight-deck operations only briefly and generally in less time than for a propeller plane crash. It took only a few minutes to replace and rig the barrier and/or barricade. The jet was almost always right-side up, which was not always the case with the propeller plane crashes, so it could be moved right away in the case of a barrier engagement and disentangled later in any event. (U.S. Navy via Tommy H. Thomason collection)

Various additions were made to the jets to minimize problems during a barricade engagement. Small protrusions were added to the wings of swept-wing jets to snag the vertical straps of the barricade and insure that deceleration was early and symmetric: On the F4D and F3H, these looked like little aerodynamic fences on the leading edge of the wing. (Don Hinton) The F11F used simple pegs extending from the leading edge slat. (Don Hinton) Other hardware was installed to keep the vertical straps from causing problems: The F9F-8 was equipped with a deflector on the nose to keep the vertical straps from snagging on the inner 20mm cannon barrels. (Robert L. Lawson collection) The F7U-3 had a set of blades between the nose wheels to cut the vertical strap if it caught there, which might result in a nose-gear collapse. (Don Hinton)

## Catapults

The original aircraft catapults used either compressed air or gunpowder, giving credence to the launch expression, "shot off." Hydraulic catapults were then developed and installed on all carriers. Up until World War II, they were infrequently used because most carrier-based aircraft could easily fly off after a short deck run with the normally available wind-over-deck. During the war, the catapult was sometimes referred to as the "Turkey Shooter," since the big Grumman-designed TBF/TBM torpedo bomber nicknamed the "Turkey" was the heaviest aircraft on board and the one most likely to be catapulted. With 18 knots wind-over-deck, which was all an escort carrier could provide in no-wind conditions, the TBM required a 400-foot deck run and couldn't carry a torpedo even with a reduced fuel load. With the aid of the CVE's catapult, under the same conditions it could take off with a torpedo and full tanks. It was also preferred for night launches because the pilot could not wander off track as he might during a deck run. By the end of World War II, 40 percent of the takeoffs from the Essex-class carriers were catapult-assisted, almost 100 percent from the escort carriers.

The catapults were actuated by a hydraulic accumulator and piston mounted crossways beneath the flight deck. They were connected to the shuttle in the catapult track by a continuous cable not unlike a streetcar's. The cable ran through a series of pulleys that turned it fore and aft and ran it back and forth along the catapult track. One characteristic of the hydraulic catapult was that the initial acceleration of the hydraulic piston was taken up in the slack of the cable system, so there was a "snatch" effect on the aircraft and pilot when the motion got to the shuttle.

Deck runs instead of catapulting were desirable due to the time it took to position an aircraft on the catapult and launch it. However, catapulting became standard procedure for jets. Using two catapults, aircraft could be launched at 25-second intervals, which was an acceptable rate.

As jets began to enter service, higher end speeds were needed and aircraft began to be heavier. The new H-8 catapult met the requirement, but it was close to the upper limit of hydraulic catapult capability and jets were getting heavier. This threatened to restrict jet aircraft to very modest ranges and endurance. The Navy evaluated the German hydrogen peroxide catapult used to launch V-1s and elected instead to develop catapults that used gunpowder in the belief that they were simpler, weighed less, and required less space. Electromagnetic concepts were also considered. In 1948, however, Colin Campbell Mitchell, who had been designing catapults and arresting gear for Brown Brothers in Edinburgh, England, since 1928, began to develop one powered by steam from the ship's main boiler that proved to be the answer.

*The hydraulic catapult machinery was large and mounted across the ship. As a result, the catapults had to be staggered fore and aft with the starboard catapult machinery forward of the one for the port catapult. Note that before afterburning, the deck surface aft of the exhaust was still wood planking. The launching Panther has not yet reached the end of the catapult stroke and the blast deflector is already being lowered so the next jet can be taxiing into position. (National Archives 80-G-448886)*

*The hookup to the catapult also required the attachment of the holdback to a fitting on the bottom of the fuselage. Here two of the catapult crew are lying down waiting for the Banshee to taxi over them so they can attach the holdback to the aircraft. The man on the left has the holdback pendant. The catapult bridle has been hooked around the shuttle and is lying on the deck between the two men, who will attach it to the catapult hooks on the aircraft. (Robert L. Lawson collection)*

*For the steam catapult evaluation aboard Hancock in July 1954, NATC gathered up as many different aircraft as it could, preferably but not necessarily instrumented. Some of them are pictured here – two F7U-3s, an FJ-3, two FJ-2s, and an F3D-2M. (National Archives 80-G-640347)*

A prototype of Mitchell's catapult was installed on the deck of the HMS *Perseus* at Belfast, Northern Ireland. Extensive evaluations were conducted while the ship was tied up to the pier. One of the first observations was that the launch was much smoother with acceleration sustained over the entire stroke. The Campbell catapult also stopped the shuttle in only five feet at the end of the launch stroke, whereas hydraulic catapults required 50. The trials on *Perseus* during 1950-1952, demonstrated that aircraft weighing up to 30,000 lbs could be launched with an end speed of 90 knots, a substantial increase in capability over the H-4 hydraulic catapult.

The steam catapult was demonstrated to the Navy in February 1952. An F9F-2 was flown up to Mustin Field adjacent to the Philadelphia Naval Shipyard and hoisted aboard the anchored *Perseus*. It was then catapulted off with a five-knot tailwind, albeit

at a relatively low gross weight. The demonstration was repeated the next day with two launches in tailwinds with even higher end speeds and then again at sea on 12 February. The most dramatic shot was an F3D that was fired off with a 10-knot tailwind; an H-8 catapult would have required a 30-knot headwind. At that point, the Commander Naval Air Atlantic, Vice Adm. John J. Ballentine, turned to his staff and said, "I want that steam catapult."

Five Brown Brothers steam catapults were procured, one for the Navy's test facility at Philadelphia and two pairs to be installed as soon as possible in Essex/Ticonderoga class carriers. The *Hancock* was selected for the first installation of the C-11 steam catapult because it was already in dry dock for repair and upgrade. It was recommissioned in February 1954, and operational testing of the new catapult, Project Steam, commenced on 1 June off San Diego, California, with the launch of an S2F-1. During the rest of

## Angled Deck

For decades, the layout of the carrier deck was long and narrow as it had been with *Langley*. The aft end of the deck was used for landings and the forward end for takeoffs. The hangar deck wasn't large enough to house all of the aircraft embarked and, in any event, bringing aircraft up for launch or taking them below after landing using the elevators was really too slow to be accomplished to any degree during the process of launches or landings. As a result, at least some of the carrier's aircraft were on the flight deck during takeoff and landings. This pack had to be pulled aft for takeoffs and forward for landing. The barrier/barricade system was almost always effective in preventing a jet from crashing into the pack. However, the aircraft was damaged, sometimes to the point of not being repairable, and flight operations were disrupted while the crash was cleared and the system reset. Occasionally, a pilot managed to evade the barriers and barricade and crash into the pack, with extensive damage to several aircraft and the almost certain likelihood of deaths and injuries. Taking too much care to avoid landing long and crashing into the barrier system increased the likelihood of a ramp strike, which was even worse.

It is hard to believe that it took so long for the benefits of the angled deck to be realized. Apparently, barrier crashes were infrequent enough that they were accepted as a reasonable cost of doing business. One rationalization was that the concept would use up too much deck space and reduce the number of aircraft that could be launched and recovered during high-rate operations. Jets, however, were coming aboard much faster and straining both the limits of deck length previously used for landings and the skill and courage of the pilots. In the early 1950s after the angled deck had been proposed, Capt. Sheldon W. Brown, director, Ships Installation Division, said, "Upon hearing of the angled deck concept, many people have wondered why such a simple idea wasn't adopted long ago. Perhaps the best answer is that a compelling necessity for seeking such a means of relief did not previously exist."

In late 1951, the Royal Navy evaluated the concept, with HMS *Triumph* modified to have a temporary wooden deck extending out from the port side. No arrested landings were made due to the limited structural capability of the addition, but approaches and then touch-and-goes were more than adequate to demonstrate the benefit. They, however, elected to wait for new-build carriers to implement it.

The concept was reviewed with the head of the Flight Test Division, Capt. R. E. Dixon at NATC in September 1951, by Lt. Cdr. Eric "Winkle" Brown, Royal Navy, assigned there on

*Some steam inevitably escaped from the catapult slot. Here a Project Steam aircraft, an F3D-2M from VX-4 laden with four Sparrow I missiles to provide a maximum gross weight challenge for the catapult, is about to be launched. (National Archives 80-G-640341)*

the month, 254 launches were made with every NATC instrumented carrier suitability aircraft that could get to the West Coast and then some.

All subsequent steam catapults were made with design improvements to allow higher pressures and additional length for higher end speeds. These were designated the C-11-1 and the C-7, with the C-11-1 having a stroke of 211 feet and the C-7, 250 feet. The steam catapult dramatically increased the launch capability over the standard H-8 hydraulic catapult:

|  | H-8 | C-11-1 | C-7 |
|---|---|---|---|
| 20,000 lb End Speed (kts) | 104 | 150 | 160 |
| 30,000 lb End Speed (kts) | 89 | 144 | 155 |

After *Hancock, Intrepid* was next to be recommissioned with a steam catapult installation in mid-1954 and *Ticonderoga* followed later that year. Because of their age, only four more Essex/Ticonderoga carriers received steam catapults. *Shangri-La, Lexington,* and *Bon Homme Richard* were modified in 1955 with *Oriskany* following up the rear in 1959.

The pilot of even a relatively easy-to-land Banshee could get into trouble with the flat approach to an axial-deck carrier, as seen here on the Oriskany on 2 March 1954. However, he wasn't even injured, as the cockpit wound up on the flight deck clear of the fire after the ramp strike. (Robert L. Lawson collection)

Antietam was expeditiously modified to evaluate the angled deck concept. An extension was added to the left side of the flight deck up to the outboard edge of the elevator, which was locked up. The arresting wires were repositioned and reduced in number. A crosshatched area was painted on the deck to provide guidance to the pilot as to his position in the landing area. This was subsequently deemed to be unnecessary. (National Archives 80-G-477585)

exchange duty as the Resident British Test Pilot. The advantages were immediately apparent and BuAer authorized an evaluation program. The landing areas of *Wasp*, an Essex-class carrier, and *Midway* were remarked using the deck-edge elevator to provide a touchdown area at an eight-degree angle to the fore and aft axis of the ship. On the *Midway*, a yellow line was painted across the deck 340 feet from the ramp to indicate where takeoff power should be applied if arrestment had not occurred. All barriers and the barricade were removed along with all the arresting wires forward of the first six.

Field landing trials were first accomplished at Patuxent River to include adding power after touchdown to insure that a successful takeoff were possible in the event that the hook missed all the wires. Two test days were devoted to the evaluation, the first on 2 March 1952, with *Wasp,* and the second on 27 May with *Midway.* Twelve NATC pilots and four fleet pilots participated in the trials flying jet fighters and the AD Skyraider. NATC recommended that a fleet carrier be modified with an angled deck for further evaluation.

This was immediately implemented with *Antietam*, having just completed a Korean War deployment in August 1952, designated as the first carrier to receive what the Navy was then calling a canted deck. In an expedited and temporary modification at the Brooklyn Navy Shipyard, New York, the port deck-edge elevator was locked in place and the deck edge extended out to incorporate it into the new landing area, which was angled to port at eight

*The angled deck did not eliminate the occasional need for the barricade to "trap" an airplane that could not make a normal arrested landing. The flight deck crew therefore periodically practices rigging the emergency barricade. In the upper left photo, it is being towed across the deck into position. The deck crew then lays out the barricade and attaches the bottom edge to the flight deck as shown in the upper right photo. Next, the barricade is attached to the stanchions and arresting engine and raised into position. A practiced crew can deploy and raise the barrier in less than two minutes. (Dick Spivey)*

degrees. The existing arresting wires were removed and replaced by six wires aligned with the landing area between 80 to 180 feet from the ramp. A no-engagement area was marked across the deck, 20 feet wide and crosshatched. The modification was completed in December.

During a four-day period in January 1953, NATC pilots evaluated and qualified the angled deck with just about every carrier-based aircraft they had available, including the XFJ-2. Landing intervals as low as 12 seconds were achieved, approximately 10 seconds less than the usual best. The tendency toward a "heavy" landing was greatly reduced since there was no pressure to land or else – average touchdown sink rates were cut in half compared to typical axial-deck landings. Crosswinds due to the ship steaming ahead in low wind conditions were not a problem. Night

landings were less stressful. Simultaneous launches using the catapults on the bow and deck runs off the angled deck were accomplished without any problem.

The ship was then cleared for operations by CVG-8, flying Panthers and Skyraiders. After the initial CVG-8 shakedown that ended in March, the deck was remarked to increase the angle to 10.5 degrees, taper the edges of the landing area so that the visual appearance was more funnel-like, and delete the no-engagement marking. A portion of the air wing was then embarked to seek "heavy weather" to explore the upper sea-state limit on flight operations compared to the axial deck. The final event of the six-month initial evaluation was a cruise to Portsmouth, England, for joint flight operations with the Royal Navy, which took the opportunity to fly on and off with Attackers, Sea Hawks, and

Wyverns. One report stated that 14 aircraft of all types and both nationalities were launched in three minutes and landings were averaging 23 seconds between aircraft, with both takeoffs and landings occurring simultaneously.[4]

During the first six months of *Antietam* operations, more than 4,000 touchdowns were made during both day and night in all kinds of weather with just about every type of carrier-based aircraft available. There were no major accidents and only eight minor ones, none attributable to the angle-deck concept. An article in the December 1953 *BuShips Journal* reported:

> The final detailed report on the evaluation of the canted flight deck installed in USS *Antietam* (CVS-36) reveals that the operational trials have met with a high degree of success. The canted deck aircraft carrier appears to provide the safest, most desirable, and most suitable platform for all types of aircraft – those currently in use as well as those still on the design board – and is superior to the axial flight deck carrier in these respects.

The Royal Navy referred to the concept as the angled deck. For some reason, the U.S. Navy had called it the canted deck, among other things, until the CNO issued OpNav Notice 9020 on 24 February 1955 stating that it would henceforth be referred to as the angled deck and the modifiers "slanted" and "slewed" were not to be used.

Since there was less of a tendency to avoid the barriers, ramp strikes decreased. As long as the pilot had enough fuel for another pass (and the availability of airborne tankers minimized that concern as well), there were fewer hard landings resulting from pushing over to get down. The hook-to-ramp distance using a constant rate of descent approach was more consistent. Since there were no barrier/barricade engagements except when necessitated by an aircraft equipment problem, operating delays to untangle and reset the barriers and/or barricade were rare.

There were other benefits as well. The area added by widening the deck and going to a 10-degree angle made it more practical to launch and recover aircraft at the same time, improving the ability to keep interceptors positioned on the forward catapults.

In order to be able to recover aircraft that were at risk of not being able to make an arrestment, a modified barricade was developed that could be laid out on the deck and erected quickly – this drill was practiced so it could be done in literally a minute when the need arose.

Topside weight on modified carriers increased, somewhat affecting sea-keeping capability. However, removal of the now unnecessary barriers and most of the cross-deck pendants, and more importantly, the heavy arresting machinery for each one, helped compensate.

*From time to time, LSOs either invented or were presented with aids to their ability to judge the acceptability of a landing approach. This late 1948 creation provides an airspeed readout and alignment reference. (National Archives 80-G-416453)*

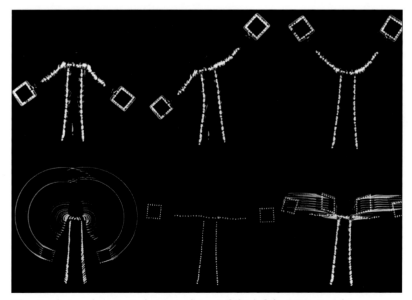

*The simplest and most used approach to visibility of the LSO at night was a combination of a flight suit modified with strings of light bulbs and paddles outlined with light bulbs. (National Archives 80-G-709044)*

Cdr. Robert Dose, on the left, and Cdr A. J. Vescovi of VX-3 examine the prototype installation of a mirror landing system aboard Bennington in August 1955. The horizontal lights provide a reference line for the ball position, which is created from the reflection of a light source mounted aft of the mirror. (National Archives)

The ball is centered in the mirror with respect to the horizontal array of lights, indicating the approaching aircraft is on the glide slope. (Robert L. Lawson collection)

Shangri-La was recommissioned in early 1955 with an angled deck and steam catapults, as was Bennington. Lexington and Bon Homme Richard were next. Hancock sallied forth with an angled deck to go along with its steam catapults in 1956, too late to minimize the damage to the Cutlasses' reputation. Intrepid and Ticonderoga followed in 1957 and Oriskany in 1959. Most of the remaining Essex/Ticonderoga carriers received the angled deck but

not the steam catapult because they were to become Antisubmarine Warfare carriers that would no longer operate high-performance jets.

### Mirror Landing System

There were many attempts to improve the LSO's ability to land aircraft and to be more visible, particularly at night. Jets had made the LSO's job more difficult because of the shorter time to signal corrections and the criticality of the wave-off/cut judgment.

A Royal Navy pilot, Cdr. Nicholas Goodhart, invented the final element in making carrier landings safer, the mirror-landing system. He had been an exchange pilot at Patuxent River during early investigations into quicker feedback to the pilot on his landing approach, necessitated by the higher speed of the jet. He continued to ponder the requirement after he returned to England and developed a solution. According to legend, to demonstrate the concept he stood a stenographer's mirror on edge on a desk and put her lipstick standing on end in front of it. He found that if you kept the reflection of the tip of the lipstick in the center of the mirror while you approached the desk, your eyes stayed on a fixed glide slope leading down to the desk. His paper on the concept resulted in the Royal Aircraft Establishment, Farnborough, being directed to design and build a prototype and evaluate it. The first full-scale mirror made of polished aluminum was ready for shore-based trials in late 1953. It was five and a half feet wide by four feet high, cylindrically concave on a 10-foot radius around the vertical axis. There were four reference lights on each side of the mid-point of the mirror. The light source for the meatball, later shortened to ball, was located 160 feet aft of the mirror. Lt. Cdrs. Donald D. Engen and R. C. MacKnight flew some of the initial evaluations in November 1953, while they were at Farnborough attending the Empire Test Pilot School.

The shore-based trials were cut short when it was recognized that the concept worked as planned and was easy to fly – if the ball was above the row of lights, the aircraft was above the glide slope and vice versa. The mirror was therefore moved to HMS Illustrious for sea trials later that month. These proved equally straightforward with only minor comments about light intensity (poor resolution when the sun was at a low angle behind the ship), possible changes to light colors, etc. The conclusion was that the mirror-landing system and the angled deck provided significantly increased safety

The mirror and exterior light source were soon replaced by a five-cell Fresnel lens array with an internal light source that provided the same approach-angle guidance. The mirror was not useable when the sun was low on the horizon behind the ship, and the very bright exterior light source was a problem for deck personnel at night. The top four cells of the lens projected a yellow light and the bottom one a red light. (Dick Spivey)

At touchdown, the pilot applied full throttle to provide maximum thrust as soon as possible in the event that the tail hook missed all the wires, which meant he had "boltered." If he felt the unmistakable tug of deceleration, then he knew he was aboard and reduced the throttles to idle. It was still a challenging process, but not quite as difficult and certainly not as worrisome as an axial deck landing with the prospect of crashing into the barriers and barricade, or even the parked aircraft forward.

The glide slope was adjustable, with 3.5 degrees being nominal. With 20 knots wind-over-deck and depending on the approach speed, that resulted in a 12- to 13-foot-per-second sink rate or eight to nine mph, more than enough to damage a car bumper but normal for a carrier landing. (The landing gear could sustain almost twice that without damage.)

The number of landing wires was eventually reduced to four. The first one was about 100 to 150 feet from the ramp, with the last of the four only about 120 feet from the first, a very small touchdown area. The hook clearance with the ramp was (and still is) only about 15 feet, assuming the deck is not pitching. The glide slope was set to the aircraft type and wind over deck, targeting the third wire.

In conjunction with the angled deck, an improved "constant run out" arresting-gear control was added to the Mk 5 arresting gear. The system applied only enough load to stop the aircraft in the available distance, as opposed to a fixed setting that had to account for the possibility of a high-speed engagement. This resulted in lower loads on the aircraft and the arresting cable, decreasing the likelihood of structural damage or a cable failure. It required that the arresting gear be set for the landing weight of the aircraft, but this was considered an acceptable increase in workload given the benefits.

In the late 1950s, the visual presentation of the proper glide slope was significantly improved by substituting a stack of five precisely aligned Fresnel lenses for the mirror. The "ball" was now a horizontal strip of light generated by a bulb within the lenses stack with the ball turning red when it was located in the bottom lens, an attention-getter meaning the approaching aircraft was dangerously low. These changes resulted in a smaller unit that was independent of a separately located light source. This allowed the Fresnel Lens Optical Landing System to be stabilized in pitch, roll,

and should become standard as soon as possible. These were followed by trials with an improved mirror aboard *Indomitable* in June 1954.[5]

The first evaluation of the mirror landing aid aboard a U.S. Navy carrier was accomplished in August 1955, with *Bennington,* newly modified with the angled deck. VX-3's Commanding Officer, Cdr. Bob Dosé, made the first at-sea landing in an FJ-3. Lt. Cdr. R. C. MacKnight, flying an F9F-8 Cougar, made the first night landing using the mirror on the third day of the trials – the mirror was far more visible at night than the LSO. Pilots from VX-3 and VC-4 (the all-weather fighter squadron) made 536 landings without incident during the day and night evaluation. VX-3's report was very enthusiastic, "successful beyond expectations," and went so far as to suggest that an LSO was no longer required.[6]

### Final Solution

In November 1955, OpNav directed that all angle-deck carriers would have mirror-landing systems, with procurement in FY 1956 and 1957. Early in 1956, the requirement was extended to all shore stations in the interest of safety and maintaining proficiency in using the mirror. The mirror-landing system in conjunction with angle-of attack-indication was the final major step in allowing supersonic jets to safely operate from aircraft carriers. Instead of a curving approach, a straight-in approach was used. The technique was to fly down the glide slope, maintaining the target angle of attack all the way to touchdown. This minimized landing dispersion and reduced the need for finesse by eliminating the flare. It also provided slightly better visibility over the nose than the flat approach.

and heave, providing a more stable glide slope that was independent of ship motion and making it easier to keep the ball centered. Elimination of the mirror meant elimination of the reflection of the sun when it was low and behind the approaching aircraft, which made the correct ball hard to see. Elimination of the external light source meant that the array could be located off the deck itself and lower, clearing the deck of an obstruction. The external light source had also been a problem for deck personnel during landing operations after dark, adversely affecting night vision.

When the mirror and angled deck were first introduced, it was thought that the Landing Signal Officer would no longer be required. It was soon realized that the LSO was able to see a trend developing in the final approach quicker than the pilot could. Now, the LSO, instead of signaling by arm motions, was talking on the radio to the pilot about corrections needed. He could also signal a mandatory wave-off by flashing the lights on the mirror and making a radio call.

When a barricade arrestment was considered necessary, the LSO also had to command a "cut" by radio, since minimum airspeed on contact with the barricade was desirable. At the cut, the pilot reduced the throttle to idle. The timing of this was critical, since too early meant a ramp strike, and too late meant the possibility that the barricade would not stop the aircraft. The LSO also had to insure that a wave-off, if required, was given early enough to insure that the aircraft would miss the top of the barricade on the missed approach.

## Smile — You're On Camera

Virtually every takeoff and landing was photographed for use if an accident investigation was required. The LSO also graded each approach and landing with detailed comments for review with the pilot. In 1954, VC-3 introduced moving pictures as a means of improving feedback. They set up 16mm movie cameras loaded with gun-camera film cartridges labeled with individual pilot names. The cameras were located on the starboard side aft of the island so that the aircraft, LSO, and deck were all in the picture. The camera was started when the aircraft was at the 90-degree position and kept running until the aircraft was on the

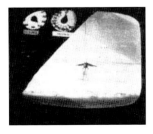

It's difficult to get a good picture off a television, and early television quality wasn't that good to begin with. However, the PLAT video was better than film because it required no processing and was available immediately following a recovery. Note the data board superimposed in the upper left-hand corner and the crosshairs that represented the desired position. (U.S. Navy via Tommy H. Thomason collection)

*Midway in a gale in February 1949 demonstrates how far out of the water her bow could go while heaving and pitching. (National Archives 80-G-399181)*

*What goes up must come down. Note the length and depth of the trough that Midway is traversing. Landing under these conditions would be all but impossible. (National Archives 80-G-399180)*

The initial layout of the super-carrier Forrestal as depicted in this September 1951 sketch was very similar to the canceled United States: no island, four catapults with the two aft canted outboard, and an axial landing area. The aircraft are notional, with the bomber similar to the A3D, and the fighter a ship-based look-alike to the F2Y Sea Dart. (National Archives 80-G-433021)

deck or waved off. The ship's photo lab would develop the film as soon as possible so the pilot and LSO could review it later. This added detail and credibility to the LSO's debriefing and eliminated any discrepancy between the pilot's memory and that of the LSO.

The 16mm gun-camera recording continued to be used for several years, with the camera moving to the mirror when it was implemented. In the early 1960s, a much-improved capability was introduced with PLAT (Pilot/LSO Landing Aid Television). This system consisted of three video cameras: one embedded in the centerline of the angle deck pointed up the glide slope; one on the island, manually operated to follow the aircraft through the landing or wave-off; and one recording a data board showing the date, the time, the wind-over-deck, and the SPN-12 radar reading of the aircraft speed. Any deviation from the correct course and glide path was immediately obvious on the centerline picture. The data board picture was superimposed on the centerline camera picture to provide a single record. PLAT recorded all landings including the radio transmissions from the LSO and the pilot on videotape, which meant it was immediately available for review, and could be paused and shown in slow motion. PLAT was installed in *Coral Sea* in late 1961 and evaluated at sea. It was subsequently made standard.

## Bigger Carriers

The final step in aircraft carrier development was that they got bigger. The smallest carriers from which jets regularly operated were the Essex class, named for the lead ship, CV-9 *Essex*, which was launched in 1942. These displaced about 35,000 tons when loaded. This class of 24 ships was followed by three of the Midway class, which displaced 60,000 tons and were too wide to transit the Panama Canal. The *Midway* was begun in 1943 and launched in 1945, just missing being in the Pacific war, and followed by the *Franklin D. Roosevelt* and the *Coral Sea*.

As built, Forrestal was conventional in layout but huge. The flight deck wasn't much longer than the Midway's, but it was almost twice as wide. The two unfolded AJ Savage bombers aft of the island provide a sense of scale. (National Archives Color Photo Collection)

Forrestal could accommodate 80 to 90 aircraft depending on the type. The notional air wing depicted here was comprised of 16 F3Hs, 32 F8U fighters, 6 F8U photographic, 18 A4Ds, and 12 A3Ds. With the hangar deck packed like this, Forrestal could launch aircraft from three of the four catapults and land a few aircraft if necessary. (National Archives 80-G-667536)

| CVA59 | | |
|---|---|---|
| VFAW | F3H | 16 |
| VF | F8U | 32 |
| VFP | F8U | 6 |
| VA | A4D | 18 |
| VAH | A3D | 12 |
| | | 84 |

Even bigger carriers were desired, in part to accommodate 100,000-lb gross weight aircraft, the projected size necessary to carry a 10,000-lb atomic bomb 2,000 miles and then return. The *United States* was begun in 1949 for this requirement with the approval of the Secretary of Defense, James V. Forrestal. It would have displaced 80,000 tons, twice the weight of the Essex class, and would have been 1,090 feet long. However, Forrestal resigned in ill health, and the incoming Secretary of Defense, Louis Johnson, sided with the majority of his Joint Chiefs of Staff in favor of the new United States Air Force as having the primary responsibility for strategic nuclear weapon delivery. As a result, the *United States* was canceled less than a week after its keel had been laid.

The Korean War revalidated the usefulness of the aircraft carrier and new construction began in July 1952, with the laying of the keel for CVB-59, *Forrestal*, named in honor of the Secretary of the Defense who had approved the *United States*. The *Forrestal* was almost as big as the *United States*. Displacing nearly 80,000 tons and measuring 1,036 feet long, it was the biggest warship in the world. It was the first carrier to be designed specifically for jet aircraft operations (and also built, unlike *United States*). Size was important for several reasons, but one was that it meant an inherent increase in stability. In some important operating areas, like the Formosa Strait or the Norwegian Sea, the Essex-class carriers could safely conduct flight operations only two days out of three on average due to sea conditions. The *Forrestal* would have to suspend flight operations on only about 20 days out of a year.

The *Forrestal* was the first U.S. carrier to be built with the angled deck, although it was not in the original design. The hangar deck had a higher overhead, 25 feet compared to 17.5 feet on the *Midway* class, and the flight deck was 237 feet wide at its most extreme.

*Forrestal* was christened on 11 December 1954 by Mrs. Forrestal and commissioned on 1 October 1955. The first arrested landing was made on 3 January 1956, which was followed by a short shakedown cruise with Air Task Group 181 (ATG-181). The first extended deployment began in January 1957, with CVG-1

It's surprising that the pilot, Eric Brown, and the Royal Navy persevered in flex-deck development after this incident, but they did. Commander Brown was not injured, except for his pride, after his ramp strike and subsequent crash into the deck. (Terry Panopolis collection)

aboard, operating the McDonnell F3H-2N and the Douglas A3D Skywarrior for the first time.

The *Forrestal* was followed by several carriers of the same size, with one, CVAN-65 *Enterprise*, launched in 1961 as the first nuclear-powered aircraft carrier. The benefit to safety as well as the ability to operate in worse sea conditions was soon obvious. In fiscal year 1959, as reported in the September issue of *Naval Aviation News*, the landing accident rate on Forrestal-class carriers was half that of the Essex-class. Moreover, there had been only one fatal accident on the big carriers versus 10 on the small carriers. However, Essex-class carriers remained on the line through March 1976, when *Oriskany* returned from the western Pacific after its last deployment.

*Commander Brown and the Royal Navy continued the development up through and including at-sea trials aboard HMS Warrior in 1948 using the Sea Vampire. Only one arresting wire was used, with the aircraft essentially making a low fly-by. (Terry Panopolis collection)*

*The Royal Navy's flex trials were successful in that the capability was demonstrated. The U.S. Navy not only monitored the trials, but its test pilots also participated in them. (Terry Panopolis collection)*

## Flex Deck

The British made innovative and significant contributions to the safety of aircraft-carrier operations – the angled deck, mirror-landing system, and in-flight refueling – in addition to being the first to fly jets, both straight and swept-wing, from carriers. Not all of their innovations were successful, however, or even a particularly good idea to begin with. In early 1945, for example, they began a project to evaluate operating aircraft with no landing gear from aircraft carriers, being catapult-launched off a trolley and landing on a flexible deck equipped with the usual arresting gear. The concept was that the deletion of landing gear would save on aircraft empty weight and provide more internal volume for fuel.

Takeoff was no problem – a trolley had been standard procedure with seaplanes launched from cruisers and battleships since the days of the biplanes. The German Me 163 rocket fighter, which used one for takeoff. Handling after landing was more problematic – one concept was that the aircraft would be slid down a chute onto a trolley in the hangar deck. The shock-absorption function of the landing gear, particularly necessary when landing on a pitching deck, was to be provided by a flexible landing surface – a rubber carpet that was suspended from shock absorbers or mounted on air-filled bags.

After satisfactory results were obtained from scale-model dynamic tests, drop testing of a weighted airframe onto the landing area, and arrestment of a full-scale airframe (a modified Hotspur glider) that was catapulted onto the landing area, piloted tests using a Vampire were authorized. The carpet configuration now consisted of a rubber sheet supported by rubber tubes inflated to a low pressure. A single arresting wire was used, but it elevated by two feet to make engagement more of a certainty.

An RAF Vampire was fitted with a Sea Vampire landing hook and a beefed-up belly. The first landing, on 29 December 1947, onto the land-based deck was nearly a disaster, as the pilot allowed the aircraft to get too low on short final resulting in the equivalent of a ramp strike but with relatively minimal damage to the aircraft and no injury to the pilot. After the addition of a more observable air-speed indicator and an LSO, the land-based tests resumed with another aircraft in March 1948. No major difficulties were encountered, and at-sea tests were approved using a modified aircraft carrier, HMS *Warrior*.

The at-sea tests commenced in November 1948 and continued through May 1949, during which nine pilots successfully accomplished 200 landings. The flexible-deck concept was proved workable and British experiments with it continued into the mid-1950s. However, operation of a true flexible-deck–configured aircraft, i.e., one with no landing gear, would be restricted to carriers and air

*The U.S. Navy duplicated the Royal Navy's land-based trials using a somewhat modified F9F-7 Cougar. (National Archives)*

bases equipped to accommodate them. The limited benefit far outweighed the investment required in ship- and shore-based facilities and the loss of flexibility in aircraft use.[7]

The U.S. Air Force had a mission requirement that was a little more appropriate for the concept. It wanted to launch a fighter-bomber armed with a nuclear weapon from a truck trailer using a large solid rocket (which they were doing with large jet-propelled missiles like the Martin Matador) so no runway was required. Since a landing gear was not necessary for takeoff, it seemed superfluous to have one for landing, particularly since it was probably a one-way mission anyway. In Project Zelmal (Zero Length Launch and Mat Landing), they modified an F-84G Thunderjet with a tail hook and attach points for a solid rocket. The first landing attempt, in June 1954, went badly with hook skip, an inadvertent flap retraction precluding any chance of flying away, and a crash landing on the far side of the mat. A second pilot in another aircraft made a more or less successful landing on 8 December, but was injured on the second one on 11 December when, in spite of his seat belt and shoulder harness, he was tossed around the cockpit by the wild gyrations of the F-84 after it touched down. As a result, the Air Force kept working on the Zero Length Launch part of the concept, which actually worked quite well, but retained a conventional landing gear.

*NATC's conclusion from the land-based trials was that it would be difficult in most at-sea conditions to make carrier landings with the precision required. There were several other shortcomings, such as expeditious deck handling once aboard. (National Archives)*

The F3D modified with Bell Aerospace's Automatic Carrying Landing System touches down, hands-off, on Antietam in August 1957. The two containers in the foreground house the ship-based avionics and control stations for the system. (National Archives 80-G-1020797)

The U.S. Navy established an independent program but had the good sense to consult with the British and learn from their experience as well as the Air Force's. Unfortunately, the good sense did not extend to a determination that it was impractical before partially redoing the British evaluation program. The strong interest in spite of the obvious shortcomings was the result of a study that projected a 30- to 40-percent reduction in gross weight if an aircraft were redesigned for the same mission without the landing gear. For example, the F3H-1, which was to have a gross weight of 29,650 lbs, would supposedly only weigh 20,150 lbs if full advantage of not having a landing gear were taken in an all-new design. In addition, the resulting fighter would be somewhat smaller, so that 77 aircraft of the all-new design could be accommodated on an Essex-class carrier, as compared to 56 of the original F3H design.

Although both the weight and size reduction seem optimistic, they were accepted as justification to go forward with a proof-of-concept evaluation. BuAer took the possibility seriously, inserting the following into the Outline Specification for the 1953 Day Fighter Competition:

Considerations shall also be given in this arrangement of the airplane to facilitate its redesign to a configuration without undercarriage for operation in a flexible landing mat.

In 1951, BuAer contracted with Grumman to modify two Cougars for the evaluation and with Firestone Tire and Rubber Co. to build a shore-based flex deck. The first Grumman test pilot, Norm Coutant, went to Farnborough and made eight landings on the flex deck there in one of the Vampires. In his opinion, having suffered a sore neck, a successful landing required too much pilot skill and/or luck, so he withdrew from the program. Another Grumman pilot, John Norris, and an NATC pilot, Lt. John Moore, picked up the gauntlet, both making landings onto the Farnborough deck.

In the meantime, Grumman had modified two F9F-7 Cougars for the project, the major change being the addition of a flat false bottom to the fuselage to provide more clearance for the flaps and provide a more stable and level static attitude than the Cougar's existing barrel shape. (They also replaced the Allison engine with the more powerful P&W of the F9F-6.) After considering the Air Force experience, they developed an elaborate restraint system for the pilot's torso and head to keep his mouth from engaging the top of the control stick as the Air Force pilot's had. The flex deck was similar to the British one, being 80 feet wide and 570 feet long, equivalent to the landing area on a carrier. The surface, a series of rubberized fabric mats, was supported by 30-inch-diameter inflated "logs" laid out crosswise to the landing direction. A single arresting cable with an arresting engine was positioned at the beginning of the ramp.

The actual tests were accomplished at Patuxent River beginning in February 1955. Norris made 10 landings without any significant problems to demonstrate the system, followed by 13 landings by NATC test pilots Lt. John Moore and Maj. Ralph Feliton. Two of the landings were made without the protective harness, with no ill effects to the pilot. There was no follow-on at-sea testing, as there were doubts that the shore-based success could be repeated at sea, due to the skill required to land on the stationary deck.

Grumman's Design 113 was a study of the benefits for the Super Tiger if it were redesigned for flex-deck operation and a point-defense mission operating from CVEs modified to have a flex deck. The assessment was that the gross weight of about 22,000 lbs would be reduced by 4,300 lbs: 1,425 lbs of landing gear and associated structure, 1,110 lbs for reducing the size of the aircraft, and 1,775 lbs less fuel. This was not only less than predicted by the F3H study, but also a large portion of the weight reduction resulted from the restatement of the mission, not the elimination of the landing gear.

For more general use in the fleet, nobody was able to justify the operational penalties the concept imposed – a longer interval between landing aircraft, inability to operate from a carrier or an airfield not flex-deck equipped, and incompatibility with conventional carrier-based aircraft. The project was terminated in March 1956.[8]

## All-Weather Carrier Landing System

One obvious answer to making safe landings at night and in poor-visibility conditions was to directly link an aircraft's autopilot to a guidance system, bypassing the need to have a pilot accurately interpret instrument indications, quickly determine what to do with the controls as a result, precisely move them to obtain the desired change, and repeat until touchdown. In 1951, BuShips awarded contracts to both Bell Aircraft and Minneapolis-Honeywell to develop feasibility models of an automatic carrier landing system. The first fully automatic landing using the Bell prototype system was accomplished at Niagara Falls, New York, using a F3D in May 1954. The Skyknight was equipped with a modified Bendix autopilot, a Bell Aerosystems data link, and an auto throttle. The rest of the equipment was to be ship-based – a precision radar that tracked the aircraft and a computer that compared the actual track to the desired one and transmitted corrections to the aircraft's autopilot. Following the successful trials at Bell's facility, the equipment was transferred to the Naval Air Test Center at Patuxent River for installation, formal acceptance, and evaluation. More than 250 automatic field landings were accomplished in the trials that ended in March 1955.

The next step was to account for ship's motion. (When ship-based, the computer would be getting ship-motion data and modifying the corrections sent to the aircraft accordingly.) Bell obtained motion data from various carriers during the latter half of 1955, analyzed it, and in March 1956, submitted a proposal to BuShips to develop a ship-based feasibility demonstrator that was accepted. An improved F3D autopilot was also developed and demonstrated in response to deficiencies noted in the NATC shore-based evaluation. The new system was designated SPN-10.

In January 1957, in a blinding snowstorm at Niagara Falls, Cdr. A. G. Russell was the pilot/passenger of an F3D that made three hands-off landings using the SPN-10. Maximum longitudinal dispersion was 25 feet. The prototype system was accepted for shipboard evaluation in February after additional flights. NATC Carrier Suitability pilot Lt. Cdr. Donald Walker rode through the first carrier landing on *Antietam* in August 1957. All the pilot had to do was fly the aircraft through a "gate" that was four miles behind the ship, 10,000 feet wide, 640 feet deep, and 1,200 feet long. The tracking radar then locked on to the aircraft and the system began to send signals to put it on the final approach course and glide slope. During the last 12 seconds before touchdown, the system introduced ship-motion compensation. At a second or two from touchdown, the autopilot stopped applying corrections and simply maintained pitch and bank. With reasonable sea states, very little dispersion of landing points occurred, with most resulting in hooking the number-three wire as targeted.

There were three modes of operation. ACLS Mode I was hands-off, with the pilot monitoring his instruments, especially attitude, angle of attack, and the needles indicating position relative to glide path and slope. He could take control back at any time and continue the approach or wave-off. In Mode II, the pilot hand flew the aircraft as directed by the cross pointers for glide path and slope. In Mode III, a ship-based controller used the radar information to provide verbal corrections to the pilot with respect to the glide path and slope as in the traditional Ground Controlled Approach (GCA).

A production contract was finally awarded to Bell in March 1960. The first fully automated carrier landing (ACLS Mode I) using the production SPN-10 system was accomplished on 13 June 1963, on *Midway* by a specially equipped Phantom and a similarly modified Crusader flown by NATC pilots.

The next trial, which followed another round of development and improvements, was accomplished aboard *Kitty Hawk* from 23 August to 7 September 1965, using McDonnell F-4Gs that were equipped with a data-link capability. The SPN-10 system was then installed on fleet carriers for operational use.

## TACAN

Navigation was greatly simplified when aircraft carriers began to be equipped with TACAN beginning in the mid-1950s. The pilot of an aircraft equipped with the proper receiver was provided with bearing and slant-range distance to the TACAN station. The bearing was accurate to one-quarter of a degree, and the distance to less than a mile. Depending on altitude, because the signal was line of sight, the receiving range was almost 200 miles. Prior to TACAN, the pilot was provided only with ADF, Automatic Direction Finding, which provided the bearing to the ship or a thunderstorm, whichever was the stronger signal, and no distance information. The other navigation aid was vectors by controllers using the ship's radar.

## Summary

While the carrier changes made a significant and essential contribution to the increased effectiveness and safety of jet operations and permitted the introduction of higher-performance aircraft, they were not in and of themselves sufficient from the standpoint of reducing accidents to a minimum. That would take a parallel effort focused on the pilot and the aircraft.

## CHAPTER TWELVE

*Pilots preferred speed brakes that could be kept extended through touchdown for wave-off responsiveness. The F8U was an exception. This lower fuselage location turned out to be best aerodynamically and for internal volume usage. However, the raised wing provided part of the benefit of a speed brake, which was higher drag on approach that kept the engine in a higher rpm range for quicker response to throttle movement. (Jay Miller collection)*

# SAFETY IMPROVEMENTS

During the time when carrier-based jet fighters were introduced and improved, there were hard-earned lessons that resulted in changes and improvements in both aircraft systems and training. These had a gratifying impact on both the safety and effectiveness of fighter operations.

## Flight Control Assistance

The major innovations in aircraft systems required for safe and effective operation of jets were hydraulic flight controls, stability augmentation, speed brakes, and angle-of-attack display.

### *Hydraulic Flight Controls*

As higher and higher speeds were reached, boosted controls became necessary to handle the loads. This was already the case with the ailerons on the Lockheed P-38 propeller-driven fighter. Even though the need was even greater at jet-fighter speeds, manufacturers were still reluctant to incorporate hydraulic-powered controls because of the weight and complexity. Grumman strove mightily

to avoid them on its F10F, ironically contributing to the program's failure. When the requirement was finally accepted, begrudgingly, it was implemented with a single system backed up by the means to operate the controls without boost in an emergency. Satisfactory handling qualities proved to be hard to achieve with a manual backup. (In the case of the F7U, automatic reversion initially had a fatal flaw.) The initial use of the same hydraulic system for other functions such as operating the landing gear and flaps/slats was also ill-advised. The eventual result was three separate hydraulic control systems, two for the flight controls and one for the so-called utility requirements, i.e., other than flight controls. Single-engine aircraft were also equipped with an extendible airstream-driven turbine to provide a source of hydraulic power in the event of an engine failure.

Simply boosted controls turned out to be unsatisfactory at transonic speeds. The unsteady flow behind the shock wave on the wing resulted in unacceptable control-surface motions being fed back to the pilot through the mechanical control system. It was as if the pilot's arm was a shock absorber on a car going down a rutted road at high speed. Isolation from the feedback was easily accomplished with so-called irreversible controls, where the pilot's input moved a valve on the boost actuator to position the control surface. The actuator held the position within its force capability, but even if it did not, the control-surface movement was not fed back to the pilot. This, of course, eliminated "feel" from the surfaces, a key input to the pilot for precise and safe flight control, so artificial feel systems using airspeed compensation, bob weights, springs, etc., acting on the stick and pedals had to be developed to restore the feedback previously provided by control-surface hinge moments. Until electronics became lighter, less expensive, and more reliable, the creation of ingenious

F8U Ram
Air Turbine

*As a backup to the engine-driven hydraulic pumps (and in some cases generator), an air-stream-driven fan called a Ram Air Turbine could be deployed to provide energy for a standby hydraulic pump and/or emergency generator. The RAT on the Crusader furnished backup electrical and hydraulic power, but the drag reduced range by almost 20 percent, which had to be taken into account when it was deployed. (Vought Heritage Center)*

mechanical devices positioned in series and parallel with the mechanical controls was required.

### Stability Augmentation

The thin air at altitude was good for a jet's performance, up to a point, but it adversely affected the fixed surfaces' ability to provide stability, specifically damping from random upsets in both yaw and pitch. Stability augmentation was first provided in yaw, as higher altitudes revealed the necessity of providing the pilot with an assist. Swept wings made an effective yaw damper even more essential. Pitch stability augmentation soon followed.

Figure 12-1 illustrates the complexity of the F3H pitch-control system. In addition to the usual mechanical control linkage that leads from the pilot's control stick to the stabilator, operating in parallel with it are a bob weight for increasing stick force with *g* level, a stabilator trim, a feel system modified by airspeed, an irreversible boost system, and a viscous damper. The next generation of fighter control systems would increase the electronic content of the stability and control augmentation systems.

The increasing emphasis on all-weather and night operations, not to mention the added workload of operating and interpreting a visual-assist radar, necessitated the addition of an autopilot. An essential feature for single-seat night fighters, autopilots of at least minimal capability became more common with the reduction in the weight of avionics.

### Speed Brakes

It was obvious early on that jet aircraft were not only slow to accelerate but, almost as disconcertingly, they were slow to decelerate. In addition, the jet engine itself was slow to develop thrust if allowed to slow to its idle rpm. The answer was speed brakes, not to be confused with dive brakes used on dive-bombers or the dive-recovery devices being added to some propeller-driven fighters. Speed brakes provided for rapid deceleration when desired. They were also often deployed during the approach for a landing because that required a higher engine rpm for a given airspeed. In the event that the landing had to be rejected, retraction of the speed brakes effectively resulted in an immediate reduction in drag — indistinguishable from an increase in thrust — and the engine acceleration time to maximum power was reduced. A few

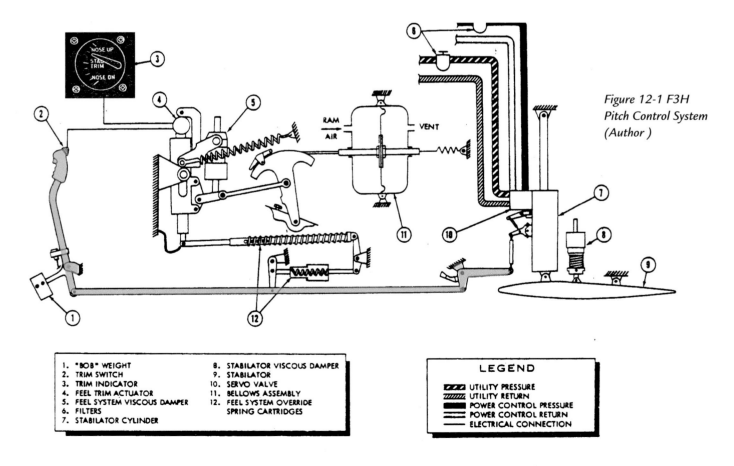

*Figure 12-1 F3H Pitch Control System (Author)*

| LEGEND | |
|---|---|
| 1. "BOB" WEIGHT | 8. STABILATOR VISCOUS DAMPER |
| 2. TRIM SWITCH | 9. STABILATOR |
| 3. TRIM INDICATOR | 10. SERVO VALVE |
| 4. FEEL TRIM ACTUATOR | 11. BELLOWS ASSEMBLY |
| 5. FEEL SYSTEM VISCOUS DAMPER | 12. FEEL SYSTEM OVERRIDE |
| 6. FILTERS | SPRING CARTRIDGES |
| 7. STABILATOR CYLINDER | |

LEGEND

UTILITY PRESSURE
UTILITY RETURN
POWER CONTROL PRESSURE
POWER CONTROL RETURN
ELECTRICAL CONNECTION

aircraft were designed with wing-mounted drag devices. The standard, however, became either belly-mounted or aft fuselage-mounted panels.

Speed-brake effectiveness became an issue on the F7U-1 program because its flight controls were powered by a single hydraulic system with automatic reversion to a manual backup. Since the manual control loads became quite high with increasing speed, pilots insisted on a very quick deceleration capability in the event that the changeover occurred at high speed. The existing speed brakes on the inboard trailing edge of the wings were determined to be inadequate. Another set was therefore added to the fuselage under the engine inlets. These were eliminated on the F7U-3, since it had a dual hydraulic system for the controls.

In February 1952, NATC sent a memo to BuAer complaining that the speed brakes in some aircraft were too small, "considering the tactical significance of this component." They suggested the following requirements:

- Three seconds maximum for full extension or retraction
- One *g* deceleration
- Sixteen seconds, including extension time, to go from maximum level flight speed to minimum fighting speed or best climbing speed, whichever is higher
- Minimum buffet and trim change, particularly nose-down, on extension
- Actuated by a switch on the throttle and variable as to extension angle
- Retractable in the event of the failure of the power source for extension

This suggestion was incorporated in the 1953 Day Fighter specification.

### Angle of Attack Display

One of the basic parameters of flight is the angle of attack of the wing, the angle between the wing and the relative wind. This determines the lift from the wing along with airspeed and significantly, when the aircraft will stall at a given flap/slat configuration, regardless of weight, indicated airspeed, or nose attitude relative to the horizon. It is what the pilot is changing when he moves the control stick forward or aft. It is what the LSO uses to determine whether the aircraft is at the right approach speed, not the rate of closure, which will vary with the wind over deck. In addition to being an accurate indication of stall margin, it can be used to establish other desired flight conditions.

The meaningfulness of angle of attack was well known, but for many years it was not provided to pilots, in part because it was impossible to measure in the propeller slipstream. Instead, the pilot determined the right approach airspeed by estimating the aircraft's weight and remembering or looking up the airspeed for

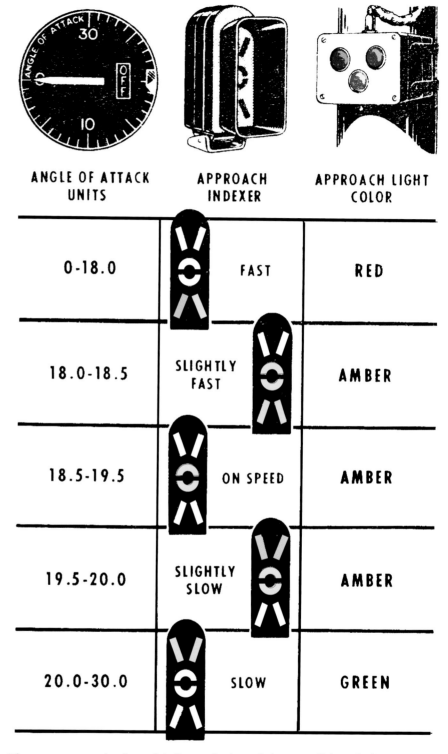

| ANGLE OF ATTACK UNITS | APPROACH INDEXER | APPROACH LIGHT COLOR |
|---|---|---|
| 0-18.0 | FAST | RED |
| 18.0-18.5 | SLIGHTLY FAST | AMBER |
| 18.5-19.5 | ON SPEED | AMBER |
| 19.5-20.0 | SLIGHTLY SLOW | AMBER |
| 20.0-30.0 | SLOW | GREEN |

*There were two angle-of-attack indicators in the cockpit, one a dial marked in units on the instrument panel and the other, an approach indexer mounted on or above the left side of the glare shield. Another set of lights was mounted on the airframe facing forward to provide angle-of-attack indication to the LSO. (Author from F3H Flight Manual)*

that weight. That wasn't so hard for the pilot of a propeller-driven fighter, since fuel was a smaller percentage of the total weight. It was a different story with jets with their much higher fuel capacity and consumption.

An experienced pilot might also know that he was at the right airspeed by the feel of the controls and the response of the aircraft. However, flight-control systems with power boost did not provide as much feel. Finally, carrier approaches were being made on the backside of the power curve, where aft stick to stop a descent will result in increased drag and a greater rate of descent. Thrust response in a propeller-driven aircraft was immediate and would stop the descent; jet-engine thrust lagged throttle application and might not increase quickly enough to stop the descent in time. With jets landing at speeds straining the capacity of the arresting gear, safely maintaining as low an approach speed as possible was critical.

The solution was to provide the jet pilot with an angle-of-attack indicator for more precise control of approach speed. Fortunately, angle of attack was easy to measure in the absence of propwash. In 1950, BuAer contracted to modify equipment originally designed to provide data to fire-control computers for the purpose of providing angle-of-attack indication. The first systems were evaluated at NATC at Patuxent River, VX-3 at NAS Atlantic City, and VMF-122 flying FJ-2 Furies at Cherry Point, North Carolina. Refinements to the indication system followed, and the installation then became standard beginning with all the swept-wing fighters and the F2H-3/4.

Measurement was provided by a small probe mounted on the side of the forward fuselage. It was free to rotate so that it aligned itself with the airstream. That angle was transmitted to the indication system, which consisted of a dial indicator in the cockpit, a small three-light display on the glare shield, and a similar three-light display visible to the LSO. The dial indicated angle of attack in units over a large range of angles of attack. The pilot used the three-light display on approach to maintain the proper angle of attack. The pilot referred to the dial for management of flight performance with the measurement in arbitrary units for a given aircraft. For example, best rate of climb might be 5.5 units, maximum endurance 8.5 units, optimum approach speed 19.2 units, and stall 22.3 units.

The three-light cockpit display

*An indication of angle of attack was also provided to the LSO via three lights located on the nose gear strut, nose gear door, or left wing. It was particularly helpful at night. (Jay Miller collection)*

was similar in format to a stoplight, with a downward-pointing chevron at the top, a circle in the middle, and an upward-pointing chevron at the bottom. If the upper chevron were lit, it meant the angle of attack was too high and that the pilot should push the nose down as indicated by the downward pointed chevron. If only the center circle, also known as the doughnut, were lit, the aircraft was "on speed" at the desired angle of attack for approach. A slightly higher degree of precision was provided by having either the upper or lower chevron light up along with the doughnut to indicate that the aircraft was a little slow or a little fast, respectively, so five conditions of approach angle of attack could be displayed.

The same fast/on speed/slow concept was used to relay the aircraft's approximate angle of attack to the Landing Signal Officer via a set of three lights mounted on the left wing, nose, or nose landing gear. The LSO saw a green light for too slow, a red light for too fast, and an amber light for on-speed. This was superior to the previous method of eyeballing the attitude of the aircraft to determine whether it was flying too fast or too slowly, particularly with jets, since the changes in attitude with speed were smaller than with propeller-driven aircraft. It was even more useful during night operations.

## In-Flight Refueling

One equipment innovation adapted by the Navy for jet aircraft stemmed from the nuclear weapon delivery mission as accomplished by the F2H-2B. First deployed in the early 1950s, it was qualified to carry nuclear weapons on a special rack located on the nacelle under the left engine. The weight and asymmetry of the load meant that it couldn't be catapulted with full fuel. However, at the higher speed of climb and cruise, the additional weight and load asymmetry of full tanks could be easily accommodated.

The probe-and-drogue method of transferring fuel in flight between two aircraft was developed by a British company, Flight Refueling Ltd., which they first demonstrated in April 1949. The U.S. Air Force adapted it to extend the range of its F-84 jet fighters and used it in combat in Korea, with a B-29 as the tanker. The Navy quickly recognized that in-flight refueling provided the ability to not only top off the tanks after takeoff when asymmetric loading at low speeds was no longer an issue, but also to greatly extend the bomber's range by refueling it not only on the way to the target but, hopefully, on its way back. As a result, a -2B was modified to incorporate an in-flight refueling probe installation in the area previously occupied by one of the 20mm cannons.

To demonstrate the capability, a prototype AJ-1 Savage was configured with a refueling package in the bomb bay. To simplify the installation, the jet engine was removed and the hose and

*Initial U.S. Navy in-flight refueling trials were accomplished with a refueling package temporarily installed in the jet-engine compartment of this XAJ Savage beginning in August 1952. (National Archives 80-G-708695)*

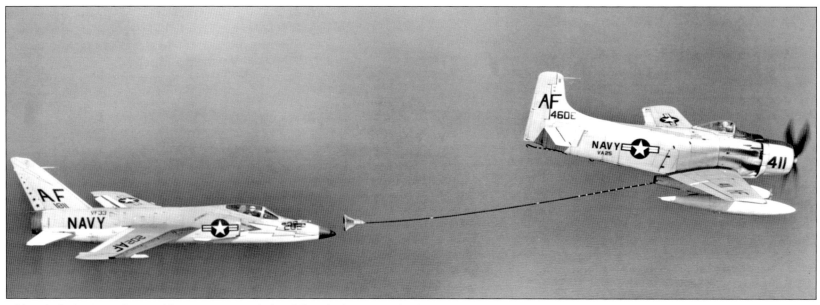

*Although the big jet tankers could give away more fuel and fly at higher airspeeds, the AD Skyraider equipped with the Douglas buddy pod provided more operational flexibility and could loiter efficiently. However, its maximum speed at altitude only marginally overlapped the low-speed capability of the jets. (At 18,000 feet an AD had to be in a slight descent on a hot day to maintain a 200-knot indicated airspeed.) (Hal Andrews collection)*

drogue were routed directly out through the tail-pipe opening. Flight tests began in April 1952, with probe-equipped Panthers and Banshees, and included carrier operations. These successful demonstrations resulted in the decision to purchase tanker kits for the AJs, with the production design having the drogue extend from a refueling package installed in the bomb bay, and add refueling probes to all Banshees assigned to squadrons with a nuclear weapon delivery mission. First flight of the production tanker configuration was accomplished in March 1953. After evaluation by NATC and trials by VX-3, AJ tankers were deployed with car-

*Not to be left out, Vought also created a tanker package, which appears to have been tested in flight. It was a hard-line system as opposed to a hose. This retouched photo shows a tanker with two external tanks, one fitted with a pole and drogue, and a belly tank. The receiver is fitted with the belly pod external tank and is carrying two Mk 7 nuclear weapons. (Vought Heritage Center)*

rier air wings having a nuclear strike capability.

It soon became obvious that in-flight refueling had a much more general application for carrier-based jet operations. Without in-flight refueling capability, maximum landing-weight limits meant that a jet pilot only had enough fuel for a few landing attempts before he had to divert to a shore-based landing, the dis-

tance to which determined the number of attempts that could be made. If the landing area were fouled for too long by a crash or equipment malfunction, or if the carrier could not escape poor visibility conditions, the jets would also be forced to divert or much worse, ditch. The availability of in-flight refueling provided the ability to reset the game clock. In September 1955, the Navy announced that all carrier-based jet aircraft were to have the capability to be refueled while airborne, to include retrofit to almost all aircraft then operational.

The final step was to develop buddy tanks with a self-contained refueling system to allow tactical jets and the propeller-driven AD Skyraider to serve as tankers. Similar in size and shape to an external fuel tank, the Douglas-developed buddy tank or refueling store contained the drogue, hose, powered hose reel, and fuel-transfer pump along with about 300 gallons of jet fuel. A ram air turbine on the nose of the store drove a hydraulic pump that powered the transfer pump and hose reel. Other than requiring the jet pilot to fly more slowly than he might like while refueling, the AD Skyraider was perfect as a tanker. In addition to the fuel in the refueling store on its centerline station, one or both of its 400-gallon drop tanks

There were various responses to the requirement to retrofit all fighters with in-flight refueling capability. The FJ-3's was mounted on the left wing and extended forward ahead of the pilot's eye line. (Robert L. Lawson collection)

The F4D probe installation was simple, having been devised at the squadron level, but it was one of the hardest to use because of the location of the tip. However, it was a handy place to temporarily hang personal equipment. (Robert L. Lawson collection)

could also be filled with jet fuel for a total of 1,100 gallons of give-away fuel at 200 gallons per minute. On its 380 gallons of internal fuel, the AD had an endurance of two hours, permitting it to loiter through a complete carrier launch and recovery cycle. The first AD-6 tanker became operational in 1957.

In-flight refueling minimized the last of the jet's penalties relative to operating from an aircraft carrier. If a pilot couldn't land aboard when planned for whatever reason, the capability now existed to accommodate the delay and reduce the anxiety that can lead to mistakes of judgment and errors in execution. Ed Heinemann of Douglas stated that keeping the first two aircraft out of the water by tanking "roughly paid for the development costs of the entire buddy store program."[1]

## Ejection Seat Development

Fighter pilots had worn parachutes since World War I. However, even before World War II, propeller-driven aircraft were capable of speeds that made avoiding the horizontal stabilizer in a normal bailout over the side an uncertain proposition. Jets were routinely cruising at those speeds and higher. The solution was the ejection seat. When activated by the pilot, the seat was literally fired out of the cockpit by a powder charge large enough to have it clear the vertical fin at high speed.

An English company, Martin-Baker, an early developer of ejection seats, was asked to develop one in 1944 for the first British jet fighters. One of the company's innovations was activation of the seat by pulling down a face curtain located at the

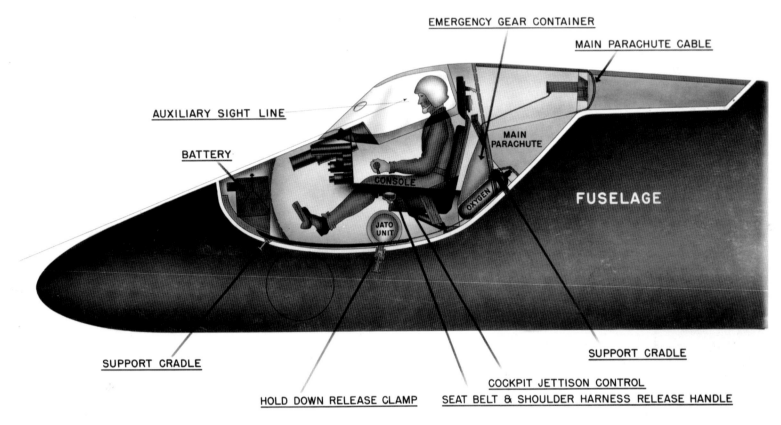

EMERGENCY GEAR CONTAINER

MAIN PARACHUTE CABLE

AUXILIARY SIGHT LINE

MAIN PARACHUTE

BATTERY

CONSOLE

FUSELAGE

OXYGEN

JATO UNIT

SUPPORT CRADLE

SUPPORT CRADLE

HOLD DOWN RELEASE CLAMP

COCKPIT JETTISON CONTROL

SEAT BELT & SHOULDER HARNESS RELEASE HANDLE

*Because of concerns about the survivability of ejection at supersonic speeds and/or high altitude, BuAer accomplished and funded design studies of cockpit capsules that could be jettisoned with the pilot protected from those hazards. This Douglas concept weighed about 1000 lbs including the pilot and was propelled away from the aircraft by a 9,000-lb thrust JATO unit. Ground testing was accomplished in 1951 including high-speed sled tests. (National Archives 80-G-432601)*

top of the headrest. This was believed to result in an orientation of the torso that minimized the risk of spinal injury from the force of the ejection and provided some protection for the face from the windblast on exiting the cockpit.

Over the years, alternatives were proposed to the ejection seat in view of the higher speeds and altitudes being reached. These were generally either encapsulation of the seat and pilot before the ejection or detachment of the portion of the forward fuselage that contained the cockpit. A few of these concepts were developed and installed in U.S. Air Force aircraft. The Navy played an active role in research and evaluation of enclosed escape systems but never procured an aircraft that incorporated one other than a few F-111Bs.

The first Navy fighters did not have an ejection seat, but it soon became a requirement. The Navy's relationship with Martin-Baker dated from its first seat tests. In 1946, the Navy procured a 105-foot-tall test tower and some ejection seats from them for evaluation at the Philadelphia Navy Yard. Although the Navy allowed the manufacturers to furnish the ejection seats in their

*James Martin, later knighted as Sir James, visited the Philadelphia Navy Yard in August 1946 in conjunction with the Navy's initial tests of an ejection seat test tower and ejection seats bought from his company, Martin-Baker. (Martin-Baker)*

aircraft as contractor-furnished equipment for more than a decade, their specification was closely modeled on the Martin-Baker seat philosophy of operation, including the face curtain. However, no U.S. manufacturer chose to buy Martin-Baker seats.

Some pilots were understandably apprehensive about sitting on a seat that had the potential to malfunction and catapult them out of the aircraft. Like a safety on a gun, the first installations were required to have a two-step ejection procedure, partly to insure that the seat could not be fired inadvertently, but also that it would not fire before all the prerequisite actions had taken place. First, a handle was pulled that decompressed the cockpit, repositioned the seat (if necessary), jettisoned the canopy, and armed the seat. Then the Martin-Baker-type face curtain was pulled to fire the seat. Once out of the aircraft, the pilot had to unbuckle his seat belt, kick clear of the seat, and pull his ripcord to open the parachute.

In addition to the test tower, the Navy modified a Douglas JD-1 (B-26) with an aft pseudo cockpit for in-flight tests. Following tower tests with both dummies and live subjects and in-flight ejections of dummies, Lt (jg) A. J. Furteck ejected himself from this aircraft on 30 October 1946, at 250 mph and 5,000 feet over Lakehurst, New Jersey, using a Martin-Baker seat. Testing was subsequently moved to NAS El Centro, California.

The first American use of an ejection seat in an actual emergency occurred in August 1949. Lt. Jack L. Fruin of VF-171 lost control of an F2H-1 after an encounter with icing conditions at 39,000 feet near Walterboro, South Carolina. He successfully ejected at

*Both dummy and live tests were accomplished from the JD test bed. (U.S. Navy via Tommy H. Thomason collection)*

After a decade of allowing its aircraft contractors to provide the ejection seats installed in their designs, the Navy invited Martin-Baker to demonstrate its latest seat at Patuxent River. This was a live test, with Flying Officer Sidney Hughes, Royal Air Force, as the subject. (Grumman Aircraft History Center)

Hughes ejected from the F9F-8T during the takeoff run while the aircraft was still on the ground but had accelerated to 100 knots. Ejection in Navy fighters at the time was discouraged below 500 to 700 feet. (U.S. Navy via Tommy H. Thomason collection)

*The Martin-Baker seat, unlike some installed in Navy fighters at the time, was fully automatic. Other than initiating the ejection by pulling the face curtain, F/O Hughes did nothing until his parachute opened. (U.S. Navy via Tommy H. Thomason collection)*

an estimated speed of 600 knots in the spiral dive that resulted.

One of the early changes to the two-step ejection process was the addition of a handle on the seat headrest that could be pulled to arm the seat in the event that negative *g*-forces precluded pulling the pre-ejection lever or the canopy jettison failed to occur. This allowed the pilot the option of ejecting through the canopy. The next major change was to eliminate the pre-ejection lever and have face curtain actuation jettison the canopy, arm the seat, etc.

The early seats were simply bailout aids and provided little, if any, altitude advantage relative to the standard bailout. Martin-Baker continued to improve its seat, however. In September 1955, it demonstrated a zero-altitude ejection with a live subject from a two-seat Meteor while it was still on the runway during the takeoff roll.

In rough weather with a pitching deck, this landing was too hard for the right main landing gear and resulted in fuel-system damage that caused the engine to flame out. (U.S. Navy via Tommy H. Thomason collection)

The pilot pulled the face curtain as his aircraft went off the angle, ablaze and without power. (U.S. Navy via Tommy H. Thomason collection)

Although his parachute was only beginning to open as he descended below the deck edge, just ahead of the huge splash his fighter made, the pilot was unhurt and rescued a few minutes later. (U.S. Navy via Tommy H. Thomason collection)

One of the several capsule concepts that was studied but not implemented was this one by Vought, Project Oscar for Optimum Survival Containment And Recovery, which involved separating the entire nose of the F8U using shaped charges which minimized the weight penalty of a separate capsule. (Vought Heritage Center)

BuAer maintained a close relationship with Martin-Baker and kept up to date on the capabilities of the company's seats. Martin-Baker's successful demonstration of a ground-level ejection made an impression, promising to significantly reduce fatality rates experienced in crashes on takeoff or landing and ejections at low altitudes. In 1956, BuAer contracted with Grumman to install the latest version of the Martin-Baker seat in the F9F-8T. After a successful demonstration of this capability at Patuxent River in August 1957, BuAer elected to make the Martin-Baker Mk 5 seat, which provided zero-altitude capability at speeds above 100 knots standard in all their fighters, both those in production as well as active aircraft already delivered. The exception was the F11F that had been relegated to training and the Blue Angels. Although 200 seats were bought for the fleet, only two were ever retrofitted.

The goal of "zero-zero" capability, so that a pilot could eject while sitting on the ramp and have his parachute open high enough that he would not be injured on landing, was eventually attained by adding a rocket to the seat. Martin-Baker demonstrated its Mk 7 zero-zero seat design in 1961, with the Navy buying it in 1965.

BuAer and manufacturers continued to explore more protected ejection concepts, but none was implemented. Operationally the high-speed, high-altitude portion of the flight envelope was seldom visited. Supersonic emergencies requiring immediate bailout were far less frequent than those on takeoff and landing. The weight and complexity of the capsule systems simply was not justifiable, particularly if they compromised zero-zero escape performance.

## Safety Programs: Aviation Safety Center/RAGs/NATOPs

In the early 1950s, the Navy's Class A Aviation Mishap rate was more than 50 per 100,000 hours, a horrendous toll and a major crash every 2,000 hours of aircraft flight time. In fiscal year

At convenient points during a carrier's deployment, crash-damaged aircraft that could not be repaired on the ship were off-loaded to make room for replacements. This barge is loaded with three Cougars, an F2H-2P, an F9F-5, and an F2H-3, all from Oriskany's 1953 Air Group 19. The preponderance of Cougars is an indication of the teething problems with carrier-basing swept-wing fighters. (U.S. Navy via Tommy H. Thomason collection)

1953 (June 1952 to July 1953), with the Korean War winding down, Naval aviators destroyed 714 aircraft, almost two a day. There were 2,229 major accidents, which meant about one out of every six of the Navy's aircraft suffered major damage that year. Many pilots went down with the ship, with more than one in 10 accidents being fatal. The Air Force was also experiencing an increasing accident rate.

The Air Force took a major, high-level, and draconian approach to stem the rising tide of accidents. In 1953, it formed a Directorate of Flight Safety Research staffed with 525 officers, civilians, and enlisted personnel, headed by a major general who reported to the Inspector General of the Air Force. This directorate instituted professional, and even more importantly, independent aircraft accident investigation and took disciplinary action when culpability could be assigned. Major commands adapted something close to a no-excuses policy when an accident occurred. Gen. Curtis LeMay, for one, became well known for his off-with-their-heads approach when one of his Strategic Air Command bombers was lost or seriously damaged. The U.S. Air Force accident rate declined.

The Navy had taken action earlier but less enthusiastically. The Naval Aviation Safety Office was formed in December 1951, reporting to the Deputy Chief of Naval Operations, but it was initially headed by a commander (equivalent to a lieutenant colonel in the Air Force) and staffed by only 25 officers, civilians, and enlisted men. By contrast, that many officers in the Air Force Flight Safety Directorate were senior to the rank of Navy commander alone. The Navy's office was also located in Norfolk, Virginia, not Washington, D.C., which further reduced its perceived importance.

Fortunately, a captain was in charge of the Navy office in 1953, and he was James F. "Jimmy" Flatley, a fighter pilot's fighter pilot. He noted, "The U.S. Air Force may have gone overboard in its aviation safety program, but it is increasingly obvious that Naval Aviation hasn't even gotten its feet wet." In September, he submitted a report, "Review of Naval Aviation Accident Prevention Methods," to the Chief of Naval Operations that contained both blunt criticism and well thought-out recommendations. The Flatley Report, as it became known, resulted in organization and process changes. The Safety Office itself was beefed up, specifically with new sections or departments for Analysis and Research, Accident Investigation, and Aviation Safety Literature. A computer was installed for record keeping and analysis. The Accident Investigation section included four accident investigators who were to become graduates of the University of Southern California's Aviation Safety School and provided special ID cards signed by the Deputy Chief of Naval Operations (Air), which gave them access to an accident investigation in a fleet command or squadron. The Aviation Safety Literature department began to pro-

duce *Approach* magazine, a monthly periodical that featured summaries and discussion of aircraft accidents.

Further, the Chief of Naval Operations began to insist on increased attention to accident avoidance through training and analysis. Major commands were encouraged to send representatives to the University of Southern California's safety school. Within squadrons, the Safety Officer was to be a senior officer, not the most junior. Flatley's successor, Capt. J. W. "Wes" Bing convinced the CNO to elevate the importance of the Navy's safety organization by designating him the director of the Naval Aviation Safety Center.

Another action was the formation of Cougar College at VC-3. Jets, axial-deck carriers, and a large influx of pilots needed by the Korean War had proved to be a recipe for a higher accident rate. The Navy's first swept-wing jet, the F9F-6 Cougar, was not helping matters. VC-3 was the West Coast squadron that provided night fighter and intruder detachments to deploying air groups. As such, they were big, operated different aircraft, and were in permanent residence at Moffett Field, California. In early 1954, ComNavAirPac, Vice Admiral Martin, directed that VC-3 establish a Transitional Training Unit with the mission of familiarizing four senior pilots from each squadron transitioning to a new type of aircraft and some of its maintenance personnel with the new aircraft. In addition to the Cougar and the new FJ-3, VC-3 was to take personnel from the Project Cutlass

*This is an early version of the NATOPS manual before they were published with blue plastic covers and became known as the Big Blue Sleeping Pill.*
*(U.S. Navy via author's collection)*

group and set up an F7U-3 familiarization program. Soon to follow at VC-3 would be the F3H Demon, beginning with two aircraft arriving in April 1956. The F4D Skyray would be next. While this was far better than the previously employed casual and informal approach, it was still inadequate from the standpoint of safety. Only a cadre of pilots was trained, with the majority of pilots in a squadron being trained on the job, as it were.[2]

One example of the lack of connectivity between NATC/BuAer, contractors, and the East- and West-Coast fleets was the dissemination of information about the F7U "post stall gyration" problem and recovery technique. In January 1955, a VC-3 student had to eject after losing control of his Cutlass and not being able to recover. Within days, one of the VC-3 instructors, repeating the maneuver that the student had attempted, had also been unable to recover and had to eject. Information about the problem, much less the action to be taken, not only hadn't been developed and promulgated, but the VC-3 instructor also apparently didn't even bother to inquire as to whether Vought, BuAer, or NATC knew something about it before engaging in their own incipient spintest program.

The accident rate in 1956 reflected the introduction of an increasing number of swept-wing aircraft. The situation resulted in an expansion and assignment of shore-based training squadrons to an air group on each coast dedicated to training Naval aviators in the aircraft type and mission that they were to be assigned in the fleet. These two Replacement Air Groups (RAGs) were established in 1958. For example, on the West Coast, VF(AW)-3 (the former VC-3), which already had a jet transition responsibility, became VF-124, operating various models of the F8U Crusader, as part of Replacement Air Group 12 at NAS Miramar, California. VF-121 was a sister squadron, operating the F3H Demon. An instrument training squadron with two-seat aircraft was also assigned. (Some of the RAG squadrons were operated from bases other than Miramar, being collocated with the fleet squadrons with a similar mission.) Specialized training units like Fleet All Weather and Fleet Air Gunnery were absorbed in the RAG organization.[3]

RAG training was intensive and thorough, including in-depth understanding of the aircraft's systems, emergency procedures, and tactical use. Flight training included familiarization, instrument proficiency, mission tactics, weapons indoctrination and actual live fire, night flying, and both day and night carrier-landing qualifications. The curriculum was expanded to about 20 weeks compared to Cougar College's six weeks, and all pilots went through the course, not just the squadron leadership. The result was a standardization of procedures, at least on a coast-wise basis, and no training activity was required of the fleet squadron itself. The new guy arriving at a squadron was knowledgeable about his aircraft and mission and theoretically ready for combat operations, if not particularly experienced.[4]

The final step in safety improvement was NATOPS, Naval Air Training and Operating Procedures Standardization. Early in 1961, Vice Admiral Robert Pirie, DCNO (Air) was observing A4D carrier qualifications and observed that some pilots had the speed brakes open on approach and some did not. When he asked why, he was told that it depended on whether the pilot had been to the A4D RAG on the East or West Coast. After much debate and discussion, OpNav declared that they would coordinate reconciliation and standardization of East- and West-Coast procedures via the NATOPS program. The most obvious output was a NATOPS manual of standard operation procedures and flight instructions for each naval aircraft type, the first being produced for the Sikorsky HSS-1 (later SH-34) antisubmarine warfare helicopter and distributed in July 1961. In December 1963, the first manual that consolidated flight and operating instructions in one book was issued for the Grumman TF-9J (previously F9F-8T), insuring that newly designated Naval aviators got an early introduction to NATOPS.

The NATOPS manual itself was not very different in content from previous flight manuals. The program's main contribution to safety was that it used the manual issued by OpNav as the focal point for training, both initial and periodic refreshment, and as an imperative for safe operation: "Compliance with the stipulated manual procedure is mandatory except as authorized herein." Because of concerns that NATOPS would stifle innovation, the standard Letter of Promulgation contained in each manual stated:

> Commanding Officers of aviation units are obligated and authorized to modify procedures contained herein, in accordance with the waiver provisions established by OPNAVINST 3510.9 series, for the purpose of assessing new ideas prior to initiating recommendations for permanent changes.

The emphasis on and enforcement of NATOPS was the main feature critical to its success. Annual standardization checks with written examinations and performance demonstrations on the ground and in the air were now required. The use of flight simulators for evaluation of a pilot's knowledge of aircraft systems and emergency procedures was emphasized. Each squadron was to have a NATOPS Standardization Instructor. Standardization Evaluators for each model aircraft and a Standardization Coordinator were assigned to each major aviation command.[5]

## Summary

As a result of innovation and continuous improvement of the aircraft carrier, aircraft systems, and operating procedures, as well as Navy leadership emphasis on training, standardization, and safety, the introduction of even bigger, more complex, and faster jet aircraft was made feasible and the major accident rate declined significantly.

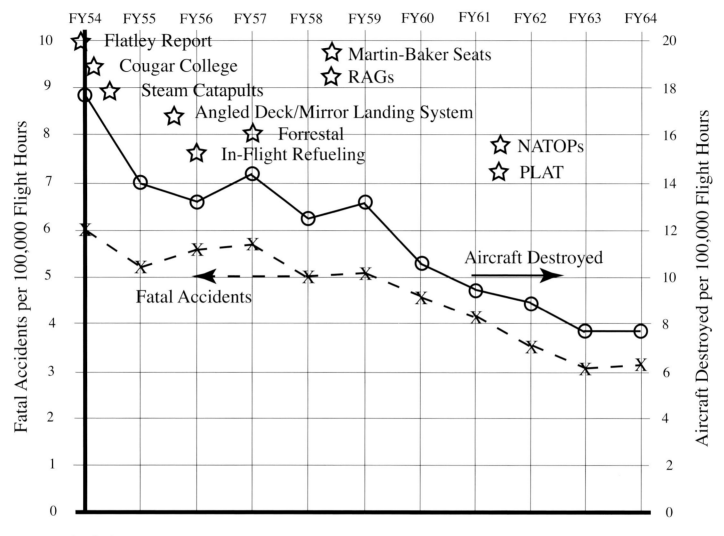

Figure 12-2 (Author)

In 1954, the accident rate had been 35 per 10,000 landings. By the end of 1957, the angled deck and the mirror-landing system, in conjunction with the other changes that had been made, had helped reduce the landing accident rate to 9 per 10,000.

By fiscal year 1964, the accident rate was down from more than 50 in fiscal year 1954 to 14 per 100,000 flight hours. Unfortunately, while there were fewer accidents, a greater percentage of them resulted in destroyed aircraft and fatalities. This was, in part, a reflection of the introduction of the higher-performance aircraft. In 1964, the Crusader represented only six percent of the total hours flown but was involved in 17 percent of the accidents – and that was one of its good years! However, as shown in Figure 12-2, the rate of both fatal accidents and aircraft destroyed was still cut in half between FY 1954 and FY 1964.

Without all that effort, it would have been a lot worse. And it continued to get better over time.

## CHAPTER THIRTEEN

*The area rule was seldom as beautifully and completely rendered as it was on the F11F. (National Archives 80-G-682572)*

# REALLY SUPERSONIC

In the early 1950s, each of the five companies that were developing and building jet fighters for the Navy was eager for a follow-on fighter program and each chose, or was chosen, to take a different path toward that end with varying degrees of success. The next step was true supersonic flight capability. At that time, most swept-wing fighters still had to dive to go supersonic. The F9F-6 Cougar was the Navy's first operational fighter capable of safely breaking the sound barrier, but only in a vertical dive started from 45,000 feet at full power. Some of the first fighters with afterburning engines still needed to unload (push over to reduce the drag due to lift) and even dive to be supersonic.

In one of the great aerodynamic eureka moments, the concept of area rule to reduce transonic drag became apparent to NACA's Richard Whitcomb in late 1951.[1] He proved its benefit in wind-tunnel tests and conveyed the data to aircraft manufacturers in September 1952. The principle was that lower transonic drag could be achieved by having the total cross-section area of the aircraft – including the wings, canopy, and empennage – increase and decrease smoothly. Up until then, the cross-section area usually changed somewhat abruptly where the wing met the fuselage, as well as where there were canopies, engine inlets, etc. The change was less abrupt on swept-wing aircraft, and that is one of the aerodynamic benefits that enabled them to fly closer to and even exceed the speed of sound. An application of area rule was most obvious when the cross section of the fuselage was reduced at the wing root. The results were very gratifying, with no dive required to slip through the sound barrier with afterburning engines.

In 1952, there were several engines powerful enough for a single-engine fighter. Of those with the better thrust-to-weight ratios, the smallest was the Wright J65, and the most powerful was the Pratt & Whitney J57, with the General Electric J79 being in between:

|  | J65-W-6 | J79-GE-2 | J57-P-8 |
|---|---|---|---|
| Thrust in Afterburner (lbs) | 11,000 | 14,350 | 16,000 |
| Military Thrust Sea Level (lbs) | 7,600 | 9,300 | 10,200 |
| Empty Weight (lbs) | 4,000 | 3,700 | 5,180 |
| Weight – engine plus Fuel system plus fuel[2] | 9,360 | 10,550 | 12,650 |

If one assumed that addition of afterburning would be straightforward, the J65 was the most mature engine of the three, being derived from the Armstrong-Siddeley Sapphire. It had been flying since November 1951, in the Gloster Javelin and had been selected to power the Hawker Hunter and the English Electric Lightning. Wright purchased a license for the Sapphire in 1950 to supply engines for the Republic F-84F Thunderstreak, the swept-wing derivative of the Thunderjet. The first production F-84F flew in November 1952, and production quickly built to a high rate. The J65 was also selected to power the FJ-3, the prototype flying in July 1953, and the A4D, which was to fly in June 1954. However, it had yet to be run with an afterburner.

The least mature but the most promising was the J79. It was not scheduled for its 50-hour test until mid-1955, or the 150-hour qualification test until late 1956. In 1952, it had not yet been run on a test stand. Moreover, its performance depended on the successful development of an untried axial-flow compressor feature. The angle of flow redirection provided by the stators had been fixed in engine designs up until that point, positioned at an angle to provide adequate margin from compressor stall during engine acceleration, not maximum compressor efficiency. GE's legendary Gerhard Neumann led the team that designed mechanization of the first six rows of stators in the J79's 17-stage compressor so that their angle could be optimized for different airflow conditions. Because of the lack of test experience, it was not on the Navy list of approved engines for the 1953 Day Fighter Competition.

## Air Force Supersonic Fighter Program Summaries

After fielding the F-86 and its derivatives and the F-84F, the Air Force did not have any success developing new swept-wing aircraft for operational service until its Century Series.

|  | F-100 | F-101 | F-102 | F-104 |
|---|---|---|---|---|
| Manufacturer | North American | McDonnell | Convair | Lockheed |
| Predecessor |  |  | F-88 | F-92 |
| Engine | J57 | 2xJ57 | J57 | J79 |
| Contract | 11/51 | 11/51 | 9/51 | 3/53 |
| First Flight | 5/53 | 9/54 | 10/53 | 3/54 (J65) |
| In Service | 1954 | 1957 | 1956 | 1958 |

*The first four U.S. Air Force Century Series fighters were all present for this 1957 photo opportunity. The lead is the F-100, the slot is the F-101, and left wing and right wing are the F-104 and the F-102, respectively. Note the mix of wing planforms and number of engines. (National Archives 199549)*

The F-100 was the first fighter to be capable of supersonic speed in level flight, and it did so during its first flight in May 1953. With the F-100 and the F-102, the Air Force maintained a very slight lead in operational fighter performance through 1957, when the first F11F and F8U squadrons stood up.

It is noteworthy that the Air Force also spread the development of its first four Century Series fighters among four manufacturers, and two of the four were preceded by a similar design that was not accepted for production. All were troubled by problems during development, and initial operation required substantial design changes. However, the Air Force-developed J57 and J79 engines proved to be critical to the success of Navy fighter programs.

### Navy 1953 Fighter Programs Summary

BuAer issued contracts for four fighter programs in 1953, only one the result of a formal competition. Two, the F9F-9/F11F and the FJ-4, were to be powered by the J65, and two, the F8U and F5D, by the more powerful J57.

The two smaller fighters were the result of one of the periodic backlashes against the trend toward bigger, more complicated, less maneuverable fighters and a campaign to field a smaller, simpler, more maneuverable one. Small meant more could be parked on the limited deck space of an aircraft carrier. Simple meant no search radar. Small and simple meant inexpensive so many more could be bought. Cost is usually the justification, but the archetypical fighter pilot wants to fly a dogfighter, a very agile fighter

with only one engine and minimal avionics that is light in weight relative to thrust. The F8F-1 Bearcat is an example — the smallest airframe that could be wrapped around an R-2800 engine and control its torque.

Cdr. Pete Aurand, who had introduced the FJ-1 into service and was the BuAer project manager of the FJ-2 and FJ-3 programs, was an advocate of simplicity and the importance of maneuverability at altitude. More controversially, he thought that subsonic performance was adequate for a day fighter – specifying that Mach 1 as the maximum speed at 35,000 feet avoided the complexity, empty weight, and fuel consumption penalties of the afterburner, which was carrying small and simple to an extreme.

The first two day-fighter programs begun by BuAer in 1953, the F9F-9/F11F and FJ-4, were done so without benefit of a formal competition, which meant that the new fighters could be in the fleet sooner. The two contractors of the day fighters then in production, Grumman and North American, were happy to oblige.

Douglas was also the beneficiary of this practice, receiving a contract for the F4D-2, which became the F5D. In this instance, the designation change did not result from a change of the engine but a redesign of the airframe, which had been literally holding the Skyray back from supersonic speeds in level flight.

Vought was the winner of the formal competition. That left only McDonnell standing when the music stopped in 1953.

### Grumman F9F-9/F11F

Grumman provided the Navy with a brochure proposal for its Design 98, the antithesis of its humongous XF10F, in late 1951. It was originally referred to as the Sapphire Cougar because it was ostensibly an F9F-6 derivative to be powered by that British engine. In April 1953, by all accounts and to the relief of both Grumman and BuAer, the XF10F program was terminated, and Grumman got a contract modification to develop its Design 98 using funds from the Cougar production program. In keeping with the convenience of contracting for a major change as if it were a minor one, the new aircraft was initially designated F9F-8. This was almost immediately changed to F9F-9 when the Navy decided to buy a derivative of the Cougar with a modified wing and wing fillet for which the F9F-8 designation was more appropriate. In recognition of the difference with its predecessor, however, the Model 98 was given a new name, "Tiger." The subterfuge, if there was any, was eventually dropped and the Tiger was re-designated F11F in April 1955.

The Tiger appears to have been an overreaction to the F10F experience by both Grumman and the leadership of the fighter-design group in BuAer at the time. Like its previous growth-trend breaker, the F8F Bearcat, it was to have a short operational career. It could have been worse – the original intent was that it not have

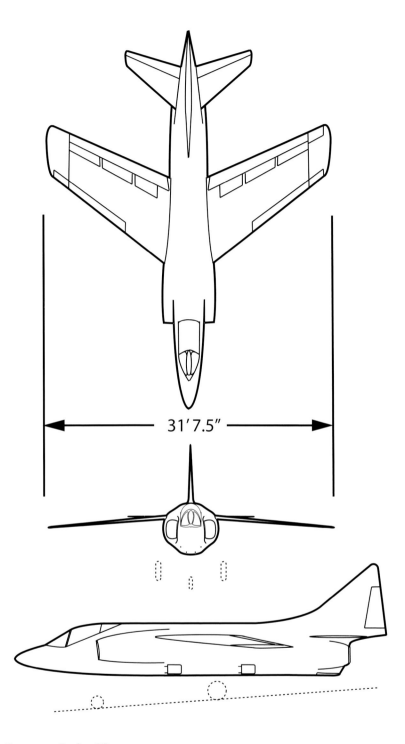

*Grumman Design 98*
*December 1951*
*The Grumman F11F began as a derivative of the F9F-6/7 with a new shape and a new engine. It was briefly designated F9F-8 and then F9F-9. To be fair, the shape of the vertical fin and far aft fuselage are Cougar-like. Then that too was changed. (Author)*

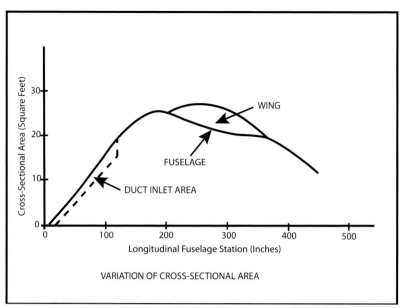

*Figure 13-1 (Author)*

an afterburner like the other "simple" day fighter, North American's FJ-4, which the Navy initiated about the same time, also using funds from an existing production contract. That might have resulted in the Tiger having no career as a Navy fighter at all.

Except for the vertical fin, the fin and the tailpipe interface, and roll-control system, the first iteration of Design 98 already bore no resemblance to the Cougar. It was a much bigger change than the Cougar was from the Panther, not even resembling the Cougar in a dim light. Gone, in order to minimize transonic drag, were the Cougar's barrel fuselage, the prominent wing-to-fuselage fairings, and thick wing. In their place were an area-ruled fuselage and a much thinner wing. The troublesome stabilizer was lowered and subsequently lowered even more. The portly centrifugal-flow J42 was replaced by the sleek axial-flow Wright J65. As Grumman engineers refined the configuration and incorporated an afterburner, even the aft fuselage resemblance to the Cougar disappeared.

Grumman engineers seem to have independently and empirically recognized the benefit of area ruling about the time Whitcomb did, a year before he published his report. A Design 98 General Arrangement drawing dated 11 December 1951 clearly depicts a pinched-in fuselage. The Design 98 sales brochure includes an illustration (See Figure 13-1) that depicts and promotes the smooth buildup of cross-sectional area for reduced transonic drag.

The selection of the J65 undoubtedly seemed like a good idea at the time. Unfortunately, the development of an afterburner for the first time proved difficult for Wright. Not only did Grumman have to accomplish the first flight of the F9F-9, in July 1954, without one, but also it was not to fly with one until January 1955.

*If they hadn't before, all mockup reviews now included a demonstration of cockpit visibility on final approach, however simple in presentation. (Grumman Aircraft History Center)*

G-42112

investigation into the cause of George Welch's fatal crash in an F-100. The typical supersonic fighter configuration of a long fuselage combined with small wings and a small vertical tail was susceptible to inertia coupling in rolling maneuvers. That led to a loss of control and subsequent structural overload. As a result, the Tiger's vertical fin and rudder were increased in size, and the buildup in the rate of transonic and supersonic rolls was carefully accomplished so that the risk of catastrophic onset of inertial coupling was minimized.

Only 201 F11Fs were built, including the prototypes and the two converted to the J79-powered F11F-1F configuration. The first 44 were so-called short-nose Tigers, most completed with an in-flight refueling probe built into the tip of the nose. None was ever deployed. For the second production lot of 157 aircraft, the nose was enlarged to accommodate the installation of visual-assist radar, the APS-50, and the refueling probe relocated to a retracted position on the right side of the nose. The radar, however, was never fitted. In keeping with the lightweight philosophy, the F11F initially had only one pylon on each wing for external stores. A redesigned wing was subsequently qualified that had provisions for four pylons.

(Four more Tigers were to make first flights without afterburners.) What was worse, on the first test flight with the afterburner, before it failed almost catastrophically, it was apparent that the thrust improvement was disappointing. The shortfall in J65 schedule and thrust (it was finally rated at 10,500 lbs instead of 11,000) was part of the reason that Grumman was unable to capitalize on the schedule advantage it had over Vought.

The basic engine was also not as reliable as Grumman had supposed, based on its maturity. The first Tiger was lost on 19 October 1954, at the start of its first Naval Preliminary Evaluation when the engine flamed out in flight. The Navy pilot was forced to belly it in short of Grumman's field when he could not get it restarted. The number-four aircraft was lost at Edwards AFB, in April 1956, due to an engine accessory driveshaft failure. The Grumman pilot ejected successfully.

Although the Tiger's handling qualities were good to excellent from the first flight onward, airframe changes proved to be required, some in pursuit of more speed since the guarantee was not being met. To reduce drag, the aft fuselage was reshaped and the nose extended. One potential disaster was averted by the

At-sea carrier suitability tests were successfully accomplished from *Forrestal* in April 1956. The scheduled BIS and FIP trials were postponed, however, because the Tiger did not have the endurance needed for the requisite 90-minute cycle time.[3] Grumman had to add more internal fuel capacity, which was accomplished by putting tanks in the tail fin and the space between the inlet ducts and fuselage skin, allowing BIS trials to begin in November and FIP, in early 1957. As a result, VX-3 did not receive Tigers for initial operational evaluation until February 1957, a few months after they had begun flying the F8U, and the same month that VF-32 received its first Crusaders to prepare for operational deployment.

*The last vestige of resemblance to the F9F Cougar had disappeared by first flight except for the wing fences. (Grumman Aircraft History Center)*

*Grumman became so enthusiastic about the area rule that it created area-ruled external tanks, with what might be tiger teeth on the Tiger tanks. This is an early aircraft with the in-flight refueling probe in the extreme nose. It has also been involved in gun-firing tests as evidenced by the powder marks. (Grumman Aircraft History Center)*

The first fleet squadron to get F11Fs was VA-156 on the West Coast, functioning as a fighter squadron within Air Group 15 in spite of its attack designation. Some of the squadron's pilots and mechanics had participated in the FIP program. They deployed on *Shangri-La* from May to November 1958 and were designated VF-111 in January 1959. Only four more West-Coast fleet squadrons were to be equipped with the F11F, and only two of them made extended deployments – of the other two, one was the F11F training squadron and the other transitioned to the F4D after less than a year of Tiger operation.

The first East-Coast squadron, VF-21, took delivery of F11Fs beginning in June 1957. They were to make only short deploy-ments on shakedown cruises before they became the East-Coast training squadron for the F11F. However, VF-33 was the only other East-Coast fleet squadron to receive Tigers. They deployed twice aboard *Intrepid*, once in 1959, and then again from August 1960 to February 1961.

The Navy got its money's worth from the Tiger eventually. After its brief career in fleet operations, it was assigned to pilot training and the Blue Angels flight-demonstration team, where speed and endurance did not matter and excellent handling qualities and good looks did. The last Training Command F11F was not retired until 1967. The Blue Angels flew their Tigers until 1969, when they were finally replaced by the F-4 Phantom.

Carrier qualifications were accomplished aboard Forrestal in April 1956. The tail hook was stowed upside down and backwards. It was double-jointed at the attach point so it could be rotated out to the side and then back under the fuselage. (U.S. Navy via Hal Andrews collection)

The F11F is fondly remembered as being very easy to fly with virtually no vices or shortcomings other than marginal endurance and less thrust than fighter pilots had come to expect. (U.S. Navy via Hal Andrews collection)

At least three Grumman flight-test aircraft were involved in external stores envelope expansion and jettison testing. Only the Sidewinder was routinely carried during its limited service with the fleet, however. (Grumman Aircraft History Center)

Most F11Fs were used to provide fledgling fighter pilots with their first experience with afterburners and supersonic performance. It was an ideal next step after two-seat trainers because it was easy to fly. (U.S. Navy via Hal Andrews collection)

The Blue Angels began giving demonstrations with the last six Tigers from the first production lot in 1957. They switched to the long-nose F11Fs for the 1959 season and flew them through the 1968 season. (Grumman History Center)

## FJ-4 Fury

Shortly after initiating Grumman's F9F-9 program, in June 1953, BuAer contracted with North American for a redesign of the FJ-3. The FJ-4 was an anachronism because it was not required to be supersonic in level flight. Like the FJ-3, it was to be powered by a non-afterburning J65 engine. However, it was to be otherwise optimized for the high-altitude dogfight.

Without the time pressure that resulted in the FJ-2 and -3 being simply overweight Sabres, North American could completely redesign the airframe to maximize the FJ-4's mission performance. The internal fuel capacity was increased by more than 100 percent. The FJ-4 wing and the evolution of the Sabre wing are shown in Figure 13-2. Although the FJ-4 wing was more tapered than the FJ-3's, it had more area because two feet were added to its span and more than a foot to its mean aerodynamic chord, which contributed to the reduction in thickness to 6 percent. The airfoil was also more cambered, with twist added to the wing tip to avoid tip stall-induced pitch-up. The ailerons were moved inboard, which reduced the flap span, but with the additional wing area and airfoil chosen, there was still no need for leading edge slats. Armament remained unchanged: four 20mm cannons and provisions for up to four AIM-9 Sidewinder air-to-air missiles.

The result was an aircraft that closely matched or even bettered a clean FJ-3 in performance in almost all respects yet had better range and endurance on internal fuel alone than the FJ-3 did with two drop tanks:

|  | FJ-3 | FJ-4 |
|---|---|---|
| Fuel (lbs) | | |
| Internal | 2,610 | 5,712 |
| External | 2,400 | 0 |
| Total | 5,010 | 5,712 |
| Combat Ceiling (ft) | 47,000 | 46,800 |
| ROC Sea Level (fpm) | 9,400 | 7,660 |
| Max Speed (kts) | | |
| Sea Level | 599 | 591 |
| 35,000 feet | 530 | 548 |
| Combat Radius (nm) | 385* | 450 |
| Mission Time (hrs) | 2.0* | 2.3 |
| Stall Speed, Power On (kts) | 97.4 | 103 |
| *With external tanks | | |

First flight of the FJ-4 was accomplished in October 1954, piloted by Richard Wenzell. In spite of the major changes, it was virtually trouble-free in development (the empennage required a little tweaking). It was a brilliant achievement, up to and including meeting the design specification of Mach .95 in level flight without afterburner.

Unfortunately, Aurand's was a minority view with respect to the tradeoff of supersonic speed versus simplicity, weight, and cost. Almost all of the 152 FJ-4s produced were therefore delivered to Marine Corps fighter squadrons. The Marines loved it. The FJ-4 got rave reviews for handling qualities – both at 45,000 feet in a turning fight and at sea level on approach – as well as gunnery accuracy.

*The FJ-4 Fury was yet another example of how much an aircraft design could be improved by evolution. Here, the main difference was the wing – the engine was the same, and the fuselage, especially the empennage, was not significantly changed. The change in camber at the leading edge of the wing can be seen at the juncture of the wing to the fuselage. (Hal Andrews collection)*

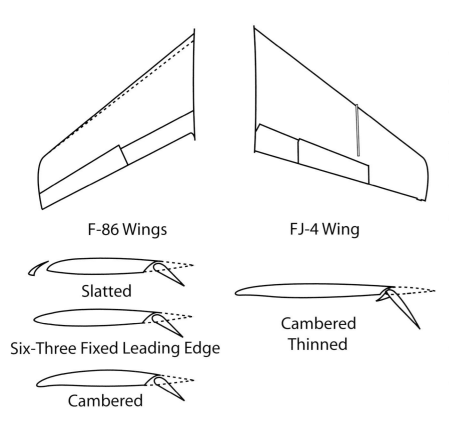

F-86 Wings      FJ-4 Wing

Slatted

Six-Three Fixed Leading Edge

Cambered

Cambered Thinned

*Figure 13-2 The FJ-4 wing was based on North American development of the F-86 wing, with the addition of even more chord to reduce the thinness ratio and increase the wing area. The critical Mach number and high-altitude maneuverability were increased as a result. (Author)*

Carrier suitability tests were accomplished aboard *Randolph* in March 1956, and *Saratoga* in August. As a fighter, the FJ-4 did eventually make at least part of one deployment. A Marine FJ-4 squadron, VMF-451, and a Navy F11F fighter squadron were aboard *Lexington* as part of CVG-21, which deployed in 1959 to the western Pacific.

North American was able to demonstrate what the FJ-4 could have done with an afterburner. In 1957, the second and fourth production FJ-4s, BuNos. 139282 and 139284, were modified to add a Rocketdyne 5,750-lb thrust liquid-fueled rocket that burned JP-4 with hydrogen peroxide as the oxidizer. With this thrust augmentation, the FJ-4F demonstrated a maximum speed of Mach 1.4 and altitude of 71,000 feet. This was one of the periodic revisits to the concept that a rocket could not only substitute for the afterburner but also provide thrust at higher altitudes than a conventional jet engine, enabling a fighter to intercept a bomber cruising at 60,000 feet or more.

## 1953 Day Fighter Competition

In addition to the two product-improvement programs contracted for with production contract funds, BuAer's Fighter Class Desk initiated a day fighter competition using development funds. When first issued in September 1952, the requirement represented the views of the smaller, simpler day-fighter contingent in BuAer. That focus was clearly stated in the introduction to the outline specification:

Primary Mission – The primary mission of this airplane shall be to maintain air superiority in daylight fair weather, both over friendly task forces and over hostile target areas, during the period of task force strikes when the enemy will mount large numbers of aircraft.

Basic Features – While speed, rate of climb, and combat ceiling are important features of this airplane, the basic features desired are those which will allow adequate numbers of the aircraft to be operated by carrier task forces to insure successful fulfillment of the mission

*Thrust augmentation with a liquid fuel rocket was sometimes considered and even proposed but seldom evaluated and never deployed. The closest the concept came to production appears to have been the FJ-4F, and even then it may have just been a test bed for an A3J derivative. It did demonstrate the performance potential of the FJ-4 had it had an afterburner. (Hal Andrews collection)*

stated above. These basic features are minimum size, maximum carrier spottability, low gross weight, low initial cost, simplicity of concept, ease of maintenance, reliability, and versatility in the air-to-air combat role.

The maximum speed at 35,000 feet was only to be Mach 1.0. That, and a change to the General Purpose and Escort Fighter mission definition that increased the time at maximum power, virtually eliminated the employment of afterburning.

This philosophy was not widely shared within BuAer. There was little support in the fleet for a fighter designed to this requirement. After Cdr. Aurand, the chief advocate for the lightweight fighter, left BuAer for his next assignment on 1 August 1952, the supersonic lobby was successful in changing the specification. It was reissued to the bidders' list in November 1952, this time with a desired speed of at least Mach 1.2 in level flight at 35,000 feet. The cover letter pointedly explained the reason for the change:

"(The original) specification place(d) undue emphasis on weight and size in an attempt to specify the effort to be made to reduce the trend toward increasing complexity in recent designs."

The Basic Features wording was revised to:

Speed, rate of climb, combat ceiling, and maneuverability are the primary features of this airplane. In addition to these primary features there are other char-

acteristics desired which will allow these adequate numbers of the aircraft to be operated by carrier task forces to insure successful fulfillment of the mission cited above. These other characteristics are minimum size, maximum carrier spottability, low gross weight, low initial cost, simplicity of concept, ease of maintenance, reliability, and versatility in the air-to-air combat role.

The mission definition change increasing the time at maximum power was deleted. In addition to these and other changes, the spotting requirement was changed from "at least 25 airplanes" in the specified area to: "The desired sizes (sic) of the airplane is such to permit spotting of 25 airplanes…Any increase in spottability beyond this requirement, should not compromise the airplane in any respect." In other words, the size requirement had gone from at least 25 airplanes to no more than 25 airplanes, and less would not disqualify the proposal.[4]

The remainder of the mission requirements remained essentially the same. Maneuverability was one of the most challenging: Limit gun platform $g$ (normal acceleration) greater than 4.5 $g$ at 35,000 feet – this was with respect to the buffet boundary, not the structure's strength. Combat ceiling remained at 52,000 feet, although now an afterburner could be used to be there. Normal radius of action was 300 nautical miles on internal fuel with external fuel extending that to 400 nautical miles.

The FJ-4, as opposed to the FJ-4B, was flown almost exclusively by the Marine Corps. Its only deployment appears to have been a month-long period during late 1959 that VMF-451 spent with CVG-21 aboard Lexington in the western Pacific. (U.S. Navy via Hal Andrews collection)

There were some carrier-suitability requirements aimed at avoiding the F7U's problems in the future:

- Takeoff, landing, wave off on military power.
- An airplane that sits close to and nearly parallel to the deck for easy handling, servicing, and maintenance.
- Catapulting without excessive dynamic rotation, ramps, or other trick means and with no sink off the bow of the ship.
- Excellent carrier-approach vision.[5]

Prospective carrier innovations were also to be taken into account by requiring adaptability to future operating techniques such as the canted deck and the flexible deck.

Surprisingly, the specification did not require armor plate, bullet-resistant glass, or self-sealing fuel tanks. It did state that, "Particular attention shall be given in the design to reducing vulnerability and in particular to arrange and group airplane components to provide mutual screening from attack," i.e., minimal vulnerability for the weight.

Eight manufacturers submitted proposals in February 1953, with Vought proposing two similar designs, one powered by the Wright J65 (the smallest possible) and the other by the new Pratt & Whitney J57 (the best performance possible). Both featured a variable-incidence wing, primarily to provide excellent over-the-nose visibility on approach, but with other carrier suitability advantages as well. Even though they were in the process of receiving contracts for derivatives of existing fighters, Grumman and North American proposed J57-powered designs.

## Grumman Design 97

Grumman's Design 97 solution to the carrier-suitability emphasis and maneuverability at altitude requirement was a wing of extremely large area relative to the overall size of the aircraft. It resembled the company's Design 98 (F9F-9) but with a bigger wing with 45 degrees of sweep and a low thinness ratio. The aspect ratio was only 2.65, and the wing loading was only 50 lbs per square foot.

In addition to its approach speed and high-altitude performance attributes, the large wing provided volume for 494 gallons of fuel. However, it hurt range and speed relative to Vought and North American's proposal. To keep the aircraft simple, there were no leading-edge devices. Grumman also took advantage of the maximum folded width limitation of 27 feet, six inches to eliminate powered wing fold as they had on the F11F. The deck crew was to manually lower the folding wingtips after landing.

The cockpit was situated well forward to provide a good field of view on approach. The landing gear was relatively long to provide ground clearance for external stores mounted on the belly. As with the other competitors, the optional two-inch rocket armament was carried internally. Like the Vought proposal, the overload fuel capacity was internal, not relegated to external tanks.

Based on conversations with BuAer personnel, some at Grumman were led to believe that their proposal had been scored the highest. In their view, the contract went to the second-best proposal because Grumman had received a letter of intent for the J65-powered F9F-9 in February. According to George Spangenberg, they were in third place at best.

## North American F2J and Super Fury

Like Vought, North American submitted a J57-powered, variable-incidence wing design for the 1953 Day Fighter Competition. In his oral history, George Spangenberg remembers the results of the competition this way:

> Vought won the competition hands down. Their big competitor… was North American. (We) knew the Vought design was underweight as proposed. It was in the low 20s… for the design mission. But North American came in close to 30,000 pounds for an airplane that was almost the same. They each had variable incidence wings. They were necessary in those days in order to solve the angle of attack problem and get back aboard in the best manner.
>
> In our mind Vought was going to be something over 1,000 pounds overweight but even at 1,000 pounds overweight or 1,400 or whatever it was we thought, it would still be a better airplane and perfectly acceptable in the fleet. North American at 30,000 pounds though would be about where we thought that the airplane might end up as a top of its growth line and there it was starting that way. And obviously if you propose a 30,000 pound airplane you can build it. Eventually we decided that we had to go with Vought. It was a better airplane of all those that were proposed.[6]

North American did not give up, however. In November 1953, they proposed a carrier-based derivative of its F-100 Super Sabre to the Navy. At that time, BuAer was reviewing Vought's F8U production proposal. Since the XF8U would not fly for another 16 months, North American apparently hoped to change BuAer's mind about its original choice.

North American's J57-powered Super Fury was a navalized version of its F-100B design study, which was an F-100A redesign that incorporated the latest supersonic flight technology and almost doubled the internal fuel capacity. The inlet was now swept back and incorporated variable geometry, with a horizontal ramp on the upper side used to establish and control the shock wave associated with supersonic flight. Unlike the F-100A, the fuselage was to be area ruled for improved transonic performance and lower supersonic drag. It had also been lengthened by almost four feet to increase its fineness ratio and add more fuel. The main landing gear now featured dual wheels. The wing was very similar in planform, but it was thinner and designed to hold fuel.

In the Super Fury proposal, in addition to adding the requisite tail hook, wing folding, catapult hooks, etc., other changes were made to the early F-100B design study to further improve the prospect of carrier suitability. For slower takeoff and landing speeds, the wing slats were extended farther inboard, flaps were added, and boundary layer control was incorporated. When the flaps were lowered, the folding portion of the wings was repositioned to provide 15 degrees of anhedral to improve lateral stability and aileron control at low speeds. The fuselage speed brake was to be deployed for approach and retract automatically on touchdown. The cockpit was raised to increase the over-the nose visibility. The gun sight was retractable for the same reason.

The proposal's most compelling point was that a prototype of sorts had flown in April so the first production delivery could be made in early 1956. As it turned out, the Air Force decided not to proceed with the F-100B. What's more, the first production F8U-1 flew on 30 September 1955, five months earlier than North American had projected for the first production Super Fury. In this case, development and production concurrency was warranted because the Crusader proved not to have any problems that could not be quickly rectified, particularly engine-related ones.

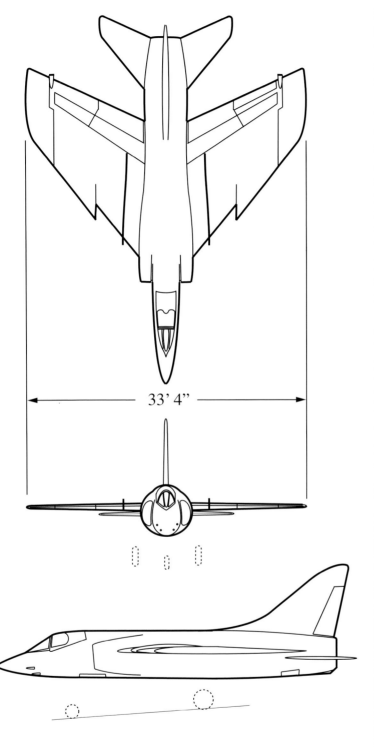

*Grumman Design 97*
*"Big wing" doesn't really do the Grumman Design 97's wing justice. Grumman was clearly emphasizing maximum combat ceiling and maneuverability at altitude. (Author)*

*North American proposed alternatives with a variable-incidence wing in the 1953 Day Fighter Competition. This one was powered with a J57. The original illustration had the designation F2J-1 above the bogus BuNo. (U.S. Navy via Jan Jacobs)*

If aircraft procurement commonality had been imposed on the services in the mid-1950s as it was in the mid-'60s, a carrier-based version of the North American F-100 shown here would have almost been a certainty. Instead, BuAer was free to choose the Vought F8U for its next day fighter. (National Archives)

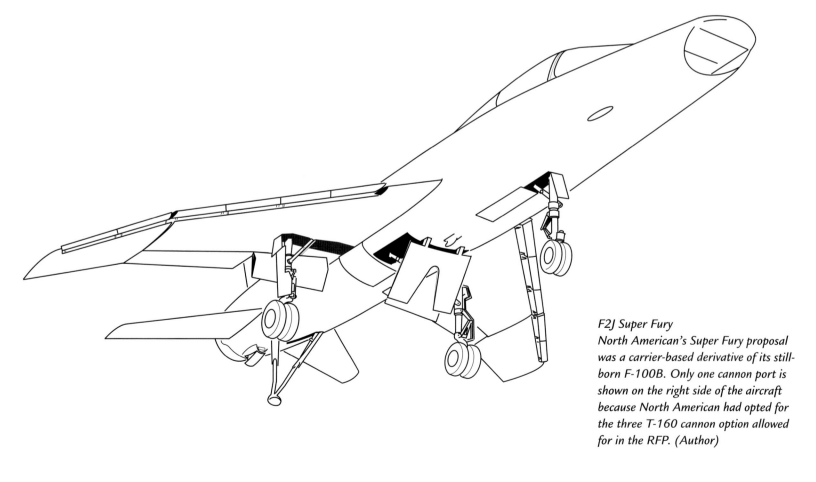

F2J Super Fury
North American's Super Fury proposal was a carrier-based derivative of its still-born F-100B. Only one cannon port is shown on the right side of the aircraft because North American had opted for the three T-160 cannon option allowed for in the RFP. (Author)

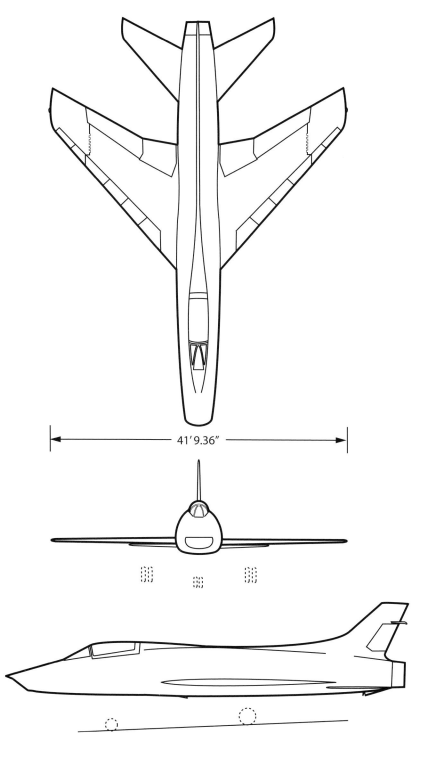

## Proposal Comparison

| | Vought V-383 Proposal | North American Super Fury* | Grumman Design 97 |
|---|---|---|---|
| Takeoff Weight (lbs) | 22,600 | 28,130 | 21,456 |
| Weight Empty (lbs) | 15,100 | 18,121 | 13,721 |
| Vmax 35K ft (M) | 1.50 | 1.63 | 1.37 |
| Approach Speed (kts) | 125 | 129 | 122 |
| Spotting (aircraft) | 25 | 22 | 25 |
| Time to Climb (min) to 35,000 feet | 1.7 | 1.8 | 1.7 |
| Mil Power Ceiling (ft) | 49,800 | 45,900 | 56,700 |
| Approximate Wing Loading (lbs per sq ft) | 60 | 72 | 50 |

*F-100B derivative

Note: All of the above powered by the Pratt & Whitney J57 engine

## Chance Vought F8U-1 Crusader

In May 1953, the Navy announced that Vought's V-383 won the competition.[7] The mockup review was accomplished in September 1953, followed by the cockpit lighting review in November. Both resulted in only minor changes. All was not going well, however. Wind-tunnel tests indicated that the top speed would only be Mach 1.3, significantly lower than the guarantee of Mach 1.45, which Vought had thought to be conservative. The projected shortfall was even more embarrassing than usual because Vought had gone counter to prevailing wisdom with respect to area ruling. Specifically, they didn't want the forward fuselage cross-sectional area to be larger than required in order to be able to indent it in the region of the wing. In making the decision, they had consulted with NACA and gotten agreement that a minimal frontal-area fuselage of maximum length would be equivalent in transonic and supersonic drag to an area-ruled one. According to Vought, NACA also agreed with them that the fairing of the aft fuselage was more important than the mid-fuselage indentation from a drag standpoint.

Based on wind-tunnel evaluations and increasing pressure from BuAer to reconsider its area rule position, Vought began design work on fuselage indentations and bulges. It was too late to incorporate all the shape changes in the first two XF8U aircraft, but Vought was able to modify the nose cone, the engine inlet duct (for improved pressure recovery), and the aft fuselage. Happily for their reputation and the success of the program,

*F2J Super Fury*
*Relative to the F-100A, the F-100B/Super Fury fuselage was longer for a better fineness ratio and to carry more fuel, as well as being area-ruled. It also had flaps, which the first F-100s did not. (Author)*

41' 9.36"

these proved to be adequate – on the first flight, in March 1955 at Edwards AFB, John Konrad was able to take the XF8U supersonic – so incorporation of the more drastic changes was canceled.

Vought and the Navy were able to field the F8U in a remarkably short time, particularly considering how much of a performance advancement it represented. The fourth production F8U-1, BuNo. 140446, was on *Forrestal* for carrier suitability tests in April 1956, little more than a year after the first flight of the XF8U-1. Two months later, the Crusader was qualified on *Bon Homme Richard*, an Essex-class carrier. VX-3 began receiving production F8Us in December to begin its operational evaluation.

F8U development, like that of the F3H and the F7U, was marred by accidents, however:

In February 1956, Vought test pilot Harry Brackett was killed when the first production F8U-1, BuNo. 140444, disintegrated during a high-speed pass at an air show at MCAS Mojave near Edwards AFB. The cause was attributed to an aileron hinge failure.

In May, Marine Corps Maj. James Feliton ejected from BuNo. 141337 near Greenville, Texas. While checking the yaw stabilization during a maneuver, he inadvertently engaged the cruise droop of the leading-edges flaps, leading to a PIO and disintegra-

tion of the aircraft. He successfully ejected just as the Crusader came apart.

A year later, in June 1957, Vought pilot James P. Buckner was killed when his F8U disintegrated after he pulled up from making a high-speed pass during a flight demonstration at the Vought plant. Under the pull-up loads, the long, slim fuselage had bowed slightly, enough to cause the mechanical control system to put in enough additional nose-up pitch for a structural overload.

Although improvements were made to correct most of the early problems, the F8U-1 was not without its faults. Directional stability at high speed, admittedly higher than Vought expected to achieve, was inadequate. It had a tendency for PIO at high airspeeds early on, but that was reduced by trim-system modifications. If anything, its gyrations after an accelerated stall were worse than those of the Cutlass. When it departed from controlled flight, it was likely to tumble end over end until it slowed to 170 knots, at which point it entered an upright spin with the pitch varying from as much as 90 degrees nose-up to 120 degrees nose-down in a single turn. Fortunately, recovery was relatively straightforward.

The Crusader's major fault, if for no other reason than that it would be encountered on every flight, was speed stability on

*The forward fuselage of the XF8U mockup was somewhat different from the aircraft as built. The speed brakes had already been moved from their proposal position on the upper aft fuselage, the cannons were under the nose, and the canopy was part of a dorsal fairing. However, the only mockup comment in this area had been a request to try to add more rearward visibility, which was one of the changes that didn't happen. (Jay Miller collection)*

Vought addressed the all-important issue of cockpit vision by mounting a mockup of the forward fuselage on scaffolding at a 25-foot wheel height and a variable nose-up attitude. This September 1953 picture represented the LSO's view of the aircraft when it was 150-feet out in the groove. (U.S. Navy photo via Tommy H. Thomason collection)

approach. According to former Crusader pilot Tom Weinel, "One of the nicknames for the F-8 was the 'Gator, because it would eat you alive if you let it." Another pilot described flying the F8U on approach to be like dancing with a mechanical bear.

None of this was likely to dampen the Navy's enthusiasm for the F8U, however. In August 1956, Cdr. R. W. "Duke" Windsor flew a stock production Crusader, BuNo. 141345, at an average speed of 1,015.4 mph over a 15-km course at 40,000 feet near China Lake, California. The only special preparation was to cool the fuel going in the aircraft to maximize the amount available. Although the course was only nine miles long and it only had to be flown once in each direction, getting turned around and reaccelerating to maximum speed used up a lot of fuel.

Unfortunately, it was not a world record, since that had been set earlier in the year at 1,132 mph by a British research aircraft, the Fairey Delta 2. More importantly, it was almost 200 mph faster than the mark posted by the Air Force's F-100C a year earlier, a very impressive difference given that the same basic engine, the J57, powered both aircraft, and the F8U design was penalized by its carrier-basing requirements.

The next year, Crusaders were used for two cross-country records that demonstrated their range and speed. The first was for the benefit of then-President Eisenhower, who was spending the 1957 D-Day anniversary aboard *Saratoga*, 50 miles east of Jacksonville, Florida. A flight of two VX-3 F8U-1s piloted by Capt. Bob Dosé and Lt. Cdr. Paul Miller launched from *Bon Homme Richard* 50 miles west of San Diego and recovered aboard *Saratoga* only three hours and 28 minutes later to demonstrate the carrier-to-carrier range of the F8U with one in-flight refueling.

The other 1957 showcasing of the F8U's speed and range capability occurred in July, when an F8U–1P photoreconnaissance

It's very hard to see any family resemblance between the F7U-3 and the XF8U. One is Vought engineering's penchant for early adoption of materials technology. In the case of the F8U, it was making the aft fuselage out of an alloy of titanium, one of the first aerospace applications of this metal. It is light, strong, and corrosion- and heat-resistant, but the most useful alloys are difficult to form. This is just the sort of benefit and challenge that some engineers live for. (Jay Miller collection)

*From the beginning, the Crusader exhibited good catapult-launch behavior. Its big, raised wing and the thrust of the afterburning J57 meant plenty of lift and thrust. (U.S. Navy via Hal Andrews collection)*

The variable-incidence wing made a huge difference in landing attitude. Unfortunately, the poor handling qualities on approach could never quite be eradicated by any amount of tweaking its mechanical control system. (U.S. Navy via Hal Andrews collection)

variant flown by future astronaut and U.S. Senator John H. Glenn was used to set a coast-to-coast speed record in Project Bullet. He was then a major in the Marine Corps and assigned to the Fighter Class Desk at BuAer. In spite of having to slow down three times to refuel from propeller-driven AJ-2 tankers, Maj. Glenn achieved an average speed of 725 mph between Los Angeles and New York City.

VF-32 at NAS Cecil Field, Florida, began receiving Crusaders in early 1957, followed by deployment aboard *Saratoga* before the end of that year. VF-154 traded in its FJ-3s for F8Us to be the first West Coast Crusader squadron, deploying on the smaller *Hancock*, albeit equipped with an angled deck, in February 1958. They got off to a bad start during carrier qualifications, losing three F8Us with two pilots killed. From the first receipt of F8Us through the end of the squadron's first deployment, there were 14 major accidents. Main landing-gear collapses in hard landings, double wire engagements that caused hook-point failure, and ramp strikes were the notable causes. VF-32 also experienced landing-gear failures.[8]

As remembered by Paul Gillcrist:

(T)he most exacting attention to power control was required if a Crusader pilot was to stay within plus or minus two knots while trying to get the airplane aboard a carrier, perhaps under horrendous circumstances. Just a trifle too much power, and the airplane would accelerate several knots too many for a safe carrier landing. To correct such a situation, the pilot reduces power to a throttle position that's just a trifle low. The airplane instantly begins to decelerate several knots below the speed considered safe for a carrier-arrested landing approach.[9]

But for the timely arrival of the angled deck and the constant angle-of-attack approach using the mirror-landing system, the F8U might well have suffered the same short operational life as the F7U.[10] However, like the World War II F4U Corsair, its superlative performance made up for its shortcomings on approach.

*The F8U probe was added after production began, but it was more streamlined than most of the retrofits. The refueling probe was mounted on the outside of the fuselage skin but retracted into a pod that had been added for that purpose. (Vought Heritage Center)*

The Navy replaced the legacy fighters, the F9F-8 and FJ-3, with the F8U as soon as possible, with the F11F helping to accelerate the fleet's transition to supersonic air superiority. As additional F8Us became available, the F11Fs were sent off to the training command. The F8U was significantly faster at altitude (it was engine-limited at sea level) and had more range.

|  | F9F-8 | FJ-3 | F11F-1 | F8U-1 |
|---|---|---|---|---|
| Gross Weight (lbs) | 20,098 | 19,360* | 21,035 | 26,969 |
| Speed SL (kts) | 561 | 599 | 654 | 637 |
| Speed 35K (kts/M) | 515/0.89 | 530/0.92 | 632/1.10 | 880/1.53 |
| Combat Range (nm) | 1,050 | 995* | 1,108 | 1,280 |
| Mission Time (hrs) | 2.06 | 1.70* | 1.57 | 1.73 |
| Approach stall (kts) | 93.8 | 94.4 | 103.3 | 108.2 |

Internal fuel only except as noted by * which include two 200-gallon drop tanks.

Length didn't matter on the deck-edge elevators, but the Crusader was still not so long that it didn't fit on the forward Essex-class elevator. It was a little awkward to spin one around, but a top speed of 1,000 mph got it a lot of slack. (Robert L. Lawson collection)

Because of the long slender fuselage and the 45°-swept wing, Vought got away without strictly adhering to the area-rule concept of a pinched-in mid fuselage. (Jay Miller collection)

*It took time for all the day-fighter squadrons to transition to the new supersonic fighters, but it was finally completed in June 1959, when VF-84 traded in its FJ-3s for gaudily painted F8U-2s. (Hal Andrews collection)*

The variable-incidence wing feature proved to be relatively trouble-free. Since the center of pressure was aft of the wing's hinge point, the wing was really held down by its own pitching moment. There was a lock on the actuator, but its primary purpose was to prevent the pilot from inadvertently raising the wing above the 220-knot limit speed. While there were a few in-flight structural failures where the wing came off, they were not precipitated by an actuator failure.

## Douglas F5D Skylancer

By late 1952, it had become clear to Douglas and BuAer that the F4D shortcomings could not be improved with just aerodynamic tweaking. The drag rise at near sonic speed was too much to overcome other than in a descent. It was also short on range and endurance because it was optimized to be a deck-launched inter-

ceptor. The resulting major redesign retained the same wing plan-form, but with a 30-percent thinner wing section to increase the critical Mach number. The wing-to-fuselage fillet was also made thinner. The fuselage was lengthened about eight feet to increase the internal fuel capacity, which increased its fineness ratio and directional stability as well. The vertical fin was increased in size almost 50 percent to provide better directional stability and control, particularly at high angles of attack. The fuselage-mounted trimmers were now to function as elevons, although after flight-test evaluation this was changed to pitch-control augmentation only.

The rocket armament was now to be housed in four retractable launcher trays with 72 two-inch rockets; these trays could be replaced with a gun package of four 20mm cannons with 500 rounds of ammunition. The fire-control system was to be the Aero 13G, which was made up of the APQ-50A radar and the Mk 13 sight. This allowed the Sparrow I missiles to be an armament option.

The production F5D was to be powered by the J57-P-8 with

As hard as it may be to believe, the forward end of the wing was only attached to the fuselage by a single hydraulic actuator as shown here. The wing was held on by the very sturdily built pivot points and stayed down because the center of lift was behind the pivot point. (Vought Heritage Center)

16,000 lbs of thrust in afterburner, the same as the F4D. The high-speed improvement was to come entirely from aerodynamics. The internal fuel capacity of 1,333 gallons was more than double that of the F4D, which eliminated the necessity for external tanks.

The two aircraft compared as follows in 1956:

|  | F4D-1 | F4D-2 |
| --- | --- | --- |
| Gross Weight (lbs) | 28,000* | 28,000** |
| Fuel (lbs) | 8,432 | 8,665 |
| Vmax @ 35,000 feet (kts/MN) | 550/0.95 | 806/1.40 |
| Combat Radius (nm) | 300 | 400 |
| Stall Speed, Landing (kts) | 100 | 110 |

* Four 19-shot rocket pods, full internal fuel, and two 300-gallon tanks,
** 72 two-inch rockets, full internal fuel

Two prototypes of this improved Skyray were contracted for in October 1953. Initiated a few months after the F8U, the Skylancer was to be the high-performance all-weather interceptor counterpart to the Crusader day-fighter. The Navy also considered it employable as an all-weather general-purpose fighter.

The mockup review was satisfactorily accomplished in November 1953. By mid-1954, it was apparent to Douglas and BuAer that the Aero 13G development was not making satisfactory progress. As a result, Douglas proposed to develop a system unique to the F4D-2 using existing hardware. The Navy agreed with the approach, and in November 1954 it ordered 18 sets of the Douglas Aero-X24A armament control system. Some were to be installed in

F3D-1s and F4Ds for development. The F4D-2 (re-designated F5D in February 1955) was now to be armed with two of the Douglas/Bendix Sparrow II air-to-air missiles carried on external racks in addition to either unguided rockets or the 20mm cannons.

The Navy ordered nine production F5Ds via a letter of intent in March 1955, and a further eight in January 1956. Procurement of an additional 43 F5Ds was included in the next fiscal-year budget plan. Douglas test pilot Bob Rahn made the first flight of the F5D in April 1956. Like the F8U, the F5D flew well enough to be taken past Mach 1 on its first flight. The first NPE was accomplished in July. As usual, several deficiencies and shortcomings were identified, but none were serious and certainly not beyond correction. However, BuAer was having to take a hard look at its all-weather fighter program budgeting.

The problem was that the F5D development, particularly the all-important fire-control system, was not nearly far enough along to meet near-term fleet requirements. Even if qualified on schedule, it would probably not be deployed for long before either the F4H or F8U-3, both of which were on contract and projected to have better performance and useful load, were available. In November 1956, OpNav therefore decided not to procure additional F5Ds and cancel the eight most recently ordered. To meet fleet-deployment requirements until one of the Mach 2 fighters was available, they ordered more F3Hs. The Navy still hoped to qualify the Aero X24 fire-control system and the Sparrow II missile, complete the 11 F5Ds still on contract, and conduct BIS trials to have the F5D/Sparrow II capability available if both the F4H or F8U-3 were delayed or neither measured up. In early 1957, this plan was also deemed to be unaffordable. On 1 March 1957, the Navy directed Douglas to terminate work on the fifth and subsequent aircraft that were still on order. Flight testing continued on the first four for a time. Two were then delivered to NACA for high-speed research projects, one being retired in 1968 and the other in 1970. The other two were retained at Douglas for chase and research assignments.[11]

Everything undesirable about the F4D was corrected in the design of the F5D without significantly diminishing the configuration's strengths: rate of climb and maneuverability at altitude. The top speed was increased by 50 percent with the same engine, a very successful aerodynamic do-over. For example, the Douglas F4D Skyray's design-limit Mach number of 1.5 was demonstrated at 35,000 feet while in a 45-degree dive and descending at 62,000 feet per minute, more than 1,000 feet per second. The F5D was capable of Mach 1.5 in level flight at 35,000 feet.

Douglas test pilot Bob Rahn remembered the F5D fondly. In his autobiography, he called it a "Cadillac," which was at the time both a compliment and a comparison to the F4D in a play on words, since the Skyray was commonly referred to as the "Ford."[12]

*The F5D versus the F4D: Same wing planform, same engine, but no external tanks required and almost Mach 0.5 faster. Even Ed Heinemann could do better the second time around. (National Archives 80-G-677189)*

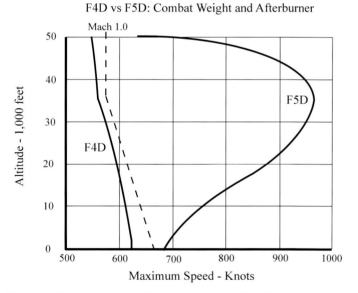

F4D vs F5D: Combat Weight and Afterburner

## Navy Fighter Program Status in 1958

In 1958, the standard day fighter was the F8U-1 Crusader, rapidly replacing all the other swept-wing day-fighters that had preceded it, including the F11F, which served only briefly in a few squadrons. The standard all-weather fighter in air groups was either the F4D-1 Skyray or the F3H-2 Demon.

The Sparrow air-to-air missile had been developed, demonstrated, and fielded to a limited degree with the F7U-3M. It had reached full potential with the F3H-2. The F4D was armed only with the cannon and

*The level flight airspeed vs. altitude envelopes of the F4D and the F5D, which were powered by the same engine, clearly demonstrate the aerodynamic benefit of raising the critical Mach number and reducing the transonic drag rise through shaping and thinning. Using only military thrust, the F5D was as fast as the F4D in afterburner. In afterburner, it easily went through the sound barrier to significantly higher speeds. (Tommy H. Thomason collection)*

The F5D is undoubtedly a close runner-up to, if not tied with, the F8U-3 for the best fighter that the Navy didn't put into production. Unfortunately, the Navy had already started deploying the F8U and started developing the F4H. The F5D was simply being developed too late to either challenge the F8U for the day-fighter role or be an interim supersonic all-weather fighter before the advent of the F4H. (Hal Andrews collection)

The pace of development in fighters (and the Marine Corps' willingness to take whatever they could get) is illustrated by this Vought AU-1 (an early '50s attack derivative of the venerable F4U Corsair) taxiing past an early F8U-1. (U.S. Navy via Hal Andrews collection)

Sidewinders, the barrage of unguided rockets proving to be much less lethal in practice than hoped. The next Navy programs were already in place to generate a successor to the F4Ds and F3Hs, and these were to be Sparrow III-equipped.

A winnowing down of the five Navy fighter manufacturers was in progress. In 1953, each of them had ongoing fighter-development programs. In 1958, three of them did not. Douglas delivered its last fighter in December. North American had delivered its last Navy fighter in 1957. Grumman was delivering F11Fs, but production would be completed in January 1959, and they did not have any product improvement prospects for it, much less a new development program.

BuAer favored Grumman for many years. Although Grumman built thousands of Navy jet fighters, they won only two formal fighter-program competitions. The first was as a runner-up and did not result in the F9F-1 prototype contracted for. The other, the F-14, was still in the future. From the F9F-2 through the F11F, Grumman was awarded successive development and production contracts without having to compete formally for them. Beginning in 1946, the stillborn F9F-1 night fighter begat the F9F-2 Panther and the F10F Jaguar. The Panther begat the Cougar, which begat the Sapphire Cougar, which became the Tiger. Both the Panther and the Cougar begat photoreconnaissance derivatives and the Cougar, a two-seat jet trainer. It was quite a run, an example of the Navy's ability to work closely with its manufacturers to perfect the breed.

Nevertheless, competition existed in actuality. That was demonstrated by Tiger production ending at 201 aircraft and

Crusader production totaling more than 1,200. Ironically, Grumman, which had two huge successes in a row from a production standpoint, the Panther and the Cougar, then produced a fighter with ho-hum performance with its original engine and limited potential due to its small size. Vought, with two or three failures in a row, depending on how you keep score, produced a best-in-class fighter, still revered by its pilots.

Next it would be Vought and McDonnell going head to head.

The F8U quickly became the sole day fighter deployed with carrier air wings. Here VF-154 is teamed with VF-23's F4D Skyrays aboard Hancock in 1958, the first West Coast deployment of the Crusaders. (U.S. Navy)

*The F3H-G/H design study was for a general-purpose fighter powered by either two Wright J65s or two General Electric J79s. The most innovative concept of the study was the use of interchangeable noses so that it could better perform a wide range of missions. (Author)*

# ACHIEVING MACH 2

In order to stay in business, an aircraft company had to be building and delivering aircraft at a fairly high and consistent rate. However, in the 1950s, even a successful fighter might only be in production for a few years because of the rapid changes in technology, particularly jet-engine performance. Considering the relatively long time required to develop and transition a new aircraft to production, the successor to the one on the production line had to have flown, and the successor of the successor had to have been proposed to the customer. In other words, there had to be a continuous replenishment of contracted development programs in order to provide a continuous level of production. Both the development and production sides of the company had to be kept relatively busy all the time. As the Red Queen said, "It takes all the running you can do, to keep in the same place."

In 1955, by somewhat different routes, McDonnell and Chance Vought received contracts for what would become the Navy's highest-performance fighters, the culmination of the transition from propeller-driven fighters to jets that had begun in the early 1940s.

## F3H-X to AH-1 to F4H-1

The founder of McDonnell Aircraft, James S. McDonnell, had built his company up literally from scratch beginning in 1939. Unlike most of the other aircraft companies, he had sold development programs to both the Navy and the Air Force, and what's more, most of them had or were resulting in production. In 1953, however, he was not producing as many F3H-1s as he and the Navy had planned and was facing the prospect that the F3H-2 might not result in production. As a result, he initiated an effort to sell a new general-purpose supersonic fighter program to the Navy. The result was one of the most convoluted BuAer fighter procurements and developments ever. It also resulted in an outstanding aircraft.

His proactive campaign to replace the F3H with another McDonnell aircraft as soon as possible began with a study of successively more significant iterations of the F3H-2 basic design. McDonnell had unsuccessfully proposed an all-new design for the 1953 Day Fighter Competition, a remarkably ugly straight-wing configuration with J57- and J65-powered alternatives. The fuselage started with the pointed nose of the F3H but ended with a vertical fin resembling that of the F2H. The wing was only 4.5 percent thick to provide supersonic speed capability and straight to eliminate the high angle-of-attack approach and landing problem of the swept and delta wings. Like the F11F, the main landing gear was attached to the fuselage and retracted into the fuselage under the wing.

The Navy's aircraft suppliers, who were both good and lucky, would have a new program in development to replace the aircraft that was currently beginning production. Here, in November 1955, the F4H mockup is ready for review while the F3Hs behind the wall are in flight-test development or being prepared for delivery. (Hal Andrews collection)

Following its loss in the day-fighter program, McDonnell did a design study of supersonic general-purpose fighters based on the F3H but powered by different engines. It compared the J71-powered F3H with two slightly different single Wright J67-powered variants (the J-67 was a license-built Bristol Olympus with 13,200 lbs military rating and 21,500 lbs in afterburner) and two twin-engine designs, one powered by the Wright J65 and the other, the General Electric J79. These latter two designs were identified in the McDonnell studies as the F3H-G and the F3H-H, respectively. All were 45-degree swept-wing aircraft with conventional tails. These were provided to BuAer in September 1953, more than a year before the baseline aircraft, the F3H-2N, was to fly.

It would appear that only the twin-engine versions elicited any interest, because all of the subsequent studies only address multi-engine fighters. The F3H-H had better performance than the F3H-G but its General Electric J79 hadn't powered an aircraft yet. The J65 was a more mature engine, having completed its 150-hour qualification and flown in the FJ-3, among other aircraft, although the afterburning version had yet to fly. George Spangenberg describes the Navy's practice at the time:

> In those days we did not allow an airplane to start until the engine had reached PFRT, which is a preliminary flight rating test, (a) fifty-hour test on that engine. If you did that, by the time you got to your full qualified engine test you had a production airplane ready to go.[1]

In January 1954, McDonnell completed an F3H-G study that described a very innovative feature, interchangeable noses, including the cockpit, allowing any F3H-G airframe with the appropriate nose installed to be used for:

- Day attack
- All-weather attack
- Photographic reconnaissance
- Day interceptor
- All-weather interceptor
- Electronic ferret/countermeasures
- Two-place strike coordinator

These noses would be stored aboard ship and installed overnight – four men could accomplish a removal and replacement in eight hours. Nine wing stations were to be provided for the attack role. The day interceptor nose contained an APQ-51 radar for control of Sparrow I missiles while the all-weather interceptor was equipped with an APQ-50 radar and armed with unguided rockets in two retractable launchers and nine pods on the external racks.

This was the ultimate general-purpose fighter. One benefit of the interchangeable nose was that "the total number of aircraft assigned to a Carrier Air Group might be reduced from 74 to 69,

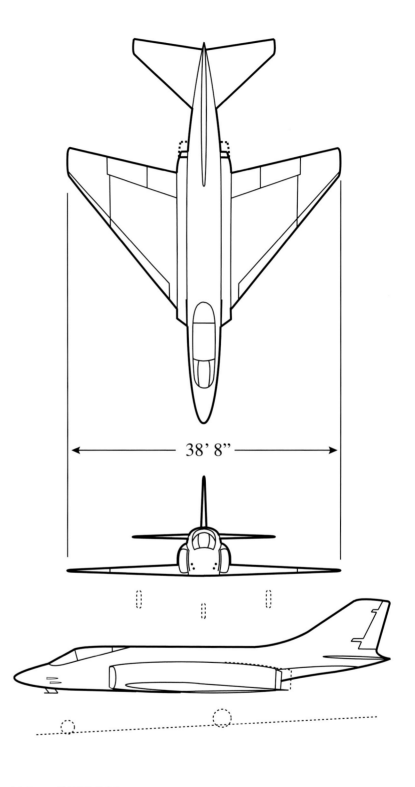

*McDonnell F3H-G/H*

providing more room on the carrier hangar deck even after allowance for storage of alternate nose assemblies." Moreover, more of the aircraft on board would be of a common design to the benefit of unit cost, pilot/maintainer training, and spare-parts stocks. Another major advantage was the flexibility to meet different tactical situations, limited only by the number of extra mission noses. For example, if a conventional Air Group had eight all-weather interceptors and 12 all-weather interceptor noses, the Task Force Commander could, overnight, increase the number of aircraft with that mission capability from eight to 20. Alternatively, if there was no air threat, the maintainers could convert some or all of the eight interceptors to attack aircraft.

The Navy was not immediately enthusiastic about the McDonnell proposal, already having the F8U and the F5D programs in place. However, in early 1954, the Navy became increasingly concerned about the status of its General Purpose Fighter programs. The XF10F had been canceled in 1953, and both the F7U-3 and F3H programs were having engine problems. The F5D had just been placed on contract the year before and was therefore an unknown quantity. As a result, in April 1954, there was a joint BuAer-CNO conference to discuss the procurement of the twin-engine J65-powered F3H-G in lieu of the single-engine J71-powered F3H. No decision was reached at that time.

The next step in McDonnell's marketing campaign was the manufacture of a full-scale mockup. It was available for Navy review in May 1954. It was not very detailed and did not even include a landing gear. It did provide a sense of size and simply depicted both engine options, with the external portion of the J65's afterburner on one side and the J79's on the other. The J79 clearly provided more performance, including a projected top speed at 35,000 feet of Mach 1.97 compared to the J65's Mach 1.52, but if BuAer had not been conservative about committing aircraft to a new engine too early before, it was now.

There has been speculation, and it is believed by some, that at McDonnell the project was temporarily stashed in the Attack branch until Fighter branch funds were available. This is entirely possible, given BuAer's ends-justify-the-means-driven approach to program starts. In this scenario, the Navy reviewed its future all-weather fighter needs, all of the unsolicited proposals in hand, the current status of fighter programs in development, McDonnell's business situation, and the upcoming fiscal year funds available for fighter and attack programs. It then issued a letter of intent to McDonnell in September 1954, for a jet-attack aircraft similar to the F3H-G/H (negotiations for the requisite specification to follow) as a placeholder for its next all-weather fighter program.

There are also reports that an RFP had been issued in June 1954. However, in his oral history, without being specific about the time frame, George Spangenberg stated: "We did an informal competition, as it were, but without getting formal bids from any-

body." He remembered that the F5D was possibly one of the alternatives considered, along with a twin-J79-powered, rocket-assisted Grumman proposition:

> The F4H as it started didn't look quite as strange. Didn't have the droop tail yet and the wings didn't have the broken wing look that they eventually developed. But it was a single-place airplane and armed only with guns. (There was) a hell of a lot of pressure from the industrial statesmanship side of the Navy organization, as well as from McDonnell saying we have to have something to keep the factory going and so on and so forth. I remember writing the memo, it's back there in Navy files somewhere, that the only way you could possibly justify the F3H-G was to buy it as a stepping stone while you awaited the arrival of the J-79s, which, as it turned out, is exactly what they ended up doing. And manipulations that I wasn't involved in ended up then with them giving a contract to McDonnell for the AH-1. Lo and behold it had become an attack plane. An afterburning twin-engine single-place attack plane. A type that didn't exist in any plan that I knew anything about. Short on range. Very strange and I don't know how it all happened. After about, I suppose, six months there was a big reconfiguration study and the airplane then was changed over to that which we know today. Became a two-place airplane, no guns, except in a pod and armed with four Sparrows as primary armament with a fair amount of emphasis still on the air-to-ground mission.

A McDonnell F4H-1 Phantom History log, dated 14 January 1958, prepared by Vought corroborates this scenario. According to the log, BuAer evaluated the McDonnell study aircraft in early 1954 along with unsolicited Douglas, Grumman, and North American proposals against an apparently urgent OpNav requirement for an all-weather attack aircraft. BuAer recommended the F3H-G/H with a preference for the J79 and then initiated the procurement of two AH-1s in September. Instead of having a sub-rosa plan to start a fighter program with Attack branch funds, it is therefore likely that BuAer's initial intent really was to procure the F3H-G/H as an attack aircraft.

As originally proposed in the January 1954 report, it was clearly intended for a multi-role capability with the emphasis on air-to-ground weapons delivery. On a chart showing 23 different external load options for the nine weapons stations, the Sparrow load-out is fourth from the bottom, below an Aero 14B Spray Tank and above a pod for loose equipment and two different variants of external tanks.

In any event, in October 1954, the Navy provided McDonnell with a letter of intent for two prototypes and a static test article of the AH-1 and McDonnell announced the receipt of a $38 million

After the McDonnell's new program was redirected to missile-armed fleet defense, Design 98 was reconfigured as a two-seat, Sparrow-missile carrier. This iteration of the mockup has some anhedral in the horizontal tail but does not yet have the dihedral in the wing tips, and inlet refinement is still in progress. (Hal Andrews collection)

contract to begin development of an all-weather attack aircraft. McDonnell submitted a detail specification to the Navy for discussion in November. In December, however, BuAer and OpNav held a conference that addressed forthcoming all-weather attack and fighter requirements. The outcome was that the McDonnell program was to be redirected to a single-seat all-weather fighter for fleet air defense, and a new requirement would be issued for a longer-range, two-seat, all-weather attack aircraft. (The latter eventually resulted in the J79-powered A3J Vigilante for supersonic nuclear weapon delivery, also without benefit of a formal competition.)

In the meantime, McDonnell was continuing with the pre-design of, and supporting tests for, a single-seat, twin-engine, attack aircraft. In March 1955, BuAer and OpNav met again to review the McDonnell program and decide whether to proceed with it as the F4H or cancel it. The agreement was to continue with initial fleet delivery slated for mid-1959. In April 1955, BuAer representatives, Cdr. Noel Gaynor and Cdr. Francis X. Timmes, the Fighter Class Desk and the AH-1 project manager, respectively, visited the McDonnell plant in St. Louis to begin the redirection of the Model 98 from an attack aircraft to a fleet-defense fighter.

The Russian bomber threat to the carrier, which had been a theoretical concern in the late 1940s based on them developing a bomber comparable to the Air Force B-47, had become reality in the early 1950s. The Tu-16 Badger continued to be upgraded and, worse, armed with better and better air-to-surface missiles. Standoff ranges had increased, and it was becoming even more important to shoot down the archer, as opposed to dealing with each individual arrow, a much more difficult task. The Navy had concluded that it needed a missile-armed aircraft, capable of loitering for two hours on a Combat Air Patrol station 250 nautical miles from the carrier. In June 1955, BuAer formally re-designated the AH-1 as the F4H-1 in accordance with the new OpNav requirement for a two-seat, all-weather interceptor. By the end of July, McDonnell finally had an approved detail specification and a contract for two prototypes.

The F4H Specification SD 513-1, dated 25 July 1955, called for a gross weight of 39,839 lbs with 1,972 gallons of internal fuel. This also included 1,700 lbs for four Sparrow IIIs and their rails. The empty weight was to be 24,083 lbs. J79-GE-2 engines were to be furnished weighing 3,300 lbs each and producing, in afterburner, 14,350 lbs of thrust. First flight was scheduled for October 1957.

The cockpit and aircraft mockups were reviewed with the Navy in November 1955. The second seat had been incorporated. The horizontal tail was now mounted with anhedral to move some of the surface below the wing wake at high angles of attack. The four Sparrow missiles were mounted in recesses on the bottom of the fuselage, to be deployed for launch on individual trapezes.

At the February 1956 design review, the Sparrow II was still being considered as an alternative to the Sparrow III. The Sparrow deployable-rail launch mechanism had yet to be designed. (This approach was eventually dropped in favor of positively jettisoning the Sparrow via small explosive charges before its rocket motor fired.) A feasibility study was being accomplished on an infrared search-and-track capability.

After further wind-tunnel tests, McDonnell decided that wing dihedral was needed for lateral stability. In order to retain the wing spar already designed with forgings in work, they simply modified the outer wing-panel attachment to add 12 degrees of dihedral outboard of the wing fold. Longitudinal stability at high angles of attack was also a concern, so the leading edge of the outboard wing panels was extended. This "snag" generated an aerodynamic fence at high angles of attack to minimize pitch-up from span-wise flow of the air over the wing causing a loss of lift aft of the center of gravity. The vertical tail area was increased (aft, not up, because of the hangar height restriction) to increase static directional stability at supersonic speeds, and even more anhedral was added to the horizontal tail. Spoilers were added for roll-control augmentation, with the ailerons only deflecting down.

The Navy continued to expand the mission-equipment list while the F4H was being designed as they often did. In May 1956, OpNav revised the F4H requirement to delete the Mk 7 nuclear weapon, continue to accommodate Sparrow II capability as a "back-up," and provide for simultaneous carriage of Sidewinders with Sparrows. An infrared scanner with tracking capability was added. In addition, ground-attack capability was to be retained.

As the weight grew, the low-speed lift configuration evolved:

|  | July 1955 | April 1958 |
|---|---|---|
| Leading Edge Flaps | Two-panel | Three-panel |
| Trailing Edge Flaps | Flaps Only | Flaps and Ailerons |
| Boundary Layer Control | Trailing Edge Only | Trailing Edge and |
|  |  | Outboard and Center |
|  |  | Leading Edge |

Due to the late definition of the low-speed lift configuration, the first five aircraft were completed to the July 1955 specification. The sixth (which became the carrier-suitability aircraft) and subsequent were to the April 1958 specification.

The engine inlet was complex in order to cope with the Mach 2 conditions. In addition to the traditional boundary layer divider that kept the slow moving air next to the surface of the fuselage from entering the inlet, it had a variable ramp to control the amount of inlet

air. This addressed the issue of changing mass flow with speed – at low speeds, air was being sucked into the inlet, and a big bell-mouth was the best inlet configuration to feed the maw of the jet engine. At high speeds, with air being rammed into the inlet, it needed to be smaller so as not to choke the engine. The ramp was also designed to generate a shock wave that reduced the airspeed at the inlet from supersonic to subsonic speed. Finally, the ramp was perforated to bleed off the slow-moving boundary layer of air on the ramp itself. An electronic inlet controller set the ramp angle. It and the pilot's instruments, autopilot, and other subsystems requiring air data were provided it by the new Central Air Data Computer, which integrated all of the sensor readings of ram air, static pressure, outside air temperature, angle of attack, etc.

In another change made before first flight, approved in February 1958 and not incorporated in most of the first 18 aircraft built, the nose was increased in size to accommodate a bigger radar dish. The longer detection range it afforded was required to cope with the closing speed of the Mach 2 Phantom II and the incoming bomber raid so that there was enough time for the Radar Intercept Officer (RIO) to identify, target, and guide the Sparrow missile to the interception. The radar designation was changed to APQ-72. This bigger radome required a downward droop in the nose to retain adequate visibility on approach, generating the last of the Phantom II's signature features. The cockpit was also raised to improve visibility on approach.

The first F4H, BuNo. 142259, flew on 27 May 1958, at St. Louis piloted by Robert C. Little. The first flight

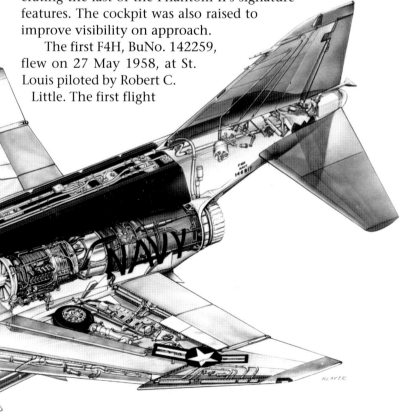

*The F4H interior was dominated by fuel tanks and engines. In addition to four semi-submerged Sparrows, two more could be carried on wing pylons. This is a cutaway of the aircraft before the bigger radar dish was adopted. (McDonnell Aircraft via Tommy H. Thomason collection)*

did not go as well as hoped, shortened to 22 minutes by a hydraulic line failure, but was otherwise satisfactory. The second was also limited because a landing gear safety pin had not been removed. Little was finally able to go supersonic on the third flight on 31 May, reaching Mach 1.3. On 2 June, he further expanded the envelope to Mach 1.68 and 50,000 feet. After 11 flights, the Navy cleared the Phantom to be ferried to Edwards Air Force Base where it was to meet its competition, the F8U-3, the Navy's other Mach 2 all-weather fighter program.

## Vought F8U-3

Vought did not initially appear to be anywhere near as aggressive as McDonnell about obtaining a new program, perhaps because it was in the midst of development and initiating production of the company's Crusader, a program that was going well, in sharp contrast to McDonnell's F3H.[2] In April 1955, the same month that Navy representatives visited McDonnell to redirect the AH to be a high-performance, all-weather, missile-only fighter for fleet air defense, Vought's contacts in the Navy informed them about the requirement. Vought also learned that there were those in BuAer who would be interested in a proposal for a single-engine fleet defense fighter powered by the Pratt & Whitney J75 engine. As a result, Vought engineering immediately initiated a design study of a derivative of the F8U. Mach 2+ required an increase in vertical fin surface area for adequate directional stability, a new engine inlet to control the mass flow and pressure, and materials changes because of increased aerodynamic heating. Vought also elected to incorporate more aggressive area ruling. The missile armament necessitated a large radar and appropriate missile mounting and launching capability compatible with the speed. Because of the higher speed, big-

ger engine, and different armament, a complete redesign of the F8U resulted, although it bore a very close family resemblance – a younger brother on steroids, perhaps.

In August 1955, BuAer issued a formal request for proposal for a fighter that met the following requirements:

- Performance: Greatest premium of Vmax over broadest possible altitude band, and on acceleration and maneuver capability at all altitudes, particularly high altitudes. Minimum performance armed:
    - Combat Ceiling, 55,000 feet;
    - Vmax of at least Mach 2;
    - CAP cycle time of 3 hours (with JP-5 fuel);
    - In-flight refueling provisions;
    - Arrested landing requirements armed, 1.3 V1 and 15 knotswind-over-deck.
- Primary Weapons System:
    - APQ-50 radar, modified to provide CW radar illumination;
    - Missile auxiliaries permitting the efficient storage, combat operations, and launch of Sparrow III missiles;
    - A battery of four Sparrow III missiles submerged, semi-submerged, or externally positioned so as to reduce drag.
    - BuAer also requested studies on weight and performance penalties incurred by the provision of a second seat for a radar operator/navigator.
- By the end of August, Vought engineering concluded that:
    - Adequate directional stability at Mach 2 would require folding ventral fins.
    - The increased cost and weight of a second seat was not justified by the limited increase in mission effectiveness.
    - An approach speed of 130 knots was achievable with a

Most of the early F4H flights were accomplished solo. Note that the spoilers in front of the ailerons are perforated as they were on the F3H. (Hal Andrews collection)

Rare for a carrier-based aircraft, the F4H was equipped with a drag chute. McDonnell had experience with drag chutes because it also designed and produced U.S. Air Force fighters. (Hal Andrews collection)

wing of 425 square feet (later increased to 450 square feet) given a double-droop leading edge slat and boundary layer control.

- An ejector nozzle was desirable for maximum thrust and center- of-gravity placement.

In addition, an inlet configuration was selected, budget weights were established, and the armament and avionics systems were defined. In order to accomplish the mission with no radar operator, the pilot was provided with an automatic flight-control system. In addition to the usual capability, it would establish and maintain the appropriate Mach number for best climb, best range, or greatest endurance, taking into account weight, outside air temperature, altitude, etc.

The resulting V-401 was significantly heavier than the XF8U-1:

| | XF8U-1 | V-401 Proposal |
|---|---|---|
| Total Structure | 7,071 lbs. | 9,602 lbs. |
| Surface Controls | 900 | 1,031 |
| Total Propulsion | 5,974 | 7,769 |
| Total Equipment | 1,506 | 1,842 |
| Weight Empty | 15,451 lbs. | 20,244 lbs. |
| Useful Load | 9,145 | 15,656 |
| Gross Weight | 24,596 lbs. | 35,900 lbs. |
| Engine | J-57 | J-75 |
| Thrust w/AB | 16,000 lbs. | 25,000 lbs. |

The V-401 was very similar in layout to the F8U-1, including the two-position wing. However, Vought made detailed wing changes in adding a second segment to the leading edge flap (later adapted to the F8U-2), boundary layer control for low-speed lift (also employed on the F8U-2), and spoilers to augment roll control. The result was a lower stalling speed than the lighter F8U-1's. The engine inlet was changed to a Ferrari-type scoop that did not require variable geometry other than the dumping of excess inlet air at high speeds. Additional vertical-fin area was provided by two ventral fins that were raised when the landing gear was extended and by a broader chord vertical fin. Internal fuel was increased to 2,000 gallons from 1,261 gallons. Virtually all of the avionics were different.

In October 1955, Vought submitted the engineering proposal for its Model V-401.[3] A cost proposal followed in December. Vought provided the following guarantees:
- Maximum speed – at 35,000 feet, maximum thrust, level flight, combat weight of 28,420 pounds: 1,265 kts. (Not less than) (Mach 2.2)
- Combat ceiling – minimum altitude for 2.5 minutes at 1.5 G. at combat weight of 28,420 pounds: 58,000 ft.
- Stalling speed – power off landing configuration, landing weight of 24,150 pounds: 108 kts.
- Weight empty: 20,244 pounds

Only three Sparrow missiles were to be carried instead of four, and the second seat was not proposed. Otherwise, the proposal exceeded the requirement.

The two-place study was accomplished at BuAer's request for "an indication of the airplane weight and performance penalties that would be associated with the addition of a second place for a radar operator/navigator." The second crew position required stretching the forward fuselage by 50 inches. It was configured with the primary APQ-50 radar indicator and navigation instruments. In order to maintain the three-hour CAP cycle, 108-knot stall speed, directional stability, and weight and balance, the following changes were also made:

- Added 59 gallons of fuel capacity, 20 in the larger wing and 39 in a tank located between the main landing gears
- Increased wing area by 27 square-feet
- Added nine square feet of vertical fin and six of ventral fin
- Shifted wing and main gear forward 11.8 inches

The second seat could not help but reduce the performance. Empty and gross weight increases were estimated to be 1,157 lbs and 1,820 lbs, respectively. Maximum speed at 35,000 feet was reduced by Mach 0.1 and combat ceiling by 2,000 feet. Time to

*The difference between the aft fuselage of the J57-powered F8U-1/2 and that of the J75-powered F8U-3 was another indication of the difference in engine size. The ventral fins in the horizontal position are mostly evident in this photo by their shadow on the ground. (Jay Miller collection)*

*Except for the speed brake and the cockpit, the F8U-3 was bigger in all respects than its older brother, the F8U-1/2. The gapping maw of the engine inlet is one indication of its bigger engine. (Jay Miller collection)*

accelerate from Mach 0.9 to Mach 1.7 was increased by 36 seconds. Finally, the deck spot number was decreased from 21 to 18. However, from a competitive standpoint, the performance degradation was not significant and was within the accuracy of the projections. The cost impact reduced its advantage over the bigger, twin-engine F4H, but not to a worrisome degree. Vought clearly believed that the second crew position was not warranted by the increased mission effectiveness and that the Navy, having up until then demonstrated a clear preference for single-seat carrier-based fighters, would agree. Vought probably spent more time doing studies and analyses, including building a cockpit simulator for workload studies, on justifying the single-seat version than it did on the two-seat study itself.

The cost proposal was submitted in December. After a review and evaluation of the proposal, BuAer decided, in June 1956, to procure the V-401 as the F8U-3, the F8U-2 now being on order. Detail specification and contract negotiations began in July. Detail Specification SD-525-1 was finally signed in early October 1956, which included a change from the JT4B-21 engine with 25,000-lbs static thrust to the JT4A-27 with 24,500 lbs. The empty weight had increased to 21,767 lbs, the useful load to 15,733 lbs, and the gross weight to 37,500 lbs. At the time, the performance of the F8U-3 and F4H-1 was projected to be virtually identical:

|  | F8U-3 | F4H-1 |
|---|---|---|
| Maximum Speed, 35,000 ft (M) | 2.02 | 2.02 |
| Supersonic Combat Ceiling (ft) | 52,100 | 51,900 |
| Subsonic Combat Ceiling (ft) | 45,700 | 42,600 |
| Accel, .9 M to 90 percent Vmax(min). | 2.89 | 2.93 |
| Stall Speed, Landing Weight (kts) | 108 | 100 |
| Combat Air Patrol Cycle Time (hrs) | 2.98 | 3.00 |
| Engine Thrust, Sea Level Static (lbs) | 24,500 | 2x 15,600 |
| Engine Thrust, 35k ft, M 2.0 (lbs) | 23,400 | 2x 17,600 |

Chance Vought received a contract in October 1956 that covered wind-tunnel test work and mockups. In March 1957, the Navy finally provided Vought with a contract for the bulk of the program, including two flight-test articles and one static-test article, with a first flight projected for 14 June 1958.

The Navy evaluation of the aircraft, cockpit, and vision mockups was completed in early December 1956. The aircraft mockup review included presentations on the F8U-3F, which had an auxiliary rocket motor in a fairing at the base of the trailing edge of the vertical fin. The thrust could be varied between 3,500 and 8,000 lbs. It burned jet fuel with hydrogen peroxide as the oxidizer. There were about three to six minutes of oxidizer depending on the level and duration of thrust. The main benefit according to the Vought analysis was the additional altitude capability of 20,000 to 25,000 feet, since the top speed was limited by

structural considerations. There was some benefit from the increased acceleration and climb rate – a deck-launched F8U-3F could get to an intercept point 75 nautical miles away in five minutes and 45 seconds after takeoff compared to a non-rocket augmented F8U-3's six minutes and 30 seconds.[4]

First flight was actually accomplished at Edwards AFB on 2 June, ahead of schedule and only a few days after the F4H's first flight at St. Louis, although the Vought go-ahead had been received about a year later than McDonnell's.

The F8U-3 demonstrated its speed potential at Edwards, flying as fast as Mach 2.38 and being flown to Mach 2 at altitudes from 35,000 feet to almost 60,000 feet. A different pitch-trim system from the J57-powered F8Us eliminated the PIO tendency. It had a simpler inlet than the F4H, requiring only that bypass doors be opened at Mach 1.4 to spill excessive air overboard to keep from choking the inlet.

The Navy fully intended to proceed into production with both aircraft. For one thing, it was too early to tell whether one aircraft or the other might suffer from a yet-to-be-revealed problem. Congress did not agree – it would only fund the continuation of one new Navy jet fighter program. The Navy argued to no avail. One of the two best jet fighters they had ever developed, both of which met or exceeded requirements and were in low-rate production, had to be canceled. It was a very tough decision because of their relative strengths and weaknesses. The F4H was the more expensive to buy and operate because of its two engines and two-man crew, but having two engines and/or two crewmembers was considered a key differentiator by some. The F8U-3 had slightly more performance and cockpit features that minimized, but did not necessarily eliminate, the mission impact of not having a second crewmember.

*In order to have room for the third semi-submerged Sparrow on the forward fuselage, the F8U-3's nose landing gear was offset to the right. This is relatively rare but sometimes has to be resorted to by aircraft designers to accommodate all the demands on internal volume. (Jay Miller collection)*

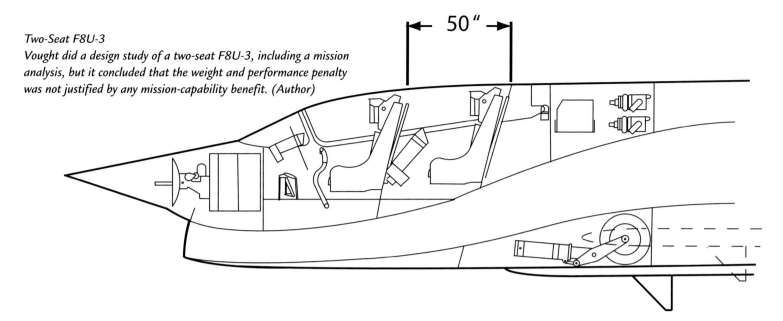

**Two-Seat F8U-3**
*Vought did a design study of a two-seat F8U-3, including a mission analysis, but it concluded that the weight and performance penalty was not justified by any mission-capability benefit. (Author)*

50 "

The competitive flight evaluation of the F4H and the F8U-3 was conducted as part of the first Naval Preliminary Evaluation on both aircraft following the initial envelope expansion by company test pilots. Eight NATC pilots headed by Capt. Robert M. Elder accomplished the NPE between 15 September and 10 October 1958. The F8U-3 was initially at a disadvantage because of engine-compressor stall incidents at supersonic speeds. Recovery required slowing to a subsonic speed. By chance, the F4H suffered an engine casualty that forced a temporary halt to the evaluation, and Vought was able to reduce the incidence and severity of compressor stalls before it resumed.[5]

In his oral history, George Spangenberg had the following to say about the decision:

> Both airplanes were scheduled for production and were designed with superb programs. Vought did a better job in development than McDonnell did. They started perhaps a year afterwards and flew at almost the same time, first flight. And then Vought did a much better job of fixing things up that showed up in flight test. In 1957, Congress was screaming. We had to cancel one. Up to that point in time the Navy had never had less than two fighters in production at the same time. Jim Russell was chief of the Bureau and he testified that we can't afford to ever get down to having our fleet defense dependent upon any one engine or any one airplane. If you have a bad episode with one and have to ground the airplanes or the engines you didn't want the fleet without some capability to defend themselves.

> (Vought was) obviously extremely disappointed. It was just one of many disappointments for (them) at about that time where the Navy was really getting itself

into a money crunch. But, in 1957, Congress told us to cancel one. We ran a big paper evaluation. Neither airplane had reached flight status, and (we) finally got Congress to delay it a year. By that time we had flight tests by PAX and could make sure that our paper estimates were all right. In the normal sense the F8U-3 won the fly-off. It had by far the best flying qualities. It was the best flying airplane, best flying fighter at least that the Navy had ever developed according to the PAX reports. Good flight control system. It carried only three Sparrows instead of four as a compromise in trying to get the best airplane. It would do everything on internal fuel that the (F4H) did with a 600-gallon tank. It had better legs. It had higher speed. Climbs were about the same. Ceilings were about the same.

> It was a one-place versus two-place (decision). At the time there was a growing conviction in the fleet that you needed two guys to do the all-weather fighter job. There was a big all-weather fighter conference at Patuxent and they came out with "a unanimous report." I can't believe that of Navy fighter pilots.

> (One versus two engines) was incidental in my opinion but it was an advantage. People would prefer two engines to one engine as long as you didn't pay too big a penalty. But the one-man, two-man decision was primary with the feeling that one man under good conditions could do the job. You had about a 20-percent advantage of cost with the F8U-3. But under the real tough conditions where the studies were done and presented, the F8U lost out. The kind of radar detection ranges we had, the conversion from when you first saw

the enemy to where you could get in a position of launching missiles, it came down to the difference of two radar sweeps that made the difference between success and failure. You sure had a hell of a lot better chance to do that with a radar operator, meaning two-man.[6]

Vought campaigned against the need for the second seat, even reportedly taking its functional, single-seat cockpit mockup to Washington in a last-ditch effort to demonstrate that the workload was acceptable. It was to no avail. The Navy's preferred fleet defense fighter configuration was two seats and two engines. As a result, the Vought F8U-3 program was terminated in December 1958, after less than six months of flight test. The three aircraft that reached flight status had flown a cumulative total of more than 200 hours with outstanding results. A fourth was nearing completion, and five more of the initial production order of 16 were in various stages of assembly. The three flying F8U-3s were transferred to NASA: BuNo. 146340 in May 1959 and 146341 the following month to NASA Langley, and 147085 to NASA Ames in May 1960. They were reportedly all transferred back to the Navy and stricken within a year or so.

Although with only 200 hours of development test and no carrier-suitability testing other than first impressions made during the NPE/fly-off, it's impossible to say how well the F8U-3 would have performed in operational service. It is remembered by some of those who flew it as having truly remarkable high-speed performance and very good low-speed handling qualities. Of course, being canceled before any shortcomings could be identified, or if identified, thought to be easy to eliminate, was a sure-fire way to claim greatness. If only…

## Grumman "F12F"

The designation F12F, two Bureau Numbers, and even a canceled contract have been erroneously associated with Grumman's Design 118, a twin-J79-powered fleet-defense fighter proposed as an alternative to McDonnell's F4H. In fact, all these were issued in anticipation of the procurement of the Super Tiger. However, Design 118 would probably have been designated the F12F if the Navy had procured it after canceling the Super Tiger plan.

Grumman proposed the J79-powered Design 98J Super Tiger to the Navy in January 1955. However, it was well aware of McDonnell's efforts to sell a twin-J79-powered fighter to the Navy and was trying to determine whether it should propose a bigger fighter as well. From 15 February through the end of March 1955, Grumman accomplished a design study of single- and multi-engine fighters using several different engines, including auxiliary engines. The engine list was established by a first flight date of late 1958 and first production in 1960. Therefore, only engines that had completed their 150-hour qualification or were likely to complete it by

1959 were to be considered. These included the J71, J79, and J75. The design number 110 was used, with different dash numbers designating different configurations. In addition, the study projected the performance and capability of the forthcoming J75-powered

*In most cases, aerodynamic changes were made to improve the performance of the original design. Because the F11F, like the F8U, was already advanced aerodynamically, Grumman also had to resort to an engine change, in this case to the General Electric J79, which wasn't mature enough when the F11F program began. (Hal Andrews collection)*

*Among the early changes to the F11F-1F was a leading edge extension (which Grumman also chose to incorporate in F11F production) and a new windscreen with a shallower slope installed for expediency over the original one. (Hal Andrews collection)*

The F8U-3 first flew at Edwards Air Force Base. Here, the first Crusader III is taxiing on the lakebed itself. The large vent above the Sparrow missile forward fins is an inlet air dump. Since the inlet itself was fixed in size, the excess air ingested at high speeds had to be removed before it got to the engine. (Jay Miller collection)

In order to provide adequate directional stability at speeds up to Mach 2.2, the Crusader III was fitted with two huge ventral fins that were repositioned after takeoff and before landing. (Jay Miller collection)

F-105 and the twin-J79-powered F4H for comparison with the Grumman designs.

The aircraft were to be single-seat and have a 24-inch radar dish and a modernized Aero 19A fire-control system. Armament included two 30mm cannons. Performance desired was the broadest attainable supersonic speed-altitude envelope, a 60,000-foot subsonic ceiling, a combat radius of 500 nautical miles, and a cycle time of 2.5 hours.

Each fighter was to be configured with a centerline recess that could be loaded with one of several "packages." Its size was established by the shape of the Mk 7 nuclear bomb, which was 183 inches long and 30.5 inches in diameter, one of the standard loads

for a general-purpose fighter. Other packages envisaged were photographic, a fuel tank, a "Buddy" refueling system, and various armament options, including two Sparrows and their launching mechanisms.

Eight different configurations were defined, including some very radical ones, the least practical being an eight-engine, General Electric J85-powered VTOL. A few had canards for supersonic trim and control. From an engine standpoint, Grumman engineers favored the General Electric J79 because of its thrust-to-weight performance over the J57 and J71. They assessed the J75-powered fighter to be inferior in operational suitability to, and 7,000 lbs heavier than, the twin-J79-powered one. It was clear to

*A late change to the Super Tiger was a dorsal fairing, adding to the bulk of the aft fuselage compared to the production F11F beside it. This aircraft has the "speed bump" in front of the engine inlet, but the retractable ventral fins have been removed as unnecessary. In production as the F12F, the wing was going to be increased in area to carry the added weight of fuel and armament. (Hal Andrews collection)*

them that the best single-engine fighter would be a growth version of the Super Tiger with a growth version of the J79. However, they also concluded that a twin-J79-powered fighter would provide a marked performance improvement over a single-engine one in addition to providing the benefit of being able to return to base after an engine failure.

Grumman therefore pursued two separate but parallel paths in order to sell its next Navy fighter program. The first was to significantly improve the performance of its fighter currently in development, the F11F. The F8U Crusader had been taken supersonic on its first flight in March 1955, and was clearly a winner in the Navy's eyes. The J65's thrust shortfall and development problems had temporarily put Grumman at a competitive disadvantage. With the Super Tiger, it was sure of outperforming the J57-powered F8U and F5D. The parallel activity based on the Design 110 study was to prepare a proposal for a twin-J79-powered aircraft because of its even better performance and payload capability.

### Super Tiger

BuAer did its part in August by accepting Grumman's proposal to build two J79-powered Super Tiger demonstrators using the last two aircraft in the first production lot. One benefit to the Navy was early experience in flight with the engine that was to power the F4H. The resulting F11F-1F first flew in May 1956, only nine months after go-ahead. After relatively minimal inlet and airframe tweaking, it demonstrated excellent high-speed and climb performance – it was flown out to Mach 2.0 in level flight, and in April 1958 Lt. Cdr. George Watkins set an altitude record on a ballistic profile with an apogee of 75,550 feet. On an earlier practice flight, a Grumman pilot had topped out at 82,000 feet.

The F11F-1F was only a performance demonstrator. The proposed Super Tiger was to have a bigger wing, visual-assist radar,

*In an overly complex attempt to address the issue of emergency egress at supersonic speeds, Grumman provided for a forward fuselage that could be separated from the aircraft and stabilized and slowed with a drag chute. The crew would then eject after it had slowed down to a safe speed. As it turned out, OpNav and BuAer were becoming more concerned about ejection capability during takeoff and landing. (Grumman Aircraft History Center)*

and more fuel. It not only received serious consideration at BuAer, but for a time it was moving toward becoming a reality. A Characteristics Summary form, dated 15 August 1955, was issued identifying it as the F12F.[7] A plan to order 23 Super Tigers was being considered in mid-1955, and a contract number issued to order two – BuNos. 143401 and 143402. However, the contract number for these aircraft was rescinded in January 1956, along with the Bureau Numbers, even before the F11F-1F flew.

Grumman still had hopes that the performance of the Super Tiger demonstrator would result in a reinstatement of the F12F. The J79 engine did make a huge difference and was actually lighter and more fuel-efficient than the J65. However, BuAer calculated mission fuel consumption at ratings, not at required thrust. Since the J79 had more thrust at every rating than the J65, it burned more fuel – 1,300 gallons vs. 1,092 for a 2.5-hour mission in the 1955 Grumman study. The bigger wing of the notional Super Tiger increased the capacity to 1,063 gallons, which at least allowed Grumman to claim a 1.5-hour cycle time on internal fuel using the Navy's fighter mission definition.

With the J79, the F11F was faster and had better climb performance than the F8U. While the Super Tiger fell short of the range and endurance of the Crusader, Grumman could credibly predict acceptable range and endurance. Unfortunately, the Navy was committed to an F8U fleet, and it was adequate to the task with arguably more growth potential.

### Design 118

In parallel with its sales efforts on the Super Tiger and in competition with McDonnell's F4H, Grumman defined and submitted the company's Design 118, a large, two-man, Sparrow-armed fighter powered by two General Electric J79 engines.[8] It was to have a throttleable rocket engine for an additional 5,000 lbs of thrust. Retractable ventral fins were provided for directional stability at high speed. For low drag, two of the Sparrows were semi-submerged in the lower fuselage and a third, or three Sidewinders with folded rear fins, housed in a box that retracted into the bottom of the aft fuselage.

Design 118 had enough internal fuel for a two-hour cycle time. With two 300-gallon external tanks, cycle time increased to three hours. The radar was to be the APQ-50 tied into a Sparrow missile-control system.

Too much innovation went into the creation of the crew's normal access to and emergency egress from the cockpit. The downward ejection seats also functioned as elevators, facilitating entry and egress for the pressure-suited crew. (Downward ejection had been used on a few other aircraft, notably the early F-104s; at the time, pilots were worried about striking the tail at high speeds – the seat was not likely to do them any good at low altitudes anyway.) Because of concerns that an ejection at Mach 2 was likely to cause severe injuries, if it was survivable at all, the nose section was to separate first and be slowed to subsonic speeds by a drag chute. The crew would then eject from the capsule. Overhead

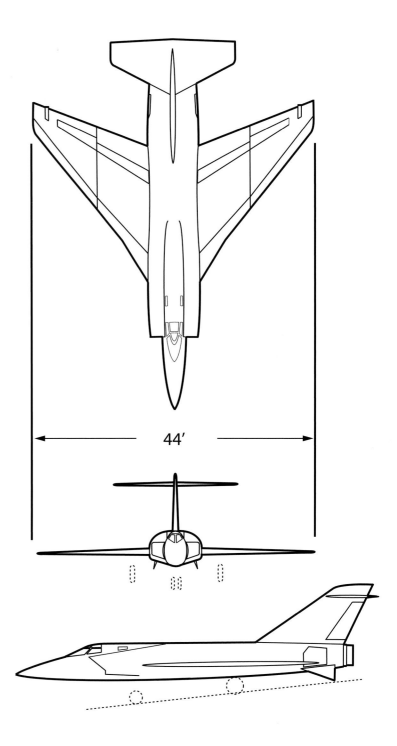

*Grumman Design 118*
*Often cited as the F12F, Grumman's Design 118 never got that far with the Navy. It was basically a late attempt to beat out the F4H, a futile effort because of the support within BuAer for "their" design. (U.S. Navy)*

hatches were also provided for emergency egress in a ditching or wheels-up crash.

Almost as unusually, the configuration included a high horizontal tail like the XF10F. Not only was it positioned high on the vertical fin, but when it was generally accepted that low speed and transonic aerodynamic considerations all but dictated a tail positioned below the wing, it was not swept. Based on analysis of wind-tunnel tests, Grumman was projecting that a low-aspect ratio, high-mounted horizontal tail would incur less trim drag than a low tail.

The rocket engine provided increased rate of climb, acceleration, and altitude performance that Grumman considered critical to the task-force defense mission. Because of airframe structural and aerodynamic heating issues, it could not be used to increase top speed, but it did allow speed to be maintained in a turn or climbs. However, it also introduced the requirement for storage and fueling of hydrogen peroxide. While not an explosive in and of itself, it was a very powerful oxidizer and demanded careful handling to avoid injury.

Grumman's sales pitch was that the Design 118 could do both the high-altitude "day" fighter mission as well as provide all-weather fleet air defense. Its argument was bolstered by detailed mission analyses. Unlike Vought, it was convinced of the advantages of a two-man crew:

• Optimum radar performance
• Increased detection and lock-on range
• Increased effectiveness in presence of Electronic Countermeasures
• Improved coordination and communications between various fighters attacking the same group of targets
• Improved navigation
• Improved ability to distinguish between targets
• Less automatic equipment
• Improved reliability and availability

Grumman proposed this aircraft to BuAer in December 1955, the same time as Vought proposed its J75-powered Crusader derivative, the V-401. According to Hal Andrews, the Navy informally rejected Grumman's twin-J79-powered proposal since it already had a similar design, the F4H, under contract. The Navy did suggest to Grumman that it change the proposal to a single-engine one for comparison with Vought's. Grumman hastily prepared an updated proposal, adding the Model 118A powered by the J75, which the company provided to the Navy in early May. It appears that the Navy already had its mind made up, as BuAer's formal response on 16 July 1956, stated, in part:

> The recent receipt of more up-to-date engine data does not alter their relative standings of your design with others already programmed in the fighter field.
> The Chief of the Bureau of Aeronautics has therefore

determined that the introduction of another design using the same engines and conforming to the same general operation requirements cannot be justified or undertaken.[9]

With this second rejection, Grumman stopped developing fighters for the Navy for a while.

*The Design 118 had relatively small ventral fins and the small leading edge extension also seen on the F11F-1F and the second lot of F11F production. One significant departure from accepted supersonic design was the high horizontal tail. (Grumman Aircraft History Center)*

*The Design 118 was to be armed with two semi-submerged Sparrow missiles and either a third Sparrow or three Sidewinders in a bay just behind them. For even more acceleration and climb performance, the Design 118 had a rocket motor, which can be seen protruding between the two ventral fins. When extended, its thrust line went through the center of gravity so no pitching moment was generated when it was firing. (Grumman Aircraft History Center)*

## CHAPTER FIFTEEN

*The next step in the development of the F8U was the F8U-2NE, the "E" designating a still bigger radar dish and the addition of an infrared scanner. Emphasis was also placed on more capability in roles for what had been known as the general-purpose fighter. Here the aircraft is burdened with a 2,000-lb bomb on each wing and two two-Zuni rocket launchers on the Sidewinder mounts on each side of the fuselage. The cartoon in front of the main landing gear well is labeled "Mad Bomber." (Hal Andrews collection)*

1953 | 1954 | 1955 | 1956 | 1957 | 1958 | 1959 | 1960

Korean War
Tachen Island ★
Suez ★
Jordan ★
Lebanon ★
Quemoy/Matsu ★
Laos ★ ★
Congo ★
Guatemala/Nicaragua
Dominican Republic
Cuban Mis.

# Summary and Epilogue

## F4H Development

On 3 July 1959, at the McDonnell 20th-anniversary celebration, James S. McDonnell announced that the F4H had been named Phantom II. The other candidates that company employees voted on included Sprite, Ghost, Goblin, and Satan. McDonnell himself reportedly preferred the name Mithras after the ancient Persian god of light, the rewarder of good and annihilator of evil. However, the final decision was the Navy's.

The F4H's first flight, in May 1958, was the beginning of an extensive development effort that was briefly interrupted by the fly-off with the F8U-3 later that same year. Due to the changes the Navy made following contract award, shortcomings revealed by flight test, the time required to perfect the mission avionics, and the initial lack of reliability inherent in new and complex aircraft systems, the F4H took somewhat longer to develop than the Navy hoped.

*McDonnell's ability to market and produce aircraft that the Navy valued is clear from this formation flight. In the lead is an F2H-3 from the Navy Reserve squadron at Oakland, California. Next is one of the last F3H-2s to be built. And just in time to replace the F3H, is the fifth F4H produced. (Hal Andrews collection)*

One troublesome innovation was the variable-area, air data computer-controlled engine inlets. Although many hours of subsonic and supersonic wind-tunnel and subsonic rocket-sled testing went into developing the inlet that first flew, it proved to be less effective than hoped at speeds above Mach 1. The first flight inlet was "hooded" and had a very small fixed ramp and a large perforated moveable ramp. The production inlet involved increasing the size of the fixed ramp relative to the moveable ramp, increasing the inlet ramp angles, revising the moveable ramp programming, and modifying the bell mouth at the engine inlet. The second prototype was used for much of this development work.

Another was the wing flap and boundary-layer control system. Aircraft six was the first to have the final configuration. It helped reduce the approach speed to an acceptable value, permitting the first at-sea evaluation to be accomplished aboard *Independence* in February 1960, almost two years after first flight.

In April 1960, suitability trials were successfully accomplished aboard the smaller *Intrepid*, an Essex-class carrier that was the design constraint for the F4H size and weight. BIS trials began in July 1960, and ran through December.

The weight of the aircraft had steadily increased in design and development, so the five-percent higher-thrust J79-GE-8 engine was to power F4H-1s after the 47th aircraft. Somewhat after the fact, the first 47 were designated F4H-1F (and then F-4A) and subsequent production, F4H-1 (later F-4B). This was due in part to the engine difference, but some F4H-1Fs were eventually retrofitted with the -8 engine. The first 47 were used for development, demonstrations, evaluations, record setting, and training. The configuration of the first 23 of these varied somewhat, as noted above. Number 24 and subsequent F4H-1Fs, however,

The F4H was finally ready for shore-based takeoff and landing trials in late 1959. The leading edge flaps have now been extended to the inboard wing and boundary layer control added to the leading edge. The nose landing gear strut was pressurized for a carrier takeoff to extend it for more angle of attack. (Hal Andrews collection)

Shore-based landing trials only required a single arresting cable because the touchdown zone could be relied upon to stay in one place. This was an in-flight engagement, which would cause somewhat higher structural loads depending on the vector of the aircraft when the engagement occurred. (Hal Andrews collection)

Successful completion of the shore-based trials resulted in at-sea trials aboard Independence in February 1960. (Hal Andrews collection)

The F4H was also qualified aboard Intrepid, an Essex-class carrier. However, Phantom IIs seldom, if ever, operated from the smaller carriers. (Hal Andrews collection)

*Here the first carrier-suitability F4H, carrying the big centerline tank, has missed all the wires and has departed the angle for another attempt, beginning to claw for altitude after sinking below the deck edge. (Hal Andrews collection)*

were indistinguishable externally from the F4H-1s, the first of which flew in March 1961.

## F4H Records

Beginning in late 1959, several of the early F4Hs were used to set performance records. Most of the record projects were distinguished by a suitable name. The first, Top Flight, resulted in a world altitude record of 98,557 feet, set in December by Cdr. Lawrence E. Flint. The next two were for speed over a closed course, 1,216 mph for 500 km in September 1960 by Marine Lt. Col. Tom Miller, and 1,390 mph for 100 km by Cdr. John F. Davis that same month. As with the F4D Skyray, the records did not really represent a practical capability. Each required extensive preparation, including envelope expansion and several flights dedicated to developing the optimum flight profile and then practicing it.

The record-setting flights were marred by two fatal crashes. The first involved the number one Phantom II on 21 October 1959, during profile development for Top Flight. An engine compartment door came off, affecting engine cooling, which caused an engine-casing failure. That allowed hot engine gases to burn through hydraulic lines to a stabilator, which caused it to go full leading edge down. McDonnell test pilot Gerald "Zeke" Huelsbeck tried to recover from the resulting spin and waited too long to eject.

The Top Flight F4H, the second one built, was as light as it could be, with no radar, fire-control system, or other extraneous equipment like a rear seat. The engine was tuned up with maximum rpm set at 105 percent, the inlet guide vanes opened up, afterburner fuel flow increased by 15 percent, and exhaust nozzle tightened. Takeoff was from Edwards AFB, and climb out to arrive over Point Mugu southwest of Edwards at 40,000 feet with about 7,800 lbs of fuel, which was just enough to fly the profile and land back at Edwards with 1,000 lbs or less. At that point, Cdr. Flint commenced an accelerating 180-degree turn to the north, manually controlling the engine inlet ramp and bellmouth positions for maximum thrust. The turn and run-in were to position the F4H back at Edwards at the coldest altitude between 40,000 and 46,000 feet at maximum speed, usually about Mach 2.35. From there, a 3.5 g pull-up produced a

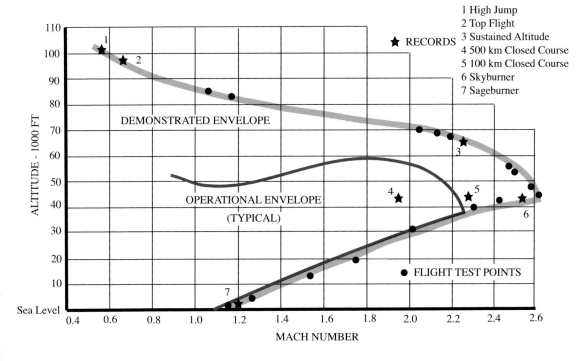

1 High Jump
2 Top Flight
3 Sustained Altitude
4 500 km Closed Course
5 100 km Closed Course
6 Skyburner
7 Sageburner

★ RECORDS

● FLIGHT TEST POINTS

*F4H Flight Envelope*
*To an even greater extent than usual, the Navy used the F4H to set world records. Most were set in the early production aircraft that had minimal mission equipment, but only a few were tweaked for added performance. However, the difference between the high and fast records versus the operational envelope is significant. (Author)*

*Sageburner, intended to capture the three-km speed record that had to be set at a dangerously low altitude at the time, proved fatal. The picture does not begin to portray the difficulty of this flight, particularly in an aircraft that was sensitive to PIO at the Q (dynamic pressure) involved. (Hal Andrews collection)*

climb angle of 50 degrees. Afterburner blowout occurred at about 72,000 feet, along with the requirement to reduce engine fuel flow to prevent overspeed and to turn off the radios to keep them from shorting out. The engines were shut down at 85,000 feet, at which point Flint's pressure suit inflated with the loss of cabin pressure. (A nitrogen bottle had been installed in the rear cockpit, which was opened at 60,000 feet to provide some cockpit pressurization and minimize the suit inflation and loss of mobility.) The flight controls were ineffective at that altitude, so the F4H coasted upward in a ballistic trajectory to the peak altitude. After the record was set, all the pilot had to do was recover from whatever attitude he was in when the aircraft fell back into thicker air, restart the engines, and land back at Edwards before running out of fuel. Total flight time was about 20 minutes.

The 500-km closed-course record took even more planning and preparation. The first problem was that the F4H couldn't fly much farther than 500 km on internal fuel while in afterburner, even at the optimum altitude of 50,000 feet. The start and finish positions could be precisely controlled using the radar at Edwards Air Force Base, but the two turn points had to be rounded visually. The solution was to place McDonnell test pilots at the turn points

with a sighting device to talk the pilot around the turn by monitoring his contrail. The fuel problem was addressed by taking off with the big 600-gallon centerline drop tank and two 370-gallon wing drop tanks and then using that fuel to take off, climb, accelerate, and position the F4H to enter the course. The wing tanks were emptied and jettisoned first and the centerline tank next, after accelerating past Mach 1. After a few practice runs to get the timing and procedures down, all that remained was waiting for a cold day at 50,000 feet. The actual record run went perfectly – 500 km in 15 minutes and 10,000 lbs of fuel, with Lt. Col. Miller coming off the course at 48,000 feet with 900 lbs of fuel remaining, just enough for a split S to a near vertical dive at idle with speed brakes out, a straight-in approach, and landing while the engines flamed out. Piece of cake…

In May 1961, in Project Sageburner, Cdr. J. Felsman attempted to set a new three-km speed record. He was killed when his F4H disintegrated during a Pilot Induced Oscillation (PIO) because he was trying to hold less than the 100-meter altitude required. In afterburner at low altitude and high speed, the early F4Hs were susceptible to PIO, which was caused by the pilot reaction time to a pitch perturbation being equal to the aircraft's self correction, causing the pilot and aircraft responses to coincide and magnify the reversal. Both would then simultaneously correct the correction and so on. In the worst case, each cycle would impose higher loads than the one before, quickly leading to a structural failure. The solution was to simply pull up, breaking the cycle. Unfortunately, the height limitations on the low-altitude run, one of them being the potential impact with the ground that was only about 200 feet away, were such that the pilot would be trying to hold altitude very precisely.

Also in May, five Phantom IIs were used by pilots from VF-74 and VF-121 in the Bendix Trophy transcontinental "race" from Ontario, California, to New York City. The fastest LANA (for 50th Anniversary of Naval Aviation, with L being the Roman numeral for 50) time was two hours, 47 minutes, and 17 seconds for an average speed of 869.7 mph. Since the cruise speed was well in excess of Mach 1, three air-to-air refuelings were necessary.

In August, the three-km low-altitude speed record was successfully reattempted and set at 902.8 mph by Lt. Huntington Hardisty with his RIO, Lt. Earl H. DeEsch, following pitch-control system changes and flight evaluation.[1] Lt. Hardisty was awarded the Distinguished Flying Cross and Lt. DeEsch the Air Medal for the flight, which the Chief of Naval Operations described as follows, alluding to some of the circumstances that affected the record flight:

The three-kilometer record graphically demonstrates several outstanding capabilities of the Phantom II, including maneuverability, flight control characteristics at high speed, pilot confidence in the aircraft, and an

*Skyburner, which strictly speaking was outside the design envelope of the F4H, was the least stock of the record-breaking Phantom IIs. This was the second F4H built, now with an engine inlet similar to the production one. For the absolute speed-record attempt, the windscreen was beefed up because of the temperatures to be encountered. The engines were also provided with water injection, for cooling and more thrust. (Hal Andrews collection)*

unmatched low altitude record. This latest record is one more bit of proof that the Phantom II is one of the best fighter aircraft in the world.

Skyburner was next, in November 1961, using the second prototype with a modified engine inlet very similar to the production design. Lt. Col. Robert B. "Robby" Robinson set a speed record of 1,606 mph, Mach 2.5, the previous record being held by an F-106 at 1,526 mph. For this flight, the engines were equipped with a water-injection system and the windscreen was beefed up. The aircraft was actually capable of a higher speed, but the record rules and the requirement to jettison the external tanks over uninhabited areas limited the ability to finish accelerating before beginning the first of two record runs, one in each direction. Legend has it that the windshield-temperature warning light was on continuously during the record runs.

Cdr. George W. Ellis accomplished the next record flight, sustained altitude, in December 1961. At 66,443 feet, it shattered the old record of 55,300 feet. It may be hard to believe, but its maximum level flight altitude was achieved at Mach 2.2. This was followed, in early 1962, by a set of time-to-climb records, accomplished with Project High Jump, from a standing start to the following altitudes above the takeoff point:

| Altitude (meters) | Time (seconds) | Pilot |
| --- | --- | --- |
| 3,000 | 34.123 | Lt. Cdr. John W. Young, USN |
| 6,000 | 48.797 | Cdr. David M. Longton, USN |
| 9,000 | 61.688 | Lt. Col. W. C. McGraw, USMC |
| 12,000 | 77.143 | Lt. Col. W. C. McGraw, USMC |
| 15,000 | 114.148 | Lt. Cdr. D.W. Norberg, USN |
| 20,000 | 178.5 | Lt. Cdr. John W. Young, USN |
| 25,000 | 230.44 | Lt. Cdr. John W. Young, USN |
| 30,000 | 371.43 | Lt. Cdr. D. W. Norberg, USN |

On the 30,000-meter record flight, the F4H coasted past 100,000 feet, unofficially breaking the altitude record.

The time-to-climb records were the only ones accomplished with F4H-1s as opposed to F4H-1Fs. They were accomplished at two different locations with a separate flight for each altitude due to the different flight paths (and fuel loads) required for maximum rate of climb. The records up through 15,000 meters were flown out of NAS Brunswick, Maine, to take advantage of cooler air. The 20,000-meter and above flights were accomplished from NAS Point Mugu, California.[2]

All of the speed records except for the three-km restricted-altitude one were broken within a year or two by Russian aircraft, except of course for the transcontinental record, which was cut in half by an Air Force B-58 in March 1962. The time-to-climb records lasted longer but were eventually surpassed by an Air Force F-15. However, none of the successor record holders, excepting a modified F-15, were even remotely capable of being carrier-based.

## F4H Introduction Into Service

VF-101, based in Key West, Florida, and VF-121, based at NAS Miramar, California, were assigned Phantom pilot training responsibility for the East Coast and West Coast, respectively. The first to receive F4Hs was VF-121 in December 1960. VF-101 formed a detachment for this purpose, which was relocated to NAS Oceana, Virginia.

One of the prerequisites to introducing the F4H into service was training for a new crewmember requirement, Radar Intercept Officer. The Phantom II was to be the first Navy fighter since the F3D, more than 10 years earlier, to have a second crewmember. Then, he had been an enlisted man, consistent with the use of enlisted men in similar positions in night-attack aircraft. However,

*VF-102, one of the early F4H squadrons, first deployed aboard Enterprise, the first nuclear-powered aircraft carrier, for a short shakedown cruise in February 1962. (Robert L. Lawson collection)*

*The position of the F4H horizontal stabilizer just after launch was very important, as in the story of the three bears. Phantom II pilots quickly learned to avoid too little or too much after their experience with either. (Hal Andrews collection)*

in this case the Navy elected to assign the responsibility to officers. They were not to be pilots, however, and there would be no flight controls in the rear cockpit of deployed aircraft. The first training was accomplished with VF-121 F3Ds modified with the APG-51C radar then equipping the F3H-2 Demon. Before their F3D flights, the training curriculum included flights in various aircraft as "Technical Observers" since the duties would include communications, navigation, and electronic countermeasures in addition to airborne intercepts; an eight-week Combat Information Center course; and a month-long Air Controller's course, where they were introduced to the responsibility of the surface-based management and direction of interceptors. The first class received their air observer wings in early 1961, just in time to take their seats in fleet aircraft.

The first F4H-1, the 48th Phantom II, flew on 25 March 1961. In June 1951, the 50th aircraft was delivered to the Navy for service use. In October 1961, aboard *Saratoga*, VF-74 became the first fleet squadron to qualify in the F4H. They made the first full deployment aboard *Forrestal* to the Mediterranean in August 1962. However, VF-102 was aboard a shakedown cruise of *Enterprise*, the first nuclear-powered aircraft carrier in February 1962.

According to Rear Admiral Pete Booth:

The Phantom was perhaps the best carrier landing airplane ever bought by the Navy. It was incredibly responsive to slight power changes and, of course, it had power like no other airplane had ever had. Its only drawback was that it couldn't come aboard with much fuel. With a tank, racks, missiles, and a not-too-recent wash job, the jet could come aboard with about 4,000 pounds of fuel, enough for four or five passes at the deck at night. It could, however, refuel airborne, which was the good news.

Bad news was that the tanker – a tiny A-4 jet – passed fuel at a rate almost equal to what we were burning in the process. At any rate, we usually had priority in the pattern, which was nice.

But, whereas the Crusader had been high workload on landing and couldn't have been easier in a catapult launch, the Phantom was just the opposite. Booth again:

> Catapulting in the F4H was kind of different because the airplane was slow to rotate at low gross weights and could have a very rapid rotation when heavy with fuel and ordnance (that) went like this: Once over the catapult shuttle and into the holdback, the nose strut was extended about two feet, which actually gave the machine a more positive angle of attack once it

left the ship. Even so, the book said to hold the stick all the way aft on the stroke, give the plane a chance to dig in and then ease off on the stick. On about one of 10 cat shots, the pilot would under-rotate and get the heart rate of the ship's captain and air boss up a peg or two, or over-rotate and get it up three or four pegs.

## F8U Derivatives and Improvements

The Navy's desire to have two different fighters with two different engines in production at all times resulted in Vought receiving a consolation prize after losing the competition with McDonnell, as there followed a long period of F8U product

improvements, new production, and major reworks. The success of the F8U and the F4H and the development cost of new fighter programs also put an end to introduction of new fighter types every few years. Now improvement was accomplished by the steady iteration of the existing basic F8U and F4H designs – airframe, engines, and avionics. As a result, new F8U production continued through 1964, and major upgrade programs to existing airframes continued for another few years after that.

The first major change to the design was made to take advantage of the availability of an uprated J57 engine, the -16 with 10,700 lbs of thrust at military power and 16,900 lbs in afterburner. Two air scoops were added to the upper aft fuselage to provide the additional cooling required by the installation of this engine. The

*The F8U-2 had a more powerful J57 with afterburner cooling scoops and ventral fins on the aft fuselage. It also had provisions for two more Sidewinders on each side of the fuselage. This picture is from one of its first deployments, here with VF-142 aboard Oriskany in 1960. (Robert L. Lawson collection)*

*The F8U-2 was subsequently provided with a small visual-assist radar for an all-weather capability and designated the F8U-2N. (Jay Miller collection)*

F8U-1's directional stability at high speed was improved by adding two ventral fins under the aft fuselage. The capability to carry two more Sidewinders was added with the provision of Y-shaped racks on each side of the fuselage, carefully configured to avoid an extended ram air turbine on the right side and the inflight refueling probe on the left. This aircraft was designated the F8U-2, with the prototype flying in August 1957. A second, more fully equipped prototype flew in January the next year, with the first production aircraft being delivered in January 1959.

F8U-2N was a further derivative of the F8U-2, closely matching the role envisaged for the General Purpose Fighter. The first example flew in February 1960. It featured a small angle track radar, infrared scanner, and a simple autopilot that would hold altitude and heading or orbit over a given point. It was therefore capable of detecting and destroying aircraft in "limited all-weather." An even more important addition for night and poor-weather capability was the Approach Power Compensator to reduce pilot workload during carrier landings. The system was engaged when the wing was raised, and it adjusted the throttle to control airspeed within a four-knot window. It was also the first Crusader model built without the rocket pack, which allowed an increase in internal fuel capacity to 1,348 gallons. The added weight was compensated for by uprating the J57 to provide 18,000 lbs of thrust in afterburner.

Even more capability was added with the F8U-2NE model. A larger, more capable radar was added under a slightly larger radome. Air-to-ground capability was added in the form of two weapons hard points stressed for up to a 2,000-lb bomb

With the F8U having all-weather capability and the Navy having enough pilots willing to land them at night on Essex-class carriers, the F4H was only deployed on the bigger decks. The air groups on the smaller carriers like Hancock had two F8U squadrons, here VF-211 and VF-24, assigned. (The four MiG markings on 213's ventral fin are a squadron tally.) (Robert L. Lawson collection)

The only thing more unimaginable in 1944, 18 years earlier, than this scene of two Mach 2 F4H Phantom IIs being launched was the thought of them landing back aboard. (Robert L. Lawson collection)

and the avionics required for launching and controlling the Bullpup air-to-ground missile. Its first flight was in June 1961. However, it had the same engine as the F8U-2N.

For various reasons, the F4H was not deployed on Essex-class carriers, but by the time the F4H was replacing the F3H, the F8U-2N and -2NE were available with a limited all-weather capability. Squadrons equipped with those more capable Crusaders therefore replaced the F3H on the smaller carriers.

There was only one foreign sale of the Crusader when it was in production, but that was a very unusual one – to the French, who typically relied on the indigenous aircraft industry for its fighters. A new wing had to be designed for the French Crusader due to the smaller size of their carrier. A 15- to 17-knot slower approach speed was provided with the incorporation of Boundary Layer Control, a two-segment leading edge flap, and a larger horizontal tail.

Even before the last of the new production Crusaders was delivered, earlier models were being returned to Vought or Navy depots for upgrades. The ultimate of these was the rebuild of surviving F8U-2NEs with the French Crusader wing and horizontal tail in an attempt to reverse the trend in higher approach speeds caused by the steady increase in weight. These were designated F-8J under the new system. The first deployments suffered from a lack of power on approach because of the BLC. This was somewhat alleviated by the incorporation of the ultimate Crusader engine, the J57-P-420 with 12,400 lbs thrust at military power and 19,600 lbs in afterburner.

Approach speed control combined with periodic weight increases caused the Crusader carrier approach to remain a challenge to the end. As Crusader pilot Wayne "Bull" Durham remembers it:

Since the Crusader was my first real airplane I didn't have much experience to judge it by. I just thought all airplanes probably flew that way, and never really gave much thought to it, then or later.

When I was at Carrier Suitability at the old Flight Test Division at Pax River, I dug up some early test reports on the F-8. The reports were pretty clear that the airplane didn't belong around the boat at night, but I guess the needs of the service trumped common sense. I also read the evaluations of BLC, which we had in the J, and of the competing Direct Lift Control. DLC rigged both spoilers up a few degrees during approach. You could beep them up or down, increasing or decreasing lift directly. The test pilots loved it. So we got BLC instead, of course. This, coupled with the P-20 engine that was worse than before. Robbie Roberts took a wave-off eight seconds out and got a one wire. Luckily, the P-420 showed up soon afterward. When I later went to a Phantom squadron and won a few Golden Tailhook awards I felt like I was cheating.

## Summary

The Navy was only just equipped with carrier-based jet fighters when the Korean War started, and they were no match for the swept-wing MiG-15. By contrast, when the Vietnam War started, the Navy had two jet fighters, the Crusader and the Phantom II, that were both the equal of any land-based one. The former was in its element as a dogfighting, gun-firing, single-seat air-superiority fighter. The latter was initially handicapped by its original function and armament as a bomber-destroyer, but it still gave a good account of itself, particularly after a short period of tactics development and crew training to maximize its usefulness, with the back-seater demonstrably worth more than his weight in mission effectiveness.

The pace of development was rapid. The original Phantom, the McDonnell XFD-1, had first flown only 20 years before the Vietnam War began. The Navy had been presented with a major technological change, jet propulsion, which affected every aspect of its operation of aircraft from wide-ranging mobile airfields, an all-important military capability. With the help of the Royal Navy and aerospace industry, they had successfully adapted it.

The XFD-1 that flew in January 1945 did not have much performance margin over propeller-driven fighters and was inferior to shore-based jet fighters. It was of primary benefit as a learning experience for McDonnell and the Navy, and was the beginning

of experiment, innovation, and development that culminated a little more than 13 years later, in May 1958, when McDonnell's fourth Navy fighter type was cleared for takeoff on its first flight. The F4H proved to be a world-class jet fighter that was also carrier-based. Within a few years after its first flight, the Phantom II had set 16 speed, altitude, and climb records. According to anecdotal reports, the loser of the fly-off with the F4H, the F8U-3, had even better performance. The F4H's eventual successor in the Navy, the F-14, was bigger and more capable in some ways, but no faster.

Perhaps most remarkable, the F4H was selected and bought by the Air Force as the F-110 following a competition with its own F-106. Better known as the F-4 after the Department of Defense standardized aircraft designations among the services in 1962, the Phantom II holds the distinction of being the only aircraft to have been flown by both the United States' premier flight demonstration teams, the Navy's Blue Angels and the Air Force's Thunderbirds. Of course, the claim of world-class is best justified by the fact that it was bought by 12 other nations, only one of which had an aircraft carrier.

The Navy's approach to creating a world-class fighter was straightforward, albeit expensive. It simply funded successive aircraft programs with five different manufacturers until experience and competition generated one:

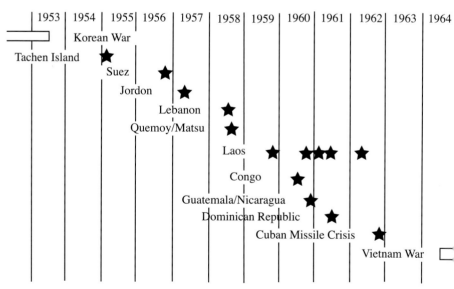

Figure 15-1 Crises Summary (Author)

| Douglas | Grumman | McDonnell | North American | Vought |
|---|---|---|---|---|
| F3D | F9F-2/5 | FH-1 | FJ-1 | F6U |
| F4D | F10F | F2H-1/2 | FJ-2 | F7U-1 |
| F5D | F9F-6/8 | F2H-3/4 | FJ-3 | F7U-3 |
| | F11F-1/1F | F3H-1 | FJ-4 | F8U-1/2 |
| | | F3H-2 | | F8U-3 |
| | | F4H-1 | | |

The Navy also did not limit itself in the beginning to traditional Navy aircraft suppliers. Both McDonnell and North American were unfamiliar with carrier-based aircraft design. It also didn't give up easily on its traditional suppliers – Vought produced two failures in a row and was given another chance with its second attempt, the F7U-1, but came up with a third disappointment, the F7U-3. Given yet another chance, after two strikes and a foul ball, Vought hit a home run with the F8U-1, one of the great fighters either land- or carrier-based, and followed up that success with the F8U-3, which a knowledgeable expert, George Spangenberg, stated was the best fighter not to get a production order.

Between Korea and Vietnam, each generation of fighters was called upon to defend the fleet and provide strike escort. As it happened, the highest priority fighter mission, defense of the carrier from attacks by supersonic bombers, was never needed. However, the need to provide air superiority for the carrier's presence and a strike group was frequently called upon. Each U.S. president sends aircraft carriers into harm's way to insure that America's interests are taken into account by foreign countries. Major international crises supported by aircraft carrier air groups are shown in Figure 15-1.

Engines were a major element. Once again, competing companies and multiple programs were key, particularly after the Navy put all its eggs in the Westinghouse basket. It was important for both the Navy and Air Force to pursue engine development, since there were fewer engine types than aircraft types. As engine companies were challenged to produce more thrust with less fuel and at a lower weight, engine durability and reliability occasionally suffered.

It is interesting to note that each of the Navy's manufacturers had distinct styles and a continuity of leadership during this period. Cdr. A. B. Metsger, the Fighter Class Desk between October 1945 and April 1949, described Grumman, possibly out of pique because it was ignoring his call for a swept-wing design but with some insight, as the company that "built yesterday's airplane today, and did it very well, indeed." The Navy benefited greatly when Grumman flew and developed the Panther and the Cougar in remarkably little time.

The exception was the XF10F, which was clearly tomorrow's aircraft, if not one for the day after tomorrow. Even the very complicated Jaguar got to first flight in about 30 months after the Navy and Grumman finally settled on its configuration.

Unlike Grumman, Vought had a reputation for pursuing engineering innovation and performance at the expense of producibility. For example, during World War II the Navy could buy three Grumman Hellcats for the price of two Corsairs. After the legendary Corsair, it designed the XF5U "skimmer" that never flew, the F6U that barely did (but Vought was inordinately proud of its aluminum/balsa sandwich skin), and the F7U-1, a flying wing on the outside and a Rube Goldberg contraption on the inside. Vought was also a little unlucky, because the F7U-3 would have been better regarded if its Navy-furnished Westinghouse engine had met specification and the angled deck had appeared sooner. In the end, the Crusader restored the company's reputation.

McDonnell is one of the standouts in this set of companies. It started with a carrier-based aircraft knowledge base of zero and created an acceptable first jet, particularly when compared to those from its more experienced competitors. The Phantom's direct descendent, the Banshee, was a cornerstone of naval fighter aviation for a decade – not flashy, but safe and reliable on a dark and stormy night. When the Navy gave McDonnell a bad engine to work with for the F3H program and then expanded the mission

## Deployments Summary

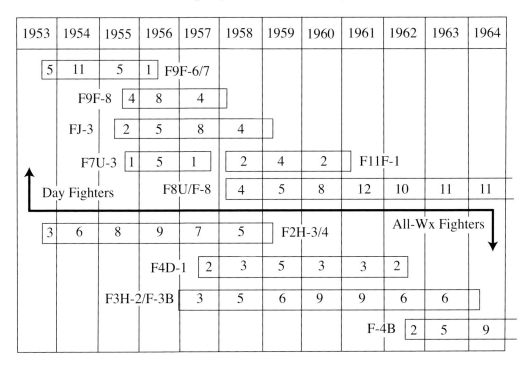

| | 1953 | 1954 | 1955 | 1956 | 1957 | 1958 | 1959 | 1960 | 1961 | 1962 | 1963 | 1964 |
|---|---|---|---|---|---|---|---|---|---|---|---|---|
| F9F-6/7 | 5 | 11 | 5 | 1 | | | | | | | | |
| F9F-8 | | | 4 | 8 | 4 | | | | | | | |
| FJ-3 | | | 2 | 5 | 8 | 4 | | | | | | |
| F7U-3 | | | 1 | 5 | 1 | 2 | 4 | 2 | | | | |
| F11F-1 | | | | | | | | | | | | |
| F8U/F-8 | | | | | | 4 | 5 | 8 | 12 | 10 | 11 | 11 |
| F2H-3/4 | 3 | 6 | 8 | 9 | 7 | 5 | | | | | | |
| F4D-1 | | | | 2 | 3 | 5 | 3 | 3 | 2 | | | |
| F3H-2/F-3B | | | | 3 | 5 | 6 | 9 | 9 | 6 | 6 | | |
| F-4B | | | | | | | | | | 2 | 5 | 9 |

Day Fighters

All-Wx Fighters

requirement without delivering the promised improvement in engine performance, McDonnell managed to salvage the situation. The Demon became a cornerstone of naval fighter aviation like the Banshee – not a fighter pilot's fighter, but one that was equipped to shoot down an incoming bomber sight unseen and then relatively easy to land back aboard regardless of conditions. If that were not enough, McDonnell followed that with the Phantom II, one of the greatest fighters, carrier-based or land-based.

Douglas and North American were out of the fighter business after the F4D and FJ-4, respectively, but both made significant contributions to the Navy's fighter needs along the way. Metsger and many others held Douglas' El Segundo Chief Engineer Ed Heinemann in very high regard, Metsger referring to him as the best in the business: "He gave us a nice balance between performance and producibility. Ed had sufficient confidence in himself and his work to give us freely the unfudged facts."

As it turned out, straight-wing jets were relatively easy to operate from aircraft carriers with minimal changes to the carrier itself. The Panthers and Banshees went directly from initial fleet familiarization into combat. The first Panthers deployed 30 months after first flight, and the first Banshees after 36 months. In both cases, an improved model quickly followed the first production design. Swept-wing aircraft took considerably longer to put into service, partly because the Navy was far too ambitious with the mission requirements in the late 1940s and partly because Westinghouse could not repeat its early engine success. The Cutlass, Demon, and Skyray finally deployed six to seven years after their first flights. The Jaguar never did. They took so long to develop that placeholders, derivatives of existing designs, had to be fielded instead. These were the Cougar, created from the Panther and deployed in record time; the swept-wing Fury, which the Navy reluctantly adapted from an Air Force design; and the F2H-3/4 Banshee, straight-winged but essential to filling the all-weather fleet defense requirement.

Figure 15-2 summarizes fighter deployments by type from 1953 through 1964, and subdivides them into day fighters and all-weather fighters, a mission differentiation that superseded the late-1940s concept of a fighter mission triad of interceptor, night fighter, and general-purpose fighter. Neither the interceptor concept nor the first night fighter, the F3D, was well received in the fleet. At some point OpNav began to reconsider the validity of the interceptor-based approach when it compared the number of aircraft required, impact on cyclic operations, and probability of splashing all of the incoming bombers compared to the mission being accomplished with guided missile-armed fighters out on stations on Combat Air Patrol. The availability of airborne early-warning radar also reduced the necessity for the interceptor concept.

Operational experience eventually resulted in the requirement for only two different single-seat fighter types, sometimes referred to as day, or air superiority fighter and night, or all-weather, fighter. The former tended to be lighter and more maneuverable; the latter was equipped with search radar, autopilot, and some form of longer-range air-to-air missile. General Purpose continued to be used to denote an attack-mission definition, however, for both day and all-weather fighters.

It's also notable that from 1955 through 1961 for day fighters, the Navy deployed more than one aircraft type, sometimes as many as three. The same is true for all-weather fighters from 1957 through 1963. This is a direct result of the continuous improvement approach that it took to developing fighters. At that point, the development of new fighters became infrequent because it had become too expensive. The Navy relied on product improvements for the two they had in service instead.

## Comparing the Day Fighters

There was more turnover among the day fighters than the all-weather fighters, in part because the emphasis for the former was keeping abreast of the performance of the best shore-based fighter.

Although their respective supporters would doubtless disagree, the F9F-8 Cougar and the FJ-3 seem to have been pretty well matched. There is no question that the FJ-4 was better than either. Unfortunately, its lack of an afterburner and therefore supersonic speed in level flight made it an anachronism. Being so closely followed by the F11F and the F8U, it was not going to be accepted by the fleet as a fighter.

The F7U was the least successful of the day fighters, if in fact it can be considered to have been one in the end. One wonders what its contribution would have been if BuAer had focused on improving the F7U-1 instead of futilely trying to perfect the F10F. The track record of the F7U-3 on axial-deck carriers suggests that would have been disastrous. On the other hand, what if the angled-deck carriers had been available a few years earlier? The F7U-3 would have still had a relatively brief career, what with the F11F and F8U introduction, but a lower accident rate and a better reputation.

The F11F cannot be said to have been a failure even though it was deployed only one more time than the F7U-3. Guided by an idiosyncratic vision of the ideal day-fighter by one clique in BuAer and making the logical engine choice at the time the program began, Grumman produced a delightful but relatively small and somewhat underpowered fighter. If Vought's F8U program had faltered, the J79-powered Super Tiger would likely have been the Navy's premier day-fighter instead for two decades. Unfortunately for Grumman, Vought quickly developed and delivered an aircraft with the performance that Navy fighter pilots wanted so much that they were willing to cope with its shortcomings much as some men take pride in riding a fast horse named *El Diablo* for good reason.

It was not hard to see why from a comparison of Standard Aircraft Characteristics data. The F8U was significantly faster at altitude (it was engine limited at sea level) and had more range.

|  | F9F-8 | FJ-3 | F7U-3 | F11F-1 | F8U-1 |
|---|---|---|---|---|---|
| Gross Weight (lbs) | 20,098 | 19,360* | 26,840 | 21,035 | 26,969 |
| Speed SL (kts) | 561 | 599 | 606 | 654 | 637 |
| Speed 35K (kts/M) | 515/0.89 | 530/0.92 | 540/0.94 | 632/1.10 | 880/1.53 |
| Combat Range (nm) | 1,050 | 995* | 800 | 1,108 | 1,280 |
| Mission Time (hrs) | 2.06 | 1.70* | 1.31 | 1.57 | 1.73 |
| Approach Stall (kts) | 93.8 | 94.4 | 93.2 | 103.3 | 108.2 |

Internal fuel only except as noted by * which include two 200-gallon drop tanks

## Comparing the All-Weather Fighters

The development of carrier-based, all-weather jet fighters was anything but smooth. The F3D-2 was very capable as demonstrated in Korea, but it saw very limited use as a carrier-based aircraft. It suffered early on when it was evaluated against a higher-performance, single-seat F2H-2N night fighter. The merits of its more capable radar system and two crewmembers went unappreciated because it was ungainly on the carrier and underpowered in the air. In any event, the Navy expected to fill the ship-based requirement with one of the interceptors that were initiated in 1949.

When both interceptor-development programs were prolonged, the F2H-3/4s, which had been initiated in 1950 as a hedge against their timely availability, filled in the gap for several years. It also facilitated the transition of all-weather fighter operation from a specialty provided by detachments to being the responsibility of one of the assigned squadrons in the air group.

The F7U, which had been designated to be a general-purpose fighter, was redirected in early 1953 to be a guided missile-carrying all-weather fighter. As the F7U-3M, it first flew in July 1954, and made a few deployments with that capability. For all practical purposes, however, its Sparrow I missile was a VFR-only weapon. In any event, because its Westinghouse J46 engines had been derated to increase reliability, it could only bring one or two back aboard. As a result, most of its deployments were with attack squadrons, where unexpended bombs and rockets could be jettisoned without concern for cost or scarcity, unlike guided missiles.

One of the interceptors, the F3H, which had also been redirected to the general-purpose fighter mission, eventually became the standard all-weather fighter, augmented by the other interceptor, the F4D-1. The F3H was preferred, however, for its all-weather Sparrow III armament and carrier-landing friendliness.

|  | F3D-2 | F2H-3/4 | F7U-3M | F4D-1 | F3H-2 |
|---|---|---|---|---|---|
| Gross Weight (lbs) | 25,414 | 21,200 | 32,974 | 27,116* | 34,641 |
| Speed SL (kts) | 477 | 513 | 579 | 625 | 627 |
| Speed 35K (kts/M) | 448 | 459 | 515/0.89 | 565/0.98 | 525/0.91 |
| Combat Range (nm) | 1,185 | 1,015 | 565 | 973 | 861 |
| Mission Time (hrs) | 3.0 | 2.5 | 1.15 | 1.7* | 2.13 |
| Approach Stall (kts) | 82 | 90 | 105 | 100 | 93 |

Internal fuel only except as noted by * which includes two 300-gallon drop tanks. F4D carrying four Sidewinders and F3H and F7U-3M, four Sparrows.

The F4D-1 and the F3H-2 were produced in about the same relatively low quantities for a successful Navy fighter, 419 for the former and 459 for the latter. Their development and service lives closely paralleled each other. Both began as interceptors to meet a 1948 requirement. The F4D retained more of its capability as an interceptor while the F3H was first transformed to the archetypical general-purpose fighter and then segued to the first effective, guided missile-armed, all-weather fighter. As a result, the F4D was better than the F3H on a time-to-climb basis but inferior as a carrier-based, all-weather fighter since it had less endurance and less likelihood of downing an incoming Soviet bomber, particularly in bad weather.

Somewhat like the FJ-3, the F4D had performance or endurance, but not both. At one point it held the time-to-climb record to 9,000 meters (29,527.5 feet) in one minute 30 seconds; on the other hand, a useful aircraft, that is to say one laden with guns and ammunition, drop tanks, and four Sidewinders, took 10.5 minutes to get to 30,000 feet. That was still better than the F3H-2M with four Sparrows that took at least five minutes more. Neither aircraft could do much more than come right back down after flying for 10 or 15 minutes in afterburner. This interceptor profile would have played havoc with a carrier's operating cycle of launch, pull forward, recover, pull aft, and repeat. As a practical matter, both fighters were mainly used on Combat Air Patrol, with deck-launched interception an available option.

On Combat Air Patrol, which was eventually judged more sensible on axial-deck carriers than trying to launch fighters like surface-to-air missiles when incoming bombers were detected, the F3H was far more useful. A Demon *without* drop tanks and carrying four Sparrows could loiter at altitude for 45 minutes at a distance of 150 nautical miles from the ship and an hour more than that with two drop tanks substituted for two of the Sparrows. The F4D *with* drop tanks, and they were never seen without them after the speed and time-to-climb records were set, was only good for 42 minutes at 150 nautical miles. (The F3H had more internal fuel capacity, 1,500 gallons, than the F4D did when carrying two 300-gallon drop tanks.)

Shooting down a fast jet bomber in a cloud, which was the worst case, was the major differentiator. The Sparrow III was effective in foul weather, whereas the Sidewinder was not since its infrared seeker needed clear air. To use its unguided 2.75-inch rockets, the Skyray pilot had to fly a collision course with the threat while on instruments, guided by the airborne radar and fire-control system, with the computer being trusted to judge when to let loose the barrage. The F3H capability, when it worked, involved a radar-beam-guided Sparrow III missile moving at Mach 4 speeds. There was no need to get too close, much less be on a collision course. Moreover, the F3H pilot could theoretically fire at four different targets whereas the Skyray pilot was limited to one or two salvos at the target of his choice, many rockets having to be fired for a reasonable likelihood of making a hit with one.

Both the Skyray and the Demon's ability to shoot down an enemy plane with their rocket-propelled weapons was therefore dependent on their avionics, totally in the case of the Demon. However, a successful kill with the Demon's Sparrow III required a bit less skill and luck on the pilot's part than with the Skyray system of a precisely flown course and barrage of unguided rockets. Demon pilots also tended to be happier about their cockpit and the outstanding visibility and good handling qualities on approach. Certainly, they crashed a bit less often than Skyray pilots. As a result, the F4D only made 18 deployments and was in service in active-duty Navy squadrons for a shorter time. However, the F4D was also operated extensively by the Marine Corps (it equipped as many USMC squadrons as Navy ones) and continued in service with them, the land-based VF(AW)-3 interceptor squadron, and the Navy reserve in parallel with the twilight years of the F3H. It cannot be said that the F4D was second best to the F3H in overall usefulness, only that the Navy preferred the latter for ship-based operation. For one thing, no Marine squadron was ever equipped with the F3H. However, when it became necessary to procure a few more all-weather fighters to bridge to the F4H introduction, the Navy bought more F3Hs, not F4Ds.

Compared to what the Navy was deploying, the F4H Phantom II was in a class by itself. Unlike the all-weather fighters it succeeded, it could fly supersonic at sea level and more than twice as fast as they could at altitude. In fact, it was almost as fast at altitude at military power as they were in afterburner. Armed and fully fueled, it could climb to 30,000 feet faster than the record set by an unarmed, minimally fueled Skyray. Full advantage could be taken of its radar and infrared tracker because it had a second crewman. Its only shortcoming was that it didn't have a 20mm cannon, consistent with its primary mission of jet bomber destroyer. It was the best general-purpose fighter of its time, accepted by not only other air forces around the world, but by the U.S. Air Force as well. And it could takeoff and land on an aircraft carrier.

It is interesting to compare and contrast the Navy's jet-fighter development record with that of the Air Force over the same period. Such a comparison is necessarily subjective but, roughly speaking, both services each contracted for about 24 jet fighter programs that reached flight status. Of those, five in each service were arguably failures, not meeting performance projections much less moving from development to operational status. Each service initiated one program that was clearly misconceived, the Navy's F2Y Sea Dart that was a supersonic jet fighter seaplane and the Air Force's diminutive F-85 parasite fighter that was to be launched and recovered from a bomber for self-protection. Three programs in the Navy – the F11F-1F, the F5D, and the F8U-3 – did not proceed to production, not because they were not adequate in performance or handling qualities, but because another fighter was chosen instead. There were four similar programs in the Air Force, the F-87, F-91, F-93, and F-107. The remainder, 15 in the Navy and 15 in the Air Force, were used operationally and were produced in the hundreds, if not thousands, each.

Because of the Navy's unique carrier-basing requirements, there was very little crossover of aircraft between the two services. The Navy bought a few P-59s, evaluated the F-80 and used some as trainers, and bought and deployed a derivative of the F-86. The Air Force on its part reportedly considered the F3D as a night fighter and evaluated other Navy fighters, at least for the fun of it, but until the F4H came along it did not opt to buy any of the Navy-developed jet fighters. There was some cross-fertilization between the services at the manufacturer level. At North American and McDonnell fighters were developed and produced for both services. On the other hand, Grumman, Douglas, and Vought never developed a jet fighter for the Air Force, and Lockheed never developed an operational jet fighter for the Navy. Convair developed fighters for the Air Force and aircraft for the Navy but never a carrier-based jet fighter, only the ill-fated F2Y Sea Dart. Both services kept a close eye on each other's technology implementation and performance achievements and evaluated each other's aircraft. However, with the notable exception of the F-86, neither service deigned to purchase an aircraft that was developed by the other until McDonnell produced the F4H.

## Epilogue

The number of different aircraft programs implemented to achieve the transition to the performance capability of the Crusader III and the Phantom II is extraordinary compared to subsequent activity. As shown in Figure 15-3, there were first flights of more than 20 different Navy jet fighter types in the 13 years between the FH in 1943 and the F4H in 1958, an average of three every two years. There have been just three first flights in almost 50 years since – F-111B, F-14, and F-18, only four or five even if you count the re-engined F-14 and the F-18E/F as different types, about one every 10 years. The F-35 is not only to be this decade's fighter, it is to be operated by both the Air Force and the Navy, without the obvious display of a shotgun by the Secretary of Defense as during the F-111 program.

As the aerospace industry has consolidated, the number of individual companies capable of building a carrier-based fighter has dwindled to basically two: the McDonnell St. Louis component of Boeing and General Dynamics Fort Worth (GD), which has yet to produce an operational carrier-based fighter. Vought is an aerospace subcontractor, what remains of North American is part of Boeing, Grumman is a vestige of its former self as a small part of a huge aerospace conglomerate, and Douglas was absorbed into McDonnell which was in turn bought by Boeing.

Grumman finally broke back into the fighter business by taking advantage of the Navy's extreme dissatisfaction with the F-111B, for which it was the principal subcontractor to General Dynamics. Using the same engines and avionics along with changes to the design requirements, it turned what most considered a sow's ear (Sea Pig was one sobriquet) into something more like a silk purse, the F-14. The Tomcat was in production for more than 20 years and in fleet service for about 35.

McDonnell also pursued a circuitous route to its next Navy fighter development program. It unsuccessfully proposed a variable-sweep F-4 and then lost to Grumman in the competition that resulted in the F-14. Success came when it teamed with Northrop to propose a fighter for the Navy's new VFAX fighter program, with McDonnell as lead. At the time, Northrop and GD were competing for the Air Force's Light Weight Fighter program. (For its carrier-based expertise, GD teamed with Vought, which was its last hoorah.) In 1974, Congress decreed in effect that the Navy buy the Air Force's Light Weight Fighter; doubtless assuming the Navy would select the winner and not the loser. However, in January 1975, the Air Force announced that it had selected General Dynamics' F-16, and in May the Navy opted for the McDonnell/Northrop proposal for an extensively redesigned YF-17.

The performance pinnacle in terms of pure speed was reached with the F4H and F8U-3 programs. They also represented the last of the parallel and duplicative development efforts.

By then aircraft development programs had gotten so expensive relative to development budgets that competitions had to be conducted on paper, if at all. Continuous improvement was still accomplished with better engines, avionics, and weapons, but seldom with airframes/aerodynamics to anywhere near the degree that it had been. Externally, the F-14 looked pretty much the same throughout its three-decade career, and in a dim light the very different McDonnell F-18E/F closely resembles its predecessor Hornets.

Another way of considering how rapidly the evolution of Navy jet fighters occurred and then plateaued is to compare the career of the F9F Panther to those of the F4H/F-4 and its successor, the F-14. If the F9F Panther had been operational for as long as the F-14, the last of them would have been replaced in 1983, more than 25 years after they actually stopped deploying on U.S. Navy carriers. The F-4 didn't serve on carriers as long as the F-14, but derivatives of the F-4 were still being flown operationally by non-U.S. military services in 2006 when the F-14 was retired. If the F-4 remains in service as long as it's projected to be, the F9F Panther would still have been flying operationally somewhere in the world in 2006.

It was an exciting time in aerospace. We will never see its like again…

## Navy Jet Fighter First Flights

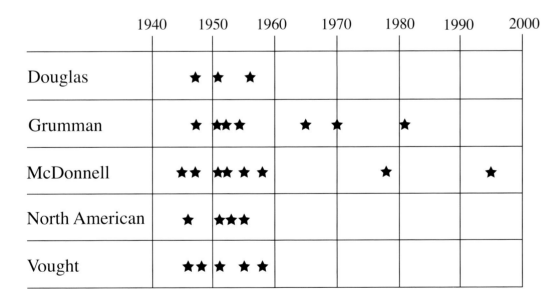

*Figure 15-3 First Flights Summary (Author)*

# APPENDIX

## Navy Aircraft Designation System

The Navy used its own designation system before the 1962 Department of Defense-mandated consolidation of the U.S. military designation systems. In addition to a first letter identifying the type's primary mission – Fighter, Attack, Patrol, etc. – the Navy designation included a manufacturer's letter – B for Boeing, F for Grumman, U for Vought, etc., and a number between the two letters. The number was sequential, corresponding to the number of different aircraft of that mission type ordered from that manufacturer, e.g., F6U stood for the sixth fighter type ordered from Vought. The number one was not used in this regard, so the first fighter from Vought was the FU. The Navy occasionally assigned designations to aircraft programs that were subsequently canceled or even when there was not yet a contract in place, which appears to have been the case with the Grumman F12F. Manufacturers sometimes jumped the gun, self-designating a proposed aircraft in marketing materials.

Aircraft were also assigned a name in addition to the designation. The practice was for manufacturers to submit a name or list of names for review by BuAer and recommendation to the Aeronautical Board. Names were generally not approved until production was authorized. This doesn't seem to have been a hard-and-fast rule, although it was occasionally invoked as with the XFV-1 and XFY-1 turboprop VTOL fighters. Both Lockheed and Convair suggested names, neither of which was approved on those grounds. Grumman, by tradition, was the only company that could use feline names for its carrier-based aircraft. Douglas had exclusive use of names with the word "Sky" included. Similarly, McDonnell was to recommend names from the spirit world, and Vought used names associated with buccaneering. Of course, when the aircraft was fielded, it often got a nickname that may or may not have been derived from its officially approved name. Banjo for the F2H Banshee and Ford for the F4D Skyray were examples.

As should already be obvious, the manufacturer's letter did not always correspond to the manufacturer's name. In 1922 when the system was developed, the first letter of the company's name was generally available and used, but later, when new aircraft companies like Bell Aircraft and McDonnell aircraft were formed and became Navy suppliers, the letter B had long since been assigned to Boeing and M to Martin. The Navy had to be flexible in this regard because there were only 24 letters – "I" not being used because of the potential confusion with the number "1" and "X"

*Hall XFH-1 (U.S. Navy via Tommy H. Thomason collection)*

not being desired – and many more companies. (One list of Navy manufacturers' letters assignments spanning the 40 years between 1922 and 1962 totals 117 different companies.) The use of two letters instead of one would have made far more identifiers available, and there are some instances of this, but almost all were for foreign manufacturers in 1922/1923 and there are none after 1933.

Using the same letter for two or more different manufacturers wasn't confusing to the Navy because when it was resorted to, the two entities were producing aircraft for different missions, patrol versus fighter for example, and not likely to change. So in 1942, "M" was assigned to General Motors for its production of the Grumman Wildcat fighter even though the Glenn L. Martin company had been assigned "M" since 1922; the Navy was not likely to buy any fighters from Martin, one of a few manufacturers of their patrol planes.

When the Navy contracted with McDonnell in 1943 for a jet fighter, "M" was not available for fighters so "D" was used, even though it was assigned to Douglas (and also Radio Plane Corp. for drones), a major supplier of Navy planes. However, since Douglas hadn't built a fighter since the one-off FD-1 biplane in the early 1930s, that seemed like a reasonable duplication. As a result, the first McDonnell fighter was designated the FD and the second F2D.

It was a shortsighted selection because Douglas was awarded a contract for a jet fighter in 1946, and the duplication was now unacceptable. As a result, McDonnell's letter was changed to "H," which was unassigned at the time. The FD-1 became the FH-1 and the F2D-1, the F2H-2. Since the F2D designation for the second

*Douglas XFD-1 (U.S. Navy via Tommy H. Thomason collection)*

McDonnell fighter was still present in many documents and minds, the new Douglas fighter, although the second for that manufacturer, was given the designation F3D.

Between 1942 and 1962, the following manufacturer's designations were used for Navy fighter manufacturers:

A   Brewster
B   Boeing
C   Curtiss
D   Douglas and McDonnell
F   Grumman
G   Goodyear
H   McDonnell
J   North American
L   Bell Aircraft
M   General Motors
O   Lockheed (Plant B – Burbank)
R   Ryan
S   Supermarine
T   Northrop
U   Chance Vought
V   Lockheed (Plant A – Vega Division)
Y   Convair

Lockheed had two letters because the Vega Aircraft Company had been a subsidiary of Lockheed and produced the Hudson, a World War II patrol plane designated PV-1. Although Vega was merged into Lockheed in 1943, for a time the Navy continued to use "V" for former Vega division products and "O" for Lockheed-Burbank products. After 1950, Lockheed aircraft with the designation "O," e.g., the TO-2 (T-33B) trainer, were re-designated with "V."

For various reasons, the number interposed between the letter for the type and the letter for the manufacturer didn't always tick up by one when an arguably new model was ordered. Instead a dash number change was used, with the intention of keeping track of derivatives of the type. The Grumman F9F series was an example of changing the dash number instead of the middle number. The XF9F-1 was to be a two-place, four-engine night fighter, but it never got off the drawing boards. When the Navy and Grumman redirected the effort to be a single-seat, single-engine day-fighter, it became the XF9F-2 Panther. When the Navy urgently needed a swept-wing version of the Panther, the next dash number, 6, was used instead of a model-letter change, but the resulting F9F-6 was assigned a new popular name, Cougar. The practice continued when the Navy contracted with Grumman for an all-new fighter with a different engine and again used the next dash number, 8. When they subsequently ordered a Cougar upgrade which was rightfully the F9F-8, the new fighter became the F9F-9 with a new popular name, Tiger. In any event, the Navy eventually had second thoughts, re-designating the F9F-9 as the F11F since F10F had already been used for Grumman's variable sweep wing fighter.

Another example is the North American FJ Fury series. The straight-wing FJ-1 was the first fighter from North American. However, the XFJ-1 was originally designated the XF4J-1 in recognition of the three previous one-off experimental biplane fighters produced by Berliner-Joyce in the early 1930s.[i] This decision was countermanded in March 1945, and the designation changed to XFJ-1, with the admonition that: "Attention is invited to the fact that this initiates a new series of "FJ" airplanes. Care should be exercised in the future to avoid confusion with the former series, XFJ-1, XF2J-1, and XF3J-1, built by the Berliner-Joyce Aircraft Corp., which no longer exists as such." It would appear that this admonition was complied with by never using the F2J and F3J designations, although it's more likely that, at least for the FJ-3 and FJ-4, it was another example of bootlegging a development program by using funds from an existing production contract.[ii]

Vought designations seem to follow the rules, with the exception of the Vought F8U-3. While it bore a definite family resemblance to the F8U-1/2, it was larger, powered by a different engine, and differently armed. It was also the result of formal competition to use budget intended for new development, not funded by production contract, the usual reason not to designate it the XF9U. Maybe the Navy was so happy that Vought had produced a successful jet fighter after the F6U and the F7U that it didn't want to jinx it with a new designation. However, the likely reason is that the Navy didn't want to make it too obvious to Congress that they were developing two all-new fighters, the F4H and the F8U-3. If so, the tactic didn't work.

One of the usual reasons for a dash-number change was a different engine, because this was important information to the maintainers. The main and possibly only difference between the F9F-2 and -3 Panthers and the F9F-6 and F9F-7 Cougars was that the engines in each case were from different manufacturers. However, the dash change was also used for other reasons, as in the F2H-1 followed by the F2H-2, F2H-3, and F2H-4. The basic aerodynamic configuration and engine model stayed the same, justifying the retention of the basic F2H designation. The dash changes reflected radar, fuel-system, control-system, and other internal and external changes.

In addition to the dash-number change indicating a difference for whatever reason, there were standard letters added after the dash number to denote subsequent modification of an aircraft to have a different or additional capability. For example, a fighter that was modified to carry cameras would get the suffix letter "P" for Photographic, as in F2H-2P. The suffix letter "F" was used to designate a modification with a special or different powerplant installation (FJ-4F); "N," a night-fighter variant (F2H-2N); and "B," a different armament configuration from the basic dash number, e.g., the ability to carry a nuclear weapon (F2H-2B).

The "B" suffix was less definitive than the others. For one thing, it did not necessarily mean the added ability to deliver a nuclear weapon. The XFJ-2B was an F-86 painted blue with Navy markings and four 20mm cannons substituted for the Sabre's six .50-caliber machine guns. This was "special" from an F-86 standpoint but was actually the intended armament for the FJ-2. The F9F-2 Panther, when modified with wing pylons to carry rockets and bombs, was re-designated F9F-2B. However, after most if not all of the F9F-2s had been so modified, the "B" was apparently dropped as no longer being needed for differentiation of F9F-2s in service.

In the Navy, the prefix "X" was applied to some prototype aircraft. The prefix "Y" for the first lot of production aircraft seems to have been rarely used by the Navy compared to the Air Force, which tended to so designate a small quantity of aircraft procured initially for service test and evaluation prior to operational use. One exception was the YF2Y-1. The F7U-1 might be considered a "Y" aircraft in that only 14 were built, but it was never designated as such. In the case of the F4H, aircraft in the initial production lots were designated F4H-1F after the fact, with the "F" standing for special (as in slightly different) powerplant installation.

In 1962, the Department of Defense decreed that the same aircraft type would be known by the same designation in all of the services, e.g., the U.S. Air Force F-110, which was its procurement of the Navy's F4H, would both become the F-4, along the lines of the Air Force system. With the exception of the F-110, Air Force

*Berliner-Joyce XFJ-1 (U.S. Navy via Tommy H. Thomason collection)*

fighters retained their designations while the Navy fighters got new ones, although similar in most cases to the original:

| Manufacturer | Before | After |
|---|---|---|
| North American | FJ | Fury F-1 |
| McDonnell | F2H | Banshee F-2 |
| McDonnell | F3H | Demon F-3 |
| McDonnell | F4H | Phantom II F-4 |
| Douglas | F4D | Skyray F-6 |
| Convair | F2Y | Sea Dart F-7 |
| Vought | F8U | Crusader F-8 |
| Grumman | F9F | Panther/Cougar F-9 |
| Douglas | F3D | Skyknight F-10 |
| Grumman | F11F | Tiger F-11 |

The inclusion of the F2Y, a jet fighter seaplane that last flew in 1957, on this list has been a mystery, sometimes explained as necessary as a way of using the number 7 (the F-5 was a Northrop fighter, Model N-156, which was being managed by the Air Force for sale to other countries under the U.S. Military Assistance Program). However, there were skips in other type lists, e.g., no P-1, and even if no skips had been the objective, the F7U would have been more appropriate, if only slightly less unnecessary. The most valid reason put forward is that one F2Y, BuNo. 135765, was not formally stricken until 10 July 1962, and therefore the type needed to be accounted for.

# GLOSSARY

**AAM:** Air-to-Air Missile

**Area Rule:** An aerodynamic concept that an aircraft will have the lowest transonic drag when its cross section smoothly increases and then decreases. The most obvious feature is an indentation of the fuselage at the wing root.

**Aspect Ratio:** The wingspan divided by the average chord of the wing. Long, thin wings have a high aspect ratio and are best for long-range cruise; short, broad wings have a low aspect ratio and are best for maneuverability.

**Barricade:** A last-chance net attached to an arresting engine to stop an aircraft on deck when the tail hook has not or will not stop the plane.

**Barrier:** A cable stretched across the deck that physically restrains an aircraft that has to be stopped.

**BIS:** Board of Inspection and Survey

**Bolter:** A touch-and-go landing on an angled-deck aircraft carrier when the intention was to engage a wire with the tail hook and stop.

**BuAer:** Bureau of Aeronautics

**CAP:** Combat Air Patrol

**cg:** Center of gravity – the point at which the aircraft is in balance longitudinally.

**CNO:** Chief of Naval Operations

**Critical Mach Number:** The Mach number at which the local airflow on an aircraft reaches Mach 1, the speed of sound.

**Cycle:** The time period that aircraft are expected to fly before being able to land back aboard the carrier.

**Cut:** Pilot – pulling the throttle(s) back to idle for landing; LSO – signaling the pilot to pull the throttles to idle.

**FCLP:** Field Carrier Landing Practice

**Fiscal Year:** Until 1977, the U.S. government's fiscal year for record-keeping purposes ran from 1 July to the following 30 June, with the fiscal year being designated by the year in which it ends.

**FIP:** Fleet Introduction Program: Intensive flight trials of a new production aircraft to establish maintenance requirements and train a cadre of pilots and maintainers.

**FIRM:** Fleet Introduction of Replacement Models: A concept instituted in the mid-'50s to limit production of a new type until it had been proven to meet requirements.

**g:** A measure of the load on an aircraft from maneuvering, either in a turn or pull up/push over, or gusts. One $g$ is unaccelerated level flight. An aircraft in a 60-degree bank in level flight is "pulling" two $g$. Fighters are generally capable of 7.5 $g$ at a given gross weight without structural damage (limit load) and 50 percent more than that before catastrophic failure of the structure.

**GFE:** Government Furnished Equipment

**Groove:** The final straight-in portion of a carrier landing approach.

**IOC:** Initial Operational Capability

**JATO:** Jet Assisted Take Off

**LSO:** Landing Signals Officer

**Mach number:** A dimensionless number equal to the aircraft speed divided by the speed of sound in the air through which it is moving.

**NAMC:** Naval Air Material Center: Located in the Philadelphia area, it was comprised of the Naval Aircraft Factory, the Naval Aircraft Modification Unit, the Naval Air Experimental Station, and the Naval Air Auxiliary Station.

**NATC:** Naval Air Test Center: Located at Patuxent River, Maryland.

**NATOPS:** Naval Aviation Training and Operating Procedures

**NOTS:** Naval Ordnance Test Station. Located at China Lake, California.

**NPE:** Navy Preliminary Evaluation: A periodic evaluation by Navy test pilots of an aircraft in development, the first occurring a few months after its first flight, to determine progress against, and potential to reach, contract performance and handling-quality requirements.

**OpNav:** Office of the Chief of Naval Operations

**PIO:** Pilot Induced Oscillation: A control situation where the pilot's control application is in phase with the aircraft's response, leading to back-and-forth movement, usually in pitch.

**RAG:** Replacement Air Group: The umbrella organization for the squadrons that trained aviators to fly a specific aircraft type.

**RFP:** Request for Proposal

**SFC:** Specific Fuel Consumption: The number of lbs of fuel burned per lb of thrust per hour.

**TACAN:** Tactical Air Navigation

**Trap:** A landing on an aircraft carrier accomplished by hooking a wire with the aircraft's tail hook.

**Vmax:** The top speed of an aircraft at a given altitude and thrust setting.

**VC:** Summary Navy designation for a Composite Squadron, which is one that has responsibility for more than one mission and has operated more than one aircraft type.

**Wave-Off:** Discontinue a landing approach and climb away.

**WOD:** Wind-Over-Deck: The perceived wind velocity produced by the carrier's speed and the existing wind, if any.

# Endnotes

Introduction

[1] An account of this conference was published in *Report of Joint Fighter Conference NAS Patuxent River, MD 16-23 October 1944* (Atglen, Pennsylvania: Schiffer Military History, 1998). It includes summary test reports and comments.
[2] Ibid., 228.

Chapter 1

[1] These dimensions varied depending on the carrier and the time frame. The forward elevator on the Essex class was eventually lengthened with a triangular forward section, for example.
[2] Ear protectors eventually became standard on the flight deck.
[3] OpNav Operational Requirement, Interceptor, August 1948
[4] OpNav Operational Requirement, General Purpose Fighter, 27 June 1949
[5] BuAer was reorganized in the mid-1950s to manage airplane procurement as "Weapon Systems." The basic practices and working relationships don't seem to have been affected much at the time.
[6] BIS Trials, *Naval Aviation News* (May 1953): 28-29.
[7] The degree of difficulty in having two qualified fighter squadrons to meet the deployment schedule was eased by having three or even four squadrons assigned to each air group; Marine fighter squadrons were occasionally impressed when required.

Chapter 2

[1] NATC report on Project No. TED No. PTR 1106 dated 21 September 1945, *Final Report on Flight Tests of Navy-owned YP-59A Airplanes.*
[2] Since low frontal area seemed important, an axial flow compressor was selected. This was also deemed to be a more efficient flow path and benefited from the company's experience with steam turbines.
[3] Kendall Perkins, presentation on "McDonnell's first Phantom" presented to the Aeronautical History Society of St. Louis, 26 June 1981. He also described the rubber-engine approach in "Design Development of the McDonnell FD-1 Phantom" in *Aviation* (November 1946): 43.
[4] For example, the daily status report for 12 January states that a two-engine "simulated takeoff" was accomplished at 75 knots; there was a problem with the right engine. On the 26th, two flights were made, both with two engines, one of which reached 300 knots indicated air speed at 7,000 feet. On the second, there was an engine vibration problem.
[5] More details can be found in NATC Report Serial: *FT-C-68 Carrier Acceptability Trials of Model XFD-1 Airplane* No. 48236 dated 15 November 1946.
[6] Captain Eric Brown, *Wings of the Weird and Wonderful* (England: Airlife Publishing Ltd., 1983): 60-70.
[7] NATC Final Report dated 23 June 1947.
[8] VF Confidential Memo Aer-R-FEB:jfm to Admiral Sallada by Commander F. E. Bakutis dated 23 April 1946.
[9] NATC Report No. M-4654 dated 16 January 1947, *Evaluation of Carrier Prototype Model P-80A Airplane.*
[10] NATC Report, Project No. TED PTR 1116 dated 23 June 1947, *Final Report of Evaluation and Carrier Adaptation of Model P-80A Airplane Bu. No. 29668.*
[11] Bureau of Aeronautics Memo Aer-E-11-JFS dated 24 July 1945 from the Chief, BuAer, to the Commanding Office, NATC Patuxent.
[12] NATC Report Serial FT-C-45, *Evaluation of German Aircraft*, dated 13 June 1946.

Chapter 3

[1] BuAer Letter Aer-E-11-JFS dated 4 September 1944, Subject: Model VF Airplane – Request for Proposal, signed by Rear Admiral L. B. Richardson.
[2] The FH wasn't all that much faster than the propeller-driven F8F Bearcat. At 28,000 feet, where the Bearcat attained its highest speed at combat engine ratings, the FH was only 14 knots faster. The FH was 80 knots faster at sea level, but couldn't sustain that advantage for long due to fuel consumption.
[3] On axial deck carriers, hooking an early wire was not frowned upon as long as there was adequate clearance with the ramp.
[4] *The Hook* (Fall 1985): 6.
[5] BuAer memorandum dated 28 November 1944, Subject: Conference on NAA Fighter Proposals signed by Commander Thomas D. Tyra.
[6] The BuNos. were lower than other aircraft contracted at that time, having been reassigned from a canceled Sikorsky HNS-1 production lot.
[7] OpNav memorandum dated 25 April 1945 from DCNO (Air), Aubrey W. Fitch, to the Assistant Secretary of the Navy for Air, A. L. Gates.
[8] OpNav Cable dated 27 February 1948 from Lt. Cdr. Young, OP55F, to Commander Air Pacific.
[9] *Aviation Week* (March 22, 1948): 13.
[10] Personal letter dated August 1946 to an acquaintance from Commander A. B. Metsger.
[11] For the next few years, most experienced aviators were informally checked out in jets at the squadron level since the training program lagged well behind the need for jet pilots.

Chapter 4

[1] *Flight Characteristics at High Mach Numbers*, Vernon Outman and G. S. Graff, McDonnell Aircraft Corporation, undated but circa late 1940s.
[2] *The New York Times* (June 2, 1949).
[3] This wasn't quite the upper limit of the Banshee's capability. In late 1952, a VCP-61 F2H-2P took a picture of San Diego from an altitude of 54,650 feet.
[4] The single-engine vs. two-engine range benefit is actually somewhat more complicated, with Vought engineers not coming to the same conclusion in an F7U analysis. Their assessment was that better range could be achieved at an altitude above the single-engine ceiling, which is correct. However, what McAir was promoting was that it was better to be on one engine if the cruise or loiter altitude was constrained to be lower than the single-engine ceiling.
[5] http://www.georgespangenberg.com.
[6] The material for the genesis of the Navy's first jet night fighter program and the XF9F-2 program was taken from a declassified document titled "Initial Steps In Development of XF9F-2, XF3D-1, and XF10F-1 Aircraft" prepared by BuAer Scientific Historical (Aer-1203) and dated 12 December 1955.
[7] Pratt & Whitney, *The Pratt & Whitney Aircraft Story* (Hartford: Pratt & Whitney Aircraft Division, 1950): 168-170.
[8] "Where Are They Now? Ed Pawka," *The Hook* (Spring 1987): 12.
[9] For a first-hand account of the F3D program, see Heinemann, *Ed Heinemann Combat Aircraft Designer* (Annapolis: Naval Institute Press, 1980).
[10] G. F. O'Rourke with E. T. Wooldridge, *Night Fighters over Korea* (Annapolis: United States Naval Institute, 1998).
[11] 1,000 Hours Between Overhaul, *Naval Aviation News* (November 1951): 37.

Chapter 5

[1] The sweep angle is measured at the quarter chord of the wing, or in other words, at a point 25 percent of the chord back from the leading edge. Since most wings are tapered in chord, being broader at the root than at the tip, the leading edge of the wing is therefore angled back more than the nominal angle of wing sweep.
[2] Arthur A. Lambert, *Flight Investigation of a Bell P-63 Airplane with 35° Swept-Back Wings*, Bell Aircraft Corporation Report No. 33-943-032 dated 1 October 1946. One reported result that calls into question the quantitative, as opposed to the qualitative, results was that the maximum coefficient of lift of the swept wing was not only roughly the same as the unswept P-63's, it was also roughly the same with and without slats, which is also contrary to aerodynamic principles.
[3] Corwin H. Meyer, *Corky Meyer's Flight Journal: A Test Pilot's Tales of Dodging Disasters – Just In Time* (North Branch, Minnesota: SpecialtyPress, 2006): p. 192.
[4] The wind-tunnel problem at transonic speeds was eliminated in 1950 with the development of a slotted throat in the wind tunnel, which bled off the excess air in the test section.
[5] The demonstration that high-speed performance could be combined with low-speed capability was not achieved with the D-558 program. In a note in the October 1947 issue of *Naval Aviation News*, the Skystreak's airspeed on approach was reported to be 220 to 250 mph with touchdown at 160 mph.
[6] The Navy and Douglas originally preferred the annular side inlets because that freed up the nose for armament in an operational airplane. At the July 1946 design review, NACA representatives recommended that the nose inlet be standard, since less was known about the pressure recovery of the annular side inlets. It was also decided that only the 10-percent wing would be flown.
[7] Phase 3, the design definition and mockup of an operational airplane, was eventually canceled. In a November 1947 Douglas D-558 report it was properly referred to as the D-558-3, a designation that subsequently became associated with Douglas' very different hypersonic proposal for the X-15 program even within Douglas. That report, ES 20912 dated 1 November 1947, was the source for the D-558-1 and -2 data in this section.
[8] Before World War I there were no regulated distances or altitudes for absolute world speed records. Between 1920 and 1923 the regulated distance was 1 kilometer, at less than 100 meters above the ground. This course had to be covered four consecutive times, twice in each direction. From 1923 to 1953 the regulated distance was extended to 3 kilometers, since the measured times had gotten too short for accurate measurements with the equipment of the time – less than 10 seconds. After 1953, a distance of 15 to 25 kilometers at any altitude was allowed as an alternative to the low-level 3 km runs. This course has to be covered only twice but in opposite directions. After 1955, almost all absolute world speed records were set using high-altitude 15/25 kilometer courses.
[9] Model D-558 Navy-Industry Conference at Douglas Aircraft Company, El Segundo Plant, Stability and Control Characteristics presentation, R. E. Heald, November 10 1947.
[10] Naval Air Test Center Report on Project No. PTR AD-349 dated 2 June 1954, F9F-4 Airplane With Supercirculation Boundary Layer Control.
[11] In another example of it taking all the running you can do to stay in place, early warning using airborne radars provided more response time just as a new weapon was being introduced and reestablishing the degree of difficulty. The Russians had paid close attention to the effectiveness of Japanese suicide tactics in disabling or sinking aircraft carriers and warships. Their substitute for Kamikazes was the anti-ship missile. This forced the Navy to develop an aircraft/weapon combination that could engage and destroy the bomber at long range, since the most effective defense against arrows was to shoot the archer.
[12] "First Round Knockout," *Naval Aviation Confidential Bulletin* (August 1955): pp. 38-39.
[13] Robert L. Lawson, *Carrier Air Group Commanders: The Men and Their Machines* (Atglen, Pennsylvania: Schiffer Publishing Ltd., 2000): p. 85.
[14] The Sparrow I was also operational on the F3D-2M, but it was only operated by one shore-based Marine Corps squadron. However, the F3D-2M was carrier qualified.
[15] Chuck Hansen, "The Emerson Aero X17A Roll-Traverse Nose Turret," *The Hook* (Fall 1984): 30-31.

Chapter 6

[1] Naval Aviation Confidential Bulletin, No. 2-49, April 1949, Navy Department, Washington, D.C. pp. 33-39.
[2] Corwin H Meyer, *Corky Meyer's Flight Journal: A Test Pilot's Tales of Dodging Disasters – Just In Time* (North Branch, Minnesota: SpecialtyPress, 2006): p. 212.
[3] Letter from Chance Vought Aircraft to the Chief, Bureau of Aeronautics; Subject: Contracts No(s)51-156-I and 51-643-I – Model F7U – Proposal for Settlement of Contract Performance Guarantee Discrepancies dated 21 October 1955.
[4] *Time Magazine*, 7 November 1955.
[5] Navy Jet Aircraft Procurement Program, Tenth Intermediate Report of the Committee on Government Operations, House Report No. 1891, 84th Congress, 2nd Session, dated 15 March 1956.
[6] William F. Trimble, *High Frontier: A History of Aeronautics in Pennsylvania* (Pittsburgh: University of Pittsburgh Press, 1982): pp. 248-250.
[7] http://www.georgespangenberg.com
[8] The stall speed, power-off, reported in the F3H-1N SAC chart dated 1 December 1954 was 95.8 knots at landing weight. However, it was 92.2 knots with approach power.
[9] Corwin Meyer, *Naval Fighters Number Twenty-Six: Grumman Swing-Wing XF10F-1 Jaguar* (Simi Valley, California: Naval Fighters Series, 1993): 10.
[10] Grumman prepared a design study of the F10F with the Pratt & Whitney J57 before the program was canceled. The resulting airplane might well have been as acceptable as any of the fighters that were produced in quantity. However, the Navy stated publicly (in Congressional hearings primarily concerning the F3H-1 program) that the XF10F was cancelled because of "basic difficulties with the airplane (that) were strictly aerodynamic in nature – beyond the state of the art" and didn't blame the J40.
[11] http://www.georgespangenberg.com

Chapter 7

[1] Ironically, both "tailless" designs, the F7U and F4D, had transonic pitch shortcomings that the transonic fighters with conventional tails did not.
[2] In November 1949, Vought proposed the V-366D with two J46 engines and the V-366E with one J40 engine for the -3. BuAer, already having multiple single-engine fighter programs in work, opted for the J46 variant, which turned out to be the lesser of two evils.
[3] Johnson's Air Decisions Upheld, *Aviation Week* (31 October

1949): 12-13.

4 Lee M. Pearson, NavAir historian, letter to Arthur L. Schoeni of Vought; AIR-953/LMP dated 5 January 1976.

5 Jan Tegler, *Flight Journal* (October 2003).

6 For the best description of the short F7U-1 tour with the Blue Angels, see Veronico, Nicholas A. *The Blue Angels, A Fly-by History, Sixty Years of Aerial Excellence.* St. Paul, Minnesota, MBI Publishing Co. 2006.

7 F. O. Detweiler, personal letter to RADM C. F. Coe, USN dated 14 December 1951.

8 R. V. Lynch, Vought internal memorandum to Paul Thayer dated 8 January 1952.

9 Letter Report F7U-3 FT01-094: Model F7U-3 airplane; preliminary evaluation of, dated 20 June 1952, From Commander, Naval Air Test Center, to Chief, Bureau of Aeronautics.

10 Naval Speed Letter F7U-3 FT31-0133 dated 15 August 1952 from Commander, Naval Air Test Center to Chief, Bureau of Aeronautics.

11 Paul. S. Baker, Vought internal memorandum to F. O. Detweiler dated 3 October 1952. The Blue Angels were based at NAS Corpus Christi in 1951.

12 In the 1 April 1956 revision of the F7U-3 flight manual, the single-engine carrier landing was to begin abeam the carrier on downwind by extending the landing gear, slats, and tail hook and commencing 'a gliding approach at "Military Power," using speed brakes as necessary to maintain 130 knots.' Just prior to entering the groove at cut altitude, the afterburner was to be lit and the speed brakes opened fully. The only way to correct settling then was to close the speed brakes.

13 W. P. Thayer, Vought letter to Bureau Aeronautics Representative, Dallas, Texas, dated 31 March 1954.

14 John Moore, *The Wrong Stuff: Flying on the Edge of Disaster*, SpecialtyPress, North Branch, Minnesota, 1997: pp. 26-27.

15 Project Cutlass, *Naval Aviation News* (June 1954): 1-5.

16 Jack Christianson, letter to the editor of *The Hook*, Winter 1989 edition, checked out in the F7U while stationed at the Chance Vought plant for production acceptance and flew at least 100 of them. He was then assigned to VX-4 at Point Mugu.

Chapter 8

1 *The Hook* (Winter 1992): The F4U-5N night fighter remained in production through late 1951 and an attack variant for the Marine Corps, the AU-1, through the end of 1952.

2 MiG stood for the design bureau of fighter designers Artem Mikoyan and Mikhail Gurevich

3 The "F2H-5" might well have been a success and available in time for the Korean War. The XF-88 that it was based on flew in April 1949. Using afterburner, it exceeded 700 mph in level flight at 20,000 feet and could climb to 30,000 feet in four minutes. The XF-88 went on to win a fly-off for the USAF's "Penetration Fighter" against the XF-90 and YF-93A in mid-1950. It was a hollow victory — funding the Korean War effort precluded a production contract.

4 Carl Mills, *Banshees In the Royal Canadian Navy* (Canada: Banshee Publication, 1991): p. 236.

5 Grumman Aircraft Engineering Report A247, Model XF10F-1 Airplane Summary of Current Status dated 23 February 1948.

6 *Naval Aviation News* (June 1954). 24-25. The F-86F flown by Colonel W. M. Millikan carried external tanks that were dropped in Lake Erie. Millikan ran out of fuel short of New York but dead-sticked the Sabre to a successful landing at Idlewild.

7 Naval Air Test Center Report on Project TED No. PTR AC-23003 dated 19 May 1959, Navy Evaluation of Model F9F-6 Airplane With F9F-8 Type Outer Wing Panels.

8 *The Hook* (Summer 1981): 30.

9 Memorandum Aer-AC-21 dated 3 December 1951, Subject FJ-3, Request for approval of, From Director, Aircraft Division to Chief, Bureau of Aeronautics.

10 Corwin Meyer, *Naval Fighters Number Sixty-Six: Grumman F9F-6/7/8 Cougar Part One* (Simi Valley, California, Naval Fighters, 2005): p. 23.

Chapter 9

1 After World War II, BuAer studied the Me 163 and gave some thought to developing an interceptor that was mostly if not wholly powered by a rocket engine. It was a concept not likely to gain much traction, and it didn't. BuAer considered rocket-augmented jet fighters but never contracted for one.

2 As it happened, annular inlets had been dropped from the D-558 program so no flight-test data was available on the configuration. While it's not clear that the Demon's performance suffered as a result, annular inlets have been rare. They provide inherently poorer pressure recovery due to the depth of the boundary layer relative to the overall width of the inlet.

3 Bureau of Aeronautics Memorandum dated 24 November 1948, VF Interceptor Competition — Recommendation for Procurement from Rear Admiral R. C. Lonnquest to Chief, Bureau of Aeronautics.

4 Edward Heinemann and Rosario Rausa, *Combat Aircraft Designer* (Annapolis: United States Naval Institute, 1980): p. 188.

5 Nicholas M. Williams, "Silver Eagle Skyrays," *The Hook* (Spring 1978): 14-17.

6 Bob Rahn, *Tempting Fate* (North Branch, Minnesota: SpecialtyPress, 1997): pp. 106-107.

7 Mike Spick, *All-Weather Warriors* (London: Arms and Armour Press, 1994): pp. 114-5.

8 Robert L. Lawson, *Carrier Air Group Commanders* (Atglen, Pennsylvania: Schiffer Military History, 2000): p. 89.

Chapter 10

1 *Time Magazine* (7 November 1955).

2 Bob Rahn, *Tempting Fate* (North Branch, Minnesota; Specialty Press, 1997): pp. 109-110.

3 McDonnell wasn't the only Navy airplane company to be useful to Congress. In March 1961, years after the last one had flown, Senator Stuart Symington used the F7U as a specific example of the Pentagon's waste of money on "unsatisfactory Navy planes, aircraft radar, and aircraft engines." Most of the more than $675 million that he cited, $417 million, he attributed to "304 F7U jet fighter planes that were faulty and had an 'accident rate more than twice that of any other jet fighter, resulting in the loss of thirty-four planes.'" See *The New York Times*, March 3, 1961.

4 Capt. Roger Carlquist, "Dead-sticking the Demon," *Foundation* (Spring 2006): 36-40.

Chapter 11

1 Strictly speaking, some U.S. carriers very similar to the *Essex* are considered to be of the Ticonderoga class. The Essex/Ticonderoga classes were further differentiated by subsequent modifications and alterations. However, for simplicity I refer to all carriers in this size range as the Essex class.

2 F9F-2s were flown from CVL-48 *Saipan* and CVL-49 *Wright*. However, there was at least one crash in both these instances, one a ramp strike and the other a hard landing.

3 A cable catcher was located on the bottom of the fuselage between the main gear and the nose gear on a few aircraft, e.g., the FJ-2. If the barrier cable had been pulled up too quickly to snag the main gear, the catcher would hold it up so it could engage the main gear. One was planned for the F8U because of the limited clearance between the fuselage and the deck and the distance between the nose gear and the main gear.

4 Cdr. Hal Buell, "The Angled Deck Concept — Savior of the Tailhook Navy," *The Hook* (Fall 1987): 13-23.

5 Vice Adm. Donald D. Engen, "Roger Ball" — How It Started," *The Hook*, (Fall 1987): 24.

6 Capt. Robert G. Dosé, "The First Mirror Landing," *The Hook*, (Fall 1987): 27.

7 For a more detailed description of the British experiments with the flexible deck, see Brown, *Wings of the Weird and Wonderful, Volume One*: 71-84.

8 Jan Jacobs, "Follow the Bouncing Cougar," *The Hook* (Spring 1984): 11-19.

Chapter 12

1 Ed Heinemann, *Combat Aircraft Designer* (Annapolis: United States Naval Institute, 1980): p. 228. North American also developed a tanker package for an FJ-4B buddy system, which became operational in June 1958.

2 *Naval Aviation News*, April 1955, pp. 1-5.

3 Capt. Michael W. Cagle, *The Naval Aviator's Guide* (Annapolis: United States Naval Institute, 1963): pp. 99-101.

4 *Naval Aviation News* (January 1959): 7-11.

5 *Naval Aviation News* (August 1961): 6-7.

Chapter 13

1 German engineers were reportedly the first to discover the area rule in wind-tunnel tests during World War II, but, unlike the swept wing, the concept was not picked up by engineers reviewing German technology after the war.

2 The weights shown are from a Vought design philosophy study dated 21 February 1953, which was submitted to the Navy in support of the F8U proposal. The fuel and fuel-system weights are estimates "to satisfy the Day Fighter radius-of-action problem."

3 Grumman also missed the speed guarantee. One bizarre consequence of even marginal supersonic performance happened to Grumman test pilot Tom Attridge. On 21 September 1956, in a contract demonstration of firing the 20mm cannon while at Mach 1.0, he entered a slight dive and through a combination of straight flying and bad luck, caught up to and intersected the ballistic path of four of his bullets, shooting himself down. As unlikely as such an encounter might seem, subsequent review of minor damage from a previous flight indicated that the aircraft was hit on at least one prior flight.

4 Amendment No. 2 To Outline Specification For Class VF Day Fighter Airplane dated 18 November 1952.

5 Outline Specification For Class VF Day Fighter Airplane dated 18 November 1952 — "Trick means" was the actual expression used.

6 http://www.georgespangenberg.com

7 Fortunately, in mid-1953, the Cutlass program had recovered from earlier disappointments and completed initial carrier qualification trials, so it was not a factor in the Navy's source selection. A year or two later and it might have been different.

8 According to one report, the Navy took delivery of 1,266 Crusaders that were involved in 1,106 major accidents with 186 pilots killed. This count did not include those lost in combat in Vietnam. It's a wonder that any are left. Of course, some F8Us were rebuilt and returned to service after a major accident. The accident rate was reduced over time, but not relative to other fighters. Its lifetime average rate was almost 47 accidents per 100,000 flight hours, more than twice that of the F4H.

9 Paul Gillcrist, "Flying the F-8 Crusader," *Flight Journal* (August 2000).

10 Actually, the orneriness of the F8U on approach appears to have been part of its cachet among Navy fighter pilots, along with its having four cannons and only one seat.

11 Most of the facts and background contained in the F5D section are from a declassified BuAer memo dated 30 October 1957, from the Chief, Bureau of Aeronautics to the Chief of Legislative Liaison, Subject: Preparedness Investigating Subcommittee request for information on aircraft not delivered to the Fleet which transmitted the response for the F5D.

12 Bob Rahn with Zip Rausa, *Tempting Fate, An Experimental Test Pilot's Story* (North Branch, Minnesota: SpecialtyPress, 1997): p. 145.

Chapter 14

1 http://www.georgespangenberg.com

2 Vought was well aware of McDonnell's activities, however. In a Vought log entitled *McDonnell F4H-1 History* dated 14 January 1958, the first entry is "3-54 McDonnell made proposal for F3H-(G); Gross Weight 3600#, Vmax at 35,000' = M 1.4, Engines 2/J65W; Navy received similar proposals on F11F, F5D and a Super Fury version of the F100."

3 Other Vought design numbers associated with the Crusader III are V-418 and V-419. The V-418 was reportedly powered by the J75 like the F8U-3 and the V-419, by Pratt & Whitney's new Mach 2.5 engine being developed for the Navy, the J58. The J58 offered even better performance, but since it hadn't even run at the time of the competition, it wasn't likely that the Navy would opt for this version initially.

4 Two F8U-1s were to be modified with the Reaction Motors LF-40 rocket motor with 8,000 lbs of thrust. Tragically, a motor blew up during a Vought test, killing two Vought employees. Vought continued to do design studies but never flew an F8U with a rocket motor.

5 Donald D. Engen, *Wings and Warriors: My Life As A Naval Aviator* (Washington: Smithsonian Institution Press, 1997): pp. 211-214.

6 http://www.georgespangenberg.com

7 The Characteristics Summary data is inconsistent. It is for a single J79-powered fighter with 350-square-foot wing area, bigger even than the 98L. However, the internal fuel capacity and gross weight listed are less than the F11F-1's.

8 Grumman Report PDR-118-5, Grumman Design 118 Task Force Defense Fighter dated December 1955.

9 BuAer letter Ae-EV-1/263 dated 16 July 1956, Subject: "Grumman Aircraft Engineering Corporation Model 111A Airplane; proposal for," from Chief, Bureau of Aeronautics, to Grumman Aircraft Engineering Corp.

Chapter 15

1 Because of the danger and measurement difficulty involved, there has apparently been only one subsequent and successful attempt to break this record, which was in 1977 in a privately owned F-104 Starfighter.

2 The takeoffs from Point Mugu, California, were initiated from a standing start at full afterburner, using a carrier catapult holdback to allow burn down to minimum fuel for the altitude being attempted. The holdback was then released, allowing maximum performance short of being catapulted. The profile was to accelerate to 400 knots, climb to 40,000 feet, accelerate to Mach 2.1, and then pull up to the optimum attitude to achieve a peak altitude.

Appendix

"i" is "Aviation Planning Directive 2-A-45 dated 9 January 1945 issued from the Office of the Chief of Naval Operations and signed by D.V. Gallery." "ii" is " BuAer Memorandum Aer-E-26-CGH dated 22 March 1945 and signed by Captain T.C. Lonnquest. In fact, North American Aviation had acquired the Berliner-Joyce Company in 1930 and dissolved it in 1933 so F4J was arguably more appropriate than FJ."

# SUGGESTED READING

Absug, Malcom J. and Larrabee, E. Eugene. *Airplane Stability and Control (Second Edition): A History of the Technologies That Made Aviation Possible.* Cambridge University Press, 2002.

Barlow, Jeffrey G. *Revolt of the Admirals: The Fight For Naval Aviation 1945-1950.* Washington, D.C.: Ross & Perry, Inc. 2001.

Brown, Charles H. *Dark Sky Black Sea: Aircraft Carrier Night and All-Weather Operations.* Annapolis: Naval Institute Press, 1999.

Brown, Captain Eric. *Testing for Combat.* England: Airlife Publishing Ltd., 1994.

Brown, Captain Eric. *Wings of the Weird and Wonderful.* England: Airlife Publishing Ltd., 1983.

Cagle, Captain Michael W. *The Naval Aviator's Guide.* Annapolis: United States Naval Institute, 1963.

Dean, Francis H. *Report of Joint Fighter Conference NAS Patuxent River, MD 16-23 October 1944.* Atglen, Pennsylvania: Schiffer Military History, 1998.

Dobronski, Joseph F. *A Sky Full of Challenges.* Atglen, Pennsylvania: Schiffer Publishing, 2004.
An illustrated and very readable autobiography by one of McDonnell Aircraft's test pilots who flew every McDonnell fighter and retired as director of Flight Test and Flight Operations.

Engen, Vice Admiral Donald D. *Wings and Warriors: My Life as a Naval Aviator.* Washington: Smithsonian Institution Press, 1997.

Freidman, Norman. *U.S. Aircraft Carriers: An Illustrated Design History.* Annapolis: Naval Institute Press, 1983.

Gillcrist, Rear Admiral Paul T. *Crusader!: Last of the Gunfighters.* Atglen, Pennsylvania: Schiffer Military/Aviation History, 1995.

Gillcrist, Rear Admiral Paul T. *Feet Wet: Reflections of a Carrier Pilot.* Novato, California: Presidio Press, 1990.

Ginter, Steve. *Naval Fighter Series.* Simi Valley, California. (self published), various.
There are more than 70 books in this series, each of which includes summary histories, both development and operational (by squadron), and detail descriptions of a particular Navy aircraft, most but not all fighters. Heavily illustrated, they are an invaluable resource for the aviation enthusiast, particularly one who builds model aircraft.

Hansen, James R. *Engineer In Charge: A History of the Langley Aeronautical Laboratory, 1917-1958.* Washington: The NASA History Series, 1987.

Heinemann, Edward. *Ed Heinemann: Combat Aircraft Designer.* Annapolis: Naval Institute Press, 1980.

Hurt, Hugh H. *Aerodynamics for Naval Aviators.* NavAir 00-80T-80, 1960, revised 1965.

Lawson, Robert L. *Carrier Air Group Commanders: The Men and their Machines.* Atglen, Pennsylvania: Schiffer Military History, 2000.

Libis, Scott. *Skystreak, Skyrocket, & Stiletto: Douglas High-Speed X-Planes.* North Branch, Minnesota: SpecialtyPress, 2005.

Lund, Frederick H. *Evolution of Navy Air-to-Air Missiles.* American Institute of Aeronautics and Astronautics Paper 2005-700, presented at the 43rd AIAA Aerospace Sciences Meeting and Exhibit, Reno, Nevada. January 2005.

Moore, Cdr. John. *The Wrong Stuff: Flying on the Edge of Disaster.* North Branch, Minnesota: SpecialtyPress, 1997.

Meyer, Corwin H. *Corky Meyer's Flight Journal: A Test Pilot's Tales of Dodging Disasters – Just In Time.* North Branch, Minnesota: SpecialtyPress, 2006.

O'Rourke, Captian G. G. *Night Fighters over Korea.* Annapolis: Naval Institute Press, 1998.

Spick, Mike. *All-Weather Warriors: The Search for the Ultimate Fighter Aircraft.* London: Arms and Armour Press, 1994.

Spangenberg, George. http://www.georgespangenberg.com/

Tilman, Barrett. *MiG Master: The Story of the F-8 Crusader.* The Nautical and Aviation Publishing Company of America, 1980.

Veronico, Nicholas A. *The Blue Angels, A Fly-by History, Sixty Years of Aerial Excellence.* St. Paul, Minn. MBI Publishing Co. 2006.

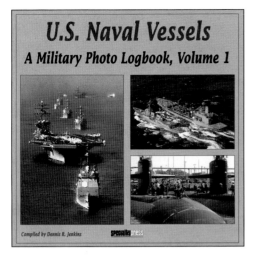

### U.S. Naval Vessels
*A Military Photo Logbook, Volume 1*

Compiled by Dennis R. Jenkins | specialtypress

**U.S. NAVAL VESSELS: A Military Photo Logbook, Volume 1** by Dennis R. Jenkins. A collection of images taken by Navy photographers with unparalleled access to ships and facilities around the world. Covers U.S. Navy and Coast Guard ships and submarines, including combat operations in Afghanistan and Iraq, humanitarian missions, training exercises, weapons testing, ship construction, and maintenance operations. Softbound, 9 x 9, 120 pages, 342 color photos. *Item # SP115*

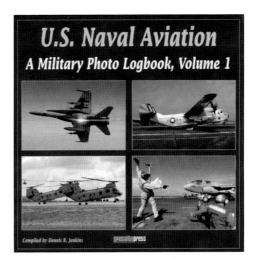

### U.S. Naval Aviation
*A Military Photo Logbook, Volume 1*

Compiled by Dennis R. Jenkins | specialtypress

**U.S. NAVAL AVIATION: A Military Photo Logbook, Volume 1** by Dennis R. Jenkins. A collection of images taken by Navy photographers with unparalleled access to facilities and aircraft around the world. Covers U.S. Navy, Marine Corps, and Coast Guard aircraft, featuring combat operations in Afghanistan and Iraq, humanitarian missions, training exercises with other nations, aerial refueling, aircraft and weapons testing, and maintenance operations. Softbound, 9 x 9, 120 pages, 350 color photos. *Item # SP114*

### U.S. Air Force Aviation
*A Military Photo Logbook, Volume 1*

Compiled by Dennis R. Jenkins | specialtypress

**U.S. AIR FORCE AVIATION: A Military Photo Logbook, Volume 1** by Dennis R. Jenkins A collection of images taken by Air Force photographers with unparalleled access to facilities and aircraft around the world. Documents all aspects of Air Force operations, including combat operations in Afghanistan and Iraq, humanitarian missions around the world, training exercises, aircraft & weapons testing, etc. Softbound, 9 x 9, 120 pages, 346 color photos. *Item # SP113*

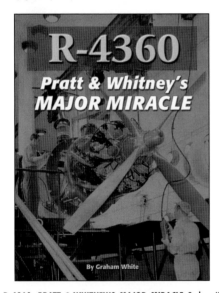

### R-4360
*Pratt & Whitney's MAJOR MIRACLE*

By Graham White

**R-4360: PRATT & WHITNEY'S MAJOR MIRACLE** Graham White Aviation technology progressed at a blindingly fast pace during the first half of the 20th century. Aircraft were asked to fly higher, fly faster, carry heavier loads, take off and land on shorter runways, fly greater distances, and consume less fuel with each new generation, and with perfect dependability. Pratt & Whitney's R-1340, or "Wasp" as it was known in the commercial marketplace, was a relatively large engine, displacing 1,344 cubic inches. The R-4360 at one time represented the largest and most sophisticated of its breed. Nothing else in the late-1940s marketplace could boast what the R-4360 did — 3,000 to 4,000 hp. By the end of the piston-engine era Pratt & Whitney had placed into mass production the largest and most powerful engine ever built in quantity. Leaving no stone unturned, this book provides a detailed account of the inner workings of the R-4360. Also covered is the engine's development history, variations, and its military, commercial, and racing applications. Hardbound, 7-1/2 x 10-1/2, 608 pages, 600+ b/w photos. *Item # SP097*

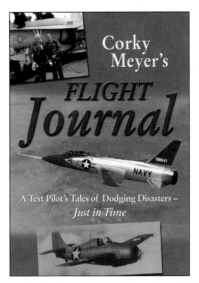

### Corky Meyer's
### FLIGHT Journal
*A Test Pilot's Tales of Dodging Disasters – Just in Time*

**CORKY MEYER'S FLIGHT JOURNAL** Corky Meyer Designing high-performance military aircraft in the slide-rule era was challenging. Being the first person to fly these airplanes and expand an aircraft's flight envelope was often very frightening, if not downright deadly. It is hard to believe that someone could really endure 22 years in this occupation, plus another 30 years in the aircraft industry, often leading the industry-wide transition from large, too-complicated piston engines to doggy, unreliable jet engines and from 300-mile-per-hour "barn doors" through slippery transonic and supersonic airframes. But this is, in fact, the truly remarkable – if not virtually unparalleled – life story of Corky Meyer. In an occupation and time which killed many, if not most, this man had the brains, skill, and good luck to meet every challenge that faced him and survive to tell his amazing story. It is a story that covers the most important era in the history of flight, told by a man at the epicenter of the activity. *Corky Meyer's Flight Journal* is an electrifying tale of a very passionate and patriotic man, his wife and family, and of course his numerous sensational close calls as an experimental fighter test pilot. Softbound, 7 x 10, 256 pages, approx. 100 b/w & 50 color photos. *Item # SP093*

### CLEAR THE DECK!
### NAVAL AVIATION ACCIDENTS OF WORLD WAR II

CORY GRAFF

**CLEAR THE DECK! Naval Aviation Accidents of World War II** by Cory Graff. Aircraft carrier operations were a dangerous business, especially in wartime. When air operations are confined to a flight deck of 50,000 square feet (escort carrier size), it was one of the most hectic and hazardous places on earth. Accidents were bound to happen. In wartime, the stakes were even higher as heavily loaded and armed combat planes went about their missions in unprecedented numbers. Commonly, there was no alternate airfield, no time to lose, and absolutely no room for error. Clear the Deck! showcases the amazing and dramatic World War II-era, U.S. Navy battle damage, and flight operations photographs gathered from the National Archives, National Museum of Naval Aviation, and many other collections. Softbound, 9 x 9, 132 pages, 250 b/w photos. *Item # SP119*

**Specialty Press,** 39966 Grand Avenue, North Branch, MN 55056. Phone: 800-895-4585 & 651-277-1400 Fax: 651-277-1203
www.specialtypress.com
**Midland Publishing,** 4 Watling Drive, Hinkley, LE10 3EY, England. Phone 01455 254 450 Fax: 01455 233 737
www.midlandcountiessuperstore.com

32' 6"